BrightRED Study Guide

Curriculum for Excellence

N5

HISTORY – SCOTLAND

Chris and Aileen MacKay

First published in 2014 by:

Bright Red Publishing Ltd

1 Torphichen Street

Edinburgh

EH3 8HX

A CIP record for this book is available from the British Library.

ISBN 978-1-906736-40-8

With thanks to:

Partnership Publishing Solutions (layout), Ivor Normand (copy-edit)

Cover design and series book design by Caleb Rutherford – eidetic

Acknowledgements

Every effort has been made to seek all copyright holders. If any have been overlooked, then Bright Red Publishing will be delighted to make the necessary arrangements. Please see page 139 for a list of acknowledgements.

Printed and bound in the UK by Martins the Printers.

CONTENTS

INTRODUCTION

NATIONAL 5 HISTORY – SCOTLAND

This book has been written to support the teaching of the National 5 qualification in History. This is the course that replaced Standard Grade History from 2013. This course will give you the opportunity to do the following:

- Develop a greater understanding of the past.
- Promote your abilities to think for yourself. You will be able to form your own opinions of historical events and support them with evidence.
- Develop the ability to reach a conclusion which is supported by evidence.
- Develop your abilities to gather and read different kinds of information.
- Demonstrate that you are able to look carefully at this information and can check it for bias or propaganda.
- Develop your abilities to communicate clearly in a variety of ways.
- Learn about the reasons why particular historical events took place.
- Learn about the impact of historical events.

History contributes to a broad general education and the wider curriculum. Studying it will help to develop informed and active citizens by helping learners to gain a greater understanding of political and social institutions and processes. You will develop skills which are transferable to other areas of study and which you will use in everyday life.

ONLINE

This book is supported by the BrightRED Digital Zone – register at www. brightredbooks.net to unlock a world of tests, videos, activities and more.

THE N5 HISTORY COURSE

This book covers four out of the five Scottish History options. It will give you the material and sources which can help you to pass the course option you are being taught.

- The Wars of Independence, 1286–1328
- Mary Queen of Scots, and the Reformation, 1542–1587
- Migration and Empire, 1830–1939
- The Era of the Great War, 1910–1928

The course is made up of three units. Each unit has a number of contexts, which means that you will have the opportunity to study a variety of historical events. Each unit also has a number of learning outcomes attached to it. You have to pass each of these to gain a unit award. You cannot pass the course without passing the units.

'Historical Study: Scottish'

The Scottish unit is where a lot of the source-handling will take place. Outcome 1 will demand that you evaluate the usefulness of a source. You will also have to say how fully a source describes or explains an event. The unit will also expect you to be able to reach a conclusion on areas of agreement or disagreement between two sources. To pass Outcome 2, you will need to describe accurately or explain a historical event connected to the Scottish unit.

'Historical Study: British'

Outcome 1 in this unit will ask you to evaluate the impact of a historical development. To do this, you will need to interpret historical information and present your evidence in a structured manner. For instance, you might need to explain how the arrival of railways affected life in Britain before 1900. Outcome 2 expects you to be able to describe or analyse historical events connected with the British unit.

'Historical Study: European and World'

Outcome 1 in this unit requires you to reach a conclusion on the factors which led to a historical development. For instance, you might need to explain why there was a revolution in Russia in February 1917. This might involve you identifying the importance of a particular reason or factor. Outcome 2 expects you to be able to describe or explain events connected with the European unit.

THE COURSE ASSESSMENT

At the course's end, you will be assessed externally by two components: the question paper and the assignment.

contd

The question paper

This will last 1 hour 30 minutes.

- It will assess Knowledge and Understanding. This means that it will ask you questions about areas of the course that you have studied. For National 5, these questions will be based on recalled evidence. This means that there will be no help or sources provided in the exam. You will have to know the material!

- It will also assess Source-Handling skills. This means that you will have to demonstrate your abilities to deal with historical evidence. That is: you will have to evaluate the usefulness of a source, compare sources to show areas of agreement or disagreement, and set sources in context.

The questions

There are six types of question that you will be faced with in the final exam: three Knowledge and Understanding, and three Source-Handling.

KNOWLEDGE AND UNDERSTANDING QUESTIONS			
Type of exam question	How many marks?	Example question	Comment
'Describe'	5 or 6	Describe the problems facing Mary Queen of Scots after her return to Scotland in 1560.	You will get 1 mark for each relevant point. It also needs to be accurate. You can also gain 1 mark for developing the point.
'Explain the reasons why'	5 or 6	Explain the reasons why Bruce was able to defeat the English army at Bannockburn.	You have to give reasons why the English army was defeated. You will get 1 mark for each relevant point. It also needs to be accurate. You can also gain 1 mark for developing the point.
'To what extent?'	8	To what extent was Scottish emigration between 1830 and 1930 due to poor living conditions?	This question expects you to reach a conclusion about the importance of a particular factor. You will have to write an extended answer. You will gain up to 5 marks for using relevant recalled evidence. A further 3 marks are available for structure. This means you should use paragraphs to deal with each factor. You should also reach a valid conclusion for a 2nd mark. For a 3rd mark, the conclusion should be supported with a reason.
SOURCE-HANDLING QUESTIONS			
'Evaluate the usefulness of Source ...'	5 or 6	Evaluate the usefulness of Source A as evidence of the problems facing Scotland after 1290.	To gain full marks, you need to look at the following areas: Authorship – who wrote it. Purpose – why did they write it? Type of source – is it a primary or a secondary source? Why is this relevant? You can get up to 4 marks for relevant comments on each of the previous areas. Comments on content can gain 2 marks. Comments on what content is missing from the source can also gain 2 marks.
'Compare the views of Sources X and Y ...'	4	Compare the views of Sources A and B about the reasons for Scots migration after 1830.	You need to show areas of agreement or disagreement. This will gain 1 mark. You will get a 2nd mark by developing the point and providing quotes to show where they agree/disagree.
'How fully does Source ...?'	5 or 6	How fully does Source A describe the impact of the Great War on Scottish industry?	In this type of question, you will have a source. You need to judge how fully the source explains or describes a particular event. You can get 3 marks for correctly identifying relevant points from the source. You can get up to 4 marks for identifying relevant points of evidence which are missing from the source.

The assignment

You will also have to produce an assignment. This will be based on a question of your choice. You research the topic and draw up a plan. You will then have one hour to write up your findings under exam conditions.

The assignment is worth 20 marks, and it is marked by the SQA. In other words, it is worth 25% of your final grade. It is a great opportunity for you to gain marks and demonstrate your research skills. The people who do well are the people who take full advantage of the opportunities presented by the assignment.

It does not have to be from the areas that you have studied. However, it's worth thinking very carefully about the topic before you start:

- Could the topic you study help you in the final exam? Picking a topic that is from the course could mean that you have a better chance of passing the final exam.

- Do you have material that could be used to support the completion of an assignment? There is no point in trying to answer a question if you don't have the material!

- Will you be able to reach a conclusion in your assignment? If you cannot, then your question is not suitable.

SCOTLAND ON THE EVE OF THE GREAT WAR, 1910–1914

THE ASSASSINATION OF THE ARCHDUKE

On 28 June 1914, the heir to the Austrian throne, Archduke Franz Ferdinand, was assassinated by members of the Serbian Black Hand movement. Just over a month later, Britain declared war on Germany. The declaration of war was greeted with enthusiasm in most European capitals. It was also greeted with excitement in the villages, towns and cities of Scotland. Crowds gathered to witness the departure of soldiers. There was a surge in patriotism. Thousands of men besieged recruiting stations in an effort to 'join up'.

The Great War lasted from 1914 to 1918. It was to lead to significant changes in Scotland and in the rest of Britain. Thousands of the enthusiastic volunteers of 1914 became casualties. Scottish industry experienced an increase in demand during the war years. Women were recruited to work in the factories and replace the men who went to fight. In 1918, some of them received the right to vote.

Post-war Scotland was not the 'land fit for heroes' that some had hoped. There was unrest among workers. Others were left wondering if their sacrifice had been made in vain.

DON'T FORGET

At this time, there was no Scottish Parliament, and all decisions about Scotland were made at Westminster in London.

VIDEO LINK

Check out a video clip about the Singer Sewing Factory strike at www.brightredbooks.net/N5History.

INDUSTRY

Scotland in 1910 was a major industrial power. Its shipyards, mills and factories supplied the needs of the British Empire. Although competition from countries such as the USA and Germany was growing, Scotland remained a manufacturing force.

- Coal output in Scotland was to reach a peak in 1913.

- Shipbuilding on the Clyde was responding to the needs of the Royal Navy. In 1913, the Clyde shipyards produced 33% of the total British tonnage. This was more than the entire output of all the German shipyards put together.

- Scottish engineering firms thrived, such as the North British Locomotive Company, which was the largest manufacturer of locomotives in Europe. It employed 10 000 people in Glasgow. Another firm, Beardmores, employed 40 000. It produced ships, engines and by 1913 even aircraft.

Industrial disputes

Workers worked long hours in dangerous conditions. In 1913, there were over 200 fatal accidents in Scottish coal mines. Strikes over pay and conditions were common in Scotland and across Britain as a whole. In March 1911, the 10 000 employees of the Singer factory in Clydebank went on strike over changes to their working conditions. These changes would also have meant a loss of pay. Industrial action by the employees failed. After a month on strike, the workers were forced to accept the changes.

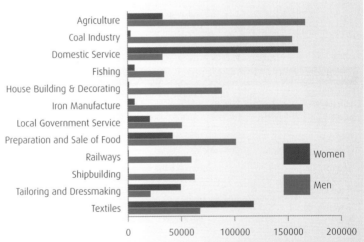

Source A shows the balance of employment in Scottish industries in 1911.

The Singer Strike was one example. Throughout 1910–1914, a number of strikes broke out across Scotland and the rest of Britain. In 1910, there were 581 disputes in Britain. By 1913, this figure had risen to 1497. All over Scotland, workers were regularly striking in order to get better pay and working hours. The strikes often resulted in scenes of violence which led to the government taking strong action.

During strikes in Dundee in December 1911, extra police and soldiers from the Black Watch had to be sent to keep order. In March 1913, another strike in the city saw 30 000 millworkers stop work. Later that year, unrest at Leith docks worried the local council. An attempt was made by some of the strikers to blow up one of the walls of the docks.

contd

Source B below is a reply by a government minister during a debate in the House of Commons in August 1913 about the strikes in Edinburgh and Leith. It shows that both the local councils and the Liberal Government were so concerned by the behaviour of the strikers that they were prepared to use the armed forces to restore order:

> *On the 17th July, the senior naval officer on the coast of Scotland ordered six gunboats then lying in the Forth to anchor off Leith. This was done at the request of the Midlothian authorities. The Navy has been called upon for aid (which, fortunately, did not have to take an active form) during certain widespread strikes in the last two years.*

HOUSING IN SCOTLAND

The 1911 **census** indicated that the population of Scotland stood at 4 760 904 people. The majority of them were crammed into the cities. Although some of the worst slums had been demolished, there were still problems. Overcrowding was the biggest issue. Many city-dwellers lived in a **single end** (a one-roomed flat) or in a **room and kitchen** (a two-roomed flat).

Diseases such as typhus and tuberculosis spread quickly in the cramped conditions and often proved fatal.

Look at the plan of one floor of a tenement. If you were to assume that one family was to live in each flat, then how many families would have lived on this one floor?

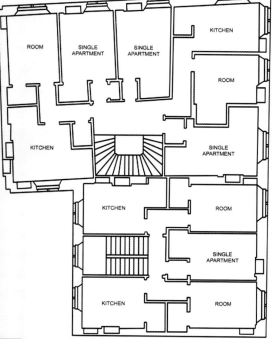

Source C shows a floor plan of a tenement in Glasgow.

Percentage of occupied houses in 1911		
Rooms per house	Scotland	England
1 room	8.4	1.4
2 rooms	39.5	6.1
3 rooms	21.1	12.8
4 rooms	9.6	24.7
5 rooms	5.4	22.4
6 rooms	3.7	14.8

Source D compares the sizes of houses in Scotland and England in 1911.
It indicates that the problem of overcrowding was more severe north of the border.

 ## THINGS TO DO AND THINK ABOUT

1. What percentage of Scots were living in two rooms or less?

2. What percentage of people were living in two rooms or less in England?

3. What strikes you about the balance of the figures in the table above?

4. What does it tell us about where and how Scots were living at the start of the 20th century?

When thinking about this, look online at http://www.gro-scotland.gov.uk/census/index.html to check how Scots are living today and how modern information compares to the data above.

POLITICAL CLIMATE, 1910–1914

WHO CONTROLLED SCOTLAND IN 1910?

In 1910, there was no Scottish Parliament. Power rested with the British Government in Westminster. Instead, Scotland was represented by 70 MPs at the House of Commons in London. These were elected by males who were aged over 21 and who owned or rented property worth at least £10 a year.

There was also the post of Secretary for Scotland. This had been recreated in the 19th century to look after Scottish affairs – which often related to issues connected with farming and fishing.

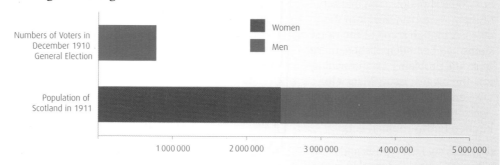

Source A shows the limited extent of the franchise in Scotland in 1911.

However, Scotland had a lot more influence than might have been thought. In 1910, nearly a third of the Liberal cabinet were Scots or represented Scottish seats. The Prime Minister, Herbert Asquith, represented East Fife. Winston Churchill was the MP for Dundee. The leaders of the opposition parties, Andrew Bonar Law (Conservative) and Keir Hardie (Labour), were Scots.

In Scotland before the Great War, the Liberals were the dominant party. In December 1910, the Liberals had won 58 out of 70 seats. In England and Wales, they had taken 212 out of 489. Labour won 3 seats in Scotland and 39 south of the border. The Unionists took 3 seats in Scotland and 238 in England and Wales.

Who was the head of state?

In May 1910, King Edward VII died. His funeral saw the gathering of a number of monarchs, including Kaiser Wilhelm II. Edward was succeeded by his son, who became George V, King of the United Kingdom and the British Dominions – and also held the title of Emperor of India. As a **constitutional monarch**, he was really just a figurehead while the real power rested with the Prime Minister and Parliament.

POLITICAL PROBLEMS

In the years before the outbreak of the Great War, there were several major challenges facing the British Government.

The naval race against Germany

The Royal Navy was important to Britain. It protected Britain, the Empire and the merchant fleet which carried Britain's trade and food. The launch of HMS *Dreadnought* in 1906 led to an increase in tension with Germany. The Germans started building their own version of the *Dreadnought*. The British public saw this as a threat. Pressure was put on the Liberal Government to spend more money on building battleships.

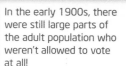

DON'T FORGET

In the early 1900s, there were still large parts of the adult population who weren't allowed to vote at all!

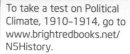

ONLINE TEST

To take a test on Political Climate, 1910–1914, go to www.brightredbooks.net/N5History.

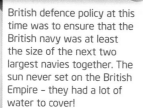

DON'T FORGET

British defence policy at this time was to ensure that the British navy was at least the size of the next two largest navies together. The sun never set on the British Empire – they had a lot of water to cover!

contd

'The People's Budget'

In 1909, the Liberal Government introduced a series of reforms to help the poor. Old-age pensions, labour exchanges, unemployment pay and sickness pay were introduced. To pay for these changes, the Liberals increased the taxes of the rich.

The 1909 constitutional crisis

The House of Lords was dominated by Conservatives. They kept rejecting the 1909 'People's Budget'. Two general elections were held in 1910. They resulted in narrow Liberal victories. 1n 1911, a Parliament Act reduced the powers of the House of Lords. The Lords could delay **bills** but could not stop them.

Ireland

This was a major issue for the Liberal Government. In the years before 1914, the demands for Irish **self-government** had grown. Irish Nationalists wanted independence from British control. The Liberal Party had introduced two **Home Rule** bills in the 19th century. Both had been defeated in Parliament. However, the Liberals' massive victory in the 1906 election had convinced Nationalists that Home Rule could be won. Two elections in 1910 had left the Liberal Government depending on Irish Nationalist MPs to get their bills passed.

In 1912, the Liberal Prime Minister, Herbert Asquith, introduced a Home Rule bill which would grant a Parliament to Ireland. This did not please the Protestants, who mainly lived in the northern part of Ireland called Ulster. In September 1912, over 200 000 Protestants signed a covenant opposing Home Rule. They believed that 'Home Rule means Rome Rule'. They feared that they would lose their jobs and influence. They also formed the Ulster Volunteers to oppose Home Rule.

Source B is a popular Unionist slogan before 1914. It indicates that the Protestants in the north of Ireland were preparing to resist Home Rule:

'ULSTER WILL FIGHT AND ULSTER WILL BE RIGHT'

ONLINE

Find out more about Lloyd George and 'the People's Budget' of 1909 at the Digital Zone – www.brightredbooks.net/N5History.

Irish Nationalists also formed a volunteer force to support Home Rule. Both sides imported weapons and armed themselves for a struggle. In March 1914, British army officers based at the Curragh in Ireland refused to obey orders. They thought they were being ordered to take action against the Ulster Protestants.

Source C is the *Glasgow Herald* of 21 March 1914 reporting on the threats of violence in Ireland. It shows that this issue was a key concern to the government and the people of Great Britain in 1914.

> **THE ULSTER POWDER MAGAZINE**
>
> It is no longer possible for any rational person, whatever his political opinions may be, however sanguine his optimism, or however limitless his irresponsibility, to blink the fact that the situation in Ulster is grave in the extreme, and that the tiniest spark may begin a conflagration whose extent and effects no human being can foresee. The Government recognises the danger at last. The War Office has issued a wholly unnecessary explanation of its action in moving troops into Ulster – unnecessary, because the movement explains itself, and is the ordinary and inevitable sequel to severe tension of public feeling, no matter whether it arises from labour troubles or political disquiet. The War Office states that 'some time ago' the Army Council issued orders to the Commander-in-Chief in Ireland that he was to take special precautions to safeguard Government property …

THINGS TO DO AND THINK ABOUT

1. Imagine you were a government leader at this time. Look at the political problems above and sketch a mind-map of the issues facing the government.
   In groups, try to decide which are the most important and how you would campaign to fix this problem and win votes.

2. Imagine you are a German agent preparing a coded message to be sent to Berlin. You have to send a 60-word summary on the major issues facing the British government in 1914. Use the following code:

A	B	C	D	E	F	G	H	I	J	K	L	M
26	25	24	23	22	21	20	19	18	17	16	15	14
N	O	P	Q	R	S	T	U	V	W	X	Y	Z
13	12	11	10	9	8	7	6	5	4	3	2	1

Give the message to a neighbour and get them to translate it. You should do the same with theirs.

THE SCOTTISH SUFFRAGE MOVEMENT

WOMEN CAMPAIGN FOR THE VOTE

Before 1914, one of the major issues facing the Liberal Government was the campaign by groups of women to be granted the right to vote (known as **suffrage**). Between 1910 and 1914, this campaign reached its peak in Scotland and across Britain.

Why were women demanding the vote?

Inequality: The 1867 Reform Act in England and the 1868 Reform Act in Scotland had given the vote to working men who owned or rented property in towns worth more than £10 a year. Many women had campaigned in support of these acts. However, an attempt to give women the vote at the same time was defeated. This resulted in women's suffrage societies being formed in several British cities. The Edinburgh National Society for Women's Suffrage was formed in 1867. A Glasgow branch was formed in 1870.

The women who demanded the vote were to become known as Suffragists. They believed that the situation was unfair. Many of the women who did not possess the vote were better educated than some of the men who did. By 1910, a number of women had qualified as doctors. This included Marion Gilchrist, the first woman to graduate in Scotland with a medical degree.

Source A is from *The Scottish Suffragettes* by the historian Leah Leneman.

> By the end of the nineteenth century, the new woman existed and had far wider horizons open to her than her mother or aunts. She could be a teacher or doctor; she could own property or even her own business, in which case she could pay taxes just as a man did – but still she could not vote for her own MP.

Changing political and legal rights

By the end of the 19th century, women had witnessed many advances in their legal protection. Some of the worst laws had been altered. Women now had the right to retain their possessions and to own property if they got married. They also could be named sole guardian of their children if the husband died.

Women also gained the right to vote for town councillors in Scotland after 1882. However, the fact remained that women could not vote in general elections.

The 1906 general election saw a landslide victory for the Liberal Party. It was hoped they would introduce reform. However, there was disappointment when the expected political changes were slow to be introduced.

DON'T FORGET

Suffragists used peaceful methods. Suffragettes used militant tactics to gain attention.

DON'T FORGET

By 1910, many women were working in important but poorly paid jobs such as teaching.

ONLINE

Find out more about the suffragettes by clicking the link at www.brightredbooks.net/N5History.

SUFFRAGE CAMPAIGN GROUPS

By 1910, newspapers were carrying reports on Suffragists, Suffragettes and the Women's Freedom League.

Who were the Suffragists?

This was the National Union of Women's Suffrage Societies. It united a number of suffrage groups which had been in existence since the 1860s. It believed that peaceful methods could be used to win votes for women. They used petitions, speeches and rallies to put over their arguments. In 1914, the NUWSS had 300000 members in Britain.

Who were the Suffragettes?

This was the Women's Social and Political Union (WSPU). It was formed in Manchester in 1903 by Mrs Pankhurst and her two daughters Sylvia and Christabel. They believed that the campaign for the vote was not making enough progress. They were a militant organisation who believed in 'Deeds Not Words'. They had 2000 members in Britain by 1914.

What was the Women's Freedom League?

This was a small group of women who split from the WSPU in 1907. They disliked how the Pankhursts were running the WSPU and the use of violence – a major part of the Suffragette campaign. Two of its leaders, Teresa Billington-Greig and Charlotte Despard, had close connections to Scotland. As a result, the WFL had a number of supporters in Scotland.

TACTICS OF THE WOMEN'S SUFFRAGE GROUPS

NUWSS	WSPU	WFL
Petitions	Petitions	Petitions
Demonstrations	Demonstrations	Demonstrations
Speeches	Speeches	Speeches
Used posters	Disrupted political meetings	Disrupted political meetings
Encouraged men to join the organisation	Did not allow men to join the organisation	Encouraged men to join the organisation
Published their own newspaper – The Common Cause	Published their own newspaper – Votes for Women	Published their own newspaper – The Vote
	Refused to fill in forms for the 1911 census	Refused to fill in forms for the 1911 census
	Refused to pay tax	
	Attacked property	
	Hunger strikes when imprisoned	

A Suffragette being arrested

What impact did these activities have?

Suffragette attacks on property increased after 1912. The government's response was to arrest those who were found to be involved in the militant activities. When the women went on hunger strike, the authorities reacted with force-feeding. In Scotland, this was often carried out at Perth Prison.

Bad publicity meant that the government introduced the 'Cat and Mouse Act' in 1913. This allowed prisoners whose health was at risk to be released. Once recovered, the prisoners would be rearrested to complete their sentences. In 1914, women had still not been given the vote.

WHY DIDN'T WOMEN GET THE VOTE?

This was due to several factors:

- The Liberal Leader, Herbert Asquith, was firmly against female suffrage. WSPU violence simply reinforced this belief.

- WSPU violence got attention. However, many men and women were horrified by the Suffragette activities. There was a backlash against the Suffragettes and other speakers who favoured votes for women.

- Who was to get the vote? The Liberals had a problem. Before 1914, many working men could not vote. Any reform which gave the vote to both working men and women would benefit the Labour Party. Any reforms which gave female householders the vote would help the Conservatives.

- In 1912, a Conciliation Bill was introduced in an attempt to solve the problem. It would give the vote to women. It was defeated. By 1912, the Liberal Party had lost its strong majority in Parliament. It relied on the votes of a number of Irish Nationalist MPs. In 1912, they voted against the bill because they believed that it would lead to a Conservative victory in a general election. The Conservatives opposed Home Rule for Ireland.

In August 1914, the Great War broke out. The campaign for the vote was put aside. Many of the Suffragettes, such as Mrs Pankhurst, put their energies into supporting the war effort. Others, such as Sylvia Pankhurst, opposed the war because they believed it was wrong.

THINGS TO DO AND THINK ABOUT

1. Go to the Digital Zone and click the link, then take some time to watch the clip about the differences between Suffragists and Suffragettes. Which group do you think was more effective? Why?

2. Explain why women had not received the vote by 1914.

DON'T FORGET

The WSPU in Scotland set fire to the stand at Ayr Racecourse as well as exploding bombs at the Botanic Gardens in Glasgow and the Royal Observatory in Edinburgh. They also tried to blow up Burns' Cottage near Ayr.

ONLINE TEST

Test yourself on the Scottish suffrage movement at www.brightredbooks.net/N5History.

DON'T FORGET

In the years up to 1914, some important topics dominated the newspaper headlines: Ireland, Germany and trade unions. Some historians believe that this made the WSPU more extreme in their attempts to get noticed.

VIDEO LINK

The link for this clip can be found at the Digital Zone www.brightredbooks.net/N5History.

Scots on the Western Front: RECRUITMENT

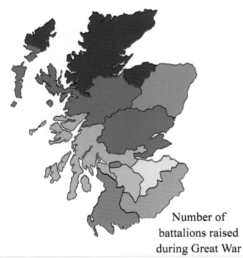

Number of battalions raised during Great War

■	Seaforth Highlanders	9
■	Cameron Highlanders	13
■	Gordon Highlanders	21
■	Black Watch	25
■	Argyll & Sutherland Highlanders	16
■	Cameronians (Scottish Rifles)	27
■	Royal Scots	35
■	King's Own Scottish Borderers	10
■	Royal Scots Fusiliers	18
■	Highland Light Infantry	26

SCOTS BATTALIONS AND THE OUTBREAK OF WAR

Source A shows the traditional recruiting areas of the Scottish Regiments. Each of these expanded during the Great War. A battalion was around 1000 men.

At the outbreak of war in August 1914, the British Expeditionary Force was sent to France. It numbered 100 000 men. The government recognised that this would not be enough. The early battles of the Great War had shocked many with their casualty figures: Mons and Le Cateau in August 1914 had resulted in 10 000 British casualties.

Field Marshal Lord Kitchener was appointed the Secretary of War in August 1914. Unlike many others, he did not believe that the war would be over by Christmas. He believed that it would last at least three years. The armed forces would need to be rapidly increased.

Some steps had already been taken. The Territorial Force had mobilised at the outbreak of war. This was made up of part-time volunteers. They had the nickname 'Saturday Night Soldiers'. However, it would take several months before they were ready for action.

A recruiting campaign was begun. On 8 August, Lord Kitchener asked for the first 100 000 volunteers. They had to be aged between 18 and 30. In September 1914, 500 000 men volunteered in Britain. By 1915, 320 589 Scots had volunteered for service. This was around 13% of the total number of British volunteers.

DON'T FORGET

Many Scots served in the army before the Great War. It was one way of escaping from boring, low-paid jobs and poverty.

ONLINE

Listen to veterans describing their experience of joining up by clicking the link at the Digital Zone www. brightredbooks.net/ N5History.

DIVISIONS OF THE SCOTTISH ARMY

Four divisions (each around 18 000 men) would be formed from Scotland's contribution:

- 9th Scottish Division
- 15th Scottish Division
- 51st Highland Division
- 52nd Lowland Division.

Source B describes the problems the Highland Light Infantry had dealing with men wishing to volunteer.

The HLI Depot at Hamilton, already worked off its feet dealing with the reservists, was thrown into a complete state of chaos lasting four days by a howling rabble arriving from Glasgow to enlist. These stout hearts declined to leave and the majority slept in the open ... until they could be dealt with – when two of them were found to only have one leg apiece one tried to get away with a wooden foot and several others had glass eyes.

Source C is C.N. Barclay, a Scot living in London, explaining his reasons for joining up.

With three or four friends I decided to join the London Scottish, and one day during the second half of August I visited their headquarters in Buckingham Gate, London, was medically examined and enlisted. My real reason for doing this was a simple one – at any age and in my circumstances and in the atmosphere of patriotic enthusiasm at the time I

contd

VIDEO LINK

Watch a great video from Education Scotland about Recruitment by clicking the link at www.brightredbooks.net/N5History.

would have been ashamed not to do so and my parents would have been ashamed of me if I had not done so. Secondary reasons were that several of my friends were joining the same regiment; also I had already decided that I did not want to be a civil engineer. It seemed likely to be a dull sort of profession.

Source D is William H. Marwick, who lived in Edinburgh, describing the reaction of his friends to the outbreak of war.

When the First World War broke out in August 1914, it came to me as to most of our contemporaries as a complete shock. But it evoked a great deal of enthusiasm at the time. Most people who had no experience of military life or any particular taste for it rallied and joined up. They were anxious to get into the war before it stopped. One of them, a friend of mine, used to say bitterly: 'But it didn't stop.'

Source E is William Murray, who was from Fife, explaining why he joined the army.

The night war was declared in August 1914 we played the final o' a football tournament in Denbeath and we won. And the whole team joined the army the next day, the whole team. 'Your King and Country need you' and all this sort of stuff – patriotism, patriotism, it wisn't the sense of excitement, it was patriotism. I said I was eighteen, and I was only sixteen.

DON'T FORGET

Thousands joined up in 1914. Most thought it would be a great adventure and 'over by Christmas'.

Source F explains why an Englishman, Norman Collins aged 18, from Hartlepool, joined the Seaforth Highlanders.

I enquired as to which was the most Northern regiment in the country, so my parents wouldn't find me easily and take me back home. They said the Seaforth Highlanders at Dingwall. I knew a little bit about the Regiment and liked their tartan. They were already fighting in France and had a good history, and when you're joining up you might as well join a good regiment and one that would see some fighting.

Army regiments had traditional recruiting areas. This meant that volunteers often came from the same area. On occasion, they had a lot more in common. In Glasgow, the 15th Battalion of the HLI was recruited in sixteen hours from the tram drivers and conductors of Glasgow Corporation. A further Battalion, the 16th, was made up of members of the Boys' Brigade. The 17th HLI was made up of businessmen.

In Edinburgh, the 16th Battalion of the Royal Scots became known as 'McCrae's Battalion', after its commander. It contained a large number of footballers, most of whom came from Heart of Midlothian Football Club.

Source G is a slogan used in 1914 to encourage Hearts supporters to volunteer.

DO NOT ASK WHERE HEARTS ARE PLAYING AND THEN LOOK AT ME ASKANCE. IF IT'S FOOTBALL THAT YOU'RE WANTING, YOU MUST COME WITH US TO FRANCE.

LORD DERBY'S SCHEME

Lord Derby was put in charge of recruitment in October 1915. At this point, the numbers of men joining up were in decline. He introduced a scheme to encourage more volunteers. Men would put their name on a register, but would not be called up until needed. Married men would not be called up until after all single men had been taken into the army. Those who volunteered were given an armband that they could wear. This had a red crown on it, showing that the wearer had put his name forward to join the armed forces. This was important, as men who were not wearing uniform were often stopped in the street and handed a white feather by women. The white feather was a sign of cowardice.

ONLINE TEST

Test yourself on Recruitment at the Digital Zone: www.brightredbooks.net/N5History

THINGS TO DO AND THINK ABOUT

A huge number of Scottish men volunteered to fight in the Great War. What do the above sources tell you about the reasons why people volunteered? Discuss this with a friend.

1914 AND THE OPENING MOVES

THE BRITISH EXPEDITIONARY FORCE

A number of Scottish regiments were part of the British Expeditionary Force (BEF) which was sent to France in August 1914. These units were made up of professional soldiers and were to play an important part in stopping the German advance at a number of battles in 1914. Over the next four years, Scottish soldiers were to have a role in every major battle on the Western Front which involved the British army.

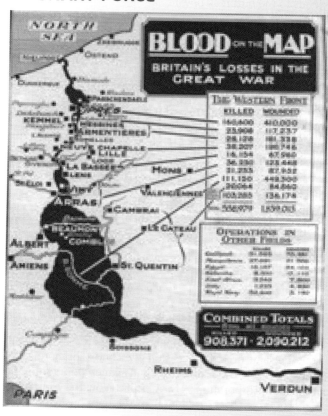

THE SCHLIEFFEN PLAN

This was Germany's war plan at the outbreak of war in 1914. Its intention was to defeat the French in six weeks. This would allow the German High Command to transfer its units to the east to face Russia. It was thought that the Tsar's army would take time to prepare for war. Speed and time were key factors if the plan was to work.

The German Army was to attack through neutral Belgium. This meant it could bypass the French Army and the forts which were massed opposite the German border.

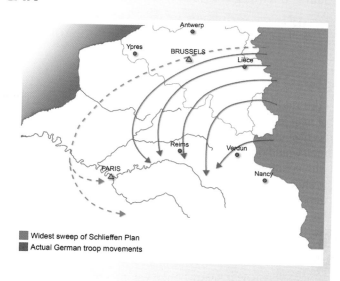

Widest sweep of Schlieffen Plan
Actual German troop movements

THE BEF ARRIVES

As the BEF was only around 100 000 men strong, it was not seen as a threat to the German plan. Kaiser Wilhelm reputedly referred to the British Army as a 'contemptible little force'. However, it was made up of experienced soldiers who had seen battle around the Empire. Many of them were to relish being known as 'Old Contemptibles'. At Mons and then at Le Cateau, the BEF slowed the Germans. They also inflicted heavy casualties on the advancing soldiers.

The Battle of the Marne and the 'race to the sea'

By mid-September 1914, the British and French armies had been forced to retreat to the River Marne. Here they faced and stopped the German Army. Both sides began a 'race to the sea'. Each side tried to 'outflank' the other. This meant that they were trying to get behind the enemy army. By Christmas 1914, both sides faced each other on a front line which stretched from Switzerland to the English Channel.

Source A is from the *Glasgow Herald* of 26 August 1914.

> The shooting of our infantry on the firing line was wonderful. Every time a German's head showed above the trench, and every time the German infantry attempted to rush a position, there came a withering fire from the khaki-clad forms lying in extended formation along a big battle front.

Source B is Sergeant I. F. Bell of the 2nd Battalion Gordon Highlanders describing the first encounter with the Germans in 1914.

> I told the men to keep under cover and detailed one man, Ginger Bain, as 'lookout'. After what seemed ages Ginger excitedly asked, how strong is the German army? I replied, 'Seven million.' 'Well,' said Ginger, 'here is the whole bloody lot of them making for us.'

Source C is an extract from the *Scotsman* newspaper of 18 August 1914.

Source D is from the *Scotsman* of Monday 31 August 1914.

BRITISH TROOPS ON THE CONTINENT

EXPEDITIONARY FORCE SAFELY LANDED IN FRANCE

The expeditionary Force as detailed for Foreign Service has been safely landed on foreign soil.

BRITISH OFFICIAL WAR NEWS

SPLENDID WORK OF THE EXPEDITIONARY FORCE
VERY HEAVY GERMAN LOSSES
ESTIMATE OF BRITISH CASUALTIES
GERMAN CAVALRY ROUTED BY SCOTS GREYS AND LANCERS

The battle on this day, August 26th, was of the most severe and desperate character. The troops offered a superb and most stubborn resistance to the tremendous odds with which they were confronted and at length extricated themselves in good order though in good order and under heaviest artillery fire. 5000–6000 British casualties.

THINGS TO DO AND THINK ABOUT

1. What was the British Expeditionary Force?

2. Look at Sources A, C and D. How do these newspaper sources make readers believe that the war is going well?

VIDEO LINK

To learn more about the reasons why the Schlieffen plan failed, watch a video at the Digital Zone www.brightredbooks.net/N5History.

ONLINE TEST

Take a test on this topic at the Digital Zone: www.brightredbooks.net/N5History

TRENCH WARFARE

ONLINE

Go to the Digital Zone and click the link to take a virtual tour of a World War One trench: www.brightredbooks.net/N5History.

VIDEO LINK

Visit the Digital Zone and click the link to view photos and listen to the experiences of a member of the Royal Scots: www.brightredbooks.net/N5History.

VIDEO LINK

Go online to watch some footage of the 5th Royal Scots training before going to the front line. www.brightredbooks.net/N5History.

THE TRENCH SYSTEM

By the end of 1914, the Allied armies faced their German opponents along the Western Front. Both sides had created a line of defence which could not be outflanked. Soldiers put a great deal of effort into creating a trench system which was to provide them with shelter from both the weather and the enemy. It was 460 miles long and was not to move a great deal in either direction for nearly four years.

The trench was a basic military position. Officers' manuals set out guidelines for their construction.

Source A is adapted from 'Notes for Infantry Officers on Trench Warfare' (March 1916).

Trench design

Trenches were supposed to zigzag. This was to prevent explosions or gunfire from causing casualties along the length of the trench. There would usually be around three lines of trenches.

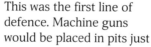

Alternative organisation of a front line

The front line

This was the first line of defence. Machine guns would be placed in pits just in front of the front line. This would give the gunners a clear field of fire. In front of the trenches would be barbed-wire entanglements.

The support trenches

This was the second line of defence. It also provided cover for soldiers to retreat to if the front line was being bombarded.

The reserve trenches

This was to be used if the soldiers had to fall back from the first two lines.

Between each of the lines, there would be communication trenches. This would allow the soldiers to move between the lines without being exposed to gunfire.

SOLDIER ROTATION

Soldiers would not be expected to spend all their time on the front line. They would rotate between the lines of trenches.

In theory, a soldier would expect to spend around four days on the front line, four days in the support trenches, four days in reserve trenches and four days out of the trenches. This, however, varied. An officer in the Argyll and Sutherland Highlanders spent six days in the trenches and six out in 1915. During an attack, however, soldiers would be expected to continue in the trenches until relieved.

Source B is an extract from the War Diary of the 5th Battalion Seaforth Highlanders.

> On 25th May 1916, the 152nd Brigade was withdrawn from the line for a rest after being for 74 days continuously in the trenches. During that time, our battalion had been 61 days in the trenches and 13 in the village of Maroeuil, which was daily under shell-fire.

contd

Source C is a diagram of a trench.

The trench had a number of features.

- It had to be at least two metres deep.

- 'Duckboards' or wooden planks were put down for soldiers to walk on.

- Trenches were supposed to have a sump for water drainage under this.

- Sandbags were used to add protection to the trench.

Within the trench, soldiers would usually build dugouts. These were placed on the side of the trench facing the enemy, and would provide a small amount of shelter. However, there were strict instructions about their construction. They had to have two entrances and were to have a wooden frame to provide support. Some soldiers took steps to make the dugouts more comfortable.

Source D is a description of a dugout by an officer who was serving in a Scottish regiment in 1915.

'It has a little door, nearly six feet high, and a real glass window, with a little curtain. Inside there is a bunk, six feet long, together with an ingenious folding wash hand stand and a flap table. The walls which are painted pale green, are decorated with elegant extracts from the 'Sketch' and 'La Vie Parisienne'.

Source E describes one of the dangers of being in a dugout. It is from the *Wigtown Free Press* of 6 July 1916.

STRANRAER SOLDIER'S THRILLING EXPERIENCES

Private A. Irving 9TH Black Watch has had the unique experience of having been twice buried alive within two months. On the first occasion a German shell struck the roof of the dugout in which he was stationed and along with five others he was entombed for two hours, three of his comrades being dead when extricated. After a few weeks' rest in hospital, he returned to his Company in the firing line and took part in a successful raid on the German trenches. It appears however that a shell struck the side of the trench which had been occupied, and sandbags, earthworks etc. collapsed on the top of the men, eight of whom including Private Irving were entombed for four hours. When the debris had been cleared away, four of the soldiers were found to be dead. Private Irving in a letter to his parents says he is back into hospital and is getting along all right, although still feeling sore from bruises.

THINGS TO DO AND THINK ABOUT

1. Explain why a line of trenches had been dug between Switzerland and the English Channel by December 1914.

2. Explain why trenches had the following features:
   a) be at least two metres deep
   b) have three lines of trenches
   c) be dug in a zigzag direction
   d) have dugouts.

3. Why do you think soldiers were only supposed to spend four days in front-line trenches?

ONLINE

Go to the Digital Zone and click the link to launch a virtual tour of a dugout: wwwbrightredbooks.net/N5History.

ONLINE TEST

To take a test on trench warfare, go to the Digital Zone: www.brightredbooks.net/N5History.

DAILY LIFE IN THE TRENCHES

ONLINE

Visit the Digital Zone to listen to veterans talking about their experiences on the Western Front: www.brightredbooks.net/N5History.

ONLINE

You can take a virtual tour of a typical day in the trenches at the Digital Zone: www.brightredbooks.net/N5History.

A TYPICAL DAY

TIME OF DAY	ACTIVITY
HALF HOUR BEFORE DAWN	Men 'stand to' in case of enemy attack. Officer checks trenches and stores.
DAWN	Men stood down. Breakfast. Officer writes report to Headquarters. Weapons cleaned and uniforms checked for lice.
DAYLIGHT HOURS	Officer's inspection of the men. This would include checking feet for signs of 'trench foot'. After inspection, the sergeant would issue duties. A third of men were put on sentry duty – 2 hours at a time. A third were sent for rations. A third were 'resting' or carrying out duties. These usually involved filling sandbags, carrying ammunition, draining trenches of water, fixing duckboards.
DUSK	Men 'stand to' in case of enemy attack. Ration parties arrive with supplies.
NIGHT	Patrols would be sent into 'No Man's Land' to gather intelligence on the enemy. Groups of men would fix the barbed wire in front of the trenches. The wounded lying in 'No Man's Land' would be recovered. A trench raid on the enemy positions might take place. Snipers would move into position.

A wiring party

Source A shows a wiring party. This group of soldiers is responsible for maintaining the barbed wire in front of a trench. Most of them are carrying 'silent pickets'. These were the posts that were used to support the barbed wire.

Source B is an extract from a diary kept by Sergeant James H. Leiper, of the Glasgow Highlanders.

18th January – was detailed for duty on a listening post so I picked on half a dozen good men whom I knew and about 7.30 pm we set out along a road towards the German line. Had the creeps up my back all the time and walked along with my rifle shoved out in front of me determined to make the best or worst of anything that turned up. About a couple of hundred yards down this road was a sort of low breastwork and we lay behind it to watch and listen. I suppose this was in case of any sudden attack on the part of the Germans when I had to send back word to the main line. That done I suppose we would then have to make a fight for ourselves or clear out the best possible way. At least I told my ½ dozen men this, but also in case of anything of the kind happening it would be better if we all kept together. United we stand, divided we fall, so to speak. It was an eerie duty – although nothing came off – except a visit from one of our own officers. Incidentally we nearly killed him as he was so slow at replying to our challenge.

I got an opportunity of crawling out in front here and was surprised at the number of dead lying about, both Germans and British. Evidently some heavy fighting must have taken place just previous to our coming up. Most of the bodies were frozen to the ground and could not be moved. During the crawling-out stunt I came upon the Germans who had gone down before our guns the previous day (I had two men with me of course – would never have gone by myself, no fear). We got a few papers etc. out of their pockets – some money and a helmet each. Turned out to be men of the Jaeger Regiment – their hats were something similar to a postman at home. About 6.30 just as dawn was beginning to come up we came back to the main line and proudly displayed our souvenirs to the rest of the Company.

DON'T FORGET

Many of the photographs would have been censored. They would not show many of the worst aspects of trench warfare. Many were posed.

FOOD IN THE TRENCHES

Life in the trenches was not made easier by the quality of food soldiers were expected to survive on. During the early years of the war, there was no provision made for hot food to be served to soldiers in the trenches. Soldiers were expected to make their own arrangements. Many units would get small stoves to cook their food on. Later, larger horse-drawn cooking wagons were used, although these were behind the lines. Food was brought up in containers which had been insulated with straw.

Many soldiers had to survive on 'iron rations'. These were a tin of 'bully beef' (corned beef), a small tin of biscuits, a small amount of tea mixed with sugar, and possibly a piece of cheese. It was an offence to eat these rations without an officer's permission.

Soldiers would often complain about the food. Most became familiar with the tins of bully beef, Tommy Tickler's Jam and Maconochie's Stew. The stew was made by the Maconochie's Canning Company, which was based in Fraserburgh. Soldiers claimed that it was 'just about edible when eaten hot but, if it was necessary to consume it cold, then it would likely kill you as surely as the Germans'.

 VIDEO LINK

Go to the Digital Zone and click the link to watch an alternative take on life in the trenches: www.brightredbooks.net/N5History.

 VIDEO LINK

You can also watch a clip of soldiers receiving their rations at the Digital Zone: www.brightredbooks.net/N5History.

Source C is from a letter by J. B. MacLean, who served with the Cameronians.

I think the principal trouble at present is the cold. We can't cook up here as the smoke would be seen, but we manage to make hot tea using a candle as the heating agent: otherwise everything is cold and a steady diet at all meals of tea, bully or cold roast, bread butter and jam with perhaps biscuits or tinned fruit, gets a bit monotonous in winter time, and one's idea of heaven is a warm room with a respectable dinner on a table and no earth mined in the grub or tea.

Source D is from the diary of Sergeant James H. Leiper, Glasgow Highlanders. He describes the difficulties of getting clean water on the front line.

Rested at Beuvry until 4th February 1915. Went up in the line on night of 5th and found things exceedingly quiet, although we had one man killed and 8 wounded. This was a funny business. All these men had been hit while getting water out of a burn which ran past the end of our trench. I went along one day to investigate and after cautiously poking my head out past the parapet I looked into the burn and got quite a shock. There was a dead German lying half in and half out of the water – but the bloomin bit was we had been making tea with this water for the past 3 days. I did not say anything however but we got a barricade up that night to stop the men going along. I made sure after that when I made tea that I saw where the water came from.

Source E is Sergeant Leiper describing one activity that the majority of soldiers took part in.

Remained at Locon till Christmas 1914. On this day we received a present from Princess Mary – tobacco, cigs, pipe – enclosed in a gilt box. Also we celebrated Xmas in our own way. Our Battalion had run out of matches here and it was a job to get a pipe or a cig lit. It was a sorry sight to see some man appear smoking a cig. He was immediately besieged for a light by about 30 or 40 men. By the time they all got lit up the original smoker's cig was crumpled to bits and he had to beg a light for another one.

THINGS TO DO AND THINK ABOUT

1. Look at Source B. What evidence is there that this duty would have involved a great deal of risk?

2. Describe the rations available to soldiers in the trenches.

3. Explain why it was so difficult to get warm food in the trenches.

 **ONLINE TEST**

To take a test on daily life in the trenchs, go to the Digital Zone: www.brightredbooks.net/N5History.

KEEPING CLEAN AND STAYING ALIVE

HEALTH AND HYGIENE

Keeping clean on the Western Front was a challenge. Most soldiers did not remove their uniform during their time in the trenches. Water was needed for drinking. Few would have the opportunity to wash. As a result, the vast majority of soldiers suffered from lice. These small insects fed on the blood of the soldiers and laid their eggs in the seams of clothing. Their main impact was to cause itching and scratching. In the trenches, this could result in boils, ulcers or impetigo – a serious skin infection.

Many soldiers spent their off-duty time in the trenches 'delousing'. They would run a candle along the seam to destroy the 'mickies', 'cooties' or 'chats', as the lice were known.

Source A (in the margin to the left) shows a group of soldiers removing lice from their clothing. The painting was made by a soldier who served on the Western Front.

A second major problem was 'trench foot'. It was caused by standing for hours in water or mud. The symptom was the loss of feeling in the feet. If not treated, it could result in gangrene. The treatment in this case was often amputation.

Source B (in the margin below, to the left) shows the effects of trench foot.

Source C (below) is an extract from the diary of a Kirkintilloch man, William St Clair, who served in the Royal Army Medical Corps:

Sunday 28th November
The trenches are in a fearful state of mud and trench feet are very common, and no wonder when fellows have to stand in mud for four days without getting their boots off and it has been very keen frost these last three nights and we had a lot of frost-bitten this forenoon and very sore some of them look.

Officers were instructed to check that each of their men regularly removed their boots and put on dry socks. Soldiers were supplied with whale oil to rub into their feet.

DEATH IN THE TRENCHES

Soldiers on the Western Front quickly became used to the sights and sounds of death. One historian has calculated the fate of one battalion that served on the Western Front.

Soldiers faced a number of challenges. Attacks or trench raids would usually result in large numbers of killed or wounded. However, casualties could occur even when the front line was quiet. Snipers would wait for hours for a suitable target. Artillery or mortar shells could drop without warning.

Served	8,313	
Killed/Died of Wounds	1,462	(17.6%)
Wounded/Gassed	3,648	(43.9%)
Invalided sick to the UK	2,066	(24.9%)
Transferred to units in the UK	227	
Transferred to other battalions and units	896	
Commissioned in the field and transferred	1	
Drowned	1	
Executed by shooting after Field General Courts Marshal	2	

Source D is an extract from the diary of Sergeant Leiper, Glasgow Highlanders.

10.45 p.m. Apr. 4th 1915
It was the same old drag. There are a few graves just at the back of the butt. One man had just had some earth piled up on the top of him as he lay. Today I saw one of his boots sticking out – the rain had washed away the earth. We covered it up. I had a shave and wash-up at the expense of running over to the ditch at the back for water at the risk of my life.

contd

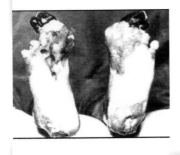

It was about two hours later and the shells had been bursting around as usual. A big one burst just outside and we remarked that it was a close one, when all of a sudden there was a deafening crash. We seemed to have been transported into hell. The place was suffocating with the stench of lyddite. Gradually we came to and looked at each other, then I looked out of the small opening into the big dugout. Oh, my God, the sight that met my eyes. The shell had come right into the opening. I don't know yet just what I saw for I didn't concentrate my gaze on it but I know it was ghastly, hellish, infernal – flesh, blood, clothing and everything. I crawled outside and looked in. The officer was sitting up with blood streaming down his face and I heard him say to someone at the other side 'For God's sake bring help or something'.

And during the forenoon our company went down the communication trench. The firing trench as we filed along was an awful sight. Dead men, wounded men and blood were scattered all over, and rifles and equipment of every description were lying thick. It was here of course that the attack had taken place a week before and had failed also. There were a few Gurkhas. At one place we had to step over a shambles of five or six dead Highlanders who had been killed in the morning by one of our own shells bursting short. They were piled one on top of the other, and our big company sergeant major was lying at the bottom. The man on top was still gasping. It was hellish.

CASUALTIES

The death of a colleague or friend could also affect soldiers. The result was that not all casualties were affected by physical wounds. Many were affected by 'shell shock'. This condition became well known during the Great War. Soldiers who suffered from it often lost control of their behaviour. Some would shake or become hysterical. Others might experience blindness or deafness. In 1914, it was reported that there were 1906 cases. In 1915, this rose to 20 327 cases. After the war ended, 50 000 men who had served in the British army were awarded war pensions because of their mental health.

During the war, a great number of hospitals were set up around Scotland and the rest of Britain to cater for the large numbers of casualties. Craiglockhart in Edinburgh was for shell-shocked officers. The poets Siegfried Sassoon and Wilfred Owen met there as they recovered from the stresses of the Western Front.

Hospitals, such as Stobhill in Glasgow, were taken over. It became the 3rd and 4th Scottish Military General Hospitals. Craigleith was the 2nd Scottish Military General Hospital and Aberdeen had the 1st Scottish Military General Hospital.

Many large houses were also taken over to provide facilities for soldiers who were recovering. While in hospital, soldiers would wear a navy blue uniform. This was to ensure that civilians realised that the individual concerned was a wounded soldier.

Sources F shows wounded soldiers who were recovering in Lenzie near Glasgow.

THINGS TO DO AND THINK ABOUT

1. Explain why almost 25% of an infantry unit might be sent back to Britain due to illness.

2. Describe the effects of shell shock.

 DON'T FORGET

Soldiers were not supposed to keep diaries in case they fell into enemy hands. However, many did. These often supply important evidence about events that the men witnessed. Unlike letters home, they were not heavily censored; but they only record the opinion of one person.

 VIDEO LINK

Go to the Digital Zone and click the link to watch a video and learn more about shell shock: www.brightredbooks. net/N5History.

 DON'T FORGET

There were usually far more men wounded than killed in a battle. The authorities had to take over a number of large houses and hospitals to deal with the casualties.

 ONLINE TEST

To take a test on this topic, go to the Digital Zone: www.brightredbooks.net/ N5History.

WEAPONS

THE CHANGING FACE OF WARFARE

During the Great War, a number of weapons were used on the Western Front. Some of these, such as the rifle and bayonet, had been in service for many years. The experience of the Western Front caused both sides to use new weapons such as poison gas, tanks and aircraft, to gain an advantage.

Source A is from the *History of the Great War Based on Official Documents*.

Causes of British Casualties 1914–1918	
Shell or mortar fire	58.5%
Rifle and machine gun bullets	39.0%
Bombs and grenades	2.2%
Bayonet	0.3%

THE RIFLE AND BAYONET

An infantry soldier would be equipped with two basic weapons. These were his rifle and bayonet. The British Army had learned some very hard lessons fighting the Boers in South Africa between 1899 and 1902. They had quickly realised the value of good marksmanship. As a result, professional soldiers in the British Army were trained to very high standards. The average soldier could fire about 15 rounds per minute. At the Battle of Mons, the British fire was so rapid and accurate that the Germans believed the British soldiers to be equipped with machine guns. This ability declined after 1914 as the pre-war British Army soldiers became casualties and were replaced by the enthusiastic recruits.

British soldiers were trained to use the bayonet. This was the knife that was attached to the front of their rifle. It was designed to be used in hand-to-hand fighting. Some officers were not impressed with its usefulness.

A British Lee-Enfield short rifle

Source B is Basil Liddell Hart, who served as an officer during the Great War, descibing the effectiveness of the bayonet.

We had a visit from Colonel Campbell's bayonet fighting team. Its worse effect was in multiplying our own men's loss of life by teaching them to push on and 'close with the bayonet' without firing, while the more cool-headed enemy, who did not fix their bayonets, went on shooting them down as they approached.

Source C is a diagram adapted from a British Army manual on bayonet fighting.

HAND GRENADES

During the war, the British organised bombing parties. These usually followed riflemen into enemy trenches. Their duty was to clear the dugouts, which they did by throwing grenades into them. By 1915, British factories were producing around 250 000 grenades a week. This was not always enough for the demands of the Western Front. Some officers believed that using hand grenades often slowed down an attack. They believed that the soldiers would have been more effective if they charged the enemy trenches rather than throwing grenades into them.

contd

Source D is a diagram adapted from a British Army manual on hand grenades.

Source E is a corporal of the Gordon Highlanders. He is a 'bomber' and is wearing a vest that was used to carry grenades.

MACHINE GUNS

Machine guns were one of the most important weapons on the Western Front. Most could fire around 500 rounds a minute. At the outbreak of the war, each battalion of the British Army was equipped with two machine guns. These were usually Vickers machine guns, which needed a crew of three men. By 1918, each battalion had around 32 machine guns. These were Lewis guns, which were lighter and needed a crew of two.

Source F is a Lewis machine gun.

Machine guns could have a devastating effect on an attack.

Source G is Lieutenant B. Meadows of the 17th Battalion of the Highland Light Infantry describing the effects of machine guns on his unit on 1 July 1916.

> *Our battalion had been badly hit. 'B' Company on our left had been caught in the wire and cut to pieces by machine-gun fire. My own company, 'A', was down to low numbers. My captain and platoon officer were both killed, all the platoon NCOS were killed or wounded. We had 17 officers killed and were working the battalion with two officers.*

During the war a new unit was set up. It was called the Machine Gun Corps. It soon gained a reputation for being one of the first units in an attack and one of the last to retreat. This meant that soldiers in this unit often became casualties. They used Vickers machine guns, which were heavier than the Lewis guns.

Source H in the margin to the right shows a Vickers machine gun.

Source I describes how one member of the Machine Gun Corps won the Victoria Cross.

> *On the 21st March 1918 Lieutenant Allan Ker of the Gordon Highlanders won the Victoria Cross while serving with the MGC. When the enemy were pressing hard, Lieutenant Ker with just one Vickers Machine Gun succeeded in holding up the German advance and was causing many casualties. He remained at his post with several of his men who had been badly wounded and personally beat off several bayonet attacks with his revolver after the machine gun had been destroyed. In spite of his exhaustion from the fighting and Gas poisoning Lieutenant Ker only surrendered after he had used all his ammunition. He managed to hold off over 500 of the enemy for more than 3 hours.*

THINGS TO DO AND THINK ABOUT

1. What caused the majority of casualties to British soldiers on the Western Front?

2. Look at Source B. Explain why some British officers did not believe that the bayonet was useful in the Great War.

3. What criticisms did officers make of hand grenades?

ONLINE

Click the links at the Digital Zone to read more about machine guns and other weapons: www.brightredbooks.net/N5History.

ONLINE TEST

Test your knowledge of First World War weapons online at the Digital Zone: www.brightredbooks.net/N5History.

ARTILLERY AND GAS

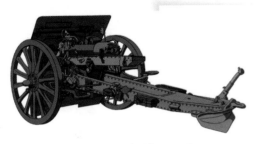

Source A shows a British 18-pounder gun.

Source B shows a British 6-inch howitzer.

ARTILLERY

Artillery could be divided into two groups:

- Guns – These were used to fire directly at targets.

- Howitzers – These could be used to lob shells from a distance at targets.

The size of guns could be measured in two ways: either by the weight of shell or by the diameter of the gun barrel. One of the most common British artillery guns was the 18-pounder. The German equivalent was the 77mm gun. The larger guns (referred to as 'heavies') were huge. The Germans used a 42cm howitzer in Belgium in 1914. The British developed a 60-pounder gun as well as making use of guns such as the 15-inch (37.5cm) howitzer. These guns could have a terrible impact on their targets. However, their effects were sometimes overestimated. Low cloud, careful camouflage and deep, well-built dugouts could often provide a measure of protection.

THE ROLE AND USES OF ARTILLERY

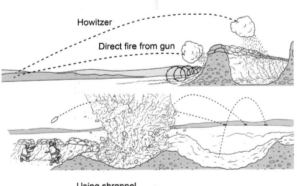

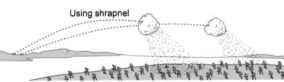

Artillery in action

Artillery was used for a number of purposes:

- Lighter guns were used to destroy barbed wire, machine guns or strongpoints.

- Howitzers were used to destroy larger targets, such as enemy artillery, roads or railways.

Artillery could be used in a number of ways:

- A **short burst** at a regular time of the day. Sometimes referred to as the 'morning hate' or 'daily hate'. This was designed to cause general difficulties for the enemy.

- An **individual shot** at a particular target. This was used to allow gunners to 'register' a target and was supposed to improve accuracy. If the enemy were suspected of preparing for an offensive, these areas would be shelled. By 1917, the commander of the 9th Scottish Division had developed methods which meant that this was no longer always needed. This helped to ensure surprise.

- A **barrage**. This was a heavy bombardment of an enemy target. At the Battle of the Somme, the British bombardment lasted a week and used a million shells. The large amounts of shells needed took the British by surprise during the first year of the war. In 1915, the British attack at Neuve Chapelle had failed. One of the reasons given was that the British guns had run short of shells.

- During the war, the barrage was further developed. The **'creeping' barrage** was introduced by 1916. During an attack, the infantry would move forward under the protection of the artillery bombardment. They were supposed to be around 45 metres from the bombardment. This was supposed to keep the enemy under fire until the infantry were very close to them. The artillery would then lift their fire onto the next line of defences.

ONLINE

Visit the Digital Zone to watch an animation of how a creeping barrage was supposed to work. www.brightredbooks.net/N5History.

contd

- In the event of a German attack, a unit could ask for **SOS fire**. This was often done by firing a sequence of coloured rockets. The artillery would react by firing on prearranged targets to break up the attack.

- Artillery could fire a number of different shells. These were: **high explosive** – designed to destroy targets; **shrapnel** – small metal balls designed to kill people; and **gas shells**.

VIDEO LINK

You can watch a short clip of soldiers moving up to the front line at the Battle of the Somme and using a Howitzer in 1916 at the Digital Zone: www.brightredbooks.net/N5History.

GAS

Gas was used by both sides during the war. On the Western Front, it was first used by the Germans at the Second Battle of Ypres in April 1915. It caused a number of casualties among the Canadians who faced it. A number of different types of gas were used.

Chlorine

This could be seen and smelt. Men could avoid some of the effects by putting a handkerchief over their mouth and keeping their head above the parapet of the trench. However, those soldiers exposed to it could be seriously wounded or killed. Many of those who breathed in the gas were still disabled at the end of the Great War.

Phosgene

This was regarded as an improvement over chlorine. Those soldiers who breathed it in would often die slowly 48 hours later. Their lungs would fill up with fluid, and they would effectively drown.

Mustard

This gas could cause massive blisters and blindness. It was very difficult to detect. There was little in the way of precautions available to soldiers. This was particularly true of Scottish soldiers who wore the kilt.

Source D to the right shows the type of gas mask in use by 1916.

Source E describes the experience of two Seaforth Highlanders who were caught in a gas attack.

> *Here they smelt gas, and could hear the peculiar whine of the gas shells and the slight 'phut' they gave as they burst. They put on their gas masks and sat tight. It is very difficult to see at night with a gas helmet on, and they had the danger of falling into the river or tumbling into a shell-hole plus their other troubles. They ultimately reached the bridge and gasped for breath for some time, as a gas mask isn't exactly the best oxygen supplying apparatus for a sprint.*

ONLINE

Visit the Digital Zone to listen to a podcast of veterans describing their experiences of gas attacks at Ypres: www.brightredbooks.net/N5History.

Source C shows British soldiers who have been blinded by gas.

Covenant with Death
(*Daily Express* 1934)

DON'T FORGET

Gas was a very unreliable weapon. Its effects could be limited by the weather. At the Battle of Loos in 1915, the wind blew the gas back onto the British trenches.

THINGS TO DO AND THINK ABOUT

Complete the following table.

WEAPON	How was it used on the battlefield?	What effect did it have on the battlefield?
RIFLE		
BAYONET		
HAND GRENADE		
MACHINE GUN		
ARTILLERY		
GAS		

ONLINE TEST

Test your knowledge of this topic online at the Digital Zone: www.brightredbooks.net/N5History.

TANKS

A NEW BREAKTHROUGH?

In 1916, the British introduced the tank in an attempt to force a breakthrough on the Western Front. The first tanks were divided into two categories:

Male tanks
Crew: 8
Weapons: 2 x 6-pdr guns;
4 x machine guns
Speed: 4–6 mph

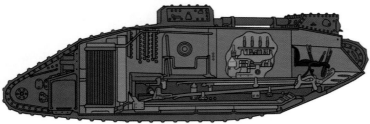

Cross-section

Male tanks – these carried heavy guns and were designed to deal with pillboxes.

Female tanks – these carried machine guns and were designed to deal with infantry.

The tanks were bulletproof and were not stopped by machine guns or barbed wire. However, they were slow, as they could only manage around four miles per hour. This made them easy targets for artillery. They were also unreliable and often broke down. They were used for the first time at the Battle of Somme in 1916, but they did not change the battle. Around 50 were originally to be used, but 19 broke down before the attack. The rest found it difficult to move on soft ground that was covered in shellholes. They were to have more success when used on well-drained ground.

ONLINE

Go to the Digital Zone to get a good look at the Mark 1 tank in action! www.brightredbooks.net/ N5History.

THE BATTLE OF CAMBRAI

In November 1917, the British launched an attack near Cambrai in France. Over 300 tanks were to be used on dry, chalky ground. The artillery bombardment by 1000 guns was very short. This meant that the Germans had little warning of the attack. The tanks crushed the barbed wire and easily crossed the trenches. Within a few hours, the soldiers had advanced over 4 miles – a distance unheard of in many of the other battles. They had also captured 4000 prisoners. However, by the end of the first day, 180 of the tanks were out of action. The majority had either broken down or got stuck.

Source A, below right, is from the *Glasgow Herald*, 23 November 1917.

The attack did not entirely go to plan. The commander of the 51st Highland Division did not want his soldiers to be too close to the tanks. He believed that the tanks would attract enemy fire. As a result, the tanks and infantry became separated. This meant that both became easy targets for machine guns and artillery.

ONLINE

Visit the Digital Zone to listen to veterans describing the impact of tanks: www. brightredbooks.net/ N5History.

TANKS VICTORY

TROOPS IN HIGH SPIRITS
SCOTTISH TERRITORIALS HARD FIGHT

English, Irish and Scottish troops went behind the tanks cheering them on and laughing and laughing when they saw them get at the German wire and eat it up and then head for the Hindenburg line and cross it as though it were but a narrow ditch.

contd

Ten days after the British attack, the Germans counter-attacked. They recaptured all of the territory they had lost. The stalemate continued.

Source B is Captain Jake Wilson describing the destruction of his tank at Cambrai in 1917.

> *Climbing the slight slope to the ridge beyond was a piece of cake, but when we showed our noses over the top we got two direct hits in as many minutes. The first smashed the left track, causing us to swing to the right to receive a broadside from the second. We had a drill for 'evacuating tank' if hit, which we put into action successfully, leaving only the driver and myself to receive the second one from which I escaped, but the driver, a young Scotsman, regrettably perished.*

VIDEO LINK

You can watch a short clip about the impact of tanks at Cambria at the Digital Zone: www.brightredbooks.net/N5History.

Source C is the mask that a tank-crew member would wear. It was designed to protect him from 'splash'. This was small bits of metal or paint which would flake off from the inside of the tank if it was struck by a bullet or shell.

Source D is a tank commander describing his experience of the Battle of Cambrai.

> *Occasionally there was a harsh metallic clang on the side of the tank as bursts of fire from rifle and machine guns struck us. With these hits came a faintly acrid odour, but no 'splash' came through, and gradually as we crunched and flattened the elaborate barbed-wire entanglements the clamour on our bulletproof plate practically ceased. The barrage had obliterated the enemy front-line defences.*

Source E describes how tanks would deal with the problems of barbed wire and trenches.

> *The tanks worked in threes. One nosed up, sought a crossing of the deep wide trench and then released a huge fascine (made of sleepers and tightly bound brushwood). The machine dipped down, and as its tracks got a purchase on the fascine its nose slowly tilted up. With hardly any exceptions, all the tanks succeeded in reaching the level ground beyond. Meanwhile the other two tanks of a group of three moved up and down along the parapet shelling any point that might have a machine gun emplacement. Then they too crossed over the fascine of their leader retaining their own to negotiate the crossing of the support and reserve lines later on.*

 THINGS TO DO AND THINK ABOUT

1. Complete the following table.

ADVANTAGES OF TANKS	DISADVANTAGES OF TANKS

ONLINE TEST

To test your knowledge of this topic, go to the Digital Zone: www.brightredbooks.net/N5History.

2. Why did the Germans have little warning of the British attack at Cambrai?

3. Evaluate the usefulness of Source B as evidence of the effects of tanks on the Western Front. You may want to comment on who wrote it, why they wrote it, what they say or what has been missed out.

AIRCRAFT

OBSERVATION AND RECONNAISSANCE

During the Great War, aircraft began to play a bigger role in the fighting on the Western Front. They were used for reconnaissance. They would fly over enemy lines and take photographs of targets. They were also used as artillery observers. As the war progressed, they were even used for bombing.

The Royal Flying Corps (RFC) was also responsible for **observation balloons** on the Western Front. These often became the focus of vicious aerial battles, as the Germans would try to shoot them down.

Source A, above right, shows a British observation balloon being inflated.

Source B, to the right, shows an aerial reconnaissance picture of the positions during the Battle of Loos in 1915.

THE FIRST ACES

The men who carried out this type of work were members of the RFC, which was part of the army. The RAF was not formed until April 1918. The pilots who served in the RFC were often young and had only a few hours of training in aircraft before they were sent to France.

Planes carried a very limited amount of ammunition. Some inexperienced pilots fired off all their bullets in a few seconds. They were then very vulnerable to the attentions of enemy 'aces' such as Baron von Richthofen, the 'Red Baron', who shot down 80 Allied aircraft on the Western Front. British pilots such as Albert Ball (44 enemy planes destroyed) also qualified as aces.

The highest-scoring Scottish ace was Major John Gilmour from Helensburgh. He had joined the Argyll and Sutherland Highlanders before transferring to the RFC. He shot down 39 German planes during the war and was awarded the Distinguished Service Order and Military Cross. Around 53 Scots were regarded as aces, which meant that they had each shot down at least five aircraft.

Major John Gilmour

DON'T FORGET

The lives of RFC pilots could be short. In April 1917, it was estimated that the lifespan of an RFC pilot on the Western Front was between 11 days and 3 weeks.

VIDEO LINK

To learn more about First World War aircraft, you can watch a video clip at the Digital Zone: www.brightredbooks.net/N5History.

THE HAZARDS OF FLYING

The biggest fear for pilots was fire. They sat close to the engine and fuel tank. This meant that, if either was struck, the flames would blow back towards the pilot. They stood little chance. Some carried pistols to shoot themselves rather than burn. Others would jump to their death. None carried parachutes although these were available. The British commanders believed that parachutes were unnecessary. They also thought that some pilots might jump from their aircraft before any 'dogfight' with the enemy.

A number of developments took place to improve the effectiveness of aircraft. Engines were improved; planes became faster and could fly higher. However, most were made from wood and fabric. This meant that, unless a bullet hit the pilot or engine, it usually passed through the plane without causing serious damage.

Aircraft were either 'pusher' (engine at the rear of the aircraft) or 'puller' (engine at the front of the aircraft). Pusher aircraft were slow but had machine guns that could fire forward. Puller aircraft were faster but usually found it difficult to fire forward.

The problem was solved in 1915 by the Germans, who immediately gained an advantage. They synchronised their machine guns with the propeller, which meant they could fire forward. The British reacted with improved pusher aircraft. Later in the war, they introduced fighter aircraft such as the Sopwith Camel.

Source C to the left is a German Fokker triplane fighter.

AIRCRAFT IN SCOTLAND

The RFC had a number of bases in Scotland, such as Turnhouse and Montrose. Many of these were situated on the east coast to defend against enemy attacks. There were also Royal Naval Air Service (RNAS) stations, which were concerned with protecting British ships against attack from U-boats (submarines). These bases operated seaplanes. Between 1914 and 1918, the main base for these aircraft was in Dundee on the Firth of Tay.

The RNAS also operated airships. These were also used to spot enemy U-boats. The first was at Luce Bay near Stranraer. Others were very soon added, including East Fortune in East Lothian. The airships were not always effective. Although they could float over areas for long periods of time, they were very vulnerable to bad weather, and a number were lost in accidents.

Source D shows an RNAS Sea Scout balloon escorting the steamer *Princess Maude* in Loch Ryan in 1916.

 ## THINGS TO DO AND THINK ABOUT

1. What was the role of aircraft over a battlefield?

2. Why do you think the life expectancy of a British pilot might have been as little as 11 days in April 1917?

 ONLINE

Visit the Digital Zone to listen to a podcast of veterans describing their experiences of air warfare: www.brightredbooks.net/N5History.

 VIDEO LINK

You can watch a clip of the RFC preparing for an attack at the Digital Zone: www.brightredbooks.net/N5History.

 ONLINE TEST

To test yourself further on this topic, go to the Digital Zone: www.brightredbooks.net/N5History.

STRATEGY AND TACTICS ON THE WESTERN FRONT

STRATEGIES

DON'T FORGET

Strategy means the overall planning and aims behind military operations during a war. This might involve armies or fleets of ships.

After 1914, the stalemate on the Western Front led to several strategies being adopted to force a breakthrough and defeat the Central Powers. Some politicians and officers believed that the deadlock could be broken by defeating Germany's allies, Austria-Hungary, Bulgaria and Turkey, as they were regarded as weaker.

Supporters of this strategy have been called 'Easterners' and included Winston Churchill. In 1915, British, French, Australian and New Zealand troops landed at Gallipoli in Turkey. The plan was to knock Turkey out of the war. The attack failed, and the soldiers were evacuated after a year.

DON'T FORGET

Tactics means the methods used to achieve a particular goal. These are used by smaller numbers of soldiers.

Many officers believed that the war could only be won in France. This group has been called 'Westerners'. It was thought that the best way to defeat the Germans was to destroy their army. This led to battles being fought which were designed to kill or wound German soldiers. The strategy was known as attrition. It was thought that this would cause the Germans eventually to run out of soldiers.

BATTLE	DURATION	DAYS	BRITISH CASUALTIES	GERMAN CASUALTIES	DAILY BRITISH RATE OF LOSS
1915 Loos	25 Sept to 18 Oct	24	61 000	25 000	2541
1916 Somme	1 July to 18 Nov	141	415 000	465 000	2950
1917 Arras	9 April to 17 May	39	159 000	120 000	4070
1917 Passchendaele (3rd Ypres)	31 July to 12 Nov	105	244 000	220 000	2121
1918 German Spring Offensive	21 March to 30 April	41	239 793	168 000	5848
Final offensive ('The Hundred Days Offensive')	8 Aug to 11 Nov	96	350 000	785 700	3645

Source A shows the estimated British and German losses during a number of battles on the Western Front.

To try to force a breakthrough, the British and French also put their faith in new weapons – but with mixed results. They did not achieve a decisive victory.

BATTLE OF LOOS, SEPTEMBER 1915

This was an attempt to break through the German lines in September 1915. The British planned to use a gas and artillery bombardment to destroy the German defences. Six divisions were to be used to exploit a breakthrough.

DON'T FORGET

The Battle of Loos was a significant part of Scottish military history. Two of the six divisions involved in the battle, the 9th and the 15th, were Scottish.

Even before the offensive, the British generals in charge, French and Haig, were not happy with the area chosen to be attacked. The ground was very flat and had little protection for attacking soldiers. Furthermore, the Germans had built a strong line of defences. These included large amounts of barbed-wire obstacles.

Source B explains why the British generals did not feel ready to fight a battle at Loos.

> *The regular troops at their disposal were mostly replacements, their officers newly promoted and inexperienced; and the few recently arrived Kitcheners battalions were at best half-trained. The shell and gun shortage had eased but not sufficiently to guarantee the success of a major offensive.*

Source C shows the tactics used during the Battle of Loos in 1915.

ONLINE

You can read a first-hand account of the Battle of Loos online at the Digital Zone: www.brightredbooks.net/N5History.

TACTIC	EFFECTIVENESS
Artillery bombardment which lasted 4 days	Failed to destroy the German positions. Warned the Germans that an attack was coming.
Use of gas	Blew back onto British positions in some areas, causing 2632 casualties including 7 deaths. In some areas, it worked and caused confusion among the Germans. Their gas masks would only provide protection from gas for 30 minutes.
Infantry attack	Advanced in waves. Some units, such as the 15th Scottish Division, captured their targets. Some soldiers lost direction and ended up in the wrong position. Very heavy casualties among the infantry units. Reinforcements were kept too far away from the battlefield. When they arrived, the Germans had reorganised their defences.

BATTLE OF THE SOMME, JULY 1916

One of the most important battles on the Western Front took place in the summer of 1916. It was an attempt by the British to force a breakthrough around the River Somme. The battle followed the same tactics as many other battles.

Source D shows the tactics used during the Battle of the Somme in 1916.

TACTIC	EFFECTIVENESS
Artillery bombardment which lasted 7 days	Warned the Germans that an attack was coming. The Germans used deep dugouts, which protected their men from shellfire. The Germans also withdrew many of their men from positions under fire. The barbed wire was not destroyed by the bombardment. It was broken in some areas but not others.
Mines	19 mines were dug under the German positions and filled with explosives. One of these was detonated 10 minutes before the attack. It gave the Germans who survived final notice of an attack.
Infantry attack	The soldiers advanced in lines or waves. They walked over 'No Man's Land' because the senior officers feared losing control over the men. The majority had volunteered at the outbreak of war. They were not seen as being fully trained. Most soldiers carried 66 lb of equipment and would have had difficulty running.

1 July 1916 is regarded as one of the worst days in the history of the British army. Over 57 000 men were to become casualties. 20 000 of them were killed. Many of them were hit by machine-gun fire in the first hour of the attack.

In **Source E** below, the War Diary of the 16th Battalion of the HLI describes the results of the first day of the Somme. They started the day with 25 officers and 755 men, but 20 officers and 534 men became casualties.

> *The advance commenced at 7.30 a.m. The enemy opened heavy Machine Gun and Rifle Fire as soon as our men jumped over the parapet. Our Platoons advanced in waves in extended order, and were simply mown down by Machine Gun Fire, and very heavy casualties resulted. On the left the Support Company got close up to the German wire, but were unable to advance. On the right we succeeded in entering German Trenches.*

The battle eventually gained around 5 miles of territory and is often seen as a failure. Some modern historians regard the battle as part of a learning curve. The disasters of the first day led to the British Army being taught some hard lessons which resulted in the victory of 1918. Others would argue that the casualties inflicted on the Germans led to the eventual collapse of their army.

BRITISH COMMANDERS

Since the Great War, the views of the British generals have been a cause of argument among historians. They are often seen as being remote from the problems faced by the ordinary soldier. While the men faced the horrors of the trenches, the generals lived in safety, in comfortable houses miles behind the front line.

Source F was supposed to have been said by the German General Ludendorff during the Great War. It was reported by an Englishwoman, Evelyn, Princess Blucher, who was married to a German prince and was told about it.

> *'The English Generals are wanting in strategy. We should have no chance if they possessed as much science as their officers and men had of courage and bravery. They are lions led by donkeys.'*

THINGS TO DO AND THINK ABOUT

1. Describe the tactics used by the British Army during the Battle of the Somme.

2. What is meant by 'attrition'?

3. Do the casualty figures support the view that the strategy of attrition was wearing down the German Army?

DON'T FORGET

Three Scottish divisions, the 9th, the 15th and the 51st, were to take part in the Battle of the Somme.

VIDEO LINK

The Battle of the Somme was filmed by the British army. You can see extracts from the film at the Digital Zone: www.brightredbooks.net/N5History.

DON'T FORGET

For much of the war, the British Army on the Western Front was commanded by a Scotsman, Field Marshal Sir Douglas Haig.

ONLINE

Were British commanders as bad as they have been portrayed? Go to the Digital Zone to look at the case studies: www.brightredbooks.net/N5History.

ONLINE TEST

Check your knowledge on this topic by taking a test at: www.brightredbooks.net/N5History.

Domestic impact of war: RATIONING

THE IMPACT OF THE BLOCKADES

British Food Imports 1909-1913

At the outbreak of war in 1914, both Britain and Germany introduced blockades of each other's countries. This meant that ships heading towards ports in those countries would be stopped. The Royal Navy swiftly cut off supplies that were heading towards Germany. This meant that Germany experienced shortages of both food and raw materials for its industries.

However, Britain was also very vulnerable to attempts by Germany to interrupt its supplies. **Source A** shows the level of food imports to Britain before the outbreak of war.

THE ROLE OF U-BOATS

DON'T FORGET

Britain is an island. Much of its food was imported.

ONLINE

Find out more about the role of U-boats during the First World War at the Digital Zone: www.brightredbooks. net/N5History.

To this end, Germany made use of its U-boat Fleet. By early 1915, many of these were based along the Belgian coast and close to Britain. At first, the U-boats would surface, and their crew would search a ship before sinking it. However, this was very dangerous for the German crew – particularly as the British often used 'Q ships'. These looked like unarmed merchantmen but were actually heavily armed warships. They would allow the submarine to come close before opening fire. A further problem was that neutral ships were not prevented from sailing towards Britain.

From February 1915, the Germans declared the waters around Britain to be a **war zone**. Any ships in that area – British or neutral – were liable to be attacked. This was abandoned when the British passenger liner *Lusitania* was sunk, killing 1198 passengers, 128 of them American. Fears that the USA might enter the war caused Germany to stop its campaign.

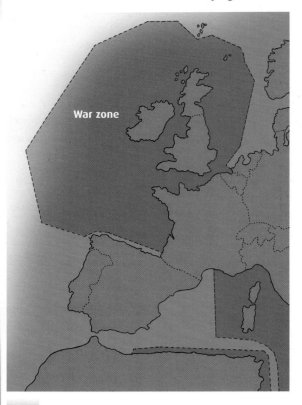

War zone

By February 1917, Germany had begun to use unrestricted U-boat warfare again. The war on the Western Front was not going well for them. They had also increased the number of submarines that they controlled. The German commanders believed that they could defeat Britain before the USA would be able to enter the war. It was a risk.

The German attacks were very successful. In April 1917, one in four ships using British ports was sunk by U-boats. Only around four days' supply of sugar and eight weeks' supply of wheat and flour were left in the country.

Shortages of food affected British civilians in a number of ways. The lack of imported wheat meant that bread was in short supply. Queues were seen outside shops. Prices of foodstuffs crept upwards. Bread and potatoes doubled in price between 1914 and 1916. This affected the poorer families, as they usually struggled to find enough money to pay the bills.

Within the poorer families, it was usually the children who suffered most. The 'breadwinner', usually the man, was given the largest portions. The rest had to depend on the leftovers.

Source B shows the war zone round Britain in 1917. Ships entering this area could be attacked without warning.

HOW THE GOVERNMENT REACTED

The government eventually took several measures to improve the situation.

- It introduced the **convoy** system. Merchant ships travelled in groups protected by the Royal Navy. Very soon, the number of sinkings began to drop.

- It used **propaganda** posters to urge people to eat less and avoid waste.

- It encouraged councils to set up **municipal kitchens** to provide cooked meals at a reasonable cost. These were popular among the poor.

- Farmland and other areas such as parks or football pitches were ploughed up and used to grow more crops.

- The **Women's Land Army** was set up to help farmers.

- The government organised 'SOS weeks' to encourage people to eat less.

- A number of foods were rationed. These were sugar, butter, jam, tea, bacon and fresh meat. Each household was sent three ration cards for sugar, meat and butter. Limits were set for the amount each adult could receive.

- The government used the powers of the Defence of the Realm Act to punish those people who tried to get more than their share. Fines were given out by the courts, and the names of offenders were published in posters and newspapers.

FOODSTUFF	WEEKLY AMOUNT FOR ADULTS
Beef, lamb, mutton or pork	15 ounces
Bacon	5 ounces
Butter, margarine or lard	4 ounces
Sugar	8 ounces

VIDEO LINK

You can watch a video clip about the Women's Land Army at the Digital Zone: www.brightredbooks.net/N5History.

Source C to the right is from the *Lennox Herald* of 26 January 1918.

WAR BREAD
The new loaf as produced from the standardised flour milled in accordance with government regulations has been officially introduced to Scotland. The new loaf differs only slightly in appearance from the bread with which the people have been long accustomed; the loaf is merely duller in appearance and the difference in taste is imperceptible.

Source D is from the *Glasgow Herald* of 11 June 1917.

A butcher shop devoted solely to the sale of horseflesh has been opened in the East end of Glasgow. The fact that the meat is horseflesh for human consumption is prominently displayed in the window and the average price is 5d per 1lb. The shop is in the neighbourhood of a poor locality and seems to be carrying on a fair trade. The scarcity of beef supplies and the consequent high prices are factors that may lead the extremely poor to buy the new form of meat.

By 1918, the food crisis had been avoided. Many people were hungry and some items were in short supply. The price of those items in short supply had also increased. However, unlike in Germany, no one had starved to death.

ONLINE

Find out more about rationing by clicking the link at the Digital Zone: www.brightredbooks.net/N5History.

Source E is from the *Dumbarton Herald* of 14 August 1915.

PATRIOTIC FOOD LEAGUE
INTERESTING DEVELOPMENT IN GLASGOW
Already much useful work has been done in Glasgow by the local branch of the Patriotic Food League which long before the public generally realised the probability of a shortage of food began an economy campaign – first by means of cookery demonstrations to women in various parts of the city and afterwards by practical lessons given in the homes of people. The latest development of the League's activity is taking the form of a food exhibition which opens today at 461 Dumbarton Road, Partick.

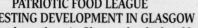
DON'T FORGET

Farming within Britain became much more important in providing food for the population during the war.

THINGS TO DO AND THINK ABOUT

1. Explain why there were shortages of food in Scotland and the rest of Britain during the Great War.

2. Describe the measures taken by the government to prevent the population from starving.

ONLINE TEST

Test your knowledge of this topic at the Digital Zone: www.brightredbooks.net/N5History.

THE DEFENCE OF THE REALM ACT AND RENT STRIKES

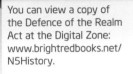

WARNING.
Defence of the Realm
Discussion in Public of Naval and Military matters may convey information to the enemy.
BE ON YOUR GUARD.

NATIONAL SECURITY

In August 1914, the British government introduced the Defence of the Realm Act. This allowed the government to introduce laws and regulations which it believed to be necessary. These were designed both to prevent information which could be useful to the enemy from being revealed, and to maintain the morale of the population. As a result of these powers, a variety of restrictions were introduced:

- Newspapers were censored.
- Restrictions were placed on any attempt to publish works or articles as to the training or tactics used by the army.
- Restrictions were placed on owning carrier pigeons, flying kites or lighting bonfires.
- Church bells were not to be rung.
- Whistling could be prohibited, as it might disturb wounded soldiers.
- The government had the right to take over land for use by the military.
- The government could take control of industries, such as the coal mines, to ensure the production of coal.
- The government had control over the railways.
- The government had the right to restrict access to areas which it considered important. In Scotland, the area north and west of Inverness and the Great Glen was heavily controlled. This was due to the large number of ships that were based at the naval bases in the Highlands and Islands. Anyone wishing to enter this area had to have permission from the army or navy.
- Daylight Saving Time was introduced in 1916. This helped to save fuel.
- After 1914, the government was concerned that drunkenness was affecting industrial production. The sale of alcohol was restricted. Pub opening hours were cut in 1916. Duty on spirits was increased. A bottle of whisky had cost 3s in 1913. During the war, its cost rose to 12s 6d. Beer was also reduced in strength.

Source A is an extract from the diaries of a Thomas Livingstone who lived in Glasgow during the Great War. He describes the introduction of Daylight Saving Time in 1916.

> **Thursday, 18 May**
> *The Summer Bill is now law. On Saturday I have to put the clock forward one hour.*

Source B shows the changes in pub opening hours during the war.

OPENING HOURS IN SCOTLAND		
1914	Monday to Friday 8am to 11pm	Closed on Sundays, except for hotels, which could serve residents and travellers.
AFTER 1916	4:30pm to 9pm	

Source C shows the convictions for drunkenness in Scotland, 1913–1919.

YEAR	MEN	WOMEN	TOTAL
1913	38443	11773	50216
1914	39306	11859	51165
1915	36438	11739	48177
1916	24388	8713	33101
1917	14922	5568	20490
1918	9168	2395	11503
1919	17722	4250	21072

ONLINE

You can view a copy of the Defence of the Realm Act at the Digital Zone: www.brightredbooks.net/N5History.

RED CLYDESIDE

During the Great War, huge numbers of workers were attracted to the west coast of Scotland. They were needed to meet the rising demand for war materials in the factories and shipyards of Clydeside. This area began to be named 'Red Clydeside' because of a number of strikes and unrest which took place during and after the war.

THE RENT STRIKES (OCTOBER TO NOVEMBER 1915)

The sudden growth in population led to problems. One of these was a shortage of housing. By early 1915, there was only around 1% of available housing left unused. As we saw on page 7, many of the existing homes in Glasgow were of a poor standard before the outbreak of war. After 1914, the shortage of skilled workers meant that there was little attempt to improve the houses or to listen to the complaints of the tenants.

Source D is historian Joseph Melling describing the housing shortage.

> *Any district which possessed a large engineering, shipbuilding or steel works – whether it was the Albion Motor Plant or North British Diesel works at Scotstoun or the great railway locomotive shops at Springburn – was facing an acute housing shortage by the early months of 1915.*

Source E is an extract from the *History of the Ministry of Munitions*.

> *The main cause of discontent was the discomfort entailed by the transfer of men to places where the housing, food and climate were worse than they had grown used to at home. Those suffered most who went from the south of England or the Midlands to the north-east coast or the Clyde. The inclemency of the weather, the overcrowding and the indifferent cooking in such lodgings as were available aggravated any weakness of health or temper that might have developed in men already worn by long hours of labour.*

Source F shows the increase in rents in Glasgow after the outbreak of war.

In 1915, the landowners began to raise rents. Many of the people living in the tenements found it difficult to cope. This was because the prices of many items such as food were also increasing. The result was that a number of tenants were threatened with eviction. Many of the people who were facing the rent increases were women whose husbands were serving in the armed forces. As a result, it was often women who took the lead in organising opposition.

The Independent Labour Party was also against rent increases.

Many of the tenants banded together to oppose the rent increases. Meetings were held and demonstrations organised. Pamphlets and leaflets demanding change were handed out. Rent strikes became a common form of defiance. Tenants refused to pay the increase in rent. When Sheriff Officers were sent to evict strikers, they were faced with a hostile reaction. By November 1915, 25 000 tenants were refusing to pay their rent. Workers in the shipyards and factories were threatening to come out on strike if evictions took place.

Source G to the right is a photograph of people demonstrating against the increase in rents in 1915.

The discontent was dealt with by the government. They were concerned at the disruption to the war effort. Rent strikes had also taken place in Aberdeen and Dundee as well as other parts of Britain. A Rent Restriction Bill was passed in November 1915. This prevented increases in rent beyond their 1914 levels for the duration of the war.

The strikes also highlighted the problems of poor housing and led to demands for the building of better houses with affordable rents. In 1917, a Royal Commission was set up to report on the state of housing in Scotland.

THINGS TO DO AND THINK ABOUT

1. Describe the government's attempts to control public life in Britain after 1915.

2. How successful were the government's attempts to reduce drunkenness in Scotland?

3. Explain why there was a shortage of housing in the West of Scotland after 1914.

4. How fully does **Source E** describe the reasons for discontent among the workers and their families on Clydeside after 1915?

 VIDEO LINK

Watch a short clip about the Rent Strikes at the Digital Zone: wwwbrightredbooks. net/N5History.

 ONLINE

You can read more about the Rent Strikes online at the Digital Zone: wwwbrightredbooks.net/ N5History.

Percentage of Glasgow rents seeing an increase between May 1914 and October 1915	Amount of increase in rent
33.9%	5%
14.6%	5–10%
7.7%	10%

 DON'T FORGET

One of the main leaders of the rent strikes was Mary Barbour. Along with other women, she led the protests against evictions. After the war, she was to become the first female Labour councillor elected to Glasgow Town Council.

 ONLINE TEST

To test your knowledge on this topic, go to the Digital Zone: www.brightredbooks. net/N5History.

PROPAGANDA AND CENSORSHIP

VIDEO LINK

Watch an example of a British propaganda film at the Digital Zone: www.brightredbooks.net/N5History.

DON'T FORGET

During the Great War, the British government used a number of powers to control the population.

THE ROLE OF PROPAGANDA AND CENSORSHIP

During the Great War, the government made use of both propaganda and censorship. This was for a number of reasons:

- to encourage the people to support the war effort
- to ensure that the population believed that they were winning the war
- to prevent information which could be helpful to the enemy from being revealed
- to prevent information which was seen as damaging to morale from being revealed.

Under the Defence of the Realm Act, the government had the powers to check what was being put in letters, newspapers and books. They could also change or ban stories which were felt to be damaging to the war effort. During the Great War, there were several propaganda campaigns that were designed to encourage people to support the war effort.

THE BELGIAN ATROCITIES

During the German invasion of Belgium, stories appeared in newspapers about the treatment of civilians. These stories usually presented the Germans as destroying or stealing property and killing men, women and children. In 1915, the British government set up a commission to look at the stories. Many of them were found to be exaggerated or untrue.

'THIS IS HOW I DEAL WITH SMALL FRY'

Source A to the left shows a British cartoon which deals with the German invasion of Belgium.

Source B to the right is from a 1915 government report.

> An hour later the women and children were separated and the prisoners were brought back to Dinant, passing the prison on their way. Just outside the prison the witness saw three lines of bodies which he recognized as being those of neighbours. They were nearly all dead, but he noticed movement in some of them. There were about 120 bodies. The prisoners were then taken up to the top of the hill outside Dinant and compelled to stay there till eight o'clock in the morning. On the following day they were put into cattle trucks and taken thence to Coblenz. For three months they remained prisoners in Germany.
>
> Unarmed civilians were killed in masses at other places near the prison. About ninety bodies were seen lying on the top of one another in a grass square opposite the convent.

EDITH CAVELL

Edith Cavell was a British nurse working in Belgium. After the German invasion, she remained to work in the hospital in Brussels. In October 1915, she was arrested by the German army because she was suspected of having helped British and Allied soldiers to have escaped. She was sentenced to death and executed by firing squad, still wearing her nurse's uniform. Many people were shocked by what had happened. Her story was used to encourage support for the war. Cavell Gardens in Inverness was named after her.

Source C shows a postcard sent from France to Scotland by a soldier in 1917.

TAKE UP THE SWORD OF JUSTICE

THE *LUSITANIA*

In May 1915, the *Lusitania* was torpedoed and sunk by a German U-boat off the coast of Ireland. It was a large passenger liner which had been launched by John Brown's shipyard in Clydebank in 1907. Around 1200 people were killed. The British government made full use of the incident to encourage people to join the forces.

Source D is a propaganda poster issued by the British government after the sinking of the *Lusitania*.

THE CORPSE FACTORY

One of the stories printed in a number of newspapers was that the Germans were using the corpses of their own soldiers to produce chemicals.

Source E appeared in *The Times* of 17 April 1917. It claimed that a German factory near Koblenz was used for the following purpose.

> Trainloads of the stripped bodies of German soldiers wired into bundles arrive and are simmered down into cauldrons, the products being stearine and refined oil.

Stearine was used to make candles or soap.

Seven years after the war was over, questions were asked in the House of Commons about the truth of the story.

Source F is an extract from a speech made by an MP, Mr Arthur Henderson, in the House of Commons on 2 December 1925.

> *The Chancellor of the German Reich has authorised me to say on the authority of the German Government that there never was any foundation for it. I need scarcely add that on behalf of His Majesty's Government I accept this denial and I trust that this false report will not again be revived.*

ANTI-GERMAN RIOTS

One of the effects of propaganda was an outbreak of anti-German riots which took place around Britain in 1915. Some of these took place in Scotland. There was trouble in Dumfries, Annan, Perth and Alloa.

Source G to the right is from the *Glasgow Herald* of 14 May 1915.

CENSORSHIP

The military and the government had the ability to censor reports which they felt could be damaging to morale and the war effort.

On 2 April 1915, Edinburgh was bombed by a Zeppelin. The reports in the newspapers were censored, although many people were aware of where the bombs had dropped. **Source H** is from the *Glasgow Herald* of 4 April 1916.

> Disturbances took place at four different points in Greenock on Wednesday evening and last night, but in each case the damage was confined to the breaking of windows in shops and dwelling houses and the destruction of the contents. The first outbreak occurred at the premises of Mr William Ohlms, hairdresser, West Blackhall Street ... About seven o'clock last night a crowd of several hundred people of both sexes congregated in the neighbourhood of the grocer's shop of Mr William Gaze, Lyndoch Street. Stones and other missiles were thrown at the windows, which were smashed. Later in the night, hundreds of young men and others assembled at the corner of Grey Place and West Blackhall Street in connection with threat to do damage to the licensed premises of Mr E. Sieger.

> **AIR RAID DAMAGE**
> **TWENTY-ONE CASUALTIES IN SCOTTISH TOWNS**
> **Story of the bombardment**
> Scotland, hitherto immune from Zeppelin raids, has at last experience of a visit from enemy aircraft. Close on midnight on Sunday evening a district in the East of Scotland suffered from an aerial bombardment. As in any other of the raids which has occurred in the south, the result of the efforts has been futile in achieving its object. No public buildings were touched and no military damage was done. All the result achieved has been the slaughter or injury of non-combatants and damage to private property.

Source I is a postcard used by British soldiers to send messages back to their families.

THINGS TO DO AND THINK ABOUT

1. What was the purpose of propaganda?

2. Which of the propaganda stories do you find the least believable? Why?

3. Why were there riots in several parts of Scotland in 1915?

ONLINE

Go to the Digital Zone to have a look at some of the British propaganda posters: www.brightredbooks.net/N5History.

DON'T FORGET

Propaganda was used to whip up hatred of Germany. The Royal Family changed its name from Saxe-Coburg-Gotha to Windsor in 1917. This was seen as patriotic.

ONLINE TEST

To take a test on this topic, go the Digital Zone: www.brightredbooks.net/N5History.

DON'T FORGET

Censorship was not always successful. Many local newspapers carried stories of casualties and experiences of the front line.

CONSCRIPTION AND CONSCIENTIOUS OBJECTORS

VIDEO LINK

You can watch a clip which tried to promote National Service at the Digital Zone: www.brightredbooks.net/N5History.

DON'T FORGET

The British army had never been as big as its European neighbours. It needed to be expanded to fight a war on land.

ONLINE TEST

To take a test on this topic, go to the Digital Zone: www.brightredbooks.net/N5History.

ONLINE

To learn more about opposition to conscription, go to the Digital Zone: www.brightredbooks.net/N5History.

ONLINE

Go to the Digital Zone to have a look at the records of people who applied to be exempt from conscription: www.brightredbooks.net/N5History.

THE DEMAND FOR MEN

By 1915, there were not enough men joining the British army. The number of volunteers in Britain had dropped from 300 000 a month to 120 000 by January 1915. A year later, that number had fallen to 80 000 men a month. As a result, the government introduced the **National Service Act** in 1916 – making it compulsory for men between the ages of 18 and 41 to join the army. Some groups were exempt from service in 1916. These groups were doing work of **national importance**. Those who wished to be exempt from military service could apply to a tribunal. This decided whether a man should be forced to join the army. They were often unsympathetic to those who did not want to join up.

Source A shows the casualties on the Western Front between 25 September and 5 October 1915 (*Glasgow Herald*, 6 January 1916).

	KILLED	WOUNDED	MISSING	TOTAL
OFFICERS	773	1288	317	2378
OTHER RANKS	10 345	38 085	8648	57 078

Source B shows the terms of the Military Service Acts.

DATE ACT EXTENDED	WHO WAS LIABLE FOR SERVICE?	WHO WAS EXEMPT?
JANUARY 1916	Men aged 18–41.	The ill. Married or widowed men with children. Reserved occupations. This was mainly those in industry who did a skilled job. It also applied to ministers or priests.
MAY 1916	The government had the right to re-examine those men previously seen as unfit for the military.	
APRIL 1917	All men regardless of marital status.	
JANUARY 1918	The government could call up those men previously exempt.	
APRIL 1918	Men aged 17–57.	

Source C (from the *Kirkintilloch Herald*, 10 May 1916) describes one attempt to gain exemption from serving in the armed forces.

An appeal was made by the father of a young baker who had three sons already serving and who had himself been disabled for a long time.

Major Hope mentioned that 47 shillings was going into the house every week and it would not be a case of hardship to let the other son go. Mr Lynch said this was a case where they should stretch a point as far as they could.

Baillie Shanks: Entirely on domestic grounds not on business grounds. The applicant stated that the boy had had bad eyesight, let them test him when they liked.

Major Hope: They are taking men with spectacles now.

The Applicant: That is why I didn't allow him to put them on. But I think I have done fairly well. I can put my finger on families not far from here with four sons and one of them away.

Baillie Lakemen: You will get other families with three or four sons away.

The Applicant: If you give him exemption till my arm is better we will both go.

The Chairman: To be fair to everyone we should dismiss this case.

Baillie Shanks: If every family was doing the same share as this one I question if there would be the same urgency in appealing for men.

Mr Bell said it would be hardship to the house to take this boy away. Although they had four sons left, all their earnings were not going into the house.

Baillie Lakeman: What would you do if the Germans were coming over? There would be no houses to keep up.

The appeal was dismissed on an undertaking by Major Hope that the lad would not be called up for two months.

contd

ONE-EYED MAN ELIGIBLE.

The next claimant for exemption was a drapery traveller who had formerly been a miner, and who had lost the sight of his left eye and whose left wrist was disabled.

Baillie Johnstone: Is this a man who would be of any use to you?

Major Hope: We do not think there is anything in this case to agree to, with regard to the eye it is for the doctor to decide, but Mr Tennant, in the House of Commons the other day, stated that the finest gunner in the British Army had only one eye. It was agreed to continue the case for further examination.

Source D is from the *Kirkintilloch Herald*, 12 July 1916. It shows how difficult it could be to gain exemption from serving in the army.

CONSCIENTIOUS OBJECTORS

Source E shows conscientious objectors at Dyce near Aberdeen in October 1916.

The Military Service Act allowed for those people with 'conscientious objections to the undertaking of combatant service' to gain exemptions. This meant that those people whose beliefs prevented them from fighting could avoid any job which might involve taking a life. There were two main groups who fell into this category:

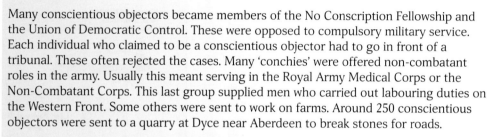

- Religious – Quakers, Plymouth Brethren and Jehovah's Witnesses

- Political – many were Socialists and members of the Independent Labour Party.

Many conscientious objectors became members of the No Conscription Fellowship and the Union of Democratic Control. These were opposed to compulsory military service. Each individual who claimed to be a conscientious objector had to go in front of a tribunal. These often rejected the cases. Many 'conchies' were offered non-combatant roles in the army. Usually this meant serving in the Royal Army Medical Corps or the Non-Combatant Corps. This last group supplied men who carried out labouring duties on the Western Front. Some others were sent to work on farms. Around 250 conscientious objectors were sent to a quarry at Dyce near Aberdeen to break stones for roads.

Source F was written by J. P. M. Millar, a conscientious objector from Edinburgh. He describes his experience of being a 'conchie':

> *These Tribunals were usually made up of elderly gents who were anxious to get the young men to do all the fighting for them. They normally gave conscientious objectors short shrift. None of my members got absolute exemption. As secretary of the No Conscription Fellowship I managed to get Non-Combatant service, which meant I became liable to go to France and do such jobs as bury the dead or paint barracks.*

Source G is by Dr Eric F. Dott from Edinburgh, who was sent to jail in 1917 for being a conscientious objector. He explains how he believes his treatment was an improvement on that given to earlier conchies.

> *The earlier men had had a far harder time. They weren't only court martialled. They were sent out to France with the real possibility of being shot there because they disobeyed an order. I believe it's true that none of them were actually shot. But they went out there fully believing they might be.*

Source H outlines the results of the cases of conscientious objectors that were heard in front of tribunals. These are figures for Britain.

DON'T FORGET

'Non-combatant' meant jobs that did not involve fighting.

DON'T FORGET

Those conchies who refused to have anything to do with the war were known as 'absolutists'. They often received extremely harsh treatment. Usually this involved being sent to prison and often kept in solitary confinement.

ONLINE

Learn more about Conscientious Objectors at the Digital Zone: www. brightredbooks.net/ N5History.

THINGS TO DO AND THINK ABOUT

1. Explain why the government had to introduce conscription by 1916.

2. Look at Sources C and D. What evidence is there that it was difficult to gain exemption from serving in the armed forces after 1916?

3. What was a conscientious objector?

4. Describe the treatment of conscientious objectors.

5. Why do you think conscientious objectors were very unpopular with many civilians during the war?

Result of case	Numbers of conscientious objectors
Individual exempted from service	6000
Individual given non combatant service	5000
Case rejected and individual conscripted into the armed forces	3000
Absolutists	2425
TOTAL	16 500

INDUSTRY AND ECONOMY

THE
VICTORIA RUBBER C⁰ Lᵀᴰ
EDINBURGH

FABRICS
FOR
RIGID
AIRSHIP BALLONETS.

NON-RIGID and SEMI-RIGID AIRSHIP ENVELOPES and BALLONETS.

OBSERVATION BALLOON ENVELOPES, BALLONETS & RUDDERS.

PROOFERS OF FABRICS FOR THE FIRST BRITISH KITE BALLOON.

Low Permeability and Maximum Durability Guaranteed

VICTORIA INDIA RUBBER MILLS, EDINBURGH

THE ROLE OF SCOTTISH INDUSTRIES IN THE WAR

In 1914, the major industries in Scotland were shipbuilding, coal mining, iron and steel manufacturing, and engineering. The outbreak of war caused a number of changes.

Some, such as the Borders woollen companies, lost business because of the loss of markets in Europe. German attacks led to a disruption of supplies. Others, such as the jute industries in Dundee, saw increased demand for their product. By 1918, a thousand million sandbags had been produced for the armed forces. Many companies, such as James Templeton's in Glasgow, changed from producing carpets to making blankets for the army. The North British Rubber Company in Fountainbridge, Edinburgh, produced gas masks, gas capes and 1 185 036 pairs of waterproof trench boots for the British army, as well as fabric for British airships. In 1914, it was the only factory with the experience to produce the materials used in observation balloons on the Western Front. Along with other factories, such as the Victoria Rubber Company, they had produced 2 million yards of balloon cloth by the Armistice.

Source A is an advert that was produced after the end of the war. It demonstrates what the company had the skill to produce.

COAL MINING

The coal mining industry saw a decline in output, for a number of reasons. Many miners decided to join the armed forces in 1914. This was often in areas such as East Lothian where there had been problems over pay and conditions before 1914. Coal mines in the west tended to do better, as they saw increased demand from the shipyards and factories around Glasgow. Newspapers such as the *Glasgow Herald* (**Source B**) also identified other reasons for the problems in an industry which had exported a third of its product. In 1917, the government took control over the production and distribution of coal in an attempt to improve the situation. As a result, miners enjoyed better conditions, with pay and safety being improved. An Act in 1919 led to the introduction of pit-head showers.

Source B is an extract from the *Glasgow Herald* of 28 December 1918.

Source C shows the output of coal in Scotland during the Great War.

When hostilities broke out, certain markets were immediately shut off such as Germany, Austria, Russia and Turkey, while trade to the remaining countries was subject to considerable interruptions through the operations of submarines and the scarcity of tonnage.

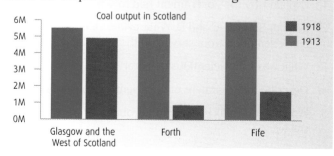

Coal output in Scotland

	1918	1913

6M
5M
4M
3M
2M
1M
0M

Glasgow and the West of Scotland   Forth   Fife

FISHING

The fishing industry experienced a number of problems after 1914. The herring markets in both Russia and Germany were closed to it. The North Sea could not be used because of the risk of German attacks. Other areas, such as the Firth of Clyde, were also off limits to fishing.

The risks involved with fishing were high, as **Source D** indicates. Over 660 British fishing trawlers were lost due to enemy action. Many fishermen became members of the Royal Navy Reserve Trawler Section. This performed many duties such as minesweeping and convoy protection. By 1918, around 25 000 out of 40 000 Scottish fishermen were working with the RNRTS. The last Royal Navy ship to be sunk during the Great War was His Majesty's Trawler *Ascot* on 10 November 1918.

Source D is from the *Glasgow Herald*, 9 April 1915.

PIRATES ON THE EAST COAST
SUBMARINE FIRES ON ABERDEEN TRAWLER
SMALL BOAT ATTACKED

Source E shows Alexander Mackay from Dunbeath in Caithness, who was drowned when his ship HMT *Ascot* was torpedoed.

Source F shows trawlers clearing mines. This was one of the activities that many former fishermen who joined the Royal Navy Reserve Trawler Section were involved in during the war.

THINGS TO DO AND THINK ABOUT

1. Which industries suffered a drop in business after 1914?

2. Explain why some companies, such as Templeton's in Glasgow and the North British Rubber Company in Edinburgh, were in demand for their products after 1914.

3. Explain why many fishermen joined the Royal Navy Reserve Trawler Section after 1914.

SHIPBUILDING

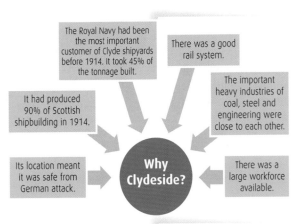

THE IMPORTANCE OF CLYDESIDE

Shipbuilding was one of the major industries before the Great War. It had reached a peak output in 1913 building ships for both the Royal Navy and the Merchant Navy. The naval race with Germany had meant that there was a demand for the construction of warships. Some, such as the Dreadnought battleship HMS *Colossus*, were built on the Clyde.

At the outbreak of war, the shipyards of the Clyde were to enjoy a sudden increase in the river's importance. This was due to a number of reasons.

THE BOOM IN PRODUCTION

Between 1914 and 1918, there were 48 shipyards along the banks of the River Clyde that were flooded with orders from the Navy for ships. Large numbers of smaller warships, such as destroyers, were required to protect merchant ships and to hunt German U-boats. Ships were also needed to replace losses. In early 1917, it was estimated that the Germans were sinking 1 in 4 of the British merchant ships heading to Britain.

At the outbreak of war, the Admiralty had taken control of the Clyde shipyards of Fairfield's, John Brown's at Clydebank and Beardmores at Dalmuir. This meant that they were only going to build warships. It also meant that they received large numbers of orders, which in turn generated huge profits for the companies involved.

The majority of ships constructed on the Clyde were built by six companies: John Brown's, the Fairfield Company, Beardmores, Scott's Company, Barclay Curle and Company, Yarrows & William Denny and Company.

By 1918, the Clyde shipyards had built the following:

ONLINE

Go to the Digital Zone to read more about Clyde shipbuilding: wwwbrightredbooks.net/N5History.

- 3 **battlecruisers** – these carried the same size of guns as battleships. They were also about the same size, but they did not carry the same amount of armour, and they were faster. The most famous ship in the Royal Navy was HMS *Hood*, which was launched by John Brown's at Clydebank in 1918.

- 11 **cruisers**

Source A shows the HMS *Hood*.

- 5 **monitors** – these were ships that carried large guns to give support to troops on land.

- 155 **destroyers**

- 36 **submarines**

- 2 **submarine depot ships** – these were designed to supply submarines.

- 3 **aircraft carriers** – these included HMS *Argus*, which was the first aircraft carrier to see service with any navy. It was launched by Beardmores in 1917.

- 2 **destroyer flotilla leaders**.

DON'T FORGET

The Clyde produced many of the smaller ships needed to protect convoys and to battle the U-boats.

contd

Source B shows HMS *Argus* in 1917.

Source C is an advert which describes some of the products of Beardmores.

Sources D to **G** are graphs which display the tonnage or number of ships that were constructed on Clydeside and in British shipyards in 1 year.

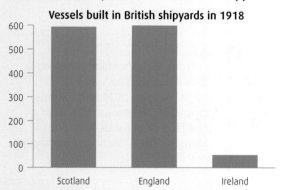

Source D shows the numbers of ships built in each country's shipyards in the last year of the war.

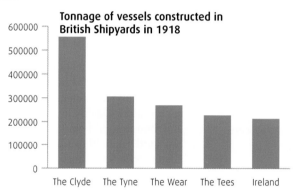

Source E shows the tonnage or weight of the ships built in British shipyards in the last year of the war.

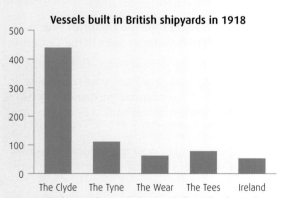

Source F shows the numbers of ships built in the major areas of British shipyards in the last year of the war.

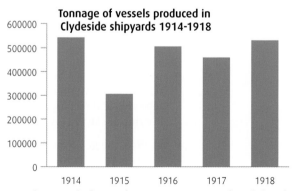

Source G shows the tonnage or weight of the ships built in Clydeside shipyards throughout the war

 THINGS TO DO AND THINK ABOUT

1. Why were the Clyde shipyards so important to the war effort after 1914?

2. Explain why Fairfield's, John Brown's and Beardmores were able to make huge profits during the Great War.

3. Describe the contribution of the Clyde shipyards to the British war effort.

 ONLINE TEST

To take a test on this topic, go to the Digital Zone: www.brightredbooks.net/ N5History.

MUNITIONS

THE SINEWS OF WAR

During the Great War, the demands on the steel industry increased considerably. Much of the demand was for the production of shells or munitions for the armed forces. As the demand increased, more factories converted to producing shells.

Source A is a painting made in 1918 by a war artist called Anna Airy. It is titled 'Shop for machining 15-inch Shells: Singer Manufacturing Company, Clydebank'.

PRODUCTION PROBLEMS

ONLINE

You can read a telegram from Weir to Lloyd George about strike action at the Digital Zone: www.brightredbooks.net/N5History.

In 1915, there was a shortage of shells on the Western Front. This shortage was seen as the reason for the failure of a British attack at Aubers Ridge in France in 1915. It soon became a political scandal and led to change. A new Ministry of Munitions was set up under David Lloyd George. Its purpose was to increase the amount of shells and ammunition being produced. William Weir was made the Director of Munitions in Scotland. He held this position until 1917. He was responsible for a dramatic increase in shell production. He took a number of steps to ensure this:

- The **Glasgow Shell Scheme**. Rather than building new factories, Weir pushed contracts towards existing firms that could make shells. This included Beardmores, Babcock & Wilcox and the North British Locomotive Company. These companies were given money by the government to help start up the manufacturing of shells.

- In June 1915, the government began building **National Projectile Factories** which could produce large-calibre shells. Six of the 15 British factories were in the Clydeside area.

- By early 1916, the **Scottish Filling Factory** at Bishopton near Paisley was operating. It filled the empty shells that were made in Glasgow. It was eventually expanded to two factories and employed 12 000 workers – mostly women. It was named Georgetown in honour of David Lloyd George.

- In 1915, the government also built a factory near Gretna Green to produce explosives. It was eventually to employ 30 000 workers. Once again, the majority of workers were female.

- These efforts succeeded in improving the flow of shells to the British army.

YEAR	WEEKLY OUTPUT OF SHELLS FROM SCOTTISH FACTORIES
1916	54 000
1917	125 000
1918	129 000

VIDEO LINK

Go to the Digital Zone to watch a clip highlighting the dangers of working in a munitions factory: www.brightredbooks.net/N5History.

A SHORTAGE OF MANPOWER

After 1914, many of the industries based in Scotland suffered from a shortage of workers. A large number of male workers answered the call from Lord Kitchener to join the armed forces. This was often in areas where unemployment had been high. By August 1915, 36.5 % of East Lothian miners had joined the armed forces. Output dropped at a time when more coal was required by the steel industry. Other industries, such as shipbuilding, also experienced a shortage of workers: 27% of apprentices working in Clydeside shipyards had joined up by September 1914, and 10% of journeymen (those workers who had completed their apprenticeship) had also enlisted. This created a labour shortage.

Source B is from the *Kirkintilloch Herald* of 24 March 1915.

Returns furnished to the Board of Trade *Labour Gazette* show that the effect of so many men being withdrawn from industries by the war, and of the great demand upon many trades to furnish munitions of war not only for our own armies, but also for the Allies, is making itself further felt in the labour market. In some industries, a shortage of male labour, especially of skilled men, is again reported. Trades affected by war contracts continue very busy with much overtime. The scarcity of agricultural labour is becoming accentuated.

NATIONAL REGISTRATION ACT

As a result of falling output, the government introduced a National Register Act in July 1915. This became known as the Derby Scheme after Lord Derby, who had pushed for its introduction. Every individual aged between 15 and 65 had to give details of their home address, marital status and dependants. They also had to indicate if they were willing to take part in war work.

ONLINE

You can read a lot more about the Derby Scheme online at the Digital Zone: www.brightredbooks.net/N5History.

RESERVED OCCUPATIONS

In November 1915, four lists of occupations scheduled as vitally important for war work and other essential requirements were published. This meant that the person doing this job was doing an important job and could not be conscripted into the armed forces. These lists were subject to change as the industrial situation of the country demanded. The following jobs were reserved:

- Those essential to the manufacture of munitions
- Certain skilled occupations in farming (this usually meant farmers and not farm workers)
- Coal mining
- Railway workers who were involved in the maintenance of lines, rolling stock and the movement of trains
- Merchant Navy
- Public utilities such as gas workers
- Those involved in what was described as 'war work'.

Workers could apply to be exempted from serving in the armed forces. They would apply to local tribunals and be given a certificate of exemption. Employers would often do this on behalf of their workers. This list was revised throughout 1916–1918 to allow more men to be sent to the armed forces.

The issue of exemption was to be a cause of discontent among workers. This was particularly the case among those men who were called up who had families. They argued that single men in the reserved occupations should be called up first.

ONLINE TEST

To take a test on this topic, go to the Digital Zone: www.brightredbooks.net/N5History.

THINGS TO DO AND THINK ABOUT

1. What measures did the government take to increase shell production after 1915?

2. Why were some workers prevented from joining the army after 1915?

WOMEN AT WORK 1

VIDEO LINK

You can watch a propaganda clip of women working at a munitions factory at the Digital Zone: www.brightredbooks.net/N5History.

MUNITIONETTES

The shortage of workers led to women being encouraged to play a role. They were presented with a number of opportunities which previously had been closed to them.

One of the growth areas of employment was in the munitions factories. The shell shortage led to large numbers of women being taken on as 'munitionettes'. They were to work long hours in challenging conditions. Thousands of women eagerly sought employment in this area, as they had been guaranteed a minimum wage of 20 shillings (£1) a week. With regular overtime, women could expect to take home far more than they ever had before. In some cases, this could be four times as much as their pre-war wages.

The work, however, was physically demanding and dangerous. Accidents were common, as were deaths. The munitionettes who worked in the larger factories were often young girls.

Source A shows munitionettes at Gretna Green mixing gun cotton with acetone to make explosives. Sir Arthur Conan Doyle, the creator of Sherlock Holmes, visited the factory in 1917 and described the material as 'the Devil's porridge'.

Source B describes the hours the women worked. It was written by the journalist and author Rebecca West, who visited the munitions factory at Gretna Green in 1916.

Every morning at six, when the night mist still hangs over the marshes, 250 of these girls are fetched by a light railway from their barracks on a hill two miles away. When I visited the works they had already been at work for nine hours, and would work for three more. This twelve-hour shift is longer than one would wish, but it is not possible to introduce three shifts, since the girls would find an eight-hour day too light and would complain of being debarred from the opportunity of making more money.

Source C is Rebecca West describing the clothing worn by the workers.

There is matter connected to these huts, too, that showed the khaki and scarlet hoods to be no fancy dress but a military uniform. They are a sign, for they have been dipped in a solution that makes them fireproof, that the girls are ready to face an emergency, which had arisen in those huts only a few days ago. There had been one of those incalculable happenings of which high explosives are so liable, an inflammatory mixture of air with acetone, and the cordite was ignited. Two huts were instantly gutted, and the girls had to walk out through the flame. In spite of the uniform one girl lost a hand.

ONLINE

Go to the Digital Zone to find out more about the munitions factory at Gretna: www.brightredbooks.net/N5History.

THE DANGERS FOR WOMEN IN THE WORKPLACE

The threat of explosion was seen as a major problem in munitions factories during the Great War. A number of precautions were taken to reduce the risk. The workers themselves wore rubber overshoes to reduce sparks. Metal objects, including hairpins, were forbidden from being taken into the workspace. Possession of matches was considered a serious offence and could lead to a court fine.

However, explosions still took place. Estimates suggest that around 200 women were killed in explosions in British factories, but some historians believe that the numbers killed could have reached 1000. Many others were seriously injured in accidents. Some workers

VIDEO LINK

You can watch a clip about the 'munitionettes' at the Digital Zone: www.brightredbooks.net/N5History.

contd

fell victim to illness. During 1916, medical cases involving diseases such as tuberculosis began to rise among young women. Some saw the working conditions in munitions factories as a major cause.

TNT poisoning also affected many of the young women. One case at the Georgetown factory involved a 22-year-old munitionette called Marion Russell. She died two days after being admitted to the Victoria Infirmary in Glasgow.

Source D was written by a doctor at the Victoria Infirmary in Glasgow.

> *Her illness began five weeks before admission with vomiting and headache ... Ten days later diarrhoea set in, and pains in the abdomen were complained of. About the same time she became jaundiced, and this condition became gradually worse. The vomited material was occasionally streaked with blood. Sleeplessness developed, and this was followed by a hysterical attack with screaming for a period of two or three days before admission.*

DON'T FORGET

Munitionettes were known as 'canaries' due to the TNT turning their skin yellow.

OTHER JOBS

Women also served in a number of other jobs that had previously been closed to them.

Source E shows conductresses of Glasgow Corporation.

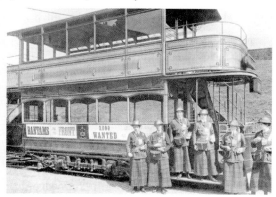

Source F is from the *Glasgow Herald* of 25 January 1916.

WOMEN OIL WORKERS

At Broxburn Oilworks yesterday female labour was introduced for the first time. The management of the Broxburn Oil Company are making the experiment in the candle-making department, where business at present is very brisk on account of the regular trade being supplemented by large special contracts. The only difficulty preventing the fulfilment of orders has been the scarcity of labour.

The women are to be paid 15/- per week during a three-week training course, after which they will receive payment according to production on the same scale as male workers. It is understood that the employment of women is not intended to be permanent, but only to continue while the present pressure lasts.

ONLINE TEST

To take a test on this topic, go to the Digital Zone: www.brightredbooks.net/ N5History.

THINGS TO DO AND THINK ABOUT

1. Explain why many women were eager to work in the munitions industry after 1914.

2. Evaluate the usefulness of Source B as evidence of the working conditions in a munitions factory during the Great War.
   You may want to comment on who wrote it, why they wrote it, what they say or what has been missed out.

3. Describe the dangers which faced women who worked in the munitions industry.

WOMEN AT WORK 2

DON'T FORGET

Many women became members of the Voluntary Aid Detachments to help with the wounded.

DON'T FORGET

Many of the women who wanted to play a role in the war effort had been involved in the pre-war campaign for the vote.

ONLINE

Go to the Digital Zone to read more about the impact of war on women www.brightredbooks.net/N5History.

VIDEO LINK

Go to the Digital Zone to learn more about the Scottish Women's Hospitals and watch a clip about the same: www.brightredbooks.net/N5History.

NURSING

Many women wanted to provide support for the soldiers in the British and Allied armies. In 1914, women joined the Voluntary Aid Detachments as nurses to help in the local hospitals. Others went further: a number of individuals set up ambulance units to treat casualties from the battlefields. Many of these had Scottish connections. The Duchess of Sutherland set up the Millicent Sutherland Ambulance and was the first of the groups to reach France in 1914.

In Edinburgh, Elsie Inglis and other members of the NUWSS set up the Scottish Women's Hospitals. This was in spite of lack of interest from the War Office, which told her to 'Go home and sit still'. This provided hospitals which were entirely staffed by women. It was eventually to set up 14 units which served in Romania, Greece, Serbia and Russia and on the Western Front.

Source A is from a history of the Scottish Women's Hospital Unit. It describes what was so special about the hospitals they organised. It was written in 1919 by a member of the unit.

> *It is this – they are 'manned' from end to end by women, and women only. Women drivers take the ambulance cars into the firing line, women stretcher-bearers lift the wounded, and place them in the ambulances, women doctors await them in the hospital. It is women who perform the operations, remaining at work in the theatres, it may be sometimes thirty-six and fifty hours at a stretch. Women nurses and orderlies attend the patients in the wards, women cook the entire food required by the hospital, and women bury amputated limbs and carry on disinfecting and other sanitary work. And he would find this too – in that the scheme for these hospitals had originated in the brain of a woman, and that they were equipped and controlled by a women's society in Britain.*

Source B was written by Winston Churchill after the end of the war.

> *The record of their work in Russia and Rumania, lit up by the flame of Dr Elsie Inglis, will shine in history. Their achievements in France, in Serbia, in Greece, and in other theatres were no less valuable, and no body of women has won a higher reputation for organizing power and for efficacy in works of mercy. It is a pleasure to me to remember that in the early days of the war I had the opportunity of furthering their efforts.*

Source C shows ambulances and the hospital which were run by the Scottish Women's Ambulance Unit at Royaumont in France.

Source D shows ambulance drivers of the Scottish Ambulance Unit.

Source E shows members of the Scottish Ambulance Unit receiving the Croix de Guerre medal from the French in 1918.

MAIRI CHISHOLM'S STORY

Mairi Chisholm was a member of a well-off Scottish family. She was 18 when she joined the Women's Emergency Corps in 1914. This organisation was set up by members of the WSPU to help the war effort. Along with her friend Elsie Knocker, she resigned from the Corps because she believed that she could save more lives if she was closer to the front line. They set up a first-aid post at Pervyse in Belgium. They would often go onto battlefields searching for wounded soldiers. Being so close to the front line, they regularly came under fire. In 1917, they were both seriously wounded when they were gassed during a German attack.

Source F is by Mairi Chisholm. She describes her experiences dealing with casualties.

No one can understand unless one has seen the rows of dead men laid out on a stretcher, the majority wrapped in a winding sheet, but here and there one is uncovered who has been left as he died. One sees the most hideous sights imaginable, men with their jaws blown off, arms and legs mutilated and when one goes into the room one is horrified at the suffering which is ghastly. I could not believe that I could have stood these sights.

Source G shows Elsie Knocker and Mairi Chisholm on their motorbike. They were warned by the Germans not to wear the helmets in case they were mistaken for soldiers when they were helping the wounded in no-man's-land.

By 1918, a number of organisations had been set up to harness the potential of women. These included:

NAME	ROLE	MEMBERS
Queen Alexandra's Imperial Military Nursing Service	Treating the wounded.	23 000
The Women's Legion	Mainly cooking and cleaning for the armed forces. This group was seen as important in convincing the government of the potential of women.	Volunteers
Queen Mary's Army Auxiliary Corps – originally known as the Women's Auxiliary Army Corps	Performed duties such as cooking and catering, storekeeping, clerical work, telephony and administration, printing, motor vehicle maintenance.	57 000
Women's Royal Air Force	Performed many duties such as mechanics, fitters, armourers, clerks and drivers.	25 000
WRNS – known as WRENS	Carried out non-combatant duties.	5500
First Aid Nursing Yeomanry	Nursing.	120 members in France.
The Voluntary Aid Detachments	Nursing and other duties.	47 000
Women's Land Army	Worked in agriculture. Provided a third of farm labour.	113 000
Women's Police Service	Used in munitions factories to search workers. Also used to try to prevent 'immoral' behaviour in public areas.	357

 DON'T FORGET

The Women's Land Army was very important in making sure that the population did not starve. They replaced the male farm workers who had 'joined up'.

 THINGS TO DO AND THINK ABOUT

The historian Gail Braybon stated that 'Women knew that they were important to the war'. To what extent would you agree with this statement?

 ONLINE TEST

To take a test on this topic, go to the Digital Zone: www.brightredbooks.net/N5History.

PROBLEMS ON THE CLYDE

	Increase in prices, 1914–1916
BRITISH MEAT	40%
IMPORTED MEAT	50%
FLOUR /BREAD	40%
BUTTER	34%
BACON	27%
CHEESE	26%
MILK	18%

RISING PRICES

After 1914, the price of goods rose dramatically. Many workers found it difficult to make ends meet. In February 1915, the engineers at Weirs of Cathcart went on strike for a pay increase of 'tuppence an hour'. This was triggered because the company had brought in American workers to work in the factory and paid them higher wages.

MUNITIONS OF WAR ACT (1915)

This act was introduced to improve the production of war materials. Munitions factories and shipyards working on orders for the Royal Navy were to be 'controlled establishments'. This meant that:

- Strikes were illegal.
- Industrial disputes would be settled by a special munitions tribunal.
- Any worker who wanted to leave his job needed a leaving certificate. It was supposed to show that the employee had their employer's permission to leave. This was nearly impossible to get.
- Dilution would be pushed as a means of increasing production.

The act was very unpopular and led to a number of strikes. In August 1915, a strike at Fairfields Shipyards took place over a minor dispute. It resulted in 17 men being convicted and fined. Three refused to pay the fine and were sent to jail. The result was threats from the unions of a much bigger strike. An inquiry was held which made recommendations about how to avoid disputes like this happening again. The jailed workers had their fines paid by the union and were released from prison.

DILUTION

The shortage of workers led the employers to take steps to improve the situation. One way of doing this was termed **dilution**. It meant that unskilled workers – often women – could be employed in jobs that were previously thought of as skilled. Other methods to improve production included using new machinery and technology to speed up work. These new methods were opposed by many workers. They believed that it was an attack on their pay and conditions by managers who wanted to increase profits.

The attempts at dilution led to a number of problems. A Clyde Workers Committee had been set up to oppose dilution and the Munitions Act. The unrest became so serious that David Lloyd George visited Glasgow to try to resolve some of the difficulties.

Source A is an extract from David Lloyd George's war memoirs. He describes his visit to Glasgow in December 1915.

Glasgow was one of the worst districts, and the agitation amongst the workers seriously interfered with the output, especially with the delivery of big guns. I decided to visit the works to see for myself what the position was, and put before the men and their leaders the exact facts with regard to the military position, and the peril in which their fellow-workmen at the front were placed by the absence of adequate artillery.

Accompanied by Mr. Arthur Henderson I arrived at Glasgow on Christmas Eve, and we both went to Beardmore's works, where the delivery of heavy artillery was being seriously retarded by labour difficulties. At my request, the shop stewards were brought together and I then told them why I had come and made my appeal for their assistance in stimulating greater activity in production. A man who seemed to be their leader stepped to the front. He struck an attitude, and in a loud, challenging voice he said, "I am as much a slave of Sir William Beardmore as if I had the letter 'B' branded on my brow," his hand

ONLINE TEST

You can take a test on this topic at the Digital Zone: www.brightredbooks.net/ N5History.

contd

passing across the wrinkled forehead. This was my first acquaintance with Mr. David Kirkwood. I discovered that he was fundamentally a reasonable man to deal with. He promised that if Mr. Henderson put our case before a free assembly of workers he would do his best to secure a fair hearing ... The visit, for a time at least, had a quieting effect and quickening influence upon production.

Some weeks later we had further trouble, and then strong action had to be taken in the way of deportation of some of the leaders, and the prosecution of others.

Five shop stewards who were regarded as the ringleaders of the strikes and unrest were deported to Edinburgh, where they had to report to the police three times a day. Some historians believe that this measure helped to reduce the opposition to dilution.

Source B to the right is an extract of an agreement from 1916 between the Boilermakers and Shipwrights Unions and officials responsible for introducing dilution.

BOILERMAKERS
Pneumatic, hydraulic and electric tools and oxy-acetylene or other cutting or welding plant to be used wherever practicable, and to be manned by skilled, semi-skilled, unskilled or women labour all as may be found suitable.

DILUTION OF SHIPYARD GENERALLY
Women to be employed as far as practicable upon the following classes of work:
(a) Clerking, tracing, timekeeping, storekeeping and checking materials
(b) Light labouring and cleaning up in shops, yard and ships, and driving light carts and vans ...
(c) Plating shed – attending machines.

RED FLAG IN GEORGE SQUARE – THE '40-HOUR STRIKE'

In January 1919, the war was over. Many servicemen were leaving the armed forces and looking for work. The STUC (Scottish Trades Union Council) and the Clyde Workers Committee made demands for a shorter working week. The STUC campaigned for a 40-hour week, while the CWC wanted a 30-hour week. This was to prevent unemployment among the returning soldiers. In many shipyards and factories, the average length of the working week was 56 hours. This meant that many ex-soldiers could not find a job. By 28 January, 70 000 workers were on strike in Glasgow.

The government feared the beginning of a revolution. Emanuel Shinwell, one of the leaders of the strikes, explains why in **Source C**, from his memoirs written in 1981.

A Labour member of the government named Roberts had told the prime minister that he thought the demonstration was intended to start a revolution, it was only eighteen months after the 1917 revolution in Russia and there was a climate of opinion – not confined or peculiar to the Clyde, but almost over the whole country – that the Russians should be supported ...

The government reacted by sending 12 000 soldiers along with tanks to Glasgow.

On 31 January, thousands of workers gathered in George Square to protest. The police baton-charged the strikers and arrested several of their leaders, David Kirkwood, Willie Gallacher and Emmanuel Shinwell. Kirkwood was found not guilty, while Gallacher and Shinwell were given short prison sentences.

 VIDEO LINK

Go to the Digital Zone to learn more about the unrest and to watch a clip: www.brightredbooks.net/N5History.

David Kirkwood

David Kirkwood was a shop steward at Beardmores in Glasgow. He helped to organise the workers in many of the disputes between 1915 and 1918. He was a member of the Independent Labour Party and elected as an MP in 1922.

Willie Gallacher

Gallacher was a Communist and president of the CWC. He was sent to prison in 1916 for criticising the war. He was heavily involved in organising and leading the disputes on Red Clydeside.

John Maclean

John Maclean was a Glasgow schoolteacher who became well known for his opposition to the war. His views caused him to be arrested in 1915 under the DORA regulations. He lost his job and spent his time promoting Marxist (left-wing) views and beliefs. This led to him being appointed the Consul of the new Bolshevik state. In April 1918, he was arrested and sent to prison again because of his views. In prison he went on hunger strike, and this led to him being force-fed. This affected his health. He died in 1923 aged 44.

 THINGS TO DO AND THINK ABOUT

1. Why would the Munitions Act of 1915 upset workers?

2. What is meant by 'Dilution'?

3. Why do you think the government sent tanks and soldiers to Glasgow in 1919?

Scotland, 1918–1928
POST-WAR DECLINE OF HEAVY INDUSTRY

CHANGES AND CHALLENGES

After the Great War, the industries of Scotland experienced a number of changes. There was a brief boom in some industries after 1918. However, for most of the industries, it was a time of great challenges.

ONLINE

Go to the Digital Zone to read more about shipbuilding after the Great War: www.brightredbooks.net/N5History.

SHIPBUILDING

The shipbuilding industry had enjoyed a large amount of work during the war, but in 1918 the demand for warships ended. The government cancelled most of the orders, as the navy didn't need any more ships. However, there was a need for merchant ships, as huge numbers had been lost to German U-boats. This kept many yards busy until 1920, when the orders dried up. Other countries could often build ships more quickly and cheaply than British yards could.

COAL MINING

The mining industry was to find the 1920s difficult. Foreign exports had dropped because coal from countries such as Poland and Germany was cheaper. Many coal mines in Britain were old and unproductive. The mine owners had not invested in new machinery. In 1928, 40% of coal cut in Scotland was still cut by hand. New fuels, such as diesel, meant that demand for coal was dropping.

As with shipbuilding, the coal mines had enjoyed many improvements in pay and conditions between 1914 and 1918. This had led many miners to believe that it would be better if the mines were nationalised. However, this did not happen. Instead, the government returned the mines to their owners in 1921. The result was a series of pay cuts. This in turn led to strikes. These were unsuccessful.

VIDEO LINK

Go to the Digital Zone to watch a clip about the General Strike and the impact it had: www.brightredbooks.net/N5History.

THE GENERAL STRIKE OF 1926

The pressure on the miners increased and eventually led to a General Strike in May 1926. Attempts were made to change the pay and conditions of miners. This meant that the miners would have been forced to accept pay cuts and a longer working day. The response of the miners' leader A. J. Cooke was: 'Not a penny off the pay, not a minute on the day'.

The miners were supported by the Trades Union Congress. Many other unions, such as those that represented the railway, transport, building, chemical, gas, print and steel workers, went out on strike. The strike was to last nine days, and it paralysed Britain. The country ground to a halt.

Source A shows an overturned bus in Glasgow. It had been attacked by strikers.

The Organisation for the Maintenance of Supplies was set up by the government to keep the country moving. However, attempts by volunteers to drive trams and buses often ended in violence. Hundreds of striking workers around Scotland were arrested for trying to stop them.

The strike was a failure. Most workers returned to work on 12 May. The miners stayed out on strike until December. When they returned, they had to accept the pay cuts and longer hours that they had fought against.

NEW INDUSTRIES

Between 1918 and 1928, a number of **new industries** were developed across Britain. These usually relied on oil and electricity for power. As a result, they could be much more flexible in their location. The most important factor in their location was, therefore, how close they were to markets. This meant that most were located in the south of England. Scotland was seen as being too far from the markets to prove attractive to many of the new industries.

The growth industries in England included the manufacture of aircraft and motor cars. There was little aircraft production in Scotland after 1919. A handful of companies, such as the Albion Motor Car Company Ltd in Glasgow, and Arrol Johnstone, produced vehicles. The latter collapsed in 1931 during the Great Depression. The 1920s did see the development of electrical power supplies. They also saw a number of bus companies begin to offer services. One of the most successful was Walter Alexander's in Larbert.

In **Source B**, the historian Richard Finlay gives examples of a number of industries that had little impact on Scotland.

> *Other industries which failed to arrive in Scotland were silk and artificial fibres and consumer durables such as radios, washing machines, vacuum cleaners and refrigerators. In electrical engineering, employment in England rose by 40 000 between 1924 and 1930 to 189 000 while in Scotland in the same period it fell from 3000 to 2300.*

Source C below shows the major employers in Scotland by 1931. Shipbuilding was included in Manufacture of metals and machines and employed 77 000 people. Transport included railways (which employed 32 000) as well as road and water transport. By 1931, there were 35 000 drivers of motor vehicles.

MAJOR OCCUPATIONS IN 1931	MALE	FEMALE
Fishing	21 585	262
Agriculture	160 545	16 187
Mining and quarrying	144 179	2218
Manufacture of bricks	12 468	2575
Manufacture of chemicals	17 177	4023
Manufacture of metals and machines	263 481	16 839
Textile manufacture	51 711	100 663
Manufacture of leather and leather Goods	4299	1517
Clothing manufacture	18 808	27 778
Manufacture of food, drink and tobacco	53 179	39 372
Wood working	39 830	4988
Paper and stationary manufacture	30 972	21 188
Building and decorating	98 362	3380
Other manufacturing industries	16 541	7953
Gas, water and electricity supply	16 807	689
Transport and communication	146 350	9453
Commerce and finance	228 350	134 840
Public administration	102 072	50 212
Professions	39 146	38 659
Entertainment	11 992	5149
Servants	54 351	168 603
Other industries	21 821	10 801

THINGS TO DO AND THINK ABOUT

1. Why did industries such as coal and shipbuilding experience difficulties in the 1920s?

2. What were 'new industries'?

3. Why were most of the new industries located in England?

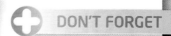

DON'T FORGET

Scotland's industries went into decline after the Great War.

ONLINE TEST

To take a test on this topic, go to the Digital Zone: www.brightredbooks.net/ N5History.

POLITICS AFTER 1918

POLITICAL CHANGE

After the outbreak of war in 1914, the Liberal government formed a coalition with members of the Conservative and Labour Parties. Herbert Asquith remained Prime Minister until he was replaced by David Lloyd George in 1916. No general election was held until 1918. By that year, a number of changes had taken place which meant that decisions had to be made about who should have the right to vote.

THE REPRESENTATION OF THE PEOPLE ACT 1918

The Great War had revealed problems with the pre-war system of awarding the vote to men on the basis of owning or renting property. Millions of men serving overseas returned to find that, as most had been out of the country for over a year, they had lost the right to vote. This, along with the high numbers of casualties, convinced many that change was required. In 1918, Parliament passed the Representation of the People Act which gave the vote to all males over 21, women who were householders or wives of householders and over 30 and female graduates. This increased the number of voters from 7.7 million in 1910 to 21.4 million in 1918.

VIDEO LINK

Go to the Digital Zone to watch a clip about women's campaign for the vote www.brightredbooks.net/N5History.

DON'T FORGET

In 1928, the voting age for women was reduced to 21. This was nicknamed the 'Flapper' vote. This referred to the way young birds flapped their wings when they first left the nest. Women now voted on equal terms with men.

Katharine Stewart-Murray, the Duchess of Atholl, Conservative MP for Perth and West Kinross

WOMEN GET THE VOTE

During the Great War, thousands of women had served in munitions factories, shipyards and the armed forces. Women had displayed abilities which some politicians had chosen to ignore prior to 1914. The events of 1914–1918 made them aware of the importance of women to the war effort. The vote was portrayed as a reward for this. However, many of the women who had carried out the war work did not actually gain the vote. Many were under the age of 30, did not own or rent property or did not have a degree.

Some historians believe that the role of the WSPU and the NUWSS was important. They presented the demand for women to receive the vote and brought it to public attention. This was at a time when many other events were dominating the news – problems with Germany, trouble in Ireland and strikes in Britain. Historians point to the example of France, where there was no pre-war demand for women to receive the vote. Although French women made huge efforts to help in the war, they did not receive the vote until 1944.

Some historians argue that the government gave women the vote because they did not want to see a return of the pre-war militant Suffragette campaigns. However, there is little evidence that the pre-war campaign gained support for the WSPU cause. In Britain in 1918 there was little appetite for more political conflict. The country was exhausted after the war.

The election was the first one in which women could vote. It was also the first in which women were elected to Parliament. The first woman to be returned was the Countess Constance Markievicz – but she was a member of Sinn Fein, which was campaigning for Irish independence, and she refused to take her seat in the House of Commons. The first woman to take her seat as an MP was Lady Nancy Astor. The first Scottish woman to become an MP was Katharine Stewart-Murray, the Duchess of Atholl, in 1923.

THE LIBERAL DECLINE

In 1918, the Liberal Party had split. The majority stayed under the leadership of Lloyd George, while a number supported the previous leader, Asquith.

contd

In 1918, Lloyd George remained Prime Minister due to Conservative support. However, the Liberal Party was to experience decline across Scotland and the rest of Britain. Divisions between Asquith and Lloyd split the party. Three general elections in six years used up party funds. The other parties, especially Labour, gained support from the increases to the electorate in 1918. Unpopular policies also caused Lloyd George to lose the support of the Conservatives and many voters. In 1922, he lost the election and was replaced as Prime Minister by the Conservative, Andrew Bonar Law. The Liberal Party was not to form a government again. Bonar Law lasted 211 days as Prime Minister.

POLITICAL PARTY	GENERAL ELECTION RESULTS 1918–1929									
	1918		1922		1923		1924		1929	
	GB	SCOT	GB	SCOT	GB	SCOT	GB	SCOT	GB	SCOT
CONSERVATIVES	359	30	334	13	248	14	400	36	250	20
LABOUR	57	6	142	29	191	34	151	26	287	36
LIBERALS	163	33	115	27	158	22	40	8	59	13
OTHER	27	2	12	2	6	1	12	1	7	2

One notable politician who lost his seat in 1922 was the Liberal MP for Dundee, Winston Churchill. He was defeated by Edwin Scrymgeour, who was a Prohibitionist (against the sale of alcohol).

THE RISE OF LABOUR

The changes brought about by the 1918 Representation of the People Act benefited the Labour Party because many of the people who gained the vote were working-class men. They were attracted to the newest of the three main political parties because of a number of factors:

- Other parties had not delivered on their promises to improve housing.
- By 1921, the economy was struggling and unemployment was beginning to rise. Labour appeared to offer an alternative.
- Labour's policies, such as nationalising the coal industry, appealed to many workers who believed that control by the government had been better than by the owners. Conditions and pay had been improved. There was also resentment that some companies such as the shipyards had made huge profits during the war.
- Some Labour politicians such as Arthur Henderson had served in the coalition government during the Great War. They had gained experience of government. This led many voters to believe that the Labour Party was a real challenger for power after 1918.

The 1923 General Election did not lead to a clear majority for any political party. Eventually, the Labour Party formed a government early in 1924. Labour were to remain in power for ten months. In that time, they passed a number of reforms which helped to ensure that the Labour Party was not seen as a threat to British society. They increased child benefit, unemployment benefit and pensions. They introduced the Wheatley Housing Act in 1924. This increased the numbers of houses that were available for workers.

In 1924, a letter which was supposed to have been written by a Communist leader, Gregory Zinoviev, was published in the *Daily Mail* newspaper. It said that Communists in Britain should support a revolution. The letter was regarded by many people as a forgery, but it led to a landslide victory for the Conservatives in the 1924 General Election. Despite this setback, the Labour Party had demonstrated that it could form a government.

THINGS TO DO AND THINK ABOUT

1. What were the reasons for the Liberal decline after 1918?

2. What were the reasons for Labour's growth after 1918?

3. Draw a line graph to show support for the Liberal, Labour and Conservative parties in Scotland between 1918 and 1929.

DON'T FORGET

The election was known as the 'Khaki' Election or Coupon Election. This was because of the large numbers of voters in uniform and also because Lloyd George had given letters of support to those Liberal MPs who were prepared to accept him as Liberal leader.

DON'T FORGET

Politics changed after 1918. Large numbers of people got the vote for the first time. The Liberal Party declined, while Labour saw a growth in support.

ONLINE

You can read more about the history of the Labour party at the Digital Zone: www.brightredbooks.net/ N5History.

DON'T FORGET

Nationalisation meant that the government would run the industries.

ONLINE TEST

To take a test on this topic, go to the Digital Zone: www.brightredbooks.net/ N5History.

A LAND FIT FOR HEROES?

ONLINE

Go to the Digital Zone to find out more about the state of housing in Scotland: www.brightredbooks.net/N5History.

HOUSING AND HOMES FIT FOR HEROES

In 1918, David Lloyd George promised that Britain would be 'a land fit for heroes'. However, the men who returned to Scotland were not always happy about the conditions they were forced to accept.

The rent strikes of 1915 and the Royal Commission of 1917 had revealed major problems with Scottish housing. The government introduced a series of reforms after 1919 to tackle the problems of poor housing. Around half of Scotland's housing was thought to be inadequate during the interwar period.

MINISTER BEHIND REFORM	NAME OF ACT	PLANS	EFFECTS
Christopher ADDISON	1919 Housing and Town Planning Act	Promised 'Homes for Heroes'. Wanted to build 500 000 low-cost homes in Britain over three years.	Built 250 000 homes in Britain, of which 25 000 were in Scotland. Money to build homes was cut after 1921.
Neville CHAMBERLAIN	1923 Housing Act	Private builders were given subsidies to build houses.	Built 438 000 private houses in Britain by 1929, of which 50 000 were in Scotland. This did not challenge the housing problems of the poor.
John WHEATLEY	1924 Housing Act	Gave a subsidy to local councils to build housing for low-paid workers.	Built over 580 000 council houses in Britain by 1935. Construction of houses in Scotland rose 140% between 1925 and 1929. These were of a better standard than existing homes.

Source A is a plan of a typical council house built after 1924.

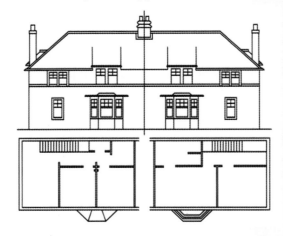

Source B is a photograph of a typical council house constructed after 1924.

Despite the attempts of the government, poor-quality housing was to remain a problem throughout the period. Large amounts of slum housing were to remain untouched until long after the Second World War. A further problem was that the rents of the new council houses were too high for the poorest workers to afford.

VIDEO LINK

You can watch a clip about the development of council houses at the Digital Zone: www.brightredbooks.net/N5History.

UNEMPLOYMENT

During the 1920s, large numbers of workers found themselves unemployed. The Unemployment Insurance Act had been introduced in 1920. It increased the amount of benefits the unemployed could receive, but it was based on unemployment remaining at 4–5%. A commission under Sir Eric Geddes was set up to look at ways of reducing government spending.

% UNEMPLOYED OF INSURED WORKFORCE	YEAR
14.3	1923
12.4	1924
15.2	1925
16.4	1926
10.6	1927
11.7	1928
12.1	1929
18.5	1930
26.6	1931

ONLINE

Go online to the Digital Zone to read an article about the challenges facing Britain after the war: www.brightredbooks.net/N5History.

Cuts were made in education, housebuilding, the armed forces and the Unemployment Insurance Act. The results are shown in the diagram below.

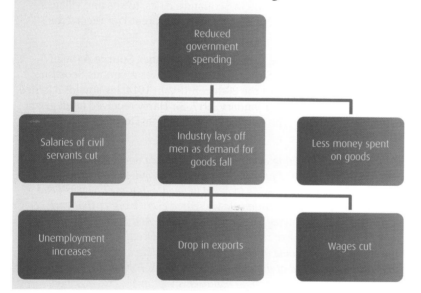

THINGS TO DO AND THINK ABOUT

1. To what extent was Scotland 'a land fit for heroes' after 1918? When you are writing your answer, use the following stages to help you:

   - Write an introduction. This should use the original question.

   - Use paragraphs to structure your answer. These should outline the evidence that is relevant, and should deal with housing, unemployment and government policy.

   - Write a conclusion which answers the original question.

ONLINE TEST

You can take a test on this topic at the Digital Zone: www.brightredbooks.net/N5History.

CASUALTIES

THE IMPACT OF THE CASUALTIES

It is estimated that around 13% of those who served in the armed forces during the Great War were Scots. During the four years of conflict, they were to serve around the globe in every battle that involved Britain. The cost of this service was huge. Estimates of the number of Scottish dead range from 74 000 to 182 000. Many historians believe that the casualties must be far more than the 100 000 which were originally estimated at the end of the Great War.

The impact of these numbers is almost beyond comprehension. Glasgow lost around 18 000 men. The Royal Scots, which recruited from Edinburgh and the Lothians, lost around 11 000 men. Other regiments, such as the Highland Light Infantry and the Black Watch, lost 10 000 men each.

These figures take no account of other casualties – the men who died prematurely of wounds in the 1920s after leaving the armed forces, or the men who were seriously injured and spent the rest of their lives trying to cope as best they could.

Evidence of the depth of the casualties is found in Scotland's cities, towns and villages. The war memorials that were constructed in the years after the Great War record the sacrifice of a nation.

Some people recorded their feelings on the loss of a family member. **Source A** (below) is an extract from 'A Minstrel in France' by Sir Harry Lauder. He was a famous Scottish music-hall entertainer during the first half of the 20th century. In 1914, his son John joined the Argyll and Sutherland Highlanders. On 1 January 1917, Sir Harry received a telegram from the War Office. It stated: 'Captain John Lauder killed in action, December 28. Official War Office.'

> *The black despair that had been hovering over me for hours closed down now and enveloped all my senses. Everything was unreal. For a time I was quite numb. But then, as I began to realize and to visualize what it was to mean in my life that my boy was dead there came a great pain. The iron of realization slowly seared every word of that curt telegram upon my heart. I said it to myself, over and over again. And I whispered to myself, as my thoughts took form, over and over, the one terrible word: 'Dead!'*
>
> *I felt that for me everything had come to an end with the reading of that dire message. It seemed to me that for me the board of life was black and blank. For me there was no past and there could be no future. Everything had been swept away, erased, by one sweep of the hand of a cruel fate. Oh, there was a past, though! And it was in that past that I began to delve. It was made up of every memory I had of my boy. I fell at once to remembering him. I clutched at every memory, as if I must grasp them and make sure of them, lest they be taken from me as well as the hope of seeing him again that the telegram had forever snatched away.*

Source B is a letter to an officer in the Seaforth Highlanders from the parents of a soldier who had been killed in battle. Officers were usually required to write letters of condolence to the next of kin, but they were not supposed to reply to letters received. The soldier who was killed was 18 when he died. He had joined up when he was 17. He should not have been serving in France for another year. Although the officer could not reply, he kept the letter for the rest of his life.

contd

671 Hawthorn St.
Springburn, Glasgow
4th Dec 1916

Dear Sir

On behalf of myself and family I have to thank you for your letter of condolence to us in our sad bereavement. Arthur was the youngest member of the family and we feel his loss more on that account. He was intensely proud of being a Scot, and proud of his Mackenzie tartan kilt. He spent the major part of his life here with us at home, but you, his officer, would see him passing from boyhood into manhood in those 4 months he was under your care in France.

We would be ever grateful to you if you could give us a little more information about the lad regarding how he died. Also if it is at all possible that we may have some little remembrance of him such as his pocket book or anything of a like nature, we would cherish and prize it above all things.

If it is not in your power to do such, perhaps some of the lads who were his companions in France would oblige us.

Again thanking you for the kindness to us in our Hour of Sorrow

I remain
Yours sincerely
Geo. Henry

VIDEO LINK

Go to the Digital Zone to watch a clip about First World War graves: www.brightredbooks.net/N5History.

Sources C and **D** show the effects of the Great War on two families – the Mochries from Kilbirnie in Ayrshire, and the Andersons from Glasgow.

Source C

James Mochrie, aged 28	2nd Gordon Highlanders	Killed on 25 September 1915
Matthew Mochrie, aged 21	9th Cameronians	Killed on 25 September 1915
Robert Mochrie, aged 19	6th Royal Scots	Killed on 25 September 1915
Andrew Mochrie, aged 38	9th Cameronians	Killed on 9 June 1917

Source D

Charles Anderson, aged 31	Highland Light Infantry	Killed on 19 December 1914
Alexander Anderson, aged 21	Highland Light Infantry	Killed on 8 October 1915
Edward Anderson, aged 21	Royal Flying Corps	Killed on 16 March 1918
William Anderson, aged 36	Highland Light Infantry	Killed on 25 March 1918

WAR MEMORIALS

In 1927, the Scottish National War Memorial was opened at Edinburgh Castle. King George V and Queen Mary put the Scottish rolls of honour into a casket within the memorial. The lists contained 100 000 names. Afterwards, thousands of people passed through the memorial and left flowers and wreaths.

Source E shows the floral tributes left outside the Scottish National War Memorial at Edinburgh Castle.

 ## THINGS TO DO AND THINK ABOUT

Do you have a war memorial near you? There may be one in your local school or church. Find out where they are located. The following websites can help, but they don't include all of the memorials.

- http://www.ukniwm.org.uk/
- http://www.warmemorials.org/links-scotland/
- http://warmemscot.s4.bizhat.com/

Once you have located a local memorial, find out more about the people who are named on it. This website can help you to start your research: http://www.cwgc.org/

ONLINE TEST

To take a test on this topic, go to the Digital Zone: www.brightredbooks.net/N5History.

SCOTLAND: A CHANGING POPULATION

WHO ARE THE SCOTS?

Scotland in 1830 was experiencing a great deal of change. The population was growing. Many were also leaving their traditional homes for new employment and new challenges.

During the 19th and early 20th centuries, Scotland witnessed the arrival of a number of immigrants. Some of these were Jews from Eastern Europe and later Germany. Other immigrants came from Italy. The largest group came from Ireland.

Source A shows the changes in Scotland's population between 1831 and 1931. It also shows the numbers of Irish, English and foreign-born inhabitants of Scotland.

	1831	1841	1851	1861	1871	1881	1891	1901	1911	1921	1931
Scottish population	2 360 000	2 439 269	2 880 000	3 062 294	3 360 018	3 735 573	4 025 647	4 472 103	4 760 904	4 882 288	4 842 980
Irish-born		126 321	207 367	204 003	207 770	218 745	194 807	205 064	174 715	159 020	124 296
English-born		37 796	46 791	54 920	69 401	90 017	108 736	131 350	161 650	189 385	164 299
Foreign-born		2776	3070	3969	4698	5585	9462	18 941	26 537	32 652	28 116

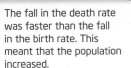

DON'T FORGET

The **birth rate** is the total number of births, and the **death rate** is the total number of deaths, per 1000 of a population each year.

FOUR MAJOR REASONS FOR POPULATION CHANGE

1. Changes in the death rate

DON'T FORGET

The fall in the death rate was faster than the fall in the birth rate. This meant that the population increased.

After 1871, there was a fall in the **death rate**. Conditions in towns were slowly improving. Diseases, such as cholera, were being brought under control. Railways and steamships meant that fresh food could be supplied much more quickly and cheaply than before.

Medical knowledge was improving, and better **welfare provision** existed by the early 20th century. The Liberal government of 1906–1914 introduced a number of reforms which tried to help the poorer members of society. The introduction of Old Age Pensions, and of school dinners for children, helped to improve the health of the population.

2. Changes in the birth rate

During the period 1831–1871, the **birth rate** was rising. A high death rate meant many children did not survive to become adults. Working-class parents needed children to look after them when they became too old to work.

After 1871, the birth rate began to drop. The 1872 Education Act in Scotland meant that children were supposed to go to school until they were 14. This meant they could no longer go out to work. Greater knowledge of contraception also played a role in explaining why the birth rate fell.

Source B shows the change in birth and death rates in Scotland between 1855 and 1940.

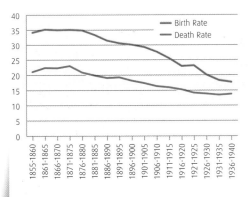

3. Emigration

This means the people who left Scotland to live abroad. Between 1830 and 1939, large numbers of Scots emigrated. Popular destinations included North America, Australia and New Zealand.

4. Immigration

This refers to the groups of people who moved to Scotland to live. During the period 1830–1939, Scotland attracted thousands of immigrants from Ireland, England and Europe.

VIDEO LINK

Visit the Digital Zone to watch a clip about Scottish emigration between 1830 and 1930: www.brightredbooks.net/N5History.

MIGRATION AND URBANISATION

After 1830, the Scottish population was on the move. In 1830, around two thirds of the population lived in the countryside. By 1939, this had been reversed. Only one third were still living in the countryside.

Many moved to the central belt of Scotland to get jobs in industry. Many of these towns had expanded during the 19th century. Cities, such as Glasgow, needed thousands of workers in shipyards, steel factories and manufacturing industries. Dundee also attracted large numbers of people to work in its textile and jute mills. Edinburgh and, further north, Aberdeen, also expanded.

Source C shows the major movements of population after 1830.

Source D shows the population growth of cities between 1841 and 1931.

	1841	1881	1931
Aberdeen	64 778	105 000	170 000
Dundee	60 553	140 000	176 000
Edinburgh	138 182	295 000	439 000
Glasgow	274 533	587 000	1 088 000

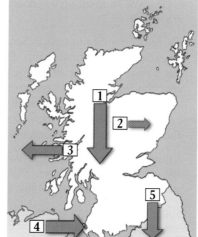

The *New Statistical Account* (NSA) is one of the main sources for historians studying Scotland in the mid-19th century. It was written by Church of Scotland ministers, who were helped by local teachers and doctors. They compiled information about local geography, industry, agriculture and population. On occasions, the writers would make unfavourable comments about the arrival of immigrants in their area.

CHANGES IN THE COUNTRYSIDE

By 1830, farms had been improved and fields had been enclosed. Hedges or walls had been built to keep animals off fields. The farms that existed after 1830 were usually much larger than the ones that had previously existed. This led to benefits for farmers and the population. The food supply was improved. Selective breeding meant that animals became bigger and healthier. The use of fertilisers helped to increase the amount of food grown. New machinery, such as the seed drill or reaping and threshing machines, meant that many tasks could be completed quickly. Those farmers who could improve their farms became wealthy.

Horses were heavily used in agriculture until the 1930s. By that time, tractors and other motorised transport had become available. This meant that the jobs for horsemen and blacksmiths began to disappear. The numbers of people employed in agriculture dropped from 200 000 in 1900 to 160 000 in 1931.

 THINGS TO DO AND THINK ABOUT

1. Design a bar graph to show the population change within Scotland after 1841.

2. Use **Source C** to complete the following task.

Arrow number	Population movement
	Population leaving the Highlands due to the demands of high rents by landowners and difficult working conditions.
	Scottish population emigrating because of opportunities in other countries.
	Rural population moving to towns and cities looking for work.
	Scots moving to England for work.
	Immigrants from Ireland moving to Scotland to find work and to escape famine.

 VIDEO LINK

Visit the Digital Zone to find out more about the growth of Scottish cities: www.brightredbooks.net/ N5History.

 DON'T FORGET

Urbanisation means the movement of people from the countryside to the city.

 ONLINE

For more on population changes in Scotland and to find out more about population changes in your area, click the links at the Digital Zone: www. brightredbooks.net/ N5History.

 VIDEO LINK

Visit the Digital Zone for a look at how the countryside changed as the Agricultural Revolution progressed: www.brightredbooks.net/ N5History.

ONLINE

Visit the Digital Zone to read more about the changes in farming and agricultural improvement: www.brightredbooks.net/ N5History.

 ONLINE TEST

To take a test on this topic, go to the Digital Zone: www.brightredbooks.net/ N5History.

JEWISH IMMIGRATION

WHY DID JEWS ARRIVE IN SCOTLAND?

In 1840, the number of Jews living in Scotland was small. Only around 200 were living in Glasgow by the mid-19th century. There were about 500 living in Edinburgh by 1900. Most of them were Dutch or German businessmen. As the numbers of Jews increased in Glasgow, they set up a synagogue and also bought a piece of ground to use as a graveyard.

The small number of Jews in Scotland was to rise after 1881. Tsar Alexander II of Russia was killed by a terrorist bomb. One of the people behind this attack was a Jew. The result was a wave of violent attacks or pogroms against the Jews living in Russia. The following year, the Tsar's government introduced the May Laws. These placed restrictions on where Jews could live and limited their chances of going to schools and universities. More than a million Jews fled from the pogroms and persecution. Many journeyed to the USA, but about 100 000 settled in Britain between 1881 and 1914.

A number of Jews settled in Scotland. A popular area of Glasgow to settle was the Gorbals. This was one of the poorest areas of Glasgow; and the Jewish settlers were joined there by the Irish and Italian communities. In 1901, there were around 5000 to 6000 Jews living in the Gorbals.

Source A is an extract from an interview with a Mrs Braverman which was carried out in 1982.

> *I come frae Dulna Guberniya in Russia and I was born, I think in 1891. Everybody was poor. The pogroms were getting so bad that I was told they used to go into a house and they'd pull a baby's tongue out! I was told that, and I felt terrible. Anyway, people were nervous in case things got worse – and that's the reason they left, because things weren't so good.*

THE JEWS DURING THE 1930s

In 1933, Adolf Hitler became leader of Germany. The Nazis had used anti-Jewish propaganda to help them come to power. Jews were blamed for Germany's defeat in the Great War and for the economic problems which followed. Throughout the 1930s, life became increasingly difficult for Jews under Nazi rule. In 1939, the numbers of Jews in Scotland rose to 15 000 in Glasgow and 2000 in Edinburgh.

Photograph of a sign on a store owned by German Jews: 'Protect Yourselves, Don't Buy from Jews'

The problem for Jews who wished to flee Nazi Germany was finding a country that was willing to take them in. One successful organisation that helped Jewish children to escape Nazi Germany was the **Kindertransport** ('children's transport'). Around 10 000 children came to Britain on their own (parents were not allowed). The children were sent to youth hostels, foster families or youth farms.

LIFE IN SCOTLAND FOR THE JEWS

The number of Jewish people in Scotland had started to increase more rapidly towards the end of the 19th century. Many settled in the Gorbals in Glasgow. Those who became more prosperous later moved to better housing in the West End of the city.

It was thought that, by 1900, over 1000 Jews were employed in 'sweat shops' (cramped, unhygienic small factories) producing garments for the tailoring trade. However, the Jewish community was also associated with the tobacco trade. One example of this was the tobacco firm Stephen Mitchell & Sons that employed Jews and whose Glasgow manager was Jewish.

contd

Jewish immigrants were helped to start their own businesses with loans from groups such as the Glasgow Hebrew Benevolent Loan Society. Other organisations existed to help those Jewish immigrants who were in extreme poverty. These included:

- The Jewish Board of Guardians
- Hebrew Ladies Benevolent Society
- Boot and Clothing Guild
- The Sick Visiting Association
- The Hachnosas Orchin (Society for welcoming strangers)
- The Hachnosas Kalla (Society for providing the bride with a dowry).

One of the major complaints of Scots about immigrants was that they were a burden on the parish Poor Relief. They had to be given money to prevent them from falling further into trouble. Few Jewish immigrants had to rely on Poor Relief in Scotland, because they received assistance from their own community.

The Jewish community was not free from criticism. This mainly centred on concerns over cheap labour bringing down the wages of Scottish workers. Also, the Church was concerned about Jews working and trading on Sundays (Saturday is the Sabbath for Jews). One reason for Jews staying in the Gorbals was that it was often difficult to rent housing in other less tolerant areas of Glasgow.

RELATIONS WITH NATIVE SCOTS

The relations between Jewish immigrants and non-Jews varied. Some experienced discrimination, while others received a warm welcome.

Source B is from the autobiography of a Jewish immigrant to Scotland, Manny Shinwell. He wrote it in 1981.

> *Many Gorbals residents were Roman Catholics, immigrants from Southern Ireland, labourers in the nearby steelworks, at the docks, in building and among the better-off publicans pawnbrokers and shopkeepers. On the whole, relations between Jews and the Irish were friendly except when the latter got too much drink. Of course there was some anti-Semitism owing to jealousy, when some Jews were flourishing and showing off a bit, but far more because some of the ignorant and bigoted Catholics could never forgive the Jews for having crucified Christ.*

Source C is from a speech made to the General Assembly of the Church of Scotland in March 1938.

> *There are only two ways to treat the Jews, and they are to fight them or to convert them, and Britain's desire is not to fight them but to see them converted to accepting the Christian religion as their faith.*

By the 1920s and 1930s, many younger Jews were becoming assimilated. Yiddish-language newspapers were closing down as demand for them declined. Younger Jews had few problems going to the cinema or theatre on a Saturday. Jewish-owned shops would also remain open on a Saturday rather than closing.

 ## THINGS TO DO AND THINK ABOUT

1. Explain the reasons why the numbers of Jews living in Scotland increased after 1881.

2. Evaluate the usefulness of Source B as evidence of the effects of immigration on Scotland. (You may want to comment on who wrote it, when they wrote it, why they wrote it, what they say or what has been missed out.)

3. Describe the reasons why Jews in Scotland did not rely on Poor Relief.

 DON'T FORGET

Anti-Semitism means hatred of the Jews.

 DON'T FORGET

Jews tended to settle into trades and industries that they were familiar with. These usually involved finance, tobacco and clothing. Jews tended to work in these areas because in Eastern Europe they had been prevented from doing other types of jobs.

DON'T FORGET

In 1905, the British government introduced an Aliens Act to prevent poor immigrants from entering the country. This reduced the numbers of Jewish immigrants arriving.

 DON'T FORGET

Between 1830 and 1939, poor people relied on help from the local authorities. This was known as Poor Relief. The money was raised through local taxes. Those in trouble could ask for help. Although they could receive money, it was only for a limited amount of time. Many ended up in the workhouse, where families were separated and conditions were harsh.

ONLINE TEST

Take a test on Jewish immigration to Scotland at the Digital Zone: www.brightredbooks.net/N5History.

THE ITALIANS

WHY DID THEY ARRIVE IN SCOTLAND?

The Premier Café, run by the Crolla family in Glasgow

In nearly every town in Scotland, the influence of Scottish Italians is clearly felt. Italians have introduced and dominated the café and restaurant culture enjoyed by Scots. Hamilton has the Equii family; Maryhill has the Jaconellis; and Largs has the famous Nardinis, to name but a few.

Many of these families can trace their immigration to Scotland back to the late 19th century. Between 1890 and 1914, the number of Italians living in Scotland increased from 750 to 5000. Most came from two distinct areas: Lucca, in Tuscany, and Frosinone, south of Rome. Their main reason for leaving Italy was to better themselves economically. Life for the Italian peasant was hard and unrelenting.

Source A is from an interview carried out in 1981 with an Italian immigrant to Scotland, Mrs D'Agostino.

I have only flashes of childhood in Italy. I remember the vast countryside, full of grapevines, lots of trees, animals and chickens. I used to run wild. I remember running barefoot – but there was no such thing as hunger, because they grew so much. There was poverty, though; it was a terrible struggle. I mean, if someone took ill or if someone needed an operation, you had to sell a cow or sell one of your mules, and that was great hardship because they would need it. Everyone was more or less the same, glad to escape the hard life they had over in Italy.

The Italian population was rising substantially during this period, and it was becoming more difficult for Italian peasants to make a good living in their homeland. The majority of Italian emigrants flocked to the USA, but many came to Britain, often making London their first port of call.

Often the Italians used agents (*padroni*) who ensured that the emigrants had work in their new country. As is often the case, the Italians moved to areas of Scotland where there were already Italian families. Often, they would join a community that had strong links to their original home in Italy.

Source B is the recollections of an Italian immigrant called Dominic Crolla.

When they came over, all the people from their own village would come over to join them. They would settle where their own villagers were, their own friends. So there's a big crowd from Barga, they've gathered together in Glasgow and the West. Most of them that came here to Edinburgh were from the villages in the Abruzzi, and they made for the Grassmarket because it was the most similar to an Italian piazza. So the Italian colony at that time was more or less centred around St Mary's Street, the Pleasance and the Grassmarket. Everybody knew everybody else.

LIFE IN SCOTLAND FOR ITALIANS

The newly arrived Italian community was involved in a variety of occupations in Scotland. The most obvious were the Italian cafés, chip shops and restaurants that spread across Scotland. They also sold ice cream on the streets from barrows. Their cry was '*gelati ecco un poco*', and they therefore became known as the 'hokey pokey' men. These street traders soon set up cafés. Leopold Giuliani was one of the most successful and had a string of cafes in Glasgow and the west of Scotland. To enable families to buy small businesses, the Società di Mutuo Soccorso was set up to loan money to Italian entrepreneurs. However, not all Italians entered the catering trade.

contd

ONLINE

Read more about Italian links with Scotland by clicking the links at the Digital Zone: www.brightredbooks.net/N5History.

DON'T FORGET

Italian families did not invent the fish supper. However, they saw the business opportunities that it provided. By 1904, the number of cafés in Glasgow alone had doubled from the previous year. This grew to 336 ice-cream shops the following year.

Source C is an extract from *Who belongs to Glasgow?* by Mary Edward. It describes some of the occupations of Italians in Scotland.

> The publication of La Scozia ('a paper for the Italian colony in Scotland') in 1908 demonstrated that there were several other Italian businesses and organisations in Glasgow, including an Italian language school for adults and children in Union Street ...
> in one family the father worked as a miner, in another the men of the family worked on the railways ... although the café business was still predominant, in 1928 a college of Italian hairdressers opened in Glasgow, and many Italians are still associated with this kind of business.

On the whole, Italians experienced less prejudice than other immigrant groups to Scotland. Their relative low numbers did not prove a threat to Scottish jobs, and they did not inspire the level of hostility which was common in dealings with Irish and Lithuanian immigrants. Italian families also married to an extent within their own community, although incidents still took place.

Source D was written by Tony Jaconelli, who was an Italian immigrant to Scotland.

> On New Year's Day 1921, I trailed along holding onto my younger brother, Michael. Our father, Domenico, carried Biagio. My oldest brother, Giacomo, brought up the rear. We had left our warm village in Italy to join Domenico's brother in some place called Scotland. School was a nightmare for me, but Giacomo, a name that was quickly shortened to Jack, revelled in school life. He was a quick learner and always able to care of himself. A few times, I found myself surrounded by classmates chanting at me because I was a foreigner. Jack scattered them, and they stopped bothering me completely. Our family moved a few times in an effort to improve our lot. Domenico took a job in the largely Italian trade of terrazzo tile workers, and my brothers followed him into that trade. Meanwhile my grasp of the Glasgow dialect improved daily. Within a couple of years, I lost trace of my mother tongue and developed a strong, guttural Glasgow accent. In no time, I was a complete Glaswegian.

One area of conflict between the Scottish Italian community and the Church centred around café opening hours on a Sunday. Opening on a Sunday was regarded by the United Free Church as a great sin. This was compounded by police reports at the time that blamed the cafés and chip shops for encouraging gambling and unsavoury behaviour. However, at the same time, the cafés were also seen in a more positive light because alcohol was not sold on their premises.

By the late 1930s, international events were causing problems for Italians living in Scotland. The leader of Italy, Benito Mussolini, was a Fascist. He had gradually become a close ally of Nazi Germany. This caused some people in Britain to view Italians with suspicion. In June 1940, when Britain was at war with Germany, Italy declared war on Britain. This led to attacks on Italian-owned businesses and to the arrest of Italians living in this country – no matter how long they had lived here.

ONLINE

Click the links at the Digital Zone to read more about the problems in the late 1930s for Italians living in Scotland: www.brightredbooks.net/ N5History.

VIDEO LINK

To watch a clip about the tragedy of the *Arandora Star* click the link at the Digital Zone: www.brightredbooks. net/N5History.

THINGS TO DO AND THINK ABOUT

1. Describe the impact of Italian immigration on Scotland.

2. Explain why Italian immigrants may have faced less hostility than other immigrant groups.

3. How fully does Source D above describe the experience of immigrants to Scotland after 1830? (Use Source D and recall.)

ONLINE TEST

Check your knowledge of Italian immigration to Scotland by taking the test at the Digital Zone: www.brightredbooks.net/ N5History.

THE IRISH

WHY DID THEY ARRIVE IN SCOTLAND?

The immigrant group that had the biggest impact on Scotland was the Irish. Although we associate Irish emigration with the Potato Famine (1848–1852), the Irish had been coming to Scotland for some time before this tragedy. With the improvements in agriculture during the latter half of the 18th century, Scotland had increased her harvests and needed willing hands at harvest time. With the introduction of cheap sailings between Scotland and Ireland, the Irish flocked to these jobs. Many were seasonal workers who found employment in farming – often as 'tattie-howkers'.

This group usually returned to Ireland when the work was finished. Many others stayed. Scotland was at the forefront of the industrial and agricultural revolutions, and this made it an attractive prospect to the Irish. Jobs were available, and wages were higher than in Ireland.

An advert for the steamships which linked Scotland and Ireland

THE POTATO FAMINE

With the onslaught of the Potato Famine, the Irish had a much more tragic reason for coming to Scotland. The Great Famine, as it is also known, killed approximately 1 million people in Ireland and forced another million to emigrate.

The **potato blight** was a fungal disease that swept through potato crops in Ireland and other European countries at this time.

The potatoes were completely inedible. This had a devastating effect on Ireland. Unlike other European countries affected by the blight, many of the poorer Irish were dependent on the potato as their main food crop. Mass starvation and disease followed the year-on-year ruined harvests. Irish labourers and their families were then evicted from their homes and often faced the stark choice of starvation or emigration.

A potato affected by the blight

Source A is from the *Illustrated London News*, 22 December 1849.

> *The Sketch of a Woman and Children represents Bridget O'Donnel. Her story is briefly this: '… we were put out last November; he [my husband] owed some rent … I was at this time lying in fever … they commenced knocking down the house, and had half of it knocked down when two neighbours, women, Nell Spellesley and Kate How, carried me out … I was carried into a cabin, and lay there for eight days, when I had the creature (the child) born dead. I lay for three weeks after that. The whole of my family got the fever, and one boy thirteen years old died with want and with hunger while we were lying sick …'*

During these terrible years, the influx of Irish into Scotland became a flood. The sheer numbers were surprising – and this had an impact on all sections of Scottish life.

Source B is the view of the historian Tom Devine:

> *In absolute terms the movement of the famine refugees to Scotland was less significant numerically than elsewhere because fewer than 100,000 came to Scotland during the crisis years, In relative terms, however, this was an enormous and unique burden for a small country which contained only 2.8 million inhabitants in 1845 and which also suffered an acute industrial depression in 1847–8, a cholera epidemic in 1848 and a subsistence crisis in the Highlands between 1846 and the early 1850s, where the potatoes also threatened an Irish-type calamity.*

WHERE DID THE IRISH SETTLE?

The majority of the Irish settled in areas where they could get work. For many, this was on the west coast where the industries were located. Many also went to Dundee and the surrounding towns for work in the mills. A large proportion of these migrants were single girls.

RELIGIOUS AND CULTURAL FORCES BINDING THE IRISH COMMUNITY IN SCOTLAND

The influx of Irish into Scotland did not cease after the famine. Scotland continued to be a popular destination for the Irish. Although the USA was the most popular, Scotland was close and cheap to travel to. Also, the emigrants knew that they would have friends, families and former neighbours whom they could easily contact and rely on for support.

Source C is Con Greene, an Irish immigrant, describing his life in the Gorbals, Glasgow.

> *It was a Donegal community and is still ye know, although they're scattered more out at all the housing schemes. But it was a good community. Well, on a Saturday night, you might go down about the Gorbals. Ye might just fall out about somethin' and ye would see a wee fight and that was that. But, for the rest of it, they were all people and they all went to their religious duties even on a workin' day, and goin' to their work you would see them goin' early to get to the early mass. They were always good livin' that way.*

Source D is from an interview with a Father Canning which took place in 1980. It outlines the importance of the Catholic Church to Irish Catholic immigrants.

> *Religion was virtually the only security they had, because they hadn't much of the world's goods, and they found comfort and strength in their religion. Also they found security, in that they could go for example to the local priest, and he was there to assist them in many ways, very often doing things that we now take for granted – like writing letters, getting houses, jobs and so on. Also fighting their battles for social security. So the priest played a very important role in their life, and also the church afforded them an opportunity for meeting their fellow countrymen or fellow county men or even fellow townsmen – and this itself was a source of help to each other.*

The church played a huge role in organising social events for the Irish community. Groups, such as the 'League of the Cross', were set up to stop heavy drinking.

By the later 19th and the early 20th century, economic factors were the main reason for Irish emigration. Construction of the railways, roads and the Glasgow Underground would have been difficult without Irish workers. In Dundee, Lochee attracted Irish textile workers to labour in the jute mills. They had worked in mills in Donegal, Londonderry, Monaghan, Sligo and Tyrone. After the Great War, Irish immigration to Scotland declined due to the post-war economic downturn.

Source E is an extract from *The Scottish Nation 1700–2000* by the historian Tom Devine.

> *Irish migration had virtually collapsed because of the slump in Scottish industry. Irish workers were among the many thousands emigrating from a distressed Scotland in the 1920s, and the vast majority of the 'Scoto-Irish' community had in fact been born in Scotland.*

THINGS TO DO AND THINK ABOUT

1. Explain why the Irish were arriving in Scotland after 1830.

2. In which parts of Scotland did the Irish settle?

3. Look at Source D. Why was the Catholic Church important to Irish immigrants to Scotland?

4. Look at Source E. Why did Irish immigration to Scotland decline after the 1920s?

ONLINE

To read more about employment options for Irish immigrants click the link at the Digital Zone: www.brightredbooks.net/N5History.

DON'T FORGET

In 1908, the Pope passed a *Ne Temere* decree. In the event of a mixed marriage between a Catholic and a non-Catholic, a priest could ask for the children to be brought up as Catholic. Otherwise he could refuse to carry out the ceremony. This was regarded as a barrier to marriage between the Scots and the Irish.

DON'T FORGET

After the Great War ended, there was a downturn in the economy. This meant that there was a shortage of jobs. This in turn led to resentment towards Irish immigrants. This was particularly true of ex-servicemen who had fought in the British army during the war and felt that many Irish had been disloyal.

ONLINE TEST

Take a test on this topic at the Digital Zone: www.brightredbooks.net/N5History.

LIFE IN SCOTLAND FOR THE IRISH

This photograph, taken in 1868, shows the living conditions which existed in Glasgow.

TENEMENT HOUSING

One of the first considerations for the Irish when they arrived in Scotland was where to live. By 1830, Glasgow had some of the worst living conditions in Britain. Overcrowding was a problem, sanitary conditions were poor to non-existent, and epidemics of cholera and typhus were common. It was into this environment that the majority of the Irish flooded – especially after the 1840s and 1850s when the famine and its aftermath were most keenly felt. The poorest sections of Scottish society lived in slums – and the Irish newcomers were often the poorest of the poor.

As well as occupying the poorest areas of Glasgow, the Irish got the reputation of being 'disease-carriers' and the cause of the ills of Glasgow. They became scapegoats for the urban problems.

Source A is from *The Irish in Scotland* by the historian J. E. Handley (1943).

The dwellings of the Irish are poorer than those of the Scotch in the same class of life; more of them are huddled together; the houses are ill furnished, ill aired and dirty in the extreme. The poor Irish frequently lie on the floor, on straw or shavings; frequently, however they have beds, it is the practice for as many to sleep in the same bed as can be crowded into it – it is not uncommon for three or four to lie in the same bed – frequently three or four beds are in the same apartment, in which males and females sleep next to one another. The Irish are, in general, dirtier and less well clothed than the native population.

ONLINE

You can read more about the Irish in Scotland by clicking the link at the Digital Zone: www.brightredbooks.net/N5History.

DON'T FORGET

12 July was the anniversary of William III's victory over the Catholic James II in 1690. The victory was celebrated with marches by the Orange Order. This was often the time when many of the troubles occurred.

SCOTS AND IRISH

The Catholicism of the majority of the Irish immigrants also became a bone of contention for many Scots. The anti-popery movement gained support in the early part of the 19th century. In 1852, the anti-Catholic 'Scottish Reformation Society' had 38 branches scattered throughout Scotland.

In the 1840s and 1850s, there were a number of riots and violence which were connected to problems between the Catholic Irish and Scots. A fanatical anti-Catholic speaker called John S. Orr caused a number of riots in Dumbarton, Greenock and Gourock in the 1850s. He summoned crowds by blowing a trumpet, and was nicknamed the 'Angel Gabriel'. Other troubles broke out across the country in the following years. There were so many problems at this time that a number of county councils (Ayrshire, Dunbartonshire, Lanarkshire, Renfrewshire and Stirlingshire) banned Orange Walks.

In Ireland, conflict had long existed between Catholics and Protestants. This was seen in the spreading of the Orange Order from Ulster to Scotland.

The photograph on the left shows a stone outside Girvan marking the site where a police constable was shot during a riot by the Orange Lodge in 1831. They were being prevented by the local inhabitants from marching through the town. A number of people were seriously injured. The man who had fired the shot was hanged in Ayr.

Before the Potato Famine, the majority of Scottish Catholics were in the Highlands and Islands, but now this shifted to the central belt.

Source B The historian Martin Mitchell describes the development of the Catholic religion within Scotland.

'the impact in Scotland was still astonishing: 83 priests, 52 permanent chapels, a nunnery and estimated 150,000 mainly Irish faithful in 1838 grew by 1855 to 131 clergy, 4 convents, about 100 chapels, and numerous Sunday and day schools for around 200,000 nominal faithful.'

The prejudice against the Catholic religion often spread into areas of employment. Catholic workers would sometimes find it difficult to get jobs because of their religion.

EMPLOYMENT OPPORTUNITIES

Although some Irish immigrants found it difficult to get a job, they were many more who provided the manpower for Scotland's Industrial Revolution. Large numbers of Irish labourers found work building canals or navigations. By 1840, many Irish "navvies" were working building new railway lines. This notoriously hard job needed strong, tough workers. All the work was done by hand with pickaxes, shovels and wheelbarrows. They quickly gained a reputation for trouble.

Source C, from the *Glasgow Herald* of 15 September 1840, describes drunken Irish navvies in the town of Hamilton.

> *Some hundreds of navigators turned out and brandishing clubs and picks broke windows, assaulted every Scotch person they could meet with, jumped, yelled and altogether frightened for their lives the peaceable inhabitants.*

In Dundee, the textile factories relied on Irish labourers. In Lanarkshire, some worked in the coal mines; and farm work in all rural areas still relied on Irish hands both seasonally and permanently. The Irish, however, often got the reputation of being strike-breakers, as sometimes factory or mine owners would use them as cheap labour during times of industrial unrest.

EDUCATION

Education was a problem for many years for the immigrant Irish. The majority of schools were strongly Protestant in ethos, and this did not encourage Catholic parents. However, within their local communities and with the help of the Church, schools and Sunday schools were set up, and in 1894 the Notre Dame training college for Catholic teachers was set up. In 1918, the Education (Scotland) Act allowed for separate Catholic schools to exist.

SPORT AND RECREATION

Another area of life where the Irish influence is most keenly felt is within Scottish football. Predominantly Irish Catholic areas began to produce their own teams. Two of the most successful were the Harp of Dundee and the Hibernians of Edinburgh. In 1888, Brother Walfrid set up Glasgow Celtic primarily as a charitable organisation to help the poor of the East End of Glasgow. These teams provided a focal point for their local Irish communities.

PROTESTANT IRISH

During the 19th century, large numbers of Protestant Irish arrived in Scotland to work. They did not face the same difficulties as the Catholic Irish. It was much easier to accept them, as they were Protestant and spoke English. Many of the Catholic Irish only spoke Irish Gaelic. Large numbers of the Northern Irish who arrived worked in the Clyde shipyards.

In Glasgow, the son of a Protestant Irish immigrant went on to become the world's most famous grocer. Sir Thomas Lipton's father came to Glasgow because of the Potato Famine. He worked in a mill and saved enough money to open a small grocer's shop. Thomas worked in the shop from a young age, emigrated to the USA at the age of 15 and returned to Scotland at age 20. He opened his own shop at 21 and was a millionaire by the time he was 30. He owned a chain of shops and tea plantations in Ceylon.

THINGS TO DO AND THINK ABOUT

1. Explain why the Irish arrived in Scotland.

2. Why were the Irish believed to be 'typhus-carriers'?

3. Evaluate the usefulness of Source C as evidence of the relationship between the Irish and the Scots. (You may want to comment on who wrote it, when they wrote it, why they wrote it, what they say or what has been missed out.)

DON'T FORGET

The Orange Order was set up in Armagh in 1795 to protect Protestants from Irish Catholics. The order had a large membership in Ulster, and lodges were set up in the West of Scotland. Orange Walks became the focus of conflicts within the Protestant and Catholic communities. Interestingly, there were fewer religious problems in Dundee, where the majority of Irish immigrants were Catholic.

VIDEO LINK

Click the links at the Digital Zone to watch clips about Irish workers in Scotland: www.brightredbooks.net/N5History.

ONLINE

You can read more about the life of Sir Thomas Lipton at the Digital Zone: www.brightredbooks.net/N5History.

ONLINE TEST

Test your knowledge on this topic at the Digital Zone: www.brightredbooks.net/N5History.

SCOTTISH EMIGRATION

Decade	Numbers of Scots emigrating
1881–1891	217 418
1891–1901	53 356
1901–1911	254 042
1911–1921	238 587
1921–1931	391 903

WHY WERE SCOTS LEAVING?

One of the main reasons, and probably the most famous reason for Scots emigration, was the Highland Clearances. However, Scottish emigration was a more complex affair and went beyond just the Clearances. Emigration was not just a Highland issue. People were searching for a new life abroad from all over Scotland during the period 1830–1939.

LIFE IN THE HIGHLANDS

Most people living in the Highlands of Scotland were crofters (small farmers). They practised a subsistence way of life where they produced enough for their family and to pay their rent. Life was hard, and living conditions were basic. The rural areas provided few medical and educational opportunities.

In **Source A**, the historian Don Watson explains why the population of the Highlands experienced problems after 1830.

> *The lack of schooling traditions, the great size of the parishes and the difficulty of travel within them, and the Gaelic language barrier, thwarted attempts ... to bring 'useful language' to the Highlands and Islands ...*

Long hours and little prospect of improvement were basic reasons to emigrate. Furthermore, the crofter did not own his land and could be evicted at any time. The attraction of cheap or even free land abroad appealed to many poor crofters.

Source B describes the plight of Murdoch MacQueen from Duirinish on Skye in 1843.

> *... seventy six: his wife seventy ... he has 4s a year from the parish: she has nothing. In the middle room one bedstead, straw and blankets, a shake-down, straw and blankets, a chest, a table, some crockery, pot, bench and several straw seats ... Daughter resides with them, and she weaves when she can obtain employment. Gets nothing but what she earns, which is from 3s to 4s a month. Before she came to this place he had some land which supported them. Their daughter and her husband have a cow.*

More modern farming methods were introduced. New crops like potatoes and turnips were seen on the land, and new types of farming machinery were brought in to replace the simple hand tools used for centuries by the crofters.

A FAMINE AT HOME

The Highlanders, like the Irish, witnessed their own famine. The potato increasingly became an important crop to the Highlander. Therefore, they too suffered the ravages of the potato blight.

In **Source C**, Osgood Mackenzie, third son of the Laird of Gairloch, describes the impact of blight in Wester Ross in the 1840s. He was writing in 1921.

> *I cannot say I can remember my first coming to Gairloch ... but there was soon to be very trying times there, due to the potato blight. I have quite clear recollections of my own small grievance at being made to eat rice which I detested, instead of potatoes, with my mutton or chicken in the years 1846–48, for even the gentry of the big house could not get enough potatoes in those hard times.*

The blight was made worse by the severe cold winters that accompanied the potato blight. During this time, deaths among the young and old increased, as did instances of influenza, typhus and dysentery.

contd

VIDEO LINK

To learn more about life in the Highlands, you can watch a clip at the Digital Zone: www.brightredbooks.net/N5History.

DON'T FORGET

In previous centuries, crofters had been protected by their clan chiefs, but by 1830 the modern world was encroaching into the rural Highlands. Clan chiefs were now modern landlords looking for ways to improve their estates and keep themselves out of debt.

ONLINE TEST

Test your knowledge of this topic online at the Digital Zone: www.brightredbooks.net/N5History.

However, the famine did not reach the level of Ireland's. Although the potato was an important crop, the people of the Highlands could also turn to grain and fish to see them through hard times. Also, the state and charities helped more in Scotland. Landowners also stepped in to help the people on their land. Sometimes this involved setting up funds to help the crofters to emigrate to a better life abroad.

Source D to the right is from the *Glasgow Herald* of 14 July 1855.

It is very clear that, even without the Clearances, there were many factors that made people wish to emigrate from their harsh working and living conditions in the Highlands.

THE HIGHLAND CLEARANCES

The crofters had been encouraged to change the crops they farmed and to use more modern techniques and tools. Greater change was afoot however.

One of the easiest ways for the landowners to make a healthy profit was to introduce sheep onto their land. Blackfaced or Linton sheep had been introduced to the Highlands by the end of the 18th century. These breeds of sheep could survive the harsh winters and produced a high-quality mutton that could be sold for a good price. Cheviot sheep were then brought into the Highlands – and they yielded even higher profits, as they could produce fine wool. These sheep needed plentiful land to graze on. Later on, the landowners found out that profits could also be made from hosting shooting parties on their estates. So, as well as sheep, the hillsides were managed for grouse and deer.

The economics were simple. Landowners could charge sheep farmers higher rents than the crofters were paying. Some Highlanders therefore had no choice about leaving their land. It was this forcible eviction of people that became known as the Highland Clearances. The most notorious of the clearances that took place were in Sutherland in northern Scotland. Like many landowners of this time, the Duke and Duchess of Sutherland wanted to maximise the potential of their estates. Sheep was the way forward, so the crofters had to go. Families had little time to clear out their possessions. They were given notice to leave, and their houses were burned to prevent them from returning.

The Sutherland Clearances' most infamous incident involved the Sutherlands' factor (manager), Patrick Sellar, who set fire to a croft in Strathnaver. Unfortunately, one of the crofts still contained Margaret Mackay, an elderly lady who refused to leave and subsequently died.

By the 1840s, the Highlands were filled with the ruins of scattered communities. Some landlords did their utmost to help their crofters, especially during the years of famine. The Duke of Argyll realised that it was cheaper to pay the poor to leave than to feed them. He helped 500 of his people on Tiree and the Ross of Mull to emigrate in 1847. Crofters who did not move abroad or to the towns and cities of Scotland's industrial central belt tried their hand at fishing on the coasts but often found it hard to profit in a very different type of work.

THE CROFTERS' ACT

The Crofters' Holdings (Scotland) Act was passed in 1886. This act was designed to give the crofters security of tenure. This meant that crofters could no longer be evicted overnight and would also be guaranteed compensation for crofts that they had improved. Rents were reduced and arrears were cancelled. Crofters now had some security, but the lure of a better life elsewhere failed to stem the flood of people leaving the Highlands. Sutherland had a population of 25 793 in 1851, but that had dropped to 17 802 in 1921.

THINGS TO DO AND THINK ABOUT

1. Explain why life for crofters was difficult.

2. You are a 19th-century crofter. Write a letter to a local newspaper describing a clearance that you have witnessed.

Famine in the Hebrides

There is not the slightest doubt that there is now and that there has been for some months back more distress in my district for want of food than has existed at any time since the failure of the potato crop in 1846. Many crofts have not had half seed put into them and some of them have got no seed at all. I daily see poor people from all quarters, and if the half of what they tell be true their sufferings must be very great, and I am only surprised how they exist at all.

 DON'T FORGET

The landlords needed to maximise the profit from their Highland estates. The crofters whose families had sometimes farmed the same land for generations were in the way of the landowners' plans for their estates.

 DON'T FORGET

The evictions in Sutherland were amongst the first and most infamous of the clearances. However, many other areas including islands such as Skye witnessed Clearances.

 DON'T FORGET

The failure of the Kelp Industry caused hardship in the Highlands. Kelp was made from seaweed which was burnt. Its ash was rich in minerals such as soda and potash. It could be used as an ingredient in glass, soap and gunpowder.

 VIDEO LINK

You can watch more clips about the Clearances and Highland emigration at the Digital Zone: www.brightredbooks.net/N5History.

 ONLINE

Go to the Digital Zone and click the links to read more about the Crofters' Act: www.brightredbooks.net/N5History.

SCOTS ABROAD

WHY MOVE ABROAD?

Simple economics was the key reason why ordinary Scots emigrated. Often, organisations were able to help with the financial costs of booking a passage abroad. The Highlands and Islands Emigration Society was formed to raise funds for emigration to the Empire. Between 1846 and 1857, the HIES helped nearly 17 000 people to move abroad.

The advent of the steamship also encouraged Scots to emigrate. Traditional ships would take months to reach Australasia, but the steamship greatly cut travelling times. Also, by the latter half of the 19th century, railways were growing in all the colonies, making easier for emigrants to reach their far-flung destinations once they disembarked from their ships. The Canadian Pacific Railway Company (CPR) actively attracted Scots.

Poster designed to attract immigrants to Canada

In **Source A**, T. M. Devine describes attempts by one overseas company to attract Scots abroad.

> *Scotland was specifically targeted, and agents of the CPR toured country areas giving lectures and providing information. The CPR even sought to reduce the hardships of pioneering by providing ready-made farms in Southern Alberta, with housing, barns and fences included as part of the sale.*

DON'T FORGET

Emigration increasingly became a business – and many businesses, charities and other benevolent groups were set up with the sole purpose of promoting emigration and also providing funds where possible.

VIDEO LINK

Go to the Digital Zone and click the link to watch a clip about Scottish emigration from the 1830s to the 1930s: www.brightredbooks.net/N5History.

Push factors	Pull factors
• Agriculture change all over Scotland led to fewer farm workers needed on the land.	• Letters from friends and family encouraged emigration.
• The Highland Clearances – crofters were being cleared off the land to make way for sheep and deer.	• Emigration Societies and government agencies gave financial help for emigration.
• Industrial change – for example, handloom weavers were no longer able to compete with textile factories.	• Land abroad was plentiful and sometimes free.
• Cities like Glasgow and Edinburgh suffered from extremely poor and unhealthy living conditions.	• Agents for many of the emigrant destinations advertised and travelled throughout Scotland encouraging emigration.
• Life in the Highlands offered little education and health care.	• The advent of steamships encouraged emigration, as the journey times were greatly reduced.
• Periods of economic depression and unemployment affected industry throughout the period 1830–1930.	

BUT WHERE TO GO?

Once Scots had decided to leave their homeland, they then had to decide where to go. Often, they looked to countries that were part of the British Empire. This choice included Canada, India, South Africa, Australia and New Zealand. Sometimes they looked to the USA. The main destination, however, was right on their doorstep.

contd

These diagrams indicate popular destinations for Scottish emigrants between 1830 and 1939.

1885-89
- USA
- South Africa
- Australia and New Zealand
- Canada

1920-24
- USA
- South Africa
- Australia and New Zealand
- Canada

SCOTS IN ENGLAND

Parliamentary Election, 1906.

Borough of Merthyr Tydfil.

Address to the Electors

J. Keir Hardie

THE

LABOUR CANDIDATE

Scots have always travelled to England to join family, search for jobs and improve their economic position. All the major English industries like coal mining, steel, textile factories and shipbuilding were prevalent in Scotland. So, Scots had the skills that were needed down south. The Scottish education system was also fairly advanced, so migrants to England often had superior literacy skills.

Scottish politicians made an impression on England. The new Labour Party that emerged at the dawn of the 20th century was often dominated by working-class Scots. Keir Hardie, a former miner from Lanarkshire, was its first leader; and Labour's first Prime Minister, Ramsay McDonald (1866–1937), was born in Lossiemouth to a farm labourer father and a housemaid mother.

DON'T FORGET

The main employer of Scots was heavy industry such as iron, steel, coal mining and shipbuilding. During the 20th century, these industries often suffered hard times which resulted in workers moving to find jobs.

SCOTTISH SUCCESS

Scottish sporting individuals have often made their way to England to further their careers. At the end of the 19th century, two English football teams showed that success could be achieved by buying Scottish players. Scottish football players who moved south were known as 'Scotch Professors' due to their skill. They were attracted by the wages offered by the professional teams in England.

In 1883, one of the best English teams was Blackburn Rovers, which regularly played at least five Scots in its team. Preston North End won the FA Cup final in 1889. The heart of the team was made up of five Scots. Millwall football club was founded in 1885 by Scottish workers. They were employed by an Aberdeen firm that had opened a factory in the area to produce canned goods. Their club colours, blue and white, reflect their Scottish origins.

By the 1930s, the town of Corby in Northamptonshire was starting to acquire its reputation of being 'Little Scotland' due to the number of Scots who came to work in its steel works. In 1931, Corby only had a small population of around 1500. In 1934, the steel firm Stewarts and Lloyds (part of the company had originated in Coatbridge) decided to build a large steelworks. This drew many Scots from the economically depressed West of Scotland. By 1939, the population had grown to 12 000, many of whom were Scots. To this day, Corby has a distinctly Scottish feel with its own pipe band and Scots club.

ONLINE

You can read more about Scottish emigration online at the Digital Zone: www.brightredbooks.net/N5History.

THINGS TO DO AND THINK ABOUT

1. What help was given to poor Scots who wanted to emigrate?

2. Why did emigration become easier by 1900?

3. Describe the reasons why many Scots were emigrating after 1830.

ONLINE TEST

To take a test on this topic, go to the Digital Zone: www.brightredbooks.net/N5History.

SCOTS IN NORTH AMERICA 1

SCOTS IN THE USA

The 1920 US census showed that 254 570 inhabitants of the USA had been born in Scotland. This was far fewer than immigrants from Ireland or England – but Scots still played a significant role in their new country. The main reason for choosing the USA as a new home was economics. Many of the Scottish emigrants were skilled workers in Scotland and took up similar roles in their new homeland.

Scotland was at the vanguard of the Industrial Revolution and had a wealth of textile workers, miners, steelmen and boilermakers. The USA was now entering its own phase of industrialisation and needed a good supply of skilled men and women.

In **Source A,** the historian Gordon Donaldson describes one area Scots became involved with.

> *One special branch of the cotton industry was the manufacture of cotton thread for sewing machines, and in this there were special links between Scotland and America. Scottish factories set up branches in America and staffed them with experienced workers from their factories at home; thus George A. Clark, from Paisley, founded works at Newark, New Jersey, and the more famous Paisley firm of Coats founded works at Pawtucket in the 1860s. Wages were nearly double those paid in Scotland.*

Scottish carpet weavers led the way in New England factories. The Connecticut village of Thompsonville was dominated by carpet workers from Kilmarnock. Scots were also popular with the owners of heavy industries. Scottish engineers brought their skills to the American iron and steelmaking industries. Shipbuilders who had served their apprenticeships on the Clyde could also work in the shipyards of Philadelphia.

The traditional image of the Scottish miner could also be found in pockets of the USA. During economic depressions in Scotland, many miners emigrated to Maryland, Pennsylvania, Illinois and Ohio. In New England, the granite quarries were populated by Scots. Many had skilled knowledge from quarries in the North-East of Scotland. Once again, they found that their wages were higher than they could earn in Scotland. Sometimes the coal and granite workers were seasonal migrants who returned to their homeland once they had saved up enough money.

Scots also played a role in journalism. One of the first popular daily newspapers was the *New York Herald*, founded in 1835 by James Gordon Bennett, a Banffshire immigrant. The high standards of literacy in Scotland made emigrants ideal candidates for journalism in their new homelands. During the time of the Civil War, Scottish journalists like James Redpath wrote passionately about their anti-slavery beliefs.

PROMINENT SCOTS IN THE USA

Andrew Carnegie

The most famous Scot in America was Andrew Carnegie, born in 1835 in Dunfermline. His first employment was as a bobbin boy in a Pittsburgh textile mill; then he became a messenger in a telegraph company. His solid Scottish education helped him to make rapid progress, and he was soon the personal telegrapher to one of the officials of the Pennsylvania Railroad Company. Carnegie then invested in many profitable enterprises including locomotive construction, bridges, railways and Pullman carriages.

Through the manufacture of iron and steel in Pittsburgh, Carnegie made his fortune. He set about forming his own charities and trusts. He spent $38 million on providing libraries for the masses. The first was in Dunfermline; and over 2500 were built in Britain, the USA and Canada.

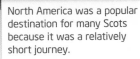

DON'T FORGET

North America was a popular destination for many Scots because it was a relatively short journey.

VIDEO LINK

You can watch a clip about Scottish emigration to North America at the Digital Zone: www.brightredbooks.net/N5History.

VIDEO LINK

You can learn more about Andrew Carnegie by watching a clip on the Digital Zone: www.brightredbooks.net/N5History.

contd

John Muir

Another Scot who played a significant role in American life, and who is much more renowned in the USA than in his home country, is John Muir, born in 1838 in Dunbar. His family emigrated in 1849 to Wisconsin.

Muir was born in 1838 in Dunbar, East Lothian, and his family emigrated in 1849 to a small township near Portage in Wisconsin. His new home was on the edge of the great American wilderness – and it was this wild, largely uninhabited frontier that Muir fell in love with for three years. He worked in a factory until an accident nearly blinded him. During this time, he went on great treks – and, for 9 years, he roamed California's Sierra Nevada Mountains taking notes and drawing nature wherever he went. Later, his expertise saw him publishing books and articles and lecturing on America's nature all over the USA.

As America grew, and cities and industrialisation started to take over the natural wilderness that he loved, Muir campaigned for these wildernesses to be saved. The result of this was the setting-up of the system of national parks in the USA. Muir's name is honoured in many geographical features of North America and in parks and reservations throughout the country.

Allan Pinkerton

Allan Pinkerton was born into poverty in Glasgow in 1819. His father died when he was a boy, and Allan left formal education at the age of 8. He was apprenticed to a cooper (barrelmaker), and qualified in 1837. Pinkerton was fully behind the Chartist movement that was protesting that more people should have the vote. Due to his protests, he had to go into hiding to prevent being arrested, and was smuggled on board a ship bound for Canada. Pinkerton eventually made his way to Chicago, where he uncovered a group of counterfeiters and exposed them.

He had found his greatest skill – solving crimes – and established himself as a sheriff in Chicago. Thereafter, he founded the Pinkerton Detective Agency and devoted his life to solving crime. He discovered an early plot to assassinate Lincoln on his way to the presidential inauguration ceremony; and, during the Civil War, he was made Chief of the Civil Service. The Pinkerton National Detective Agency still exists to this day.

Allan Pinkerton on the left, standing beside Abraham Lincoln during the Civil War

SCOTS IN CANADA

Canada was a very popular country to emigrate to. The evidence for this is clear in the place names in some areas of Canada. Settlers would often name their new homes to remind them of Scotland. Hence Canada has a Hamilton, a Banff and an Aberdeen among many other Scottish names. Also, Nova Scotia in Canada means 'New Scotland'.

A recent census in Canada showed that Canadians of Scots origin constitute the third-largest ethnic group in the country. Scots had been coming to Canada for many centuries, but from 1760 onwards this slow and steady pattern of emigration really took off. When relatives in Scotland received letters from friends and family who had emigrated, they often were encouraged to make this move themselves.

contd

VIDEO LINK

Visit the Digital Zone to watch a clip and learn more about the Scots in Canada: www.brightredbooks.net/N5History.

SCOTS IN NORTH AMERICA 2

THE CANADIAN EXPERIENCE

Source B is a letter, dated 1835, from John Scott to his uncle, Andrew Redford, in Hermiston, describing the establishment of the family farm in the area of Ontario settled by John Galt and the Canada Company.

> *He has 4 oxen 3 cows and 5 young cattle and 40 swine. He has about 70 acres clear'd now. A good house and a barn.*

Life was hard for the new farmers. They had to clear the land and build their own farms – but the important factor was that they actually owned the land and could not be evicted by landlords with little warning, as had happened during the Highland Clearances in Scotland.

When they first arrived in Canada, however, sometimes the attraction of their new home was not always evident. **Source C** is a letter of 1820 from Samuel Rogerson in St John's, Newfoundland, to his brother in Dumfriesshire:

> *This is a wild country, and from what I have seen I do not like it well ... the island is not known in the interior but it is supposed that there is nothing but Indian savages ...*
> (National Records of Scotland, Miscellaneous Gifts and Deposits: GD1/620/66)

A group of Scots leaving for Canada in the 1920s

The Scots arriving in Canada were on the whole very welcome. Scotland had been at the forefront of the Industrial Revolution and was a country with railways, factories, coalmines and foundries. Therefore they often had the skills that these new countries were crying out for.

In **Source D,** T. M. Devine describes some of the successes of the Scots.

> *In the 1880s, Scots or the sons of Scots migrants were dominant in Canadian textiles, paper, sugar, oil, iron and steel, furniture making, the fur trade and bakery products. The level of success achieved was out of all proportion to their numbers in the Canadian population.*

VIDEO LINK

Visit the Digital Zone to watch a clip about Canada's Scottish heritage: www.brightredbooks.net/N5History.

SCOTTISH SUCCESS IN CANADA

The Scots were also well thought of because of their superior standards of education. This allowed them to feature heavily in Canada's political and economic life. They also played a leading role in Canadian education and government, at times dominating the scene. Scots also invested in Canada. By 1884, 75% of colonial investment companies had Scottish origins. Scots helped to finance Canadian agriculture, fishing, mining, timber and, particularly, land purchase and development. The timber industry was very important, as it gave jobs to Scottish emigrants and supplied materials for the Scottish shipbuilding industry.

The Canadian fur trade was also dominated by Scots, and this trade played a large role in Canada's economy. Emigration has been seen as a Highland issue, as most people associate it with the Highland Clearances – but Lowland emigration was also a steady contributor to the outward flow of people from Scotland. Canada was a perfect location for Lowlanders who wished to work in agriculture, with its plentiful supply of land and a Scottish workforce who had already experienced agricultural improvements. Scots also dominated the industries in Canada, as once again the lowland Scots had experience in working in factories and manufacturing.

DON'T FORGET

Two of Canada's biggest firms involved in the fur trade had strong connections with Scotland and in particular Orkney – the North West Company and the Hudson's Bay Company.

PROMINENT SCOTS IN CANADA

Sir John Macdonald

Macdonald's family left Glasgow in 1820 and emigrated to Kingston, Ontario. He went on to become the first Prime Minister of Canada and was instrumental in the building of the Trans-Canadian railroad.

Alexander Mackenzie

Alexander Mackenzie, the second Prime Minister of Canada, was born in 1822 in Perthshire, the third of ten sons. Forced to leave school to support his family after his father died, Mackenzie was working full-time as a stonecutter and mason by the age of 13, but continued his education by reading after work. Like many Britons and Scots, he emigrated in 1842, leaving behind a depression in Great Britain to search for prosperity in Canada.

Robert Mackay

An 1855 emigrant to Montreal from his birthplace in Caithness, Robert Mackay got his start working at the Henry Morgan & Company department store. He then went to work for Mackay Brothers wholesalers, owned by his uncles. Highly successful in business, he became a close business associate of powerful Montreal entrepreneurs.

Scots also had an impact on the cultural life of Canada. From 1871 onwards, there was a Gaelic society in Toronto and also one in Vancouver. St Andrew's societies were set up in many Canadian towns.

Source E is from Gordon Donaldson, *The Scots Overseas*.

> *As an example of a 'Scottish Club' with varied activities, the Edmonton Scottish Club will serve: it organises a Scottish day in August, country dancing classes, a choir, a curling bonspiel, a Burns Supper, a St Andrew's Day Banquet and a Hogmanay Ball … There are over twenty curling clubs in Canada …, golf, introduced by the Scots, has become a popular game especially in British Columbia … that province has 66 golf courses and, it is estimated, 32,000 golfers.*

ONLINE

You can learn more about the North West Company and Hudson's Bay Company at the Digital Zone: www.brightredbooks.net/N5History.

THINGS TO DO AND THINK ABOUT

Use an atlas to identify Scottish and other British place names in North America.

Scottish place names	British place names

ONLINE TEST

Test your knowledge of this topic at the Digital Zone: www.brightredbooks.net/N5History.

SCOTS IN AUSTRALIA

TRANSPORTATION

VIDEO LINK

To watch a clip about transportation to Australia, go to the Digital Zone and click the link: www.brightredbooks.net/N5History.

Before 1830, the majority of new settlers to Australia were convicts – criminals of varying degrees of seriousness whose punishment was to be sent to Australia because of the terrible conditions in British prisons at the end of the 18th century. Up until 1868, around 160 000 convicts were transported to Australia, and about 5% of them were Scottish. Most of the convicts were young single men who had been convicted of common crimes like theft, burglary and forgery. Some were political activists, but most were common criminals.

a convict chain gang in Sydney, New South Wales

The fact that Australia was primarily a penal colony put many free men and their families off emigrating there – and, in the early years of the colony, Australia had far more convicts than free settlers. By the 1830s, the tide was changing. Many were questioning the use of transportation as a punishment; and in Australia free settlers did not like the fact that convict labour had a negative impact on the wages of free workers. Scots were also put off by the long, arduous and expensive journey. For many Scots, Canada seemed a much safer option as a future home.

In **Source A**, written on 4 February 1836, George Mackenzie describes the type of men he is looking for to work in New South Wales.

'young and either married or unmarried men at less wages than I give to older and more experienced men with families ... I can find employment for as many shepherds and farm labourers as can be procured at better wages than they can possibly procure at home and with infinitely better prospects ...'

EMIGRATION SOCIETIES AND GOVERNMENT SCHEMES

Scots were also encouraged and helped to emigrate to Australia by the setting up of organisations like the Highlands and Islands Emigration Society that helped emigrants to find jobs and escape the famines and Highland Clearances. The Scottish Australian Emigration Society was set up in Glasgow to help handloom weavers who had lost their jobs to factories and increasing mechanisation. By 1886, around 50 emigration societies were helping prospective emigrants and their families in England and Scotland.

By 1851, the movement to Australia become a flood due to the discovery of gold in New South Wales and Victoria. Gold led to Scots choosing Australia over Canada. This movement continued into the 20th century as more goldfields were discovered in Queensland and Western Australia. Gold prospectors *could* find a fortune – but often the reality was much harsher.

In **Source B**, a letter to his sister written on 8 April 1892, J. A. Dick describes waiting for a successful gold strike.

'so far my share of the profits have been nil but that may not always be the case and any day we may come across a patch of gold which would repay us our labour ... station in life now ... is as a rule a poor affair ...'

The wool industry became vital to the Australian economy, and Scots were instrumental in this area. John Macarthur introduced Merino sheep into Australia and saw that the country could provide the perfect climate and landscape for a wool industry. Wool exports were important in the early stages of the Australian economy. In 1886, the New Zealand and Australian Land Company was formed by the amalgamation of 14 Glasgow-based firms and was highly involved in the export of wool.

contd

Through farming and the wool trade, Scots inevitably came into contact with the Aboriginal communities in Australia. Early relations with Aborigines were fairly friendly; the Aborigines were given clothes and encouraged to follow the ways of the new Australians. However, Scots, along with other emigrant groups, disturbed the Aboriginal lands, and this inevitably led to tension.

In **Source C**, a letter written in 1839 to his mother from Canning River, D. S. Murray gave family news and commented on the climate and the Aborigines.

> *Our natives have been much more quiet lately and I think every year they will become more accustomed to our ways if not civilised: they now begin to find out that powder is more deadly than their spears. Many of them understand a little English and most of the settlers after being two or three years in the Colony, pick up a letter of their language so that we can manage to understand one another.*

One of the most shocking incidents in the Scots' relationships with the Aborigines happened at Warrigal Creek in 1842. A Scot, Ronald Macalister, had been murdered by Aborigines, and tension over land ownership had been simmering for quite some time. The Scots in the area, led by Angus McMillan, decided to take violent action.

In **Source D**, the historian Michael Fry describes events at Warrigal Creek.

> *McMillan called out every Scotsman who had a gun and a horse, and they rode off to extract retribution ... They found them, more than 100 men, women and children, camped by a waterhole on the Warrigal Creek. The Scots galloped up, surrounded them, then without warning began to shoot them down. The terrified people ran defencelessly hither and thither, some jumping into the water to try and hide under it. The Scots made great sport of picking them off as they had to come up for air. The creek ran red with their blood.*

PROMINENT SCOTS IN AUSTRALIA

Lachlan Macquarie

Lachlan Macquarie was Governor of New South Wales from 1810 to 1824. He was born in 1762 on Ulva in the Inner Hebrides. Although he was replaced before 1830, he is regarded as the 'Father of Australia'.

Macquarie became Governor at a time when New South Wales was still being used as a penal colony. He followed a policy of encouraging former convicts to settle in Australia – despite opposition from the 'free settlers' who wanted to retain privileges only for themselves. Australia would be a different place if he had not succeeded. He transformed it into a thriving country and Sydney from a shanty town to a Georgian city.

Andrew Fisher

Andrew Fisher's politics were formed at the coalface. At the age of 10 in Ayrshire, he became one of many boys working in Scottish mines. He was still a coalminer 13 years later when he emigrated to Queensland.

Fisher was a founding member of both the Labour Party in Queensland and of the federal parliamentary Labour Party. He held the House of Representatives seat of Wide Bay from 1901 until 1915. When Fisher was Prime Minister, a number of important projects were undertaken. The Royal Australian Navy was established, the Commonwealth Bank was set up, the Northern Territory of South Australia was transferred to the Commonwealth, the federal capital of Canberra was founded, and the construction of the trans-Australian railway line linking Perth to the other capitals was begun. As well as introducing maternity allowances, Fisher acknowledged the need for greater political equality for women.

THINGS TO DO AND THINK ABOUT

1. Explain why Scots were settling in Australia after 1830.
2. Describe the role Scots played in the political and economic development of Australia.

VIDEO LINK

Visit the Digital Zone to watch a clip about Scottish emmigration to Australia: www.brightredbooks.net/N5History.

DON'T FORGET

The arrival of Scots immigrants was marked by the setting up of Presbyterian churches.

DON'T FORGET

Scots immigrants were heavily involved in the development of education in Australia. Melbourne Academy (now known as The Scotch College) was founded by the Presbyterian Church. Scots also played an important role in setting up the University of Sydney.

ONLINE

You can read more about successful Scots in Australia by clicking the links at the Digital Zone: www.brightredbooks.net/N5History.

ONLINE TEST

You can test yourself on this topic at the Digital Zone: www.brightredbooks.net/N5History.

SCOTS IN NEW ZEALAND

A poster advertising passage to New Zealand

VIDEO LINK

Go to the Digital Zone to watch a clip about Scottish settlers in New Zealand: wwwbrightredbooks.net/N5History.

ONLINE

You can read a lot more about Scottish experiences in New Zealand by clicking the link at the Digital Zone: www.brightredbooks.net/N5History.

ONLINE

Go to the Digital Zone to find out which parts of Scotland the settlers to New Zealand came from: www.brightredbooks.net/N5History.

A PREFFERED OPTION

As well as in Australia, Scots made an important contribution to the development of New Zealand. Many Scots who made the decision to take the long journey to the Southern Hemisphere often chose New Zealand over Australia. Settlers were put off by the association of Australia with convicts. Also, the climate and farming land in New Zealand seemed to be more suited to Scots – and New Zealand had a thriving Presbyterian (Scottish church) settlement. This settlement came from an early missionary movement in New Zealand.

THE FIRST BRITISH SETTLERS AND THE ROLE OF THE CHURCH

The first settlers in New Zealand were involved in the Church and in trading and whaling; but it was a small settlement. Numbers increased after the 1830s. In 1840, the Treaty of Waitangi was signed with the Maori population, and New Zealand became part of the British Empire. Scots moved to all parts of New Zealand, but the Otago area in the south of the South Island became the main destination for most Scots.

The Otago region of New Zealand

In 1844, the Scottish Church purchased 144 000 acres of land in the Otago area, which was then sold to emigrants at £2 per acre. Dunedin became the centre of Scottish influence. Clergymen, like the Reverend Thomas Burns, travelled around Scotland and influenced Scots to make the decision to start a new life in New Zealand. Between 1848 and 1860, around 80% of emigrants to Otago were Scots.

Source A is from the *Otago News,* December 1848.

> the eye is gladdened with a goodly sprinkling of houses, some of wood, others of mud and grass; whilst numerous gardens, well fenced and cleared, and one street at least, showing a broad track from end to end of the future town, gives evidence of the progress we have made. We have two hotels, a church, a school, a wharf, small though it be. We have butchers, bakers and stores of all descriptions ... and every outward sign of commercial activity and enterprise.

The Church in Scotland was very important in promoting the Presbyterian and distinctly Scottish area of Otago. However, there were also many agents travelling throughout Scotland promoting Otago to Scots. Adverts appeared in Scottish newspapers; pamphlets were circulated; and the Otago Association organised lecture tours and published the *Otago Journal.* It contained details for would-be emigrants, letters from Scots already in New Zealand, and information about gaining financial help to get them to New Zealand. This publicity – combined with lots of good farming land, churches and schools – made New Zealand very attractive.

An advertisement aimed at domestic servants

OTHER AREAS TO EXPLORE

Another area of New Zealand that had a huge Scottish influence was Waipu in the north of the North Island. By 1860, Waipu had a 1000-strong Highland Scots community. Scots played a large role in the expansion of farming. By 1850, New Zealand had 1.5 million sheep, but by 1909 this had grown to 23 million, and Scots were heavily involved in this sector and in the new frozen-meat industry that was booming by 1900. Thomas Bruce, who was born in Jedburgh, came to New Zealand in 1859 and soon had 17 000 sheep on his land.

In **Source B**, the historian Gordon Donaldson describes some of the Scottish successes in New Zealand:

> *Thomas Brydon (1837–1904), a native of West Linton, was a pioneer in both the frozen meat and the dairy industry: Brydon was a partner with another Scot, Davidson, in the New Zealand and Australian Land Company, and loaded the first cargo of frozen meat sent from new Zealand to Britain in 1882, shipped from Port Chalmers to London on a ship called the Dunedin.*

Gold also had an obvious attraction to Scots. Discovery of gold in the Otago region in 1861 caused emigration to the region to rise sharply; and many Scots were involved in this rush for riches, as had happened before in California and Australia.

DUNEDIN

The town of Dunedin in New Zealand epitomises the strong Scottish connection. The town was set up to reflect Edinburgh in its architecture, and it gained the nickname of 'Edinburgh of the South'. It was founded by the Free Church of Scotland, and its street names like George Street, Princes Street and the Canongate show its Scottish connection. James McAndrew (1820–1887), born in Aberdeen, became an influential member of the Dunedin community. As well developing shipping, he did much to encourage the founding of the university at Dunedin and also helped to set up training colleges and schools. Today, Dunedin has its own tartan, whisky and distinct haggis ceremony.

The crest of the University of Otago in Dunedin, showing its Scottish connection in the saltire

DON'T FORGET

The arrival of large numbers of immigrants in New Zealand led to conflict with the native Maori. A series of wars took place over land between 1845 and 1872. Scots played a role in the fighting. In the 1860s, the commander of the British troops was Lieutenant-General Duncan Cameron.

DON'T FORGET

Some Scots immigrants became involved in politics. Sir Robert Stout, from the Shetland Islands, was Prime Minister of New Zealand between 1884 and 1887.

DON'T FORGET

Religion was a key part of Scottish life in the 19th century. One sign of Scottish settlement was the growth of Presbyterian churches in New Zealand.

ONLINE

Go to the Digital Zone to learn more about Scots settlers in early Dunedin and Otago: www.brightredbooks.net/N5History.

ONLINE TEST

You can take a test on this topic at the Digital Zone: www.brightredbooks.net/N5History.

THINGS TO DO AND THINK ABOUT

1. Complete the following table to show the impact of Scots settlers on Australia and New Zealand.

	Australia	New Zealand
Agriculture		
Religion		
Government		
Native Population		

2. Design a poster to attract Scots to either Australia or New Zealand.

SCOTS IN INDIA

ONLINE

Go to the Digital Zone to read more about the connections between Edinburgh and India: www.brightredbooks.net/N5History.

DON'T FORGET

India was known as the 'Jewel in the Crown' of the British Empire. It was a huge market for Scottish and other British companies. Some of them were involved in making brightly coloured cloth using the 'Turkey Red' process. Scots businessmen went to India to make sure their designs were popular. Much of the cloth was used to make saris and was decorated with birds such as peacocks.

EMBRACING THE EMPIRE

India often proved to be a popular destination for ambitious Scots who wanted to start a new and prosperous life. The famous Scottish author Sir Walter Scott referred to India as being:

'the corn chest for Scotland, where we poor gentry must send our youngest sons, as we send our black cattle to the south'.

Scott had seen generations of Scots emigrating to India to work in business, education and in the military. Scots embraced the many business opportunities that the vast Indian subcontinent had to offer. By the end of the 19th century, they dominated the tea industry and were also involved in timber, jute, coal and cotton.

In **Source A,** the historian Tom Steel describes the involvement of Scots in the jute industry.

The Scots in India were also great traders. By 1813 there were 38 trading companies in Calcutta, 14 of which were run by Scots. Scots were also responsible for the first jute mill at Baranagar, and by 1885 Dundee had supplied 24 factories in Calcutta alone with power-driven looms to make sacking. Together the factories employed more than 50 000, managed totally by Scots. During the First World War, the mills of Calcutta were to manufacture eight million sand bags a month for the British War Office. Such was the wealth made that when the Armistice came, the Scots of Calcutta called the day Black Friday.

Many of the Scots who went to India to further their business interests did not return to their homeland. This is evident by the opening of a Scottish cemetery in Calcutta in 1820. More than 1500 Scots are buried here.

The Scottish cemetery in Calcutta

THE ROLE OF SCOTS IN INDIA

Scots also played a key role in India's religious and education systems. Alexander Duff, born in Perthshire, was the first Church of Scotland missionary to India. He played a leading role in founding the University of Calcutta in 1857. He also helped to establish several girls' schools and the first medical college in India.

Scots were also influential within the military field. The most famous was Colin Campbell, the son of a Glasgow carpenter, who had joined the army at the age of 15. When news of the Indian Mutiny reached England in July 1857, the Prime Minister, Lord Palmerston, offered the then Lieutenant-General Campbell the position of Commander-in-Chief of India. He accepted, and left the following day. Quickly, he organised his troops and cleared Lower Bengal of mutineers. He then advanced with 4500 men to relieve the besieged garrison at Lucknow. His main achievement during the Indian Mutiny was the way he organised the various campaigns that systematically cleared the rebels from each region. For these services, he was given the title Lord Clyde in 1858.

ONLINE

Click the link at the Digital Zone to learn more about how Scots played a role in India: www.brightredbooks.net/N5History.

PROMINENT SCOTS IN INDIA

James Taylor

James Taylor arrived in Ceylon (now Sri Lanka) from Kincardineshire in 1852 at the age of 16. His job was to work as an assistant supervisor on a coffee plantation. Taylor began experimenting with growing tea and improving its production. He did away with a lengthy manual process by inventing the first tea-rolling machine, and pioneered the use of a new tea – Assam. In 1893, a year after his death, an amazing 1 million packets of Ceylon tea were sold at the Chicago World Fair.

Sir William Mackinnon

Mackinnon was born in Campbeltown and started work in the grocery business. He travelled to India in 1847 and joined a school friend in the coasting business, which involved carrying goods from port to port around the bay of Bengal. In 1856, he founded the Calcutta and Burma Steam Navigation Company. Within five years, it had grown hugely to become the British Indian Steam Navigation Company, trading throughout the Indian subcontinent. Mackinnon believed in eliminating the slave trade and treating nations equally.

The logo of the British Indian Steam Navigation Company

Lord Dalhousie

James Ramsay, the first Marquess of Dalhousie, was Governor General of India from 1847 to 1856. In this time, he annexed eight Indian states and created what came to be British India. He also did much to modernise the infrastructure of India. This included extending India's road system; and he was personally involved in the construction of canals and railways. Railways subsequently became vitally important in India. Many of the engines were built in Scotland and shipped to India. Dalhousie also improved communication by introducing the telegraph.

A Glasgow-built locomotive getting ready to be shipped abroad

Mountstuart Elphinstone

Elphinstone was a Scottish historian and statesman who became the governor of Bombay. During his governorship, he greatly promoted education for Indians at a time when this was unfashionable. Many regard him as the founder of the Indian system of state education. Elphinstone College in Bombay was founded in his honour.

Elphinstone College in Bombay

THINGS TO DO AND THINK ABOUT

Use the information from the previous sections about the Scots overseas to complete the following table.

Country	Business links	Military links	Political links	Cultural links
Australia				
New zealand				
Canada				
India				
USA				

 VIDEO LINK

You can read more and watch a clip about Scots who played an important role in India at the Digital Zone: www.brightredbooks.net/N5History.

DON'T FORGET

Sir Thomas Lipton, from Glasgow, was responsible for making cheap tea available. He travelled to Ceylon (present-day Sri Lanka) and bought plantations to reduce his costs.

 ONLINE TEST

You can take a test on this topic at the Digital Zone: www.brightredbooks.net/N5History.

THE IMPACT OF EMPIRE ON SCOTLAND 1

TRADE AND INDUSTRY

Just as Scots played important roles in their new adopted homelands, the places they went to live also had an impact on the country they left behind. As more Scots settled abroad between 1830 and 1939, so trade increased with Scotland – and this trade had a substantial impact on Scottish industry and manufacturing.

In **Source A,** the historian Tom Devine outlines some of the effects of the Empire on Scotland.

GNR1744 plate

This new industrial and urban society depended on a number of important foundations. Most crucially of all, the economy relied overwhelmingly upon access to overseas markets. Some 38 per cent of all Scottish coal production went abroad ... The giant North British Locomotive Company sent nearly half its engines to the British Empire in the years before the First World War, with India as the primary destination. The rise of jute was generated from the 1840s by the demand for international commodities as varied as East India coffee ... as well as the enormous requirements for sandbags during the Crimean War, the American Civil War and the Franco–Prussian War ... two thirds of Scottish pig iron was exported ... the ships that poured out from the yards of Clydeside relied on orders on the condition of international trade ... It was the same story elsewhere, from quality Border knitwear to malt and blended whiskies. As far as Scotland was concerned, the international market was the king.

Many settlers who left Scotland already had business contacts in Scotland. So, when they reached their new destinations, it made sense to use old connections to further their new business interests. Also, investors in Scotland used Scottish connections in the colonies to invest in new areas where great profits were to be made.

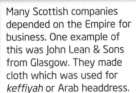

DON'T FORGET

Many Scottish companies depended on the Empire for business. One example of this was John Lean & Sons from Glasgow. They made cloth which was used for *keffiyah* or Arab headdress.

Source B is from *The Scottish Empire* by Michael Fry.

One way of feeding foreign demand was financial, out of a exportable surplus of capital that Scotland soon enjoyed ... Blackwood's Edinburgh Magazine ran an article on foreign investment from Scotland which noted three quarters of the companies formed for foreign investment overseas were said to be of Scottish origin: 'if not actually located in Scotland, they have been hatched by Scotchmen and work on Scottish models'. The article set out not just to boast. It also doubted if the outflow would be good for the country in the long run.

SHIPPING

One area where emigration had a profound effect was in shipping. Trade and transport for passengers to and from the Empire made the manufacture of ships vitally important. Before the Great War, the Glasgow shipyards built one third of all new British ships. These ships carried the wheat from Canada and the USA, the tea from India, the locomotives to India (the Indian railway system was and is one of the world's biggest) and the jute sacking from Dundee to all areas of the world.

Scotland also dominated the great passenger shipping lines. The Anchor Line and the Glen Line both provided ships for the growing number of emigrants.

Poster advertising the Glasgow-based Anchor Line

TEXTILES

Textiles were also an area of Scottish industry that benefited from overseas connections. During the 19th century, almost 18% of the labour force were textile workers. The firm of J. P. Coats of Paisley took production from Paisley to many parts of the world. By 1913, Coats was manufacturing thread in North America, Brazil, Mexico, Japan and across Europe. Their most famous product was the Paisley-pattern shawl. Its distinctive design originated in the Far East, but it was the Scottish firm Coats that sold it around the world.

A typical Paisley pattern

DON'T FORGET

One way in which the Empire affected Scotland was language. A number of words came into use due to large numbers of military and business links with India – shampoo, pyjamas, thug, bungalow and dungarees are just a few.

CASE STUDY – FINLAYS

Many Scottish communities relied heavily on trade with the Empire to provide them with their livelihoods. Catrine, a small village in the heart of Ayrshire, is a good example of a Scottish connection with the Empire. The company Finlays originated in Glasgow and were traders and manufacturers of cotton. By the start of the 19th century, Finlays had invested in a cotton mill in Catrine as well as in Ballindalloch (Balfron, Stirlingshire) and Deanston (Perthshire). Finlays' aim was to control the whole process of cotton manufacturing from the purchase of raw cotton in America to its finishing and marketing. Finlays opened branches in Charleston, New Orleans and New York, then branched out to the Far East. It was while trading with India that Finlays decided to move into the tea industry. By 1903, Finlays had some 90 000 employees in Britain and in the Far East. Finlays also invested in shipping lines.

The mill that dominated the village of Catrine

Most of the village of Catrine was reliant on the Finlay Company, with the majority of the inhabitants working in the mill or the bleachworks. Profit from the tea estates enabled continued investment in the mills of Catrine. Houses and a church were built for the mill workers; and Catrine had gas street lighting two years before London.

Today, Finlays is still one of the biggest independent tea traders in the world – but the mills and bleachworks of Catrine have long been shut down.

THINGS TO DO AND THINK ABOUT

1. Look at Source A. What evidence is there that trade with the Empire was important to the each of the following Scottish industries?
   - Coal
   - Locomotives
   - Jute
   - Pig iron

2. a) Why do you think many Scottish businessmen wanted to invest their money in companies which were set up in the Empire and North America?

   b) What do you think the author of Source B meant when he wrote that he 'doubted if the outflow would be good for the country in the long run'?

ONLINE

You can read a lot more about the history of Finlays by clicking the link at the Digital Zone: www.brightredbooks.net/N5History.

ONLINE TEST

You can take a test on this topic at the Digital Zone: www.brightredbooks.net/N5History.

THE IMPACT OF EMPIRE ON SCOTLAND 2

THE SPREAD OF WEALTH

Finlays is only one example of the Scottish businesses or individuals who amassed huge fortunes from their trade abroad. However, these vast sums of money did not always filter down to the ordinary workers like the mill workers of Catrine. Wages and working conditions were very hard – as was life in general.

Source A, historian Tom Steel describes conditions in the factories.

Whole families were employed in factories, and when gas lighting was introduced in the early part of the nineteenth century, workers were able to put in longer hours.
The abuse of children was the greatest evil of the age. By 1830, children of six or seven were put to work in cotton mills for less than two shillings a week. In Dundee, children got up at four o'clock in the morning in order to walk to the factory and be at the machines by five to five. They were expected to work all day until half past seven at night. Often they had to be beaten with straps to keep them at their machines. One Dundee mill owner employed Edinburgh orphans whom he housed in a building locked and barred at night to stop them running away.

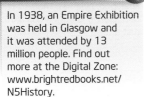

ONLINE

In 1938, an Empire Exhibition was held in Glasgow and it was attended by 13 million people. Find out more at the Digital Zone: www.brightredbooks.net/N5History.

CULTURE

Another way in which Scotland was affected by the Empire was through popular culture. Victorious battles were celebrated in Scottish music halls and later in films. Art too was used to depict the Empire.

This painting shows Lieutenant Francis Farquharson of the Black Watch winning the Victoria Cross during the Indian Mutiny.

ONLINE

There are many examples around Scotland of memorials to soldiers who saw service in the Empire. Find out about one of the most famous, 'Fighting Mac', by clicking the links at the Digital Zone: www.brightredbooks.net/N5History.

MONUMENT-BUILDING

An example of the effects of Empire in Scotland is the number of monuments that are to be found in Scotland's cities. These record the achievements and events of the Empire.

One example of these is the Doulton Fountain in Glasgow, which was presented to the city in 1888. It shows the relationship between the Empire and the 'Second City'.

This photograph shows the King's Own Scottish Borderers War Memorial in Edinburgh. It commemorates those soldiers who died between 1878 and 1902 fighting in these conflicts of the Empire:

Doulton Fountain

Afghanistan	1878–1880
Egypt	1889
Chin Lushai	1889–1890
Chitral	1895
Tirah	1897–1898
South Africa	1900–1902

THE SCOTTISH CONTRIBUTION – AN OVERVIEW

'In British settlements, from Canada to Ceylon, from Dunedin to Bombay, for every Englishman that you meet who has worked himself up to wealth from small beginnings without external aid, you find ten Scotchmen' (Sir Charles Dilke, *Great Britain*).

Religion	• In 1796, the Scottish Missionary Society was founded and had many branches throughout Scotland. This continued throughout the 19th century. • They financed and developed missionary activity abroad. • In 1821, a Ladies' Auxiliary Society was set up in Lanark to support missionary activity. This was repeated all over Scotland. • In 1824, the Church of Scotland took control of the Scottish Missionary Society. Its first missionary to India was a Donald Mitchell. He was followed by John Wilson (1804–75) from Glasgow University and Alexander Duff (1806–78) from St Andrews. They were both influential in modernising Indian education.
Soldiering	• After 1815, regiments of Scottish soldiers were stationed in Canada, including the Highland Light Infantry (1825–32), the Royal Scots (1838–39) and the Seaforth Highlanders (1850). • Regiments such as the Gordon Highlanders served in India.
Manufacturing	• The records of fur trading in Canada show that many Scots were involved (Camerons, Campbells, MacDonalds and Stewarts). • John Guthrie Wood Aitken (1849–1921) had learned the carpet-manufacturing business in Templeton's famous factory in Glasgow, and opened his own factory in Wellington, New Zealand.
Engineering	• Two Scots in Canada, Donald Alexander Smith and his cousin George Stephen, dominated Canadian railways, including the Canadian Pacific Line (completed in 1885). • Arthur Beverly (1822–1907) was a watchmaker in Aberdeen. In New Zealand, he became a geologist, botanist, mathematician and designer of optical and meteorological apparatus. • A jute mill was built in Calcutta in 1855 using Dundee machinery and a Dundee foreman. By 1900, there were 34 jute mills in Calcutta. By 1930, they were producing 70% of the world's jute.
Mining	• Scots played their parts in the gold rushes of California, Australia and New Zealand. • Some Scots stayed on in their new countries once gold fever had subsided. The Scottish-born Brown brothers of East Maitland, New South Wales, were particularly successful in various coal-related businesses, including the export of coal from Newcastle, NSW.
Agriculture	• Scottish finance and expertise helped to develop wheat and cattle farming in the US state of Oregon. • In 1883, Scottish investors bought the Swan Land and Cattle Company in Wyoming. Within a year, the Scots owned over 3 250 000 acres – all controlled from Castle Street, Edinburgh. • A Scot, Alexander Ross, founded the Agricultural Improvement Society of Canada in 1850.

THINGS TO DO AND THINK ABOUT

1. Describe the impact of the Empire on Scotland.

2. Did all Scots benefit financially from the Empire?

3. Use the internet to find out about the conflicts mentioned on the King's Own Scottish Borderers War Memorial.

4. What do you think was Scotland's biggest contribution to the Empire?

DON'T FORGET

Some of the most famous Scots who went abroad were missionaries. Mary Slessor left Dundee to travel to Africa and helped many of the local children. David Livingstone also spent much of his life in Africa.

ONLINE

Go to the Digital Zone to find out more about Mary Slessor and about David Livingstone: www.brightredbooks.net/N5History.

DON'T FORGET

Glasgow became known as the 'Second City of the Empire' due to the strength of its industry. It shipyards, foundries and factories produced much of the materials needed to develop the Empire.

ONLINE TEST

You can take a test on this topic at the Digital Zone: www.brightredbooks.net/N5History.

THE SUCCESSION PROBLEM, 1286–1296

THE DEATH OF ALEXANDER III

On 18 March 1286, King Alexander III of Scotland left Edinburgh Castle to journey to Kinghorn in Fife. There, his young wife of less than six months, Yolande of Dreux, waited for him. Alexander had spent most of the day with his leading nobles drinking French wine. Near dusk, he decided to leave. He was warned that the journey was fraught with challenges and dangers. Kinghorn was 20 miles away and was reached on treacherous roads. It would soon be dark, there was a storm raging – and he would have to cross the Firth of Forth.

Despite the warnings, Alexander set out on his journey. At Dalmeny, the ferryman at first refused to carry him across the Forth. When Alexander accused him of being afraid, the reply was: 'I could not die better than in the company of your father's son'. The king was transported across the water and landed at Inverkeithing. There, he was met by Alexander le Saucier. He was the master of the king's sauce kitchen, and warned the king not to continue with his journey. Alexander III was offered lodgings until the morning. He refused. Instead, he continued his journey, accompanied by two locals who were to show the king and his escort the correct road. During the journey, Alexander rode further ahead of the others. Eventually, they lost sight of him. The next morning, the king was found dead beneath the coastal road near Kinghorn. His neck had been broken. It appeared that he had fallen from his horse in the dark.

Source A is a song that was written in Scotland during the early 14th century.

> When Alexander our King was dead
> That led Scotland in love and law
> There was no more abundance of ale and bread
> Nor wine, nor wax; there was no more gaming and fun
> Our gold was turned into lead
> The fruit failed on every tree
> Christ, born of a virgin
> Rescue, and give a remedy for, Scotland
> That is beset with trouble.

SCOTLAND UNDER ALEXANDER III

The death of Alexander was seen as a tragedy for Scotland. He had been regarded as a good king of Scotland. During his reign, the country had enjoyed many benefits.

- The money supply of silver coin in Scotland trebled between 1250 and 1280. In England and Wales, it only doubled. Scotland was becoming wealthy.
- Threats from the kings of Norway had declined. The death of King Haakon IV after the battle of Largs in 1263 marked the end of the Norwegian or Viking raids on Scotland. The Treaty of Perth in 1266 saw the Isle of Man and the Western Isles sold to Alexander.
- Alexander built on the work of his father, Alexander II. He continued to ensure that the different parts of Scotland were brought under the control of the Scottish king. Until the reign of his father, many areas of modern Scotland, such as Lothian, Moray and Galloway, had been effectively separate regions with their own laws and customs. Under both Alexanders, powerful families, such as the Comyns, remained loyal rather than challenge the power of the king.
- During Alexander III's reign, the pope recognised Scotland as a sovereign realm. This meant that the country was regarded as an independent kingdom under its own monarch. This established that the kings of Scotland were not subservient to English kings. However, this was a position often disputed by English kings such as Edward I.

contd

VIDEO LINK

Go to the Digital Zone to watch a clip which describes the death of Alexander III: www.brightredbooks.net/N5History.

ONLINE

To read more about the succession problem, click the link at the Digital Zone: www.brightredbooks.net/N5History.

- Relations with England had improved considerably. During the reign of Alexander III, there was a time of peace between the two. In 1251, Alexander had married Margaret, the daughter of King Henry III of England. When Henry was succeeded by his son Edward in 1272, the good relations continued.

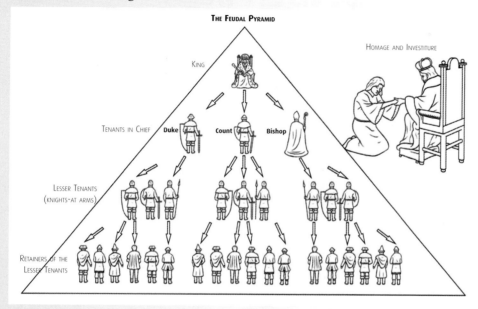

THE FEUDAL PYRAMID

KING

HOMAGE AND INVESTITURE

TENANTS IN CHIEF — Duke, Count, Bishop

LESSER TENANTS (KNIGHTS-AT ARMS)

RETAINERS OF THE LESSER TENANTS

On 29 October 1278, Alexander III paid homage (gave a formal public acknowledgement of his allegiance) to Edward I for his lands in England. He also made it clear that this did not extend to Scotland.

Alexander III:	'I become your man for the lands which I hold of you in the kingdom of England for which I hold homage saving my kingdom.'
Bishop of Norwich:	'And be it saved to the king of England if he have a right to homage for it.'
Alexander III:	'No one has a right to homage for my kingdom of Scotland save God alone, and I hold it only of God.'

THINGS TO DO AND THINK ABOUT

1. Complete an accident report on the death of Alexander III.

Ministerium Salutem et Umbra			
Name of victim		Injury sustained	
Date of accident		Location of accident	
Time of accident		Weather at time of accident	
Names of any witnesses			
Brief description of incident			
Can any blame be attached to anyone?			

2. Explain why Alexander III was considered a good king.

3. Look at Source A. What does this source tell us about the reaction of the Scottish people to the death of Alexander III?

4. What is meant by homage?

5. Why do you think the issue of homage was so important to kings such as Alexander and Edward?

THE SCOTTISH RESPONSE TO THE DEATH OF ALEXANDER III

Margaret, the Maid of Norway

A PROBLEM OF SUCCESSION

The death of King Alexander III caused a major problem for Scotland. His wife Margaret and his three children had all died before him. Debate centred on who should now succeed him.

There was one direct relative of Alexander who had a claim to the throne – his granddaughter, Margaret the Maid of Norway. She was 3 years old when her grandfather died. Being so young, she remained with her father King Eric of Norway rather than make the rough crossing over the North Sea.

However, Alexander's second wife, Yolande, was rumoured to be pregnant. This complicated matters. Should a child be born, then it would be recognised as the rightful heir to the throne. This situation continued until November 1286, when it was concluded that she would not be giving birth.

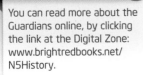

ONLINE

You can read more about the Guardians online, by clicking the link at the Digital Zone: www.brightredbooks.net/N5History.

THE GUARDIANS OF SCOTLAND

After the death of the king, a Parliament was held at Scone near Perth. It appointed six Guardians to govern Scotland in the absence of a monarch. They were:

Two earls:
   Alexander Comyn of Buchan (a supporter of the Balliol family)
   Duncan of Fife (a supporter of the Bruce family)

Two bishops:
   William Fraser of St Andrews (a supporter of the Balliol family)
   Robert Wishart of Glasgow (a supporter of the Bruce family)

Two barons:
   John Comyn of Badenoch (a supporter of the Balliol family)
   James the Stewart (a supporter of the Bruce family).

These Guardians were drawn from different areas of Scotland as well as different groups. They were faced with a difficult challenge.

There was a great deal of concern about a female being designated the heir to the Scottish throne. Some believed that she would not be able to rule a Scotland that had a number of powerful nobles. She would need others to run the country for her. Furthermore, as a girl, she would have to marry. Choosing her a husband would be difficult. He would be the next king of Scotland.

THE STRUGGLE FOR THE THRONE

Some of the most powerful families began to make their moves for the throne. The Bruce family, who held lands in Galloway as well as other parts of Scotland and England, occupied castles in Dumfries and Wigtown. This was a show of force which was meant to demonstrate their claim to the throne. They were aware of the strengths of rival families such as the Balliols. The Balliols were also powerful and possessed territory in both Scotland and England. The Balliols too wished to see their claims to the throne recognised. There was a risk of civil war breaking out.

The Guardians approached Edward I of England for advice. The result was a series of treaties involving Norway, Scotland and England.

TREATY OF SALISBURY, 1289

This treaty had the following clauses:

- The Norwegians promised to send Margaret to either Scotland or England within a year.
- Margaret would not be married without the king of England's consent.
- The Norwegians also included a clause that Edward I's advice would be sought if there was any dispute within Scotland. This was designed to ensure that the Maid of Norway would be safe and accepted within Scotland.

TREATY OF BIRGHAM, 1290

This treaty had the following clauses:

- Margaret would marry Edward's son (also named Edward).
- Scotland would remain free and separate from England.
- The Scottish Church would remain separate from that in England.
- There was to be no taxation of Scots for anything other than the needs of the Scots.

The treaty was agreed by the English king at the Treaty of Northampton.

During the summer of 1290, Edward I took control of the Isle of Man. This had been under Scottish control since the Treaty of Perth in 1266. He did not consult the Scottish Guardians. A few saw it as evidence of the English king's plans for Scotland.

VIDEO LINK

Go to the Digital Zone to watch a clip chich looks at the background of Edward I: www.brightredbooks.net/N5History.

DEATH OF THE MAID OF NORWAY

During the late summer of 1290, King Eric of Norway eventually agreed to send his daughter Margaret to the Orkney Islands to complete the complicated negotiations. On the voyage between Norway and Orkney, she took ill – with pneumonia, some have suggested. Margaret died in the Orkney Islands. Her body was returned to Norway. The risk of civil war between the rival claimants to the throne now increased.

THINGS TO DO AND THINK ABOUT

1. Why was the Maid of Norway not seen as a suitable heir by some nobles?

2. Why was there a risk of civil war in Scotland after 1286?

3. What was the significance of the Treaty of Birgham?

THE SCOTTISH APPEAL TO EDWARD I

AN INVITATION TO EDWARD I

There were 13 claimants to the Scottish throne in 1290. The danger of open warfare among them, especially between the Bruces and the Balliols, led the Scottish Parliament to ask for help from the one individual who they believed had the skill and power to prevent trouble in Scotland. An invitation was sent to Edward I, king of England, to judge the claims to the Scottish throne.

There were a number of arguments for and against asking Edward I:

FOR	AGAINST
Edward I was seen as a peacemaker. He had negotiated a settlement between rival claims to the Crown of Sicily.	Edward I had already taken over Wales and crushed several revolts.
He did not seem to have any interest in Scotland. He had visited once to see his sister Margaret.	The Treaty of Birgham suggested that Edward I wanted to increase his control over Scotland.
He had been brother-in-law to the Scottish king, Alexander III.	He had the power to enforce any decisions.
As a king, he was aware of the qualities needed to be a king.	

DON'T FORGET

Edward I was an ambitious king. He had waged war in Wales to establish his control over that country. Relations with the Scottish king, Alexander III, had been good. Edward's sister, Margaret, was the first wife of the Scottish king.

THE GREAT CAUSE

The two main claimants were Robert Bruce and John Balliol. Their claims were based on their connections to the Scottish king.

DON'T FORGET

There were three Robert Bruces alive at this time – grandfather, father and son. It was the grandfather who competed against Balliol for the throne. It was the youngest who was crowned king in 1306.

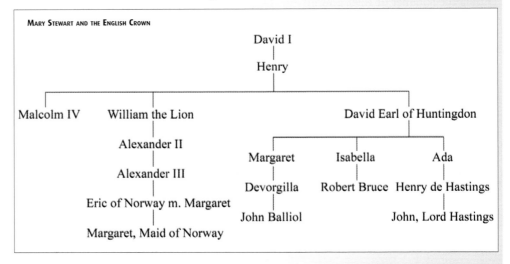

MARY STEWART AND THE ENGLISH CROWN

David I — Henry — Malcolm IV, William the Lion, David Earl of Huntingdon. William the Lion — Alexander II — Alexander III — Eric of Norway m. Margaret — Margaret, Maid of Norway. David Earl of Huntingdon — Margaret, Isabella, Ada. Margaret — Devorgilla — John Balliol. Isabella — Robert Bruce. Ada — Henry de Hastings — John, Lord Hastings.

Robert Bruce claimed that he should be king because he was the great-great-grandson of King David of Scotland.

John Balliol claimed the throne because he was descended through the eldest daughter of David, Earl of Huntingdon.

There were three Robert Bruces alive at this time – grandfather, father and son. It was the grandfather who competed against Balliol for the throne. It was the youngest who was crowned king in 1306.

ONLINE

Go to the Digital Zone to read more about the Great Cause and the events which followed: www.brightredbooks.net/N5History.

THE DECISION AT NORHAM – EDWARD'S CHOICE

Edward agreed to the request from the Scottish Parliament and arranged for the claims to be heard during the summer of 1291. He eventually decided in favour of John Balliol. However, he made each of the claimants swear an oath that he was their overlord. A number of Scottish castles were also handed over to him.

Source A is from the Chronicle of Lanercost. It gives an English version of what happened during 1291. It was written by monks who lived at the Lanercost Priory during the time of the events.

In the same year, after Easter, Edward, King of England, held a Parliament at Norham, in the nineteenth year of his reign, concerning the affairs of the realm of Scotland, where the suzerainty [overlordship] of Scotland was adjudged to him and unanimously accepted by all the magnates [powerful men] of the aforesaid realm elected for this matter and closely examined upon oath, having touched the sacred gospels.

Source B is a letter to King Edward by the monks of Croyland Abbey. It was written on 20 May 1291.

The Monks of Croyland Abbey inform King Edward that William the Lyon, King of Scotland, with all his nobles and Churchmen swore the oath of loyalty to Henry II King of England at York on 10 August 1175. Thus William the Lyon was accepted the English King as Lord Superior.

Source C is a part of a letter written by the English King on 3 June 1291.

The King of England has been saddened by the misfortunes which have descended upon the Scottish people, arising from the death of their Queen Margaret Maid of Norway. He has come from distant parts with the knowledge that as Lord Superior of Scotland he can do justice to all. In order that the business of choosing a new king of Scotland may be made easier, it is necessary that those people gathered here do King Edward the favour of accepting him as Lord Superior of Scotland.

Source D is the response of the main claimants to the Scottish throne to Edward's demands on 4 June 1291.

The nine Competitors agree to put all Scotland with all its castles under the care of King Edward until such time as he decides who from amongst us is to be King of Scotland.

VIDEO LINK

You can read more and watch a clip describing these events at the Digital Zone: www.brightredbooks.net/N5History.

THINGS TO DO AND THINK ABOUT

1. Evaluate the usefulness of Source A to historians studying the Great Cause.

2. Take each of the arguments about selecting Edward to judge the claims to the Scottish throne. Put them under the correct heading.

Arguments for choosing Edward as judge	Arguments against choosing Edward as judge

3. Look at Sources B and C. What arguments did Edward use to explain why he should be accepted as the Lord Superior of the Scottish Kings?

4. Look at Source D. Why might the nine claimants have agreed to Edward's demands?

ONLINE TEST

You can test your knowledge on this topic at the Digital Zone: www.brightredbooks.net/N5History.

EDWARD AS OVERLORD OF SCOTLAND

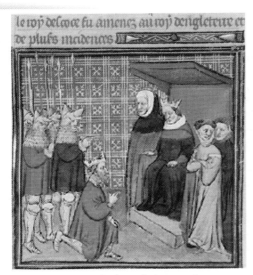

A medieval view of John Balliol paying homage to Edward I

KING JOHN

John Balliol was crowned king on Saint Andrew's Day, 1291. Very quickly, Edward began to make demands of the Scottish king.

A timeline of the demands

26 December 1292 – Edward summons John Balliol to Newcastle to pay homage. The Treaty of Birgham is cancelled by Edward.

February 1293 – Macduff of Fife had been accused of misusing his position to take over land which belonged to King John. He case was tried in front of the Scottish Parliament. When he lost, Macduff appealed to Edward I. John was summoned to Westminster in October 1293. He refused to cooperate with the English court. He was then found in contempt of court and ordered to hand over three Scottish castles. John agreed to deal with the charges at the next Scottish Parliament.

8 March 1293 – John was summoned to Westminster to answer complaints by a Gascon wine merchant called John Mazun. He was complaining about an unpaid wine bill. The wine had been ordered by Alexander III.

June 1294 – John, along with 10 earls of Scotland and 16 barons, was summoned by Edward to England to take part in war between the French and English.

This last demand was too much for the Scots nobility. They refused to attend. Instead, they formed a council of 12 nobles to make the decisions of government. Power was removed from Balliol. They decided that the independence of the country was at risk.

THE FRANCO–SCOTTISH TREATY

The Scots formed an alliance with the French in February 1296. They agreed to wage war against the English. If the English attacked the French, then the Scots were to invade England. The French were to do the same if Scotland was attacked.

A summons went out for the Scottish army to assemble near Selkirk in March 1296. The English army was ordered to assemble near Newcastle at the same time. Edward I also ordered that land held by Scottish nobles in England should be seized and that Scots living in England be arrested.

While the Scottish army moved south and laid siege to Carlisle, the English army moved to Berwick. This was one of the wealthiest and most important burghs in Scotland. Much of Scotland's trade with Europe passed through the town.

The town itself relied on a ditch and a wooden palisade for protection. Edward I asked for the town's surrender. This was refused. A dragon flag was flown. This was the sign that there would be no prisoners taken.

Source A is from the Chronicle of Lanercost. This was an English account of the events.

> *The King ... tried to persuade the head men of Berwick to surrender, promising them safety in their persons, security for their possessions, reform of their laws and liberties and pardon for their offences. But they became insulting....*
>
> *The stubbornness of these misguided people being shown, the troops were brought into action, the pride of these traitors was humbled almost without the use of force and the city was occupied by the enemy.*

contd

Much booty was seized, and no fewer than fifteen thousand of both sexes perished, some by the sword, others by fire, in the space of a day and a half, and the survivors, including even little children, were sent into perpetual exile.

According to some sources, the slaughter was only stopped when Edward I witnessed a woman who was in the process of giving birth being killed by his soldiers. The richest town in Scotland was now in English hands.

EDWARD TAKES CONTROL OF SCOTLAND

The English army then laid siege to nearby Dunbar Castle. The Scots sent their army to relieve the garrison of the castle. The Battle of Dunbar was a disaster for the Scots. Many important nobles were taken prisoner by the English. Large numbers of ordinary Scottish soldiers were killed fleeing from the English cavalry. Scottish resistance to Edward's invasion collapsed after this defeat.

The important Scottish castles of Roxburgh and Edinburgh surrendered. At Stirling Castle, the garrison fled and left the janitor to hand over the keys. During the summer, King John asked for terms of surrender. He was ordered to resign his kingdom and end the alliance with France. This he did in July 1296.

Balliol was taken prisoner. His coat of arms was stripped from his surcoat. After this, King John was referred to as 'Toom Tabard', meaning 'empty coat', or 'King Nobody'. He was taken as a prisoner to the Tower of London. Eventually, he was released and spent much of his time hunting on a comfortable estate in England. He died in France in 1314.

Edward also took a number of objects with him to England. These were:

- The Scottish records of state.
- The Holy Rude of Saint Margaret, which was reputed to be part of Christ's cross. It was considered to be one of Scotland's holiest relics.
- The Stone of Destiny. This was the stone that Scottish kings had been crowned upon. It was taken to Westminster.

In August 1296, Edward returned to Berwick. He declared that two of his nobles were to control Scotland. John de Warenne, 6th Earl of Surrey, was made Keeper of Scotland, and Hugh Cressingham was to be the treasurer. English sheriffs were also appointed to keep order within the country.

THINGS TO DO AND THINK ABOUT

1. Take the events of 1292–1294. Use them to complete the following table.

	Date	Reason for decision
Most important event in demonstrating King John's weakness		
Least important event in demonstrating King John's weakness		

2. Why would Edward feel threatened by the Franco–Scottish Treaty?

3. Describe the English attack on Berwick in 1296.

4. Why was John Balliol known as 'Toom Tabard' after 1296?

5. What did Edward do after his victory to demonstrate his control over Scotland?

WILLIAM WALLACE, 1296–1305

This painting supposedly shows William Wallace. It was made many years after he was dead.

WHERE DID WILLIAM WALLACE COME FROM?

One name that was not recorded on the Ragman Rolls was that of a William Wallace. Between 1297 and 1305, he was one of the main leaders of the Scottish uprising against the English. The main source of evidence about Wallace is a poem by 'Blind Harry' which was probably written around 160 years later. However, it could have been based on contemporary sources. Some historians believe that one of these sources was by a monk called John Blair, who knew Wallace.

Source A is a description of Wallace, written in the 15th century by a Scotsman called Walter Bower.

A tall man with the body of a giant, cheerful in appearance with agreeable features, broad-shouldered and big-boned ... pleasing in appearance but with a wild look, broad in the hips, with strong arms and legs, a most spirited fighting-man, with all his limbs very strong and firm.

Wallace was born probably at Elderslie near Paisley, possibly around 1270. It is known that he had two brothers, John and Malcolm. He was educated by uncles who were priests – one at Dunipace near Stirling, and the other in Dundee.

Source B is an extract from the poem by Blind Harry. Wallace was responsible for the killing of Haselrig, the English Sheriff of Lanark. This was in revenge for the killing of Wallace's wife Marion Braidefute.

And to their sleeping tyrants bend to their course
Where Hesilrig the cruel murderer lay
Eager on slaughter, Wallace wings his way

With beating heart he heard the warrior's voice
Soon he saw the distant beaming lance,
And trembling saw the injured man advance
'And though'st you traitor fierce' the hero cried
'When by your murdering steel she cruel died
When by thy fell hand her precious blood did spill'
Furious he spoke and rising on the foe
Full on his head he discharged the heavy blow
Down sinks the murderer headlong to the ground

There is little reliable evidence that Wallace was married or that Marion Braidefute even existed. However, it is a fact that Wallace did kill the Sheriff of Lanark in 1297. This murder may not have been an act of revenge. It was probably more likely to have been part of an uprising by Scots against Edward's control of Scotland.

VIDEO LINK

Go to the Digital Zone to watch a clip which examines the story of William Wallace: www.brightredbooks.net/N5History.

UPRISINGS ACROSS SCOTLAND

In the north of Scotland, Sir Andrew Moray led a rebellion against the English rule of Scotland. Moray had been taken prisoner at the Battle of Dunbar. He had escaped and returned to his home. He gathered support from the men on his estates, began attacking English troops, and laid siege to Castle Urquhart on Loch Ness.

There was also an uprising in the south-west of Scotland. It was led by Robert Wishart, Bishop of Glasgow, and by James the Stewart. They were later joined by the son of the Earl of Fife and the Earl of Carrick, Robert Bruce. However, in July 1297, they surrendered without much fighting to an English army at Irvine.

Wallace attacked small groups of English soldiers in central Scotland. He rapidly built up support among many of the ordinary people.

Source C is an extract from John of Fordun's Chronicle. John was a Scottish writer who recorded the events of the Wars of Independence around 50 years after they happened.

> From that time, therefore, there flocked to him all who were in bitterness of spirit, and weighed down beneath the burden of bondage under the agonizing power of English tyranny; and he became their leader. He was wondrously brave and bold of goodly appearance, and boundless generosity; and, though, among the earls and lords of the kingdom, he was looked upon as low-born, yet his fathers rejoiced in the honour of knighthood.

Source D is a letter by Hugh Cressingham to Edward I in July 1297.

> By far the greater parts of your counties in the Scottish kingdom are still not provided with helpers because they have been killed, besieged or imprisoned, or have abandoned their bailiwicks and dare not go back. And in some shires the Scots have appointed and established bailiffs and officials. Thus no shire is properly kept save for Berwick and Roxburghshire and they only recently.

THINGS TO DO AND THINK ABOUT

1. What problems are there for historians studying the life of William Wallace?

Look at Source C.

2. Why did many people look to Wallace for leadership?

3. What explanation is there for Wallace not being treated as an equal by the Scottish nobility?

4. Design a 'Wanted' poster for William Wallace. Include the following:

   - A description of his appearance

   - A description of his crimes

   - A reward.

ONLINE

You can read more about these early uprisings at the Digital Zone: www.brightredbooks.net/N5History.

DON'T FORGET

The lack of information about William Wallace indicates that he was not an important person before his rebellion. Some historians suggest he was an outlaw.

ONLINE TEST

To test yourself on this topic, go to the Digital Zone: www.brightredbooks.net/N5History.

THE BATTLE OF STIRLING BRIDGE

THE ENGLISH ARMY MOVES NORTH

The English sent an army north to restore their control. It was led by John de Warenne, Earl of Surrey, and by Hugh Cressingham. Wallace had been laying siege to the English garrison at Dundee when he received news of the English advance. He and Moray joined forces and marched towards Stirling. At that time, it was the lowest point at which an army could cross the River Forth by bridge or ford. This meant that it had been the location of a number of battles, as well as the strategic site of Stirling Castle.

- River Forth
- Ford
- Army of Wallace and Andrew of Moray (hidden)
  - Mainly foot soldiers
- Stirling Castle
- Stirling Bridge
- Army of the Earl of Surrey
  - Foot soldiers
  - Archers
  - Heavily-armed Knights

English Army	Scottish Army
350 Horse	180 Cavalry
10 000 Foot	6000 Foot

Wallace placed his men on the Abbey Craig. It provided him with good views of the surrounding land. The two armies were divided by the River Forth, which meandered across the land. Much of the ground was soft, boggy carse land. The bridge itself was a narrow wooden structure. It has been described as only being wide enough for two knights to cross side by side. To any soldier, it appeared obvious that crossing the bridge was fraught with danger. The English held a council of war to decide upon their strategy.

Plan by Sir Richard Lundie, a knight with the English army	Decision by Hugh Cressingham
• Send a group of knights to cross at the ford. • Wallace and Moray would be either surrounded or forced to retreat.	• Crossing at the bridge would take less time than the ford. • Keeping the army supplied in Scotland cost money. • The Scots were no more than outlaws. They would retreat as soon as the army crossed the bridge.

VICTORY AT STIRLING

The battle was a disaster for the English. Surrey overslept in the morning, and this delayed the advance of his men over the bridge. Some who had already crossed the bridge were recalled. An attempt by the English to convince the Scots to surrender was met with this reply by Wallace.

Source A is an extract from an English chronicle. It was written by a priest called Walter of Guisborough, and describes William Wallace's response to the English demands.

Tell your commander that we are not here to make peace but to do battle to defend ourselves and liberate our kingdom. Let them come on and we shall prove this in their very beards.

Moray and Wallace waited until around half of the English army had eventually crossed the river.

VIDEO LINK

Go to the Digital Zone to find out more about the Battle of Stirling Bridge and watch clips describing how the battle unfolded: www.brightredbooks.net/N5History.

DON'T FORGET

Few nobles actually fought alongside Wallace. Most of his army was made up of ordinary men.

contd

In **Source B**, the Chronicle of Lanercost describes the battle.

> *They [the Scots] allowed as many of the English to cross the bridge as they could hope to overcome, and then, having blocked the bridge, they slaughtered all who had crossed over, among whom perished the Treasurer of England, Hugh de Cressingham, of whose skin William Wallace caused a broad strip to be taken from the head to the heel, to make therewith a baldrick for his sword. The Earl of Warenne escaped with difficulty and with a small following, so hotly did the enemy pursue them.*

The English forces on the north bank of the Forth were cut off and destroyed. Few were able to escape. One English knight, Sir Marmaduke Tweng, managed to battle his way over the bridge. Most could not. The battle was a huge victory for the Scots – but it came at a cost. Andrew Moray was wounded at the battle and died two months later.

The battle had a number of results:

- Dundee and Stirling Castles surrendered to the Scots.

- Edinburgh, Roxburgh and Berwick were recaptured by the Scots, although the castles continued to hold out.

- The Scots raided the north of England.

- Many of the Scottish nobles, including the Comyns and Robert Bruce, joined the revolt after the victory.

THE DEATH OF MORAY AND WALLACE AS GUARDIAN

After Moray's death, Wallace assumed more power. He was knighted in 1298, possibly by Robert Bruce. This was important, as it meant that his status had been improved. He had found it difficult to gain the support of many of the Scottish knights, as they did not see him as their equal.

Wallace was also appointed the Guardian of Scotland. He was looking after the kingdom until John Balliol could return to Scotland. He therefore dealt with the business of government.

Source C shows the power that Wallace had as Guardian.

> *Written on the 29th day of March in the year of grace 1298*
>
> *William Wallace, the knight, guardian of the kingdom of Scotland, and leader of the army of the same, in the name of Lord John, king of the Scots, by the consent of the community of the kingdom, granted to Alexander Scrymgeour lands in the territory of Dundee, and additionally the office of constable of the castle of Dundee, without any reservation, for homage to be made to king and his heirs, or his successors, and faithful service and aid to kingdom, and he is to carry the banner of the king in the army from the time of the present agreement.*

THINGS TO DO AND THINK ABOUT

1. What advantages did the English have over the Scots at the Battle of Stirling Bridge?

2. How did Wallace use the land to his advantage?

3. What mistakes did the English commanders make?

4. Why was the victory at Stirling important to the Scots?

ONLINE

You can read more about the Battle of Stirling Bridge at the Digital Zone: www.brightredbooks.net/N5History.

ONLINE TEST

Test yourself on this topic at the Digital Zone: www.brightredbooks.net/N5History.

THE BATTLE OF FALKIRK

EDWARD RETURNS

Edward returned from France and began preparations to lead an army northwards. In June 1298, he assembled a large army at Roxburgh. However, his attempts to destroy Wallace met with little success. The Scots retreated in front of the advancing English. The population fled northwards, taking their supplies and livestock with them. Edward in turn destroyed the villages and farms as he advanced. This was a mistake. The English were soon to find the lack of food to be a serious problem. Edward had around 2000 cavalry and 12 000 foot soldiers. By the middle of July, they were starving. Supply ships that Edward had ordered to carry grain along the east coast of Scotland failed to appear.

By 21 July 1298, the English advance was turning into a disaster. Large numbers of Edward's army were from Ireland and Wales. Edward had given wine to his starving soldiers to drink. This resulted in fights between the Welsh and English which led to a number of deaths.

Edward had been preparing to end his campaign when two Scottish knights who owed their loyalty to him gave him important news.

Source A is taken from the English Chronicle of Guisborough (quoted in Andrew Fisher, *William Wallace*).

> *My lord king, the Scots army and all your enemies are no more than eighteen miles from here just outside Falkirk ... they have heard that you intend to retreat to Edinburgh and they mean to follow you and attack your camp tomorrow night or at least to fall on your rearguard and plunder your vanguard.*

Edward immediately moved his army towards Falkirk. He discovered the Scottish army waiting for him. They were positioned with woodland behind them and a small stream in front of them. They were drawn up into four **schiltrons**.

ONLINE

Read more about the Battle of Falkirk at the Digital Zone: www.brightredbooks.net/N5History.

A schiltron

SCHILTRONS

These were made up wholly of spearmen, standing shoulder to shoulder in deep ranks and facing towards the circumference of the circle with their spears slanting outwards at an oblique angle.

In **Source B,** the historian Patrick Traquair describes what a schiltron looked like.

> *As many as 2000 soldiers may have been in each schiltron. Outside each of the schiltrons, wooden stakes had been hammered into the ground and roped together. The schiltrons would provide an obstacle to the English cavalry. Between each of the schiltrons were placed archers. These were from the forest of Selkirk. Behind the schiltrons and archers stood the Scottish cavalry.*

Wallace appears to have been aware that his army was not as strong as the English. He had been trying to avoid a pitched battle. He is reputed to have told his soldiers:

> *I have brought you to the ring. Now dance the best you can.*

	Scots army	English army
Leaders	William Wallace	Edward I
Number of footsoldiers	1500 Longbowmen 8000 Spearmen	5500 Longbowmen 7000 Spearmen 400 Crossbowmen
Cavalry	300–500	2250

THE BATTLE BEGINS

The battle began when the English cavalry charged. The Scottish cavalry left the field almost at once.

The historian Andrew Fisher describes the effects of the Scottish cavalry leaving the battle. Extract taken from *William Wallace* (1986):	The historian Chris Brown gives his explanation of why the Scottish cavalry left the battlefield. Extract taken from *Wallace* (2005):
At the first contact, the Scottish horse fled. The inevitable charge of treachery followed in Scottish accounts. Whatever the motives of the cavalry, their flight was a disaster for Wallace. It was bad enough that they had not struck a blow. Worse still, their absence was to allow free reign of the English archers.	The Scottish cavalry force at Falkirk probably did not exceed 300 and was in no position to inflict a serious blow on the English cavalry; on the other hand, if the English cavalry brought them to battle, the Scots would assuredly be completely destroyed. The withdrawal of the Scottish cavalry may not have been glorious, but it was the only sensible course to pursue.

After the Scottish cavalry fled, the English knights destroyed the Scottish archers easily – but they could not penetrate the schiltrons. A number of English knights fell victim to the Scottish spears. They were withdrawn, and Edward's longbowmen opened fire.

The longbow was one of the most feared weapons of medieval warfare. An experienced archer would fire around 6 arrows a minute. Although they might not be accurate enough to hit a particular target over 180 metres, they would be deadly when launched in volleys. This is what happened at Falkirk.

THE EFFECT OF THE LONGBOWS

It did not take long for gaps to begin appearing in the schiltrons as men were struck by arrows. The final stroke was when the English cavalry charged again. This time, they were able to penetrate the schiltrons and destroy them. The Scottish army collapsed. Those who could, including Wallace, fled the field. The numbers of Scottish casualties was high, especially among the ordinary soldiers.

Source C is from the English Chronicle of William Rishanger and describes the battlefield.

They fell like blossoms in an orchard when the fruit has ripened. Their bodies covered the ground as thickly as snow in the winter.

These photographs show memorials to Scottish knights killed at the Battle of Falkirk. On the left is the grave of Sir John Graham; on the right is a memorial to Sir John Stewart, who commanded the Scottish archers.

THINGS TO DO AND THINK ABOUT

1. Describe a schiltron.

2. What evidence is there that Wallace was attempting to avoid a battle?

3. Who would you expect to win in a battle between the following groups, and why?
   - Knights attacking a schiltron.
   - Archers attacking a schiltron.
   - Knights attacking archers.

4. Do historians agree about the actions of the Scottish cavalry at Falkirk?

5. How long would it take the longbowmen to fire 66 000 arrows at the Scottish schiltrons?

6. Can you think of reasons why this amount of arrows may not have been fired?

 VIDEO LINK

Watch the clip on the Digital Zone to learn more about the Battle of Falkirk: www.brightredbooks.net/N5History.

 VIDEO LINK

Go to the Digital Zone to watch a clip of a longbow being fired: www.brightredbooks.net/N5History.

 DON'T FORGET

The archers were not English. They were Welsh! Their country had been conquered by Edward.

 DON'T FORGET

Sources on medieval battles such as Falkirk and Stirling Bridge often exaggerated the numbers of soldiers involved. You need to be aware that the writers often wanted to make a defeat or a victory look more impressive than it actually was.

ONLINE TEST

To take a test on this topic, go to the Digital Zone: www.brightredbooks.net/N5History.

AFTER THE BATTLE

WALLACE STEPS DOWN

After the Battle of Falkirk, Wallace resigned as Guardian. His movements thereafter are unclear. He left the country in 1299, possibly to gain support from abroad. This may have included France and Norway. Wallace also travelled to Rome.

After his resignation, Wallace was replaced by John Comyn and Robert Bruce as joint Guardians. This arrangement did not last long, as they disliked each intensely. At Peebles in 1299, a meeting between the two ended in violence.

Source A is part of a report by an English spy who was with the Scottish army at the time of the meeting between Bruce and Comyn.

> At the council Sir David Graham demanded the lands and goods of Sir William Wallace because he was leaving the kingdom without the leave or approval of the Guardians. And Sir Malcolm Wallace, Sir William's brother, answered that neither his lands nor his goods should be given away, for they were protected by the peace in which Wallace left the kingdom. At this the two knights gave the lie to each other
> and drew their daggers. And since Sir David was of Sir John Comyn's following and Sir Malcolm Wallace of the Earl of Carrick's [Robert Bruce's] following, it was reported to the Earl of Buchan and John Comyn that a fight had broken out without their knowing it; and John Comyn leaped at the Earl of Carrick and seized him by
> the throat, and the Earl of Buchan turned on the Bishop of St Andrews, declaring that treason and an insult to the King were being plotted.

AN ENGLISH CONQUEST?

Edward was unable to follow up his victory at Falkirk due to his continuing supply problems. He made some gains. Stirling Castle was recaptured; St Andrews and Perth were burned; Robert Bruce's castle at Lochmaben was captured; and at Carlisle, Edward distributed the lands belonging to the Scottish nobles who had rebelled to those English knights who had supported him. Edward knew he would continue to receive support from these knights if they wanted to take possession of their new estates.

However, large parts of Scotland, especially in the north, remained under the control of the Scots. Edward, subsequently, was forced to return to Scotland a number of times.

A timeline of conquest

1300 – Edward captured Caerlaverock Castle and defeated a Scottish army under John Comyn and the Earl of Buchan at the River Cree near Creetown in south-west Scotland. However, the Scots escaped and Edward was no further forward in controlling Scotland.

1301 – Edward brought an army north again. He captured Bothwell Castle and planned to spend the winter at Linlithgow. The Scots retreated in front of him and used guerrilla warfare. Edward agreed to a truce early in 1302.

1302 – The French were defeated and signed a peace treaty with Edward. There was no longer any chance of the French sending an army to help the Scots. This meant that there was no longer any chance of John Balliol being returned as king. Scotland was excluded from the Treaty of Paris in May 1303.

1303 – A Scottish army under John Comyn defeated an English force at the Battle of Roslin. Edward brought an army north again which marched as far north as Kinloss. He then returned to Dunfermline.

contd

1304 – In February, John Comyn accepted Edward's offer of peace. This left Stirling Castle and a handful of individuals opposing Edward. Stirling Castle resisted Edward and many of his siege weapons, such as the 'War Wolf', for three months. The eventual surrender marked the end of the Scottish resistance.

WILLIAM WALLACE'S CAPTURE

Source B is part of the orders issued by Edward I in 1304:

No words of peace are to be held out William Wallace in any circumstances whatsoever unless he places himself utterly and absolutely in our will. The Stewart, Sir John de Soules and Sir Ingram de Umfraville are not to have safe conducts nor come within the King's power until Sir William Wallace is given up. Sir John Comyn, Sir Alexander Lindsay, Sir David Graham, and Sir Simon Fraser shall exert themselves until twenty days after Christmas to capture Sir William Wallace and hand him over to the king, who will watch to see how each of them conducts himself so that he can do most favour to who ever shall capture Wallace.

This photograph shows the 'Wallace Well' near Robroyston outside Glasgow. Wallace supposedly drank from the well shortly before he was captured.

Wallace was eventually captured at Robroyston near Glasgow on 3 August 1305. He was taken prisoner by a Scottish knight called Sir John Menteith. Wallace was handed over to the English, who transported him south to London. He was put on trial at Westminster Hall, where he was charged with treason, murder, arson, destruction of property and sacrilege. Wallace denied the charge of treason, but he made no response to the other charges.

Source C is by an English chronicler called Mathew of Westminster. He disliked Wallace and describes the punishment that was inflicted on him by Edward I.

First of all, he was led through the streets of London, dragged at the tail of a horse, and dragged to a very high gallows, made on purpose for him, where he was hanged with a halter, then taken down half dead, after which his body was vivisected in a most cruel and torturous manner, and after he had expired, his body was divided into four quarters, and his head fixed on a stake and set on London Bridge. But his four quarters thus divided, were sent to the four quarters of Scotland. Behold the end of a merciless man whom his mercilessness brought to this end.

The quarters of Wallace's body were dispatched to Newcastle-upon-Tyne, Berwick, Stirling and Perth (although some sources mention other locations). Edward I may have believed that, with the death of Wallace, Scotland was now firmly under his control. He was mistaken. The struggle for Scottish independence would now take a new turn.

 ### THINGS TO DO AND THINK ABOUT

1. Evaluate the usefulness of Source A to historians studying the relationship between Bruce and Comyn.

Many of the sites connected with William Wallace and Robert Bruce have disappeared over time. Some of those that are left are under threat. Often, this is because of developments which take place close to the sites. Battlefields such as Falkirk, Stirling Bridge and Bannockburn have been built over with housing, factories and shops. The Wallace Well is at risk from housing developments. Think about these questions:

2. Should we preserve our heritage? If so, how?

3. Should this preservation be at the expense of creating jobs and homes for people who live nearby?

 ONLINE

Go to the Digital Zone to read more about the risk that faces some of the sites, such as the Wallace Well: www.brightredbooks.net/N5History.

 DON'T FORGET

Wallace was put to death in the same way as many other people who opposed Edward I. This horrific punishment was supposed to stop others from following Wallace.

 ONLINE TEST

To take a test on this topic, go to the Digital Zone: www.brightredbooks.net/N5History.

ROBERT BRUCE, 1306–1328

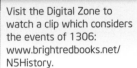

VIDEO LINK

Visit the Digital Zone to watch a clip which considers the events of 1306: www.brightredbooks.net/N5History.

ROBERT BRUCE, EARL OF CARRICK

Bruce was the grandson of one of the main claimants for the throne in 1291. His actions until 1306 have often been seen as open to debate. He changed sides and swore loyalty to Edward on a number of occasions. In 1298, he was leading a rebellion against Edward I in south-west Scotland. In 1304, he was with Edward I at the siege of Stirling Castle. However, this was not unusual. Many lords and individuals changed sides at this time. The Bishop of Glasgow, who was a firm supporter of Scottish independence, swore loyalty to Edward six times.

Self-interest was one of the key factors behind Bruce's behaviour. The Bruce family controlled lands in England and in Scotland. Furthermore, many of the Bruce lands were in Annandale in the south-west of Scotland. If there was to be an uprising, the Bruce family had a lot to lose. They would be the first to have an invading English army on their land.

One other problem for the Bruces was John Balliol. Wallace and others were fighting to get him back to Scotland. The Bruce family believed they were the rightful kings of Scotland.

In February 1306, Robert Bruce arranged to meet John Comyn (known as the Red Comyn) in Greyfriars Church in Dumfries. A church was selected, as it was seen as a safe meeting place. It was thought unlikely that either would attack or kill the other in a church. They may have wished to discuss their next steps in the struggle for independence. Edward I of England was now elderly and also suffering from illness. It was not thought that he would live much longer. Some historians believe that Bruce wanted to put forward a plan to Comyn. If the Red Comyn supported Bruce as king, then he would receive the Bruce lands. However, the meeting was to go badly. The two disagreed, and a violent struggle took place.

Source A is John of Fordun's Chronicle. This writer believed that Bruce's plans to rise up against the English had been betrayed to Edward by Comyn.

VIDEO LINK

To find out more about the death of John Comyn, go to the Digital Zone and watch the short clip: www.brightredbooks.net/N5History.

> *John Comyn is accused with his treachery. The lie is at once given. The evil-speaker is stabbed, and wounded unto death, in the church of the Friars; and the wounded man is, by the friars, laid behind the altar. On being asked by those around whether he could live, straight-way his answer is:– 'I can'. His foes, hearing this, give him another wound; – and thus was he taken away from this world on the 10th of February.*

Source B is from the Chronicle of Lanercost. This was an English account of the incident.

> *In the same year, on the fourth of February, Sir Robert Bruce, Earl of Carrick, sent treacherously for Sir John Comyn, requiring him to come and confer with him at the house of the Friars in Dumfries; and, when he came, did kill him and his uncle Sir Robert Comyn in the church of the Friars, and afterwards took [some] castles of Scotland and their wardens, and was made King of Scotland at Scone, and many of the nobles and common people of that land followed him.*

REPERCUSSIONS

The murder of Comyn was to have several results:

- The family and followers of Comyn became bitter enemies of Bruce.
- Many of the Scottish people were horrified at the murder of Comyn in a church.
- Some members of the Church turned against Bruce. He was excommunicated by the pope because of the murder. This meant that he would not able to receive the blessings or services of the Church. To a medieval Christian, this was a very serious step. They could not enter heaven if they were not cleansed of their sins. However, many, such as the Bishop of St Andrews, William Lamberton, and the Bishop of Glasgow, Robert Wishart, continued to support Bruce.
- Bruce was now an enemy of Edward. After Bruce was crowned King, Edward I sent a force to deal with him and crush the revolt.

DON'T FORGET

Religion was very important to people at the time of Bruce. As well as meeting the religious needs of the people, the Church also provided other services. It helped the sick, the old and the poor.

contd

On 25 March 1306, Bruce was crowned king at Scone. A number of nobles who were either supporters of Comyn or afraid of Edward I stayed away. The Stone of Destiny was also missing, as it had been taken to Westminster by the English. Bruce should have been crowned by the Earl of Fife. However, he was under the control of Edward. In his place, his daughter the Countess Isabella placed the crown on Bruce's head.

Source C is the English chronicler Walter of Guisborough's description of the event. The Chronicle also reveals the punishment inflicted on those who supported Bruce.

> *At the beginning of AD 1306, Robert the Bruce had himself crowned as King of Scotland at Scone, in the presence and with the agreement of four bishops, five earls and the people of the land. The Countess Isabella had been captured after this. The King of England ordered her to be placed upon the wall [the top of a tower] of the castle of Berwick, secured in a wooden cage, so that she could be seen and recognised by those passing by. And she remained many days, thus enclosed and on a strict routine.*

ONLINE

You can read more about the Countess Isabella at the Digital Zone: www.brightredbooks.net/N5History.

KING HOB

Within a short time of his coronation, Bruce was in trouble. He had been defeated at the Battle of Methven in June 1306 and his army scattered. He suffered a second defeat by the supporters of Comyn at Tyndrum. He had sent his family to Kildrummy Castle in Aberdeenshire to keep them safe. However, the castle was captured by the English after a traitor set fire to it. The Bruce women had escaped to the north before the castle fell but, they were captured by a supporter of Balliol, Earl William of Ross, and sent to the English as prisoners. After these setbacks, many of the English called Bruce 'King Hob' (King Nobody).

Many of Bruce's supporters were also taken prisoner during 1306. Edward had the majority executed, often by being hung, drawn and quartered.

After his defeats in 1306, Bruce moved around western Scotland and to the islands off the coast of Ireland. He would probably have been trying to gather support to help him destroy his enemies.

In February 1307, he travelled back to his estates in Carrick. He had sent men ahead who were supposed to light a fire as a signal that it was safe to cross to the mainland. Some time later, a fire was sighted on the mainland. Bruce crossed over – to be met by his men, who informed him that it was the English burning his lands.

Source D was written by the Scottish chronicler John of Fordun around 1360. He was describing Robert Bruce's status in 1306.

> *It came to pass that the king was cut off from his men, and underwent endless woes, and was in dangers untold, being attended at times by three followers, at times by two and more often he was left alone, utterly without help. Now passing a whole fortnight without food of any kind to live upon, but raw herbs and water now walking barefoot, when his shoes became old and worn out; now left alone in the islands; now alone, fleeing before his enemies; now slighted by his servants; he lived in utter loneliness. An outcast among the nobles, he was forsaken; and the English bade him be sought for through the churches like a lost or stolen thing. And thus he became a byword and a laughing-stock for all, both far and near, to hiss at.*

THINGS TO DO AND THINK ABOUT

1. What explanation is there for the murder of Comyn in a church?

2. Look at each of the events listed below. Use them to explain why Bruce was being referred to as 'King Hob' by the end of 1306.
   The murder of Comyn in the church; crowning himself king at Scone; defeat by an English army at Methven; defeat by the supporters of Comyn's army at Tyndrum; the capture of his wife and daughter; the execution of his brothers and supporters.

3. Evaluate the usefulness of Source D to historians studying Bruce's attempts to take control of Scotland after 1306.

DON'T FORGET

Chronicles were often written by monks and priests, as they were usually the only groups who could read and write. These were a record of events that had affected the country. However, they were often biased by the personal views of the writer.

ONLINE TEST

You can take a test on this topic at the Digital Zone: www.brightredbooks.net/N5History.

BRUCE'S FORTUNES CHANGE

VIDEO LINK

Go to the Digital Zone to watch a video considering the latter years of Edward's reign: www.brightredbooks.net/N5History.

The summer of 1307 saw Bruce's fortunes improve. In April and May 1307, he defeated English forces at Glentrool and then at Loudon Hill near Kilmarnock. On 7 July 1307, Edward I died at Burgh by Sands, near the border. His son did not have the same enthusiasm for warfare. In August, he left to return to England. This gave Bruce the opportunity to deal with his opponents in Scotland.

In **Source A,** the English Chronicle of Lanercost suggests why Bruce was becoming more successful.

> *Howbeit, notwithstanding the terrible vengeance inflicted upon the Scots who adhered to the party of the aforesaid Robert de Brus, the number of those willing to establish him in the realm increased from day to day.*

In **Source B,** the historian Geoffrey Barrow describes Bruce's strategy to defeat the English.

> *Bruce took a simple but momentous decision which changed the whole course and character of the war. He was the first of the Scottish leaders to accept the harsh logic of a situation in which the English would always have the upper hand in cavalry and siege machinery. For a great nobleman and a trained knight, it was not only a revolutionary decision; it was proof of his genius and imagination. From the spring of 1307 to the short night which fell between the first and second days of Bannockburn, all Bruce's strategy was based on belief in the supreme virtue of guerrilla warfare. Speed, surprise, mobility, small-scale engagements, scorched earth and dismantling of fortresses – these were to be the hallmarks of his campaigns.*

VIDEO LINK

You can watch a clip about Glentrool and Louden Hill at the Digital Zone: www.brightredbooks.net/N5History.

VICTORY OVER SCOTTISH OPPONENTS

Between 1307 and 1310, Bruce destroyed the Scots who opposed him and had supported Comyn and Balliol. The behaviour of his opponents often worked in his favour.

During 1307, Bruce did not have many men. One historian suggests he only had around 250–300 with him. His enemies in the north outnumbered him. Had the MacDougalls, the Earl of Buchan and the Earl of Ross combined their forces and attacked Bruce, then they could have overwhelmed him. However, the lords did not cooperate.

- In 1308, he defeated the Earl of Buchan and devastated his lands. Cattle were slaughtered, crops and homes were destroyed. Those who were loyal to Comyn were killed.

- Others, such as the Earl of Ross, were allowed to surrender and keep their lands as long as they agreed to support Bruce.

- In the late summer of 1308, Bruce defeated another of John Comyn's supporters, John of Lorn, at the Pass of Brander.

- In the south-west of Scotland, soldiers under Edward Bruce attacked their enemies. Once again, those who opposed Bruce were killed and their lands destroyed. Many fled south to England. Edward Bruce was rewarded by his elder brother with the Lordship of Galloway. However, the larger castles in the south-west remained under English control until much later.

- Within a year, Bruce had destroyed the opposition to him within Scotland.

- Bruce inspired the ordinary folk because he was seen as able to defeat his enemies. This led to an increase in support.

- In 1310, Edward II brought an army to Scotland to destroy Bruce. Bruce simply retreated and avoided a pitched battle with the English. Edward returned south.

DON'T FORGET

The destruction of the Comyn Lands in the north-east became known as the Herschip (hardship) of Buchan. This was a deliberate attempt to destroy the supporters of the Comyn family. It was very successful. It was 30 years before Comyn's successor returned to the area.

EDWARD II DOES NOTHING

Edward II did little to stop Bruce's campaigns in Scotland. The English king was experiencing serious problems with his nobles. They refused to obey his instructions because of the high taxes he was raising and his relationship with Piers Gaveston. Gaveston was a close friend of Edward and held a great deal of influence over the king. In 1310, when Edward summoned an army to invade Scotland, some of the lords failed to appear. This allowed Bruce breathing space to deal with his enemies in Scotland and to launch raids into the north of England in 1312. Areas, such as Northumberland, suffered heavily. Some of the northern towns, such as Durham, arranged a truce by paying a ransom or 'blackmail'. This money allowed Bruce to become stronger.

CAPTURING THE CASTLES

Bruce was now free to deal with the castles that held English garrisons. These were a problem for Bruce and his army. During the medieval period, castles were usually captured in one of two ways.

- **Direct attack**. This could lead to quick capture, but it could cost a lot of men. One of the major difficulties for Robert Bruce was that his army lacked siege equipment.
- **Laying siege**. This meant surrounding a castle and waiting for it to surrender. This was usually when the garrison ran out of supplies. This could take several months. It also meant that a force had to be left in place to stop food getting in.

Between 1307 and 1313, Bruce and his commanders captured many of the castles garrisoned by the English. The castles in the north of Scotland were mainly motte-and-bailey castles. These had wooden walls and small garrisons. Aberdeen could hold 55 men, while the castle at Dundee held 38. These did not pose the same difficulties as the castles in the south of Scotland, which were larger and built of stone. By 1312, most of the castles that remained in English hands were in the south of Scotland, especially around Lothian.

Stirling Castle

By the summer of 1314, the English controlled just a handful of castles. The most important one was Stirling. Bruce had surrounded the castle, hoping to starve out the garrison and left the siege to his younger brother Edward. The governor of the castle, Sir Philip Mowbray, proposed a deal. If the Scots were to lift the siege and allow food into the castle, he would write to the English king.

Source D is an extract from the *Scalacronica*, which was written by an Englishman, Sir Thomas Gray.

> *Philip de Moubray, knight, having command of the castle for the King of England, made terms to surrender the castle, unless he [de Moubray] should be relieved: that is, unless the English army came within three leagues of the said castle within eight days of Saint John's day in the summer next to come, he would surrender the said castle.*

Robert Bruce was horrified when he discovered what his brother had done. It meant that his strategy of avoiding a pitched battle with the English was going to be challenged. He knew that Edward II would be forced to send an army north, and Bruce would have to fight it. This could undo all the achievements he had made over the previous years.

THINGS TO DO AND THINK ABOUT

Give a briefing to a group of Bruce's men who are about to attack a castle. Offer them advice on how to deal with the following problems:

- What is the best time of the day to attack?
- Is it a good idea to attack on a holy day?
- What should you do to avoid the garrison being alerted to your attack?
- How should you cross the wall?
- How could you stop the gate from being shut?
- What should be done with the castle after its capture?

VIDEO LINK

Go to the Digital Zone for a look at some of the siege weapons in action: www.brightredbooks.net/N5History.

DON'T FORGET

The strongest castles were made from stone. However, these were expensive and slow to build. Many castles in Scotland had wooden walls and an earth mound. Once captured, they were destroyed to prevent their future use.

DON'T FORGET

Bruce's destruction of castles denied English garrisons the opportunity to rule from behind strong walls, but it also ensured that the two devastating invasions of the north, in 1296 and 1304, could not easily be repeated.

ONLINE TEST

To take a test on this topic, go to the Digital Zone: www.brightredbooks.net/N5History.

THE BATTLE OF BANNOCKBURN

VIDEO LINK

Go to the Digital Zone to watch the clips following the debate on the location of the battlefield at Bannockburn: www.brightredbooks.net/N5History.

BRUCE'S PREPARATION

	Scottish army	English army
Commander	Robert Bruce Highly experienced	Edward II Lacks experience of battle
Cavalry	500	2000
Footsoldiers	6000 (3000 of these may have been peasants with limited training and weapons)	18 000, including many archers

It was June 1314. Bruce spent most of the time before the English arrived training his army and preparing for the battle. One of the most important benefits of this was that the schiltrons were able to move. They could now attack rather than simply defend.

The Scottish army also dug a number of traps, called **pots**, for the English cavalry. These were shallow pits with a sharpened wooden stake at the bottom. The idea was to injure the horse and reduce the amount of cavalry available to the English.

Another device used by the Scots was a **calthrop**. This had four iron spikes, one of which always pointed upwards. They were designed to be used against horses.

DON'T FORGET

Bruce had avoided pitched battles with the English because they were stronger and better equipped.

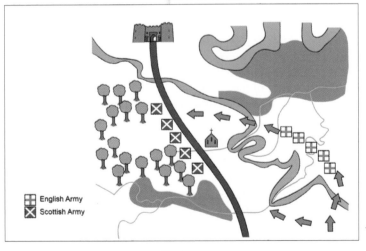

English Army
Scottish Army

The position of the two armies at Bannockburn

THE BATTLEFIELD

Bruce chose very carefully the area he was going to fight on. He knew that the English would have the advantage of heavy cavalry and more soldiers. He selected an area that was filled with streams and bogs. Behind the Scottish army was a wood which would help to protect their rearguard.

23 JUNE 1314

The English army arrived on 23 June 1314. One of the English knights, Sir Henry de Bohun, spotted Bruce inspecting his army. He saw an opportunity for glory. Bruce was easily recognisable, as he was wearing a crown and riding a small horse. De Bohun was fully armoured and carrying a lance. Bruce was able to kill his attacker with one blow.

While the Scots were celebrating this small victory, a group of English knights attempted to reach Stirling Castle. This was a threat, as they could attack the Scots on two sides. Bruce sent one of his schiltrons to move rapidly to block the threat. They managed to form in front of the English knights, who were led by Sir Robert Clifford, and to stop them. The English cavalry could not break the schiltron and resorted to throwing their weapons at it.

After this failure, the English moved to what they believed what would be safe ground, and made camp. The next day, the battle resumed.

VIDEO LINK

Watch a clip at the Digital Zone to learn more about the Battle of Bannockburn: www.brightredbooks.net/N5History.

24 JUNE 1314

On the second day, the battle went through the following stages:

- The Scottish schiltrons advanced.
- They were attacked by the English cavalry. This led to a number of casualties among the knights, who failed to stop the schiltrons.
- Edward II ordered his archers to attack. This took time, as they were at the rear of the English army.
- Bruce ordered his small group of cavalry to attack the archers. They were very successful. Their charge destroyed the archers' usefulness in the battle.
- The Scottish schiltrons continued their slow advance. This forced the English backwards. They were unable to use their numbers to any advantage.

Source A was written by Sir Thomas Grey, whose father was an English knight at the battle.

> *The Scots came in line of schiltrons and attacked the English columns, which were jammed together and could not operate against them [the Scots], so direfully were their horses impaled on the pikes. The troops in the English rear fell back upon the ditch of Bannockburn, tumbling one over the other.*

The final straw appears to have been when the English saw what they believed to be another Scottish army heading towards the battle. This was in fact several thousand camp-followers. In some accounts, they are called 'sma folk'. These were peasants who had little training and few weapons. They had probably seen an opportunity to gain riches at the expense of the English army.

Edward II was led from the battlefield by knights who feared he would be taken prisoner by the Scots. He headed towards Stirling Castle but was denied entry by the governor, as the castle was going to surrender to Bruce. With an escort of knights, he fled south, pursued closely by Scots.

RESULTS OF THE BATTLE

- Bruce had established himself as the undisputed king of Scotland.
- He had established a reputation as a great general.
- His army of foot soldiers had defeated knights in battle.
- It gave Bruce control over all of Scotland except Berwick.
- The Scots captured the English baggage train and supplies. It was estimated that this was worth £200 000.
- Important knights were captured and ransomed by the Scots. Many of these brought more money to Bruce. However, some were exchanged for Scottish prisoners held by the English. This included Bruce's wife, his daughter, his sister Mary – and Robert Wishart, the Bishop of Glasgow.

However,

- Edward II escaped capture.
- He was able to invade Scotland again.
- The war was to continue for another 15 years.

 THINGS TO DO AND THINK ABOUT

1. What advantages did the Scottish have over the English army?
2. Explain why the English army was unable to take advantage of its superior numbers at Bannockburn.
3. Why do you think the events of 23 June 1314 would have encouraged the Scots army?
4. How did the Scots deal with the threat of the English archers?
5. Describe the results of the Battle of Bannockburn.

 VIDEO LINK

Go to the Digital Zone to read more and watch videos explaining the battle: www.brightredbooks.net/ N5History.

DON'T FORGET

The battle was unusual, as it lasted two days. Most battles at this time were over in a few hours.

 ONLINE TEST

To take a test on this topic, go to the Digital Zone: www.brightredbooks.net/ N5History.

SCOTLAND, 1314–1329

VIDEO LINK

Go to the Digital Zone to learn more about the later years of Bruce's reign: www.brightredbooks.net/N5History.

WHAT HAPPENED NEXT?

After Bannockburn, Bruce was keen to see an end to the war. However, this did not happen. Although the English defeat in 1314 had come as a shock, its effects were felt much more in the north of England than in the south. Many of the English soldiers had come from the north. Moreover, Scottish raids were wreaking havoc in areas such as Northumberland. However, the war in Scotland seemed remote to many in the south of England. This meant that ending it did not seem all that pressing. Furthermore, Edward II did not wish to surrender his claims to Scotland.

The Scots continued to pile the pressure on the English king. The Scots used lightly armoured cavalrymen called 'hobelars' to raid deep into England. They returned loaded with hostages, money and materials. In one raid led by Bruce, they almost captured Edward II at Rievaulx Abbey in 1322. Edward escaped. However, his reputation among his own lords was in steep decline. He was eventually overthrown in 1327 by his wife, Queen Isabella, and by the English lords.

BRUCE IN IRELAND

Robert Bruce sent an army to Ireland in 1315 under the command of his brother Edward. The idea was to gain support from the Irish in the war against England. Ireland had been a source of money and supplies for both sides. Robert Bruce hoped to stop the flow of materials to England. Fighting raged for three years until Edward Bruce was killed at the Battle of Fochart. After this, the Scottish army was forced to retreat from Ireland. However, the amount of money that the English gained from taxes from Ireland dropped.

BRUCE AND THE POPE

After 1314, Bruce hoped to gain recognition as the king of Scotland from the pope. However, he was faced with a pope who was very hostile to him. Pope John XXII wished to see an end to the fighting, as it prevented him from organising a crusade to the Holy Lands. In 1317, he sent letters carried by two cardinals to Bruce requesting him to accept a truce. However, the letters addressed him as the Governor of Scotland. Bruce responded to these letters by stating:

> 'We cannot say anything in reply to the cardinals' letters which are not addressed to us as king. There are several Robert Bruces who in company with other barons are Governors of the Kingdom of Scotland. We will not open the Pope's sealed letters, for they carry no royal title and are not addressed to us.

THE DECLARATION OF ARBROATH, APRIL 1320

Bruce had been excommunicated from the Church after the murder of the Red Comyn. His failure to accept the truce proposed in 1317 led to further punishment. The pope placed an interdict on Scotland. This meant that the population was not able to use the services of the Catholic Church. In an attempt to put forward his case to be recognised as king, and the interdict and excommunication lifted, Bruce had a letter sent to the pope.

The letter was written on 6 April 1320 by Bernard Linton, Abbot of Arbroath, the King's Chancellor. It carried the seals and signatures of 8 earls and 31 barons. It set out Scotland's case to be recognised an independent country free of English interference.

contd

Source A is an extract from the Declaration of Arbroath in 1320.

For so long as 100 of us remain alive, we will never in any degree be subject to the rule of the English. For it is not for glory, riches or honour that we fight. But for liberty alone, which no good man loses, but with his life.

The pope eventually recognised Bruce as the Scottish king in 1324. However, attempts to negotiate an end to war failed. It was not until 1328 that a settlement between Scotland and England was reached. By this time, a number of events had led to increasing pressure on England to accept a peaceful settlement.

In 1326, Scots' the Alliance with France was renewed. This meant that England would again have been faced with war on two fronts.

In 1327, Edward II was overthrown by a rebellion led by his wife Isabella (nicknamed the 'She-Wolf') and her lover Roger Mortimer. Edward was thrown into prison, where he died. Some historians suggest he was murdered on the orders of his wife. He was replaced by his young son Edward III. Isabella ruled as Guardian. The new rulers of England were keen to end the war with Scotland, as it was expensive. They also wanted to concentrate on strengthening their own position in England.

In the same year, a Scottish raid into the north of England nearly captured the 14-year-old English king. It reminded many of the strength of the Scots and of the failure of the English crown to protect the northern counties.

THE TREATY OF EDINBURGH-NORTHAMPTON, 1328

The Scots and the English agreed to the following terms:

- Edward III would give up his claims to Scotland.
- Robert Bruce's son David (born 1324) would marry Edward III's sister Joan (born 1321). This took place in July 1328.
- The English king would help to have the sentence of excommunication against Bruce lifted. This happened in October 1328.
- The Scots and the English would help each other in the event of a foreign attack, unless this involved the French; the Scots would not help the Irish in any attack upon the English; and the English would not help any attack by the Isle of Man upon the Scots.
- Bruce would pay £20 000 to the English.

BRUCE'S LEGACY

Bruce died in 1329. However, his legacy was quickly challenged. Many of the knights who had lost lands during the Wars of Independence pressed Edward III to take action over the issue. They were known as the 'Disinherited'. In 1332, an army led by John Balliol's son, Edward, invaded Scotland with English support. Edward Balliol claimed the throne. For the next 25 years, a series of English invasions and battles took place until a further treaty was signed at Berwick in 1357. Balliol gave up his claim, and the Scots agreed to pay a ransom for the return of David II, who had been captured by the English.

 THINGS TO DO AND THINK ABOUT

You have the opportunity to interview Robert Bruce after the Battle of Bannockburn. Develop five questions that you could ask him. These need to help you to write an article of 200 words for tomorrow's newspaper or to do a short taped interview for the radio.

Remember that you want details that will inform your readers or listeners about the battle. It will also try to explain why the battle was won and lost by the rival armies.

 ONLINE

Read more about the Declaration of Arbroath at the Digital Zone: www.brightredbooks.net/N5History.

 DON'T FORGET

Bruce is buried in Dunfermline Abbey. His heart is buried in Melrose Abbey. It was carried on a crusade by Sir James Douglas. After Douglas was killed in battle in Spain, Bruce's heart was returned to Scotland.

 ONLINE

Go to the Digital Zone and click the link to play an online board game about the Wars of Independence: www.brightredbooks.net/N5History.

ONLINE TEST

To take a test on this topic, go to the Digital Zone: www.brightredbooks.net/N5History.

SCOTTISH SOCIETY AND CHURCH IN THE 1540s

DON'T FORGET

James was referring to the Stewarts as the Royal Family of Scotland. They had gained the throne when Marjory Bruce (daughter of Robert) had married Walter the Steward. The first Stewart king was their son, Robert II.

ONLINE

Go to the Digital Zone to read more about the Battle of Solway Moss: www.brightredbooks.net/ N5History.

Mary Queen of Scots' parents, James V and Mary of Guise

VIDEO LINK

Go to the Digital Zone to watch a comical take on the misfortunes which plagued the Stewarts: www.brightredbooks.net/ N5History.

ONLINE TEST

To test yourself on this topic, go to the Digital Zone: www.brightredbooks.net/ N5History.

QUEEN OF SCOTS

On 8 December 1542, Mary Queen of Scots was born at Linlithgow Palace. Her father, James V, was not present at the birth. He lay ill at Falkland Palace in Fife. When he was informed of the birth of his daughter, his reputed response was:

> *'It cam wi a lass and it will gang wi a lass'.*

Less than a week later, he died. He was 30 years old. Historians believe that it was a combination of disease (possibly cholera or dysentery) and mental collapse. Shortly before he died, he had received news that a Scottish army had been defeated by the English at Solway Moss on the border. The battle had been a disastrous rout: 1200 Scots had been captured, while many others had been killed. Only a few had died in battle. The majority of the dead had drowned while attempting to flee. The news had come as a shock to the Scottish king. His death left Scotland with a six-day-old queen. She was now the head of a country which faced a number of challenges.

CONTROLLING THE COUNTRY

Power in Scotland was held by the crown. However, there was also a Scottish Parliament which could influence a ruler. This was made up of representatives of three groups, who were known as the Three Estates. This was the Church, the nobility and the Burgh Commissioners, who came from the Royal Burghs. Parliament met once or twice a year and passed laws which maintained law and order in the country. These dealt with outbreaks of disease or problems with beggars. The members of Parliament sat in Parliament because they were wealthy. Ordinary people had no opportunity to vote for them.

THE CROWN

James V had continued the work of his predecessors in strengthening the control of the king over his country. He would use harsh punishments to restore order in those parts that were posing problems. During his reign, he went to the Borders on a number of occasions after receiving complaints. His solution was to hang those he believed responsible. These actions became known as 'Jeddart Justice' after the town of Jedburgh, where the punishments often took place.

A number of James V's predecessors had met untimely deaths:

- James I was murdered at Perth in 1437 by Scottish nobles
- James II was killed in 1460 laying siege to Roxburgh Castle, which was held by the English
- James III was killed at the Battle of Sauchieburn in 1488 fighting an army of Scottish nobles
- James IV was killed at the Battle of Flodden in 1513 fighting the English.

This made James aware of the risks posed to him from both his own nobles and the English. He was also aware of the ambitious nature of many of the nobles. After the death of his father, he was brought up under the control of a number of **regents**, who governed the country. One of them, the Earl of Angus, Archibald Douglas, kept James under very close control. James eventually escaped from his influence and attacked the castles belonging to the Douglas family.

contd

A **Privy Council** would help the king or queen to rule the country. This was a group of councillors who were nobles or members of the Church. They advised the monarch on many of the issues affecting the country, and helped to enforce many of the decisions.

THE NOBILITY

The nobles in 1542 were very influential and powerful. At the time of James V's death, there were a number of key families. These included the Hamiltons, the Campbells, the Gordons and the Lennoxes, as well as the Stewarts. As with earlier monarchs, they continued to supply soldiers when needed, as there was no full-time army. This allowed them the opportunity to make clear their feelings on major issues.

In 1542, they were less than keen to supply men to take part in any war against England. Part of the reason for this was high taxation. Some nobles were experiencing a shortage of funds. This encouraged many of them to look at the lands and possessions of the Church. It also led some to look at the views of the Protestant Reformers.

THE NATION IN 1542

Scotland at this time had a population of around 1 million people. Around 60% of the population lived in the countryside. Most were to be found in small **fermtouns**. These were small groups of houses whose inhabitants worked the land. They paid their rent to the landlord, who would provide them with protection if required. The main concern for the farmer was to keep control of the land, as his family depended on it. Many wished to pass it on to their sons, as this would be their livelihood. This in turn depended on the landlord, who had the right to object. For many of the tenants, the real problem was a rise in rents. This was increasing, and led to some losing their place on the land. It resulted in growing numbers of poor who looked to the Church for help.

Much of the business of the country took place in **burghs**. These were areas which had the right to hold a market. The most important of these were the Royal Burghs. They had the right to trade with foreign countries and were to be found on the coast or with access to a river. The majority of these were located on the east coast. These towns were small. The largest was Edinburgh, with around 8000 inhabitants. Three others, Aberdeen, Dundee and Perth, had populations of around 5000. Most would only have a few hundred.

Within the burghs, the main decisions were made by **burgesses**. These were merchants or skilled men who had been successful in trade or business. They had to pay a fee to become a burgess. However, it would increase their influence. It also opened the chance of becoming one of the burgh representatives at the Scottish Parliament.

The merchants with businesses on the east coast could make their fortune through trade. Many used this wealth to buy land, which meant that they increased their importance and influence. In turn, they became known as **bonnet** or **bunnet lairds**. This increased their ambitions.

THINGS TO DO AND THINK ABOUT

1. 'It cam wi a lass and it will gang wi a lass.' What do you think James V might have meant by this statement?

2. Why were Scottish nobles a problem for Scottish kings?

3. Explain why people living on the land might be experiencing difficulties by the 1540s.

4. Why do you think trade links and the ambition of burgesses might have led to the spread of new ideas within Scotland?

DON'T FORGET

The royal family at this time were the Stewarts. However, Mary Queen of Scots used the French spelling of the surname, which was Stuart.

DON'T FORGET

The Renaissance is the term used to describe the period after 1450. It marked a rebirth in interest in learning. This included science, literature, philosophy and music. Many of the new ideas that were spread challenged the established views.

VIDEO LINK

For an alternative take on the Renaissance go to the Digital Zone: www. brightredbooks.net/ N5History.

DON'T FORGET

Many of the merchants who worked on the continent came into contact with new ideas and customs. This included the views of religious reformers, such as Martin Luther, in Germany. Some of the merchants and burgesses believed that the new religion gave them the chance to play a bigger role in society.

Wars with England were not good for business. During the 1540s, a number of burghs, including Edinburgh, were damaged or destroyed.

THE CHURCH IN SCOTLAND

Cardinal David Beaton, the last Scottish cardinal before the Reformation

THE CHURCH AND THE CROWN

The Scottish Church in Scotland was very close to the crown. One of the closest advisers to James V was Cardinal Beaton of St Andrews. One of the reasons for this was that the king was able to appoint those he wanted into many of its positions. James V was able to do this because the popes were keen to keep Scotland a Catholic country. They were worried that Scotland would follow the example of Henry VIII's England and break with Rome. James V exploited this to his advantage. He gave well-paid positions in the Church to five of his illegitimate sons.

The Church also contained much wealth. On the eve of the Reformation, it was taking £300 000 a year. The crown earned £17 500. As a result, the Church was heavily taxed to pay for James V's ambitions. However, this position was beginning to face challenges from a number of areas.

PROTESTANTISM

In 1517, Martin Luther pinned his list of faults in the Catholic Church on the door of a church in Wittenberg, Germany. He was unhappy with the Church for a number of reasons:

- The sale of indulgences or pardons. The Church offered those people who had committed a sin an easy way of making amends. They could buy a pardon from the Church. Many nobles and kings had taken advantage of this in the past.

- The types of people who were being given important roles in the Church were often not very religious.

- The Church was earning large amounts of money. Luther felt that this was not being used correctly.

These woodcuts, made by a Protestant in 1521, were designed to show the faults in the Catholic Church. The one on the left shows Jesus chasing the moneylenders from the temple. The one on the right shows the pope selling indulgences or pardons.

Within Scotland, the Catholic Church was also experiencing difficulties. Much of the money gathered by the Church was used for the construction of many church buildings throughout the country. It was also used to build colleges at Aberdeen and St Andrews. However, this meant that many of the ordinary parishes had their funds taken. Village priests had little to live on. It meant that they had to look to other methods of earning to survive. This usually meant taking other jobs which reduced the amount of time they would spend on their religious duties. This was called **pluralism**. Furthermore, some had formed relationships with women and had had children. This was called **concubinage**. Priests were not supposed to have done this!

CHURCH REFORM

The Catholic Church in Scotland discussed reforms on three occasions – 1549, 1552 and 1559. It attempted to deal with some of the problems that it was aware of. This included the issue of priests who had taken wives and had used money from the Church to support their families. The Church also tried to improve the standard of education of many of the parish priests. It was believed that the more intelligent members of the Church would not put up with the poor conditions that often went with being a parish priest.

New methods of preaching were put forward, including pamphlets which outlined the Catholic faith. This included a 'Twapenny Faith' – a four-page pamphlet which

contd

DON'T FORGET

Protestantism got its name because the supporters of this movement were protesting about the faults of the Church.

was designed to be more easily understood by ordinary people. However, the attempts at reform were not successful – for a number of reasons:

- The leaders of the Catholic Church in Scotland did not actively enforce many of the reforms. Some historians believe that they had become too used to their comfortable positions and did not travel around the country to improve the Church.

- The archbishops of St Andrews and Glasgow did not get on and did not always cooperate with each other. On one occasion, this led to a fight between the priests and supporters of the two archbishops at Glasgow Cathedral.

- Little was done to improve conditions for the ordinary priests.

- They received little support from the crown. Between 1542 and 1560, Scotland was controlled by James V's widow, Mary of Guise. She did not take action against the Protestant 'heretics', as she needed the support of the Protestant nobles in her struggles against England.

THE SPREAD OF PROTESTANTISM IN SCOTLAND

The Reformation in Scotland was not as violent as in other countries. In England, 300 Protestants were executed by Mary I ('Bloody Mary'). 200 Catholics were put to death by her half-sister Elizabeth. In Scotland between 1528 and 1558, 28 Protestants were executed for heresy. After 1567, saying mass was made a capital crime in Scotland. However, only two executions are thought to have taken place.

Protestant reformers

One sign of Protestantism in Scotland was the number of individuals who risked terrible punishments to promote their ideas. These became known as martyrs. In 1528, Patrick Hamilton was burnt at the stake in St Andrews. He was the first martyr of the Reformation. However, his execution was seen by some as a mistake. One observer was reputed to have warned the Catholic leadership that any future burnings should take place in cellars, as the 'reek of Master Patrick Hamilton infected as many as it blew upon'.

George Wishart

In 1546, another Protestant reformer, George Wishart, was burnt at the stake. He had been accused of heresy. This meant that he held ideas which were at odds with those of the Church. Wishart was seen as a powerful speaker and a threat to the Catholic Church. One of his closest supporters was John Knox, who often attended his meetings carrying a sword.

The spread of Protestantism in Scotland was also helped by the introduction of bibles that ordinary people could understand. In England, William Tyndale had translated the Bible into English in 1526. In the 1540s, the occupation of parts of Scotland by the English meant that it was easily available.

THINGS TO DO AND THINK ABOUT

1. Explain why James V had a great deal of influence over the Catholic Church in Scotland.

2. Imagine you are a member of the Scottish Church in 1540. You have been sent to find out the problems that are facing the Church. Identify five faults in the Catholic Church. Make suggestions as to what possible improvements could be made.

3. Explain why attempts to reform the Catholic Church were unsuccessful before 1560.

4. Why did Protestantism spread in Scotland?

5. Evaluate the usefulness of the two woodcuts on page 114 as evidence of the reasons for the Reformation.

   (You may want to comment on who made them, when they were made, why they were made, what they depict or what has been missed out.)

ONLINE

Go to the Digital Zone to learn more about the Catholic Church's attempt to reform: www.brightredbooks.net/N5History.

The execution of Patrick Hamilton in 1528, drawn by an artist in 1879

Page from William Tyndale bible of 1526

DON'T FORGET

Around 1450, a goldsmith called Johannes Gutenberg developed a printing press. This allowed books and pamphlets to be produced a lot more quickly. It meant that ideas could be spread more effectively across wider areas.

ONLINE TEST

To take a test on this topic, go to the Digital Zone: www.brightredbooks.net/N5History.

THE TREATY OF GREENWICH, 1543

THE AFTERMATH OF SOLWAY MOSS AND HENRY VIII

The picture to the left was originally drawn in 1537 by the artist Hans Holbein. It is showing that Henry is a man of power. How does it try to do this?

The painting below to the left was originally created between 1545 and 1550. It shows Henry's children: his son Edward (born 1537) and his daughters Mary (born 1516) and Elizabeth (born 1533). The painting also shows the court jester.

After the Battle of Solway Moss, a large number of Scottish nobles had been captured by the English. They had been well treated and given pensions. They agreed to help ensure that Henry's son would marry the infant Mary. In July 1543, the Scots and the English signed the Treaty of Greenwich. The two sides agreed that Mary Queen of Scots would marry Edward, the young son of Henry VIII, when she turned 10 years old. This ended the war between the two sides. However, the agreement very quickly unravelled. There were a number of reasons for this:

- The Scots were split over the issue. This was on religious and political grounds. Scottish Protestants favoured the treaty, while Catholics tended to view it with suspicion.

- Mary of Guise favoured a closer relationship with France and worked against the treaty. She accepted it at first to buy time to strengthen her position.

- Many Scots saw the treaty as Henry's way of seizing Scotland.

- Some historians believe the Scots were simply buying time. When the treaty was rejected, it was too late for the English to invade Scotland that year.

- The Protestant Earl of Arran, who signed the treaty, was a weak individual. He may have signed the treaty in good faith, but, he needed the support of a number of individuals to keep his position as Governor of Scotland. His family were the next in line to the throne. However, this claim was based on the marriage of his father to James II's daughter. There was strong evidence to suggest that this marriage should not have taken place, as his father was not properly divorced from his second wife. He needed the support of Cardinal Beaton and of his own brother, John Hamilton the Abbot of Paisley, to ensure his position.

THE ROUGH WOOING

The failure of the Treaty of Greenwich led Henry to try a different approach. Between 1543 and 1551, English armies were regularly sent to Scotland to wreak havoc.

Sketch of Edinburgh in 1544

Source A is an extract from the orders given to the English commander, the Earl of Hereford, in 1544.

> *Put all to the fire and sword. Burn Edinburgh town – so razed and defaced when you have sacked and gotten what you can from it, as there may remain forever a everlasting memory of the vengeance of God lightened upon them for their falsehood and disloyalty. Put man, woman and child to fire and sword without exception where any resistance shall be made against you.*

The destruction wrought upon Scotland was severe.

Source B outlines some of the damage caused. It was written by an Englishman who was involved in the destruction. (A bastell house was a house used by a peasant. It had two floors. The bottom one was used to keep animals.)

contd

Exploits done upon the Scots from the beginning of July to 17 November 1544	
	Sum total
Town towers, Steading Barns, Parish churches, Bastell Houses cast down or burnt	192
Scots killed	403
Prisoners taken	816
Horned Cattle	10 386
Sheep	12 492
Nags or Geldings	1296
Goats	200
Bolls of Corn	850

In 1547, a Scottish army led by the Earl of Arran faced an English army outside Edinburgh. The Battle of Pinkie Cleugh was a disaster for the Scots. The English army had a large number of firearms. The Scots were carrying pikes and swords. It was a medieval army against a Renaissance army. Around 5000 Scots were killed and another 1500 captured. After the battle, the English created a base near Haddington.

This map of the Battle of Pinkie Cleugh was drawn by an Englishman who was an eyewitness in 1547.

A – English Camp
B, C & D – English Army
E – English Artillery
I – English Horsemen
M, N & O – Scottish Army and horsemen
Q – St. Michael's of Inveresk
R – Musselburgh
T – Scottish Camp
Y – Our Galley
Z – Edinburgh Castle

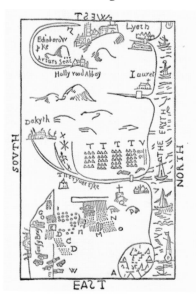

ONLINE

You can read a lot more about the Battle of Pinkie Cleugh at the Digital Zone: wwwbrightredbooks.net/ N5History.

THINGS TO DO AND THINK ABOUT

1. Look at the picture of Henry VIII with his children. What significance is there in the order that the children have been placed in the painting?

2. Explain why the Treaty of Greenwich was rejected by the Scots.

3. Describe the effects of the Rough Wooing on Scotland.

ONLINE TEST

To take a test on this topic, go to the Digital Zone: www.brightredbooks.net/ N5History.

THE PROTESTANT REFORMATION

THE MURDER OF CARDINAL BEATON

Cardinal Beaton was one of the most important opponents of Henry VIII's plans for Scotland. He was also firm in his opposition to the spread of Protestantism within Scotland. He was responsible for the execution of a number of Protestants after 1543, including George Wishart. In 1546, a group of Protestants murdered Beaton in St Andrews Castle.

In **Source A,** John Knox describes the murder.

> *While they forced at the door, the Cardinal hid a box of gold under coals that were laid in a corner. At length he asked, 'Will you save my life?' The Cardinal sat down in a chair and cried, 'I am a priest, I am a priest; you will not slay me.' Presenting the point of his sword at the Cardinal, James Melvin said, 'Repent thee of thy former wicked life, but especially of the shedding of the blood of Master George Wishart, which, although the flame of fire consumed him before men, yet cries a vengeance upon you. We are sent from God to revenge it.'*

After his murder, the body of Beaton was left hanging from the castle walls. Groups of Protestants joined the small band that had carried out the murder. One of the people who joined the 'Castilians' was John Knox. They looked to England for help. Instead, Mary of Guise was able to get help from France. The Protestants in the castle were forced to surrender and were sent to France. They were used as galley slaves. However, the death of Cardinal Beaton removed a powerful opponent to Henry's plans for Scotland.

MARY QUEEN OF SCOTS IN EXILE

The defeat of the Scots at Pinkie Cleugh led to fears for Mary's safety. She was moved around the country to keep her out of the hands of the English. Eventually, a treaty was signed at Haddington in 1548 between the French and the Scots. The young queen was to be sent to France. In return, the French would supply weapons and soldiers to fight the English. The Earl of Arran was made the Duke of Chatelherault for agreeing to the treaty.

MARY OF GUISE AND THE SPREAD OF PROTESTANTISM

Time as regent

In 1554, Mary of Guise replaced Arran as the Regent of Scotland. For the next five years, she directed the campaigns against the English and made conciliatory gestures towards the Scottish Protestants. However, by 1558, she was under a great deal of pressure. Mary needed the pope's support if she wanted to see her daughter rule England. This meant that she had to keep Scotland Catholic.

1555 – There were riots against the passing of an act which affected craftsmen in burghs. They were prevented from electing their own leaders. Mary of Guise repealed the act the following year.

1556–7 – Five separate taxes were introduced which were very unpopular.

1558 – The marriage of Mary Queen of Scots to the Dauphin Francis worried many Scots. They saw it as part of a process which would end with Scotland becoming part of France.

January 1559 – The 'Beggars Summons' was pinned on the doors of all friaries throughout the country. This demanded that friars hand over their property. Friars were members of the Catholic Church who had taken vows of chastity, poverty and obedience. They lived in the community and were supported by donations. Some historians believe they were targeted because their work in the community made them effective opponents of the Protestants.

contd

March 1559 – Mary of Guise abandoned her conciliatory policy towards Protestants. She issued a proclamation upholding the position of the Catholic Church. Anyone who did not rejoin was to be seen as a rebel.

May 1559 – A riot broke out in Perth. Protestants attacked and smashed Catholic churches and statues. They had been encouraged by John Knox.

THE LORDS OF THE CONGREGATION

A group of Scottish lords formed an alliance against Mary of Guise. Some were Protestant lords, such as the Earl of Morton, the Earl of Arran and the Earl of Argyll, who felt that their ambitions had been held back by Mary. They were known as the Lords of the Congregation. They deposed Mary as Regent and took control of Edinburgh. However, they were forced to retreat two weeks later.

February 1560 – The Treaty of Berwick was signed between the Lords of the Congregation and the English. Under its terms, an army would be sent to help the Scottish Protestants. 9000 English soldiers laid siege to Leith, where a French army was based.

June 1560 – Mary of Guise died of illness at Edinburgh Castle.

July 1560 – The Treaty of Edinburgh was signed. The French and the English agreed to withdraw their forces from Scotland.

August 1560 – The Reformation Parliament met in Edinburgh. It declared that Scotland was a Protestant country. The mass was abolished. The authority of the pope was forbidden, and Protestant beliefs were adopted.

THE REFORMED KIRK

John Calvin, a Frenchman in Geneva, was a key influence on the Protestant Reformation. His views became known as Calvinism. He believed that the ministers of the Reformed Church should be treated equally. He did not believe that there should be a hierarchy such as the bishops that controlled the Catholic Church. His followers became known as Presbyterians. After 1555, he offered shelter to John Knox in Geneva. Knox had left England after Mary I had become queen. As a result, Knox became heavily influenced by Calvin's ideas.

The new Church had a number of problems. It lacked funds and ministers. John Knox wrote the *First Book of Discipline*, which set out the rules and aims of the new Church – to seize the property and lands of the Catholic Church and to provide education and look after the poor. It set out the aims of ministers being elected by the congregation of a parish.

Source C is by a modern historian, Ian Whyte. In this extract, he describes the spread of the Protestant religion after the Reformation.

> *Of Scotland's 1080 parishes, about 240 were being served by the new church in some way by the end of 1561, perhaps 850 by 1567 and over 1000 by 1574. Adherence to Catholicism continued in many parts of the lowlands well into the 1570s and even 1580s with masses being celebrated in rural churches. In the Highlands, the structure of the old Church was dismantled but slow to be replaced. Highland Chiefs saw the new religion as a threat to their way of life and did little to help it. From the late 1570s, Jesuit missionaries succeeded in reviving the Catholic faith in parts of the Highlands.*

THINGS TO DO AND THINK ABOUT

1. Why was Cardinal Beaton murdered in 1546?

2. Why was Mary Queen of Scots sent to France?

3. What evidence is there that there was growing unhappiness with Mary of Guise's rule by 1559?

4. Explain why the marriage of Mary Queen of Scots to the Dauphin Francis would cause concern to Scots.

DON'T FORGET

The destruction of statues and other religious symbols was known as **iconoclasm**.

ONLINE

You can read more about the Lords of the Congregation at the Digital Zone: wwwbrightredbooks.net/N5History.

John Knox

ONLINE TEST

To take a test on this topic, go to the Digital Zone: www.brightredbooks.net/N5History.

MARY QUEEN OF SCOTS IN FRANCE

THE ENGLISH SUCCESSION QUESTION

While Mary was in France, the issue of who should be the ruler of England arose.

In 1558, the Catholic queen of England, Mary Tudor, died. She was succeeded by her half-sister Elizabeth, who was a Protestant. Elizabeth's mother was Ann Boleyn, the second wife of Henry VIII. He had divorced his first wife, Catherine of Aragon, to marry her. However, Catholics refused to accept that the divorce was legal. This meant that Elizabeth was not the rightful queen. In their eyes, the next in line to the English throne was Mary Queen of Scots.

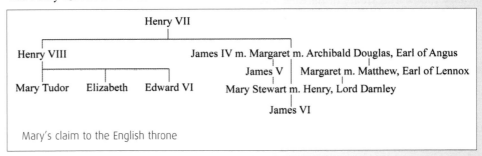

Mary's claim to the English throne

This picture shows the coat of arms that Mary used when she was married to Francis II of France. It shows the symbols of France and Scotland. It also shows the three lions of England.

Mary with Francis in 1559

QUEEN OF FRANCE

Mary spent thirteen years of her life in France. In 1558, she married the Dauphin Francis, heir to the French throne. A year later, he became king of France when his father was killed in a jousting accident. In 1560, Francis died of an ear infection. Mary was no longer the queen of France. Although there were rumours that she would marry Francis's younger brother Henry, nothing came of it. Instead, she decided to return to Scotland.

VIDEO LINK

Go to the Digital Zone to learn more about Mary's return to Scotland and watch the video clips describing her life: www.brightredbooks. net/N5History.

RETURN TO SCOTLAND

Mary arrived back in a country that she had not been in for thirteen years. She was faced with two major issues when she returned to Scotland:

* What action should she take about the religion of the country? In 1560, Parliament had declared that Scotland was now a Protestant country. However, she was a Catholic. What should she do?

* She was a widow. Scotland needed an heir. The question of whom she should marry was a major issue.

MARY QUEEN OF SCOTS AND RELIGION

Source A to the right is a painting depicting Mary's arrival at Leith in August 1561.

Mary returned to Scotland in August 1561. Her ship arrived a lot earlier than was expected, and no one was at the port of Leith to greet her. She had ignored the advice of the Catholic Earl of Huntly, who wished her to land at Aberdeen. He had promised her that 20 000 soldiers would be ready to meet her and place her on the throne. Instead, Mary preferred to try to win over the Protestant lords and avoid a civil war.

For the first few years, Mary did little to upset the Protestants. Her first privy council had twelve ministers: seven Protestants and five Catholics. She took advice from three Scottish nobles in particular:

- James Stewart, a Protestant noble who was her half-brother and a member of the Lords of Congregation. He had appointed himself Regent in 1559. As an illegitimate son of James V, he could not become king. However, as Regent, he could wield a lot of power until Mary's return. He was given the title Earl of Moray by Mary in 1561.

- Sir William Maitland of Lethington, another Protestant noble. He was on very good terms with the English.

- Sir James Douglas, Earl of Morton, who was also a Protestant.

ONLINE

Read more about Mary's return and the Scottish Reformation at the Digital Zone: www.brightredbooks. net/N5History.

None was especially friendly with John Knox, who believed in a more extreme form of Protantism.

Mary met with Knox at Holyrood Palace. They argued over religion and many of Knox's views. In 1558, Knox had written a book, *The First Blast of the Trumpet Against the Monstrous Regiment of Women*. Knox claimed he had written it as an attack on Mary Tudor's treatment of Protestants in England and that it was not meant as an attack on Mary Queen of Scots. However, neither succeeded in changing the other's opinion about religion. Mary practised her religion in private, although this did upset some in Edinburgh. On one occasion, her servants were attacked while carrying the items required to say mass.

Source B in the margin to the right is a painting, made in 1879, showing one of the meetings between Mary and Knox.

In 1562, Mary attacked the Catholic Earl of Huntly. He had failed to obey her instructions and had been upset by Mary granting the titles of Mar and Moray to her half-brother. Huntly died of a heart attack before his capture, but his corpse was put on trial five months later and his estates seized. It proved that Mary was not inclined to support the Catholic nobility in their wish to see the restoration of the Catholic Church.

Mary passed an act in 1562 which allowed money from the Catholic Church to be diverted towards the new reformed Church. It was used to pay for ministers in parishes.

In **Source C**, Sir James Melville, who worked for Mary, describes her return.

'The Queen's Majesty after returning to Scotland behaved herself so princely, so honourably and discreetly that her reputation spread in all countries.'

In **Source D**, William Lethington of Maitland describes Mary as having acted as

'reasonably as we can require. If anything be amiss the fault is rather ourselves.'

ONLINE TEST

To take a test on this topic, go to the Digital Zone: www.brightredbooks.net/ N5History.

THINGS TO DO AND THINK ABOUT

1. Explain why Catholics regarded Mary Queen of Scots as the rightful queen of England.

2. Do you agree with Sir James Melville's view in Source C of Mary's reign after she arrived back in Scotland? Give reasons for your answer.

MARY AND MARRIAGE

A HOST OF SUITORS

Within a short time of the death of her husband, Mary was faced with the question of whom she should marry next. A number of men were suggested and rejected. There were many things to consider, but the big issues were:

- What religion should her husband be?

- What status should he hold?

DON'T FORGET

Mary needed to remarry in order to produce an heir to the throne.

Name	Title	Religion	Advantages	Disadvantages
James Hamilton	3rd Earl of Arran	Protestant	Son of the Duke of Chatelherault	• Rejected by Elizabeth as a possible husband for Mary • May have been mentally ill
Robert Dudley	Earl of Leicester	Protestant	Recommended by the English queen	• May have murdered his wife • His father was a traitor • May have had a relationship with Elizabeth
Don Carlos	Son of the Spanish king, and heir to the throne	Catholic	Able to supply soldiers and money	• Marriage may upset the English • Marriage may also upset the French • His behaviour could be odd – he once tried to force a shoemaker to eat a pair of shoes that he did not like
Henry Darnley	Lord	Catholic, although he had attended Protestant ceremonies	• Had a claim to the Scottish and English thrones • Slightly younger than Mary • As tall as Mary	• Not very bright • Made a lot of enemies with his behaviour

ONLINE

You can read more about Mary's husbands at the Digital Zone: www.brightredbooks.net/N5History.

In **Source A**, Lord Melville describes Mary's opinion of Darnley.

Her Majesty took well with him, and said that he was the lustiest and best proportioned long man that she had seen; for he was of a tall stature, long and supple, even and smooth; well instructed from his youth in all honest and comely exercises.

Lord Darnley and his younger brother

MARY AND DARNLEY

Mary's control of Scotland began to unravel with her marriage to Darnley.

- She lost the support of James Stewart, who was against the marriage. He gathered forces to oppose Mary. However, his forces deserted him when faced with the superior numbers of the royal army. Moray fled to England. The episode became known as the 'Chaseabout Raid'.

- The second problem was Darnley. Mary was married to him in a Catholic ceremony on 29 July 1565. However, very quickly the relationship became strained. Darnley did not sit through the mass after the wedding.

DON'T FORGET

Darnley had a claim to the thrones of both England and Scotland through his parents – a Scottish Lennox and an English Douglas.

contd

- In late November 1565, Mary lay ill with pains in her side. Darnley spent nine days hunting in Perth.

- Mary became so fed up with Darnley that she moved to prevent him from being referred to as the king.

- After their marriage, official documents had to be signed by both Mary and Darnley. However, Darnley was absent so often that it became difficult to complete the royal business. Mary had a stamp made with Darnley's signature. It was kept by her Italian secretary, David Rizzio.

- David Rizzio and Mary spent a great deal of time together. They had a common interest in music and dancing. Some people believed that Mary was having an affair with him. Others believed that Rizzio was a spy for the pope. They believed that he was urging Mary to take action to support the Catholic Church.

VIDEO LINK

Go to the Digital Zone to learn more about Mary and Darnley by watching the clip: www.brightredbooks.net/N5History.

This painting of David Rizzio was made in the late 17th or the 18th century. Those who met him said that his face was 'considered ill-favoured and his stature small and hunched'.

In **Source B**, John Knox, in his *History of the Reformation*, describes Lord Darnley's behaviour at this time.

> *As for the King, he passed his time in hunting and hawking and such other pleasures as were agreeable to his appetites having in his company gentlemen willing to satisfy his will and affections.*

Source C is from a letter written by an English noble, Sir William Drury, to Queen Elizabeth's secretary about the relationship between Mary and Darnley.

> *All people say that Darnley is too much addicted to drinking. 'Tis certainly reported there was some jar [argument] between the Queen and him at an entertainment in a merchant's house in Edinburgh. She only tried to persuade him from drinking too much and encouraging others to drink, in both which he proceeded, and gave her such words that she left the place with tears.*

THINGS TO DO AND THINK ABOUT

1. *Blind Date* – Imagine you are a PR consultant for each of the candidates who are being recommended to Mary. Try to sell your client as having the strongest case to be married. This means that you have to promote his strengths and defend his weaknesses.

2. Was Darnley a good choice as Mary's husband? Give reasons for your answer.

3. Why did Mary become close friends with Rizzio?

4. Evaluate the usefulness of Source C above to historians studying the problems facing Mary after her return to Scotland. (You may want to comment on who wrote it, when they wrote it, why they wrote it, what they say or what has been missed out.)

5. "Mary was having an affair with Rizzio." Would you agree with this statement?

ONLINE TEST

Take a test on this topic at the Digital Zone: www.brightredbooks.net/N5History.

THE MURDER OF RIZZIO

A MARRIAGE UNDER STRAIN

By March 1566, Mary and Darnley's relationship was seriously damaged. They were spending less and less time with each other. Mary preferred the company of her secretary, David Rizzio. This relationship caused more problems. The only good news for Mary appears to have been the fact that she was pregnant.

- Darnley was jealous and concerned that he may lose his position.

- Some of the Scottish Protestants were upset at the queen spending so much time with a Catholic.

- Rumours were spreading that Mary and Rizzio were having an affair.

- Some of the lords believed that Rizzio was the obstacle to Moray and the others who were involved in the 'Chaseabout Raid' being pardoned by Mary. A number of them signed a **bond,** or agreement, to kill Rizzio. Darnley was one of the signatories.

ONLINE

Go to the Digital Zone to watch a clip abut this incident and learn more about Rizzio's murder: www.brightredbooks.net/ N5History.

Source A is John Knox's view on the subject outlined in his book *History of the Reformation*.

This David Rizzio was so foolish, that not only had he drawn unto him the managing of all affairs, the King set aside, but also his furniture and belongings did exceed the King's. He was made chancellor at the following parliament; which made the lords plot against him. They made a bond, to stand to the religion and liberties of the country, and to free themselves from the slavery of the villain David Rizzio.

A number of the Scottish lords decided to take matters into their own hands. Led by Lord Ruthven, and dressed in armour, they forced their way into the queen's apartments.

The painting in the margin to the right depicts the murder of David Rizzio. It shows Rizzio being attacked by the nobles. Darnley is holding Mary back.

In **Source B**, James Melville, who worked for the queen, describes what happened after the nobles forced their way into the queen's apartments.

This vile act was done upon a Saturday at six a-clock at night, when the Queen was at supper in her closet. A number of armed men entered within the court. One part of them went up through the King's chamber, led by the Lord Ruthven and George Douglas; the rest remained outside with drawn swords in their hands. The King was with the Queen, and was leaning upon her chair, when the Lord Ruthven entered with his helmet upon his head, and George Douglas and others with them, so rudely, that the table, candles, meat and dishes were overthrown. Riccio took the Queen about the waist, crying for mercy; but George Douglas plucked out the King's dagger and struck Riccio first with it, leaving it sticking in him. He making great shrieks and cries, was rudely snatched from the Queen, who could not prevail either with threats or requests, to save him. But he was forcibly drawn forth of the closet and slain in the outer hall, and her Majesty kept as a captive. The next morning being Sunday, I was let forth at the gate, and passing through the outer close, the Queen being at a window, cried to me to help her.

ONLINE

You can read more about the murder of Rizzio at the Digital Zone: www. brightredbooks.net/ N5History.

contd

In **Source C**, Lord Herries, who was a supporter of Mary Queen of Scots, describes what happened at Holyrood Palace.

> *The Queen was mightily terrified at the sight of the men, with drawn swords; and when she saw Ruthven the leader, she was strangely amazed. 'What strange sight (says she) is this, my Lord, I see in you? Are you mad?' Says he, 'We have been too long mad!' And with these words he pulled Signor Davie from beyond the Queen (for he was extremely terrified, and slipped himself behind for refuge, and put his arms about the Queen's middle). The Queen took likewise hold of him, spoke some words of authority, and would not let go her hold until Andrew Ker held a pistol to her breast which refused to give fire, and then by violence pulled him away. Then he was hurried to the next room, where the rest were. The Earl of Morton gave him the first stroke, and he was killed with six and fifty wounds. It is written, that in the time of this tumult, where tables, candles, and everything was overthrown, the King came in, and some plucked his dagger out of the sheath and thrust it in the dead corpse, to be seen by all, that the world might believe that the King himself was the actor!*

After the murder of Rizzio, a number of nobles, including the Earl of Bothwell, slipped away to fetch help. Mary was left alone. She eventually convinced Darnley to help her to escape. With the help of a few loyal servants, Darnley and Mary rode to Dunbar.

THE REPERCUSSIONS

- A few days after her escape, Mary returned to Edinburgh with 8000 men.
- The lords who were directly involved in the murder fled to England.
- They sent a document which showed Mary the involvement of Darnley.
- Rumours spread that Mary and Darnley were going to divorce. However, Mary was aware that any split from Darnley could cause people to question the legitimacy of the child. Some were already wondering if Darnley was the real father.
- Mary turned for support to James Hepburn, the Earl of Bothwell, who had remained loyal during the 'Chaseabout Raid' and the Rizzio murder.

THE BIRTH OF JAMES

In June 1566, Mary gave birth to a son, James, at Edinburgh Castle. The event was celebrated by the majority of the population. Scotland had an heir. The birth also strengthened the case for Mary to be recognised as the heir to the English throne, as Elizabeth was childless.

However, the relationship with Darnley fell away. They argued in public and lived apart. When Mary became seriously ill in October 1566, Darnley visited once – eleven days after she fell ill. In December, James was christened at Stirling Castle. Darnley did not attend.

Mary discussed divorce with one of her nobles, Maitland of Lethington. He suggested that he could arrange matters if she pardoned the Rizzio murderers. He also suggested 'other means' to get rid of Darnley. Mary wanted nothing to happen that would reflect badly on her or her son.

 THINGS TO DO AND THINK ABOUT

1. Explain why Rizzio was murdered at Holyrood Palace in March 1566.
2. Why do you think the nobles revealed Darnley's involvement to Mary?

 VIDEO LINK

Go to the Digital Zone to take a tour of where the murder happened: www.brightredbooks.net/N5History.

 DON'T FORGET

Mary was six months pregnant when Rizzio was murdered in front of her. Some historians believe that this may have been an attempt to cause Mary to suffer a miscarriage.

 ONLINE TEST

Take a test on this topic at the Digital Zone: www.brightredbooks.net/N5History.

THE MURDER OF LORD DARNLEY

VIDEO LINK

Go to the Digital Zone and watch the clip introducing events leading up to Darnley's death: www.brightredbooks.net/N5History.

ONLINE

You can read more about Darnley's death and tackle some tasks at the Digital Zone: www.brightredbooks.net/N5History.

VIDEO LINK

You can watch a clip which considers motives for the murder at the Digital Zone: www.brightredbooks.net/N5History.

10 FEBRUARY 1567

By January 1567, the marriage of Mary and Lord Darnley appeared to be recovering. Darnley had returned in December to Glasgow, where he had become seriously ill with a 'pox'. He was visited by Mary on 22 January. She had heard of his illness, and suggested that he should return to Edinburgh, where she could nurse him back to health.

As he was suffering from an illness which was considered contagious, he was not placed in Holyrood Palace. It was argued that there was a possible danger of young James becoming infected. Darnley was placed in a small house called Kirk o' Field, which was a short distance from the palace. On the night of 9 February, he was visited by Mary, who left at around 11pm to return to the palace to take part in a wedding masque. This was part of the celebrations for two of her favourite servants, who been married that day.

At around 2am, a loud blast rocked Edinburgh. Kirk o' Field had been reduced to rubble by an explosion. Some of the first people on the scene heard a servant crying for help. Several bodies were pulled from the rubble. More than three hours later, two other bodies were discovered in a nearby garden. They were those of Lord Darnley and one of his servants, William Taylor. An English spy compiled a picture, which was sent to Queen Elizabeth's secretary.

This picture shows the scene at Kirk o' Field in February 1567, with a number of events taking place. It shows the body of Darnley and his servant in the garden. They were wearing nightshirts. Beside them lay a fur coat, a blanket, a chair, a rope and a dagger. It also shows the ruined Kirk o' Field and Darnley's son James asking for revenge against the murders.

WHAT WAS THE MOTIVE?

The motive may have been **religion**, as Darnley was a Catholic. **Or** – was it **revenge**?

He had been involved in the murder of David Rizzio. He had then betrayed the other nobles by helping Mary to escape from Holyrood. In December 1566, Mary had pardoned a number of the nobles who had been involved in the Rizzio murder. Some of them returned to Edinburgh at this time.

DON'T FORGET

The Rizzio murder in March 1566 has been seen as a key factor in explaining what happened at Kirk O'Field.

DON'T FORGET

The evidence concerning Kirk O'Field is very unreliable. Most of the people involved had good reason not to tell the truth. It was also very convenient to blame one person – Bothwell.

WHO CARRIED OUT THE MURDER?

There were a large number of people who were seen as being involved in the plot. Nevertheless, much of the evidence connected with the murder has to be treated carefully. It suited many of the people involved to present others as having been behind the crime.

Theory 1

- Mary was involved in the plot to kill her hated husband. She brought him to Edinburgh, where he would be very vulnerable to any plots. His family's supporters were mainly based around Glasgow, while his enemies were based in Edinburgh.

- She wanted revenge for the murder of Rizzio and was reported as having said: 'No more tears now; I will think upon revenge.' She also wanted to get rid of an embarrassing husband. Being a Catholic, divorce could be difficult for her to obtain and could have consequences for her son's claim to the throne.

- She had been supposed to stay at Kirk o' Field that night but changed her mind at the last minute.

contd

However,

- Mary appears to have been deeply shaken by the events at Kirk o' Field. She may well have suffered a mental collapse after the murder.

- When she was leaving Kirk o' Field, she spotted her servant 'Frenchie' Paris. She said: 'Jesu, Paris! How begrimed you are!' Would she have drawn attention to this if she was aware of the plot?

Theory 2

- Darnley was murdered by the Earl of Bothwell. They had fallen out over the Rizzio murder.

- The Earl of Bothwell wanted to murder Darnley so that he could marry Mary.

- Bothwell was in attendance with the queen at Kirk o' Field until 11pm. He then claimed to have returned to his house in Edinburgh. At 2am, he arrived at the site of the explosion with a group of armed men.

- 'Frenchie' Paris had been one of Bothwell's servants. He could easily have gained access to Kirk o' Field to carry out any work connected with the explosion.

- Darnley or his servant became aware of the plot to kill him. They tried to leave the house quickly and quietly. However, they were caught and killed outside the house.

- A number of his followers, including a Wyll Blackadder, were executed after confessing their involvement in the plot.

However,

- Some historians argue that Bothwell was set up by his enemies. The evidence against him was compiled by his enemies after he had been forced to flee the country.

- His men confessed under torture. The evidence is unreliable.

Theory 3

- Darnley was killed by a number of Protestant lords who had quarrelled with him over the Rizzio murder. These included the Earl of Morton, the Earl of Moray and Archibald Douglas – a cousin of Darnley.

- They had returned to Edinburgh in December 1566. Darnley had left for Glasgow at that time.

- A group of women had seen a number of men running away from Kirk o' Field shortly after the explosion. An expensive slipper was found left behind. (Wearing slippers would create less noise than heavy riding boots.) Local people in Edinburgh believed that it belonged to Douglas.

- Another witness claimed that she had heard Darnley shouting: 'Pity me, kinsmen, for the sake of Jesus Christ who pitied all the world' after the explosion. Darnley was begging for his life. **Kinsmen** meant relations or cousins.

Theory 4

- The explosion was the work of Darnley. He had planned it to kill Mary and many of the other nobles.

- The plot backfired. Darnley was caught by his enemies and murdered after they discovered his intentions.

 DON'T FORGET

The only people to be executed for the murder were servants who were employed by Bothwell.

 VIDEO LINK

Go to the Digital Zone to watch a clip containing further speculation about Darnley's murder: www.brightredbooks.net/N5History.

 ONLINE TEST

To take a test on this topic, go to the Digital Zone: www.brightredbooks.net/N5History.

THINGS TO DO AND THINK ABOUT

1. Describe the events surrounding the murder of Darnley in 1567.

2. Which of the theories concerning the Darnley murder do you think is the most likely? Give reasons for your answer.

MARY AND BOTHWELL

Bothwell

THE LOSS OF DARNLEY

The murder of Darnley left Mary in a very fragile state. Her behaviour after the killing caused concern among her supporters and presented her enemies with an opportunity to attack her.

In **Source A**, John Knox gives his views on Mary in one of his books.

> *The Queen, according to the ancient custom, should have kept herself forty days within. Before the twelfth day she went out to Seton, Bothwell never parting from her side. There they went out to the fields, to behold guns and pastimes. The King's armour, horse, and household stuff, were bestowed upon the murderers.*

One of the most serious problems was when Mary was carried off by Bothwell to Dunbar.

In **Source B**, one of Mary's supporters, Lord Herries, describes what happened.

> *The Queen went to Stirling to visit her son; but Bothwell, with six hundred horsemen, went out to meet her as she was coming back. He carried her to Dunbar castle, where he detained her until she granted both to complete the marriage, and grant pardon of this ravishment; in which was included, all other treasonable acts and filthy deeds done in times past.*

In **Source C**, another of Mary's supporters, James Melville, describes why Mary married Bothwell in May 1567.

> *The Queen could not but marry him, seeing he had ravished her and lain with her against her will. I cannot tell how nor by what law he parted with his own wife, sister to the Earl of Huntly.*

This placard appeared in Edinburgh after the death of Darnley. The hare was the symbol of Bothwell. The daggers suggested that he was involved in the murder. The mermaid was the symbol of a prostitute.

ONLINE

Visit the Digital Zone and click the links to read more about Mary's third husband: www.brightredbooks.net/N5History.

DON'T FORGET

Although Bothwell was a Protestant, he had been a supporter of Mary's mother, Mary of Guise.

OTHER REPERCUSSIONS

The behaviour of Mary was seen as shocking. It caused many people to turn against her. She was with a man who was seen as the murderer of her husband. She also upset many Catholics because she had married a Protestant who had just divorced his wife. It also presented ambitious lords, such as Moray, with the chance to replace her. In June 1567, the nobles formed an army. They referred to themselves as the Confederate Lords. They claimed that they wanted to free Mary from Bothwell's influence. They also claimed that they wanted to avenge Darnley.

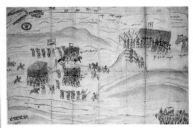

The two sides met at Carberry Hill outside Edinburgh. There was no fighting. The royal army was not as well supplied as the nobles. Furthermore, many of the queen's men started to slip away, believing they were going to lose. Mary gave herself up, expecting to be treated as a queen and thinking that she would be able to strike a deal. Bothwell fled from the field, hoping to find support. He failed, and left the country. He eventually died in a Danish prison.

This painting shows the events at Carberry Hill. Mary is positioned between the two armies. She is about to surrender. Bothwell is shown fleeing from the battlefield.

ONLINE

Go to the Digital Zone to read more about Bothwell and Mary, Queen of Scots: www.brightredbooks.net/N5History.

MARY A PRISONER IN SCOTLAND

Mary was taken as a prisoner to Loch Leven Castle near Kinross, where she spent the next eleven months. Shortly after her arrival, she miscarried with dead twins. She was also forced to abdicate in favour of her young son James, whom she was not allowed to see.

Over time, she was able to win the trust of two of the people at Loch Leven Castle. George Douglas (brother of the governor of the Castle) and an orphan, Willie Douglas, began to help her. Together they smuggled letters out of the castle to Mary's supporters. Eventually, they were able to steal the keys for the castle and escape with a disguised Mary.

In **Source D**, the Venetian Ambassador to Scotland describes Marys escape from Loch Leven. It was written around three weeks after Marys escape.

Loch Leven Castle, where Mary was kept prisoner

> *Guard was continually kept at the castle gate day and night, except during supper, and the key was always placed on the table where the Governor took his meals. The Queen arranged that a servant of the Governor's, when carrying a dish, to the table of his master, should place the napkin on the key, and in removing the napkin take up the key with it, and carry it away unnoticed by anyone.*
>
> *Having done so, the servant then went directly to the Queen, and told her all was ready. She and the servant went quietly to the door, and he having opened it, the Queen went out with him and locked the gate outside with the same key,*
>
> *They then got into a little boat which was kept for the service of the castle, and, she made a signal to those who awaited her.*

 VIDEO LINK

Go to the Digital Zone to learn more about Mary's abdication and time in captivity in Loch Leven castle: www.brightredbooks.net/N5History.

THE BATTLE OF LANGSIDE

Mary gathered an army and headed towards Dumbarton Castle. Here she hoped to be able to gain help from her relatives in France. Instead, her army was defeated at the Battle of Langside. The battle was over in 45 minutes. It was decided that Mary should flee to England.

In **Source E**, a 19th Century historian describes the results of the battle of Langside in 1568.

> *Of all the many battles in which Scots have fought against Scots, perhaps the only one which can be claimed to have had a decisive influence on the fortunes of the nation was at Langside. There was much more at stake than in any other engagement during Scotland's tragic and frequent civil wars. Compared to any of the great battles of Scottish history, the engagement was no more than a skirmish, yet it settled the destiny of Scotland. It established the reformed church, put an end to the French alliance and shattered the last hope of Mary Stuart.*

In **Source F**, a historian writing in the 21st Century discussed the results of the Battle of Langside.

> *This is somewhat overstating the case, as French influence had declined with the death of Mary of Guise in 1560 and it would in fact take several years and civil war before the authority of James VI under the Regency and Protestantism as the religion of Scotland were fully established. The immediate result of the battle was Mary's flight to England, where she was effectively held under house arrest at various castles by Elizabeth I.*

 VIDEO LINK

Watch the clip on the Digital Zone to learn more about the Battle of Langside: www.brightredbooks.net/N5History.

 THINGS TO DO AND THINK ABOUT

1. Explain why many nobles and other people turned against Mary in the summer of 1567.
2. Compare the views of John Knox and Lord Herries about the relationship between Mary and Bothwell.
3. Describe the events which resulted in Mary fleeing to England in 1568.
4. Compare sources E and F about the effects of the Battle of Langside.

ONLINE TEST

To take a test on this topic, go to the Digital Zone: www.brightredbooks.net/N5History.

MARY IN ENGLAND

MARY'S PLEA TO ELIZABETH

After her defeat at Langside, Mary fled south. She spent her last night in Scotland at Kirkcudbright. The next day, she travelled by boat across the Solway Firth and landed near Workington. She was taken to Carlisle, where she wrote to Queen Elizabeth asking for assistance to reclaim her throne.

Option	Problem
Give Mary an army and restore her to the throne.	Elizabeth preferred to have a Protestant neighbour rather than a Catholic one.
Allow Mary to go to France.	Mary may receive military support from Catholic France which could threaten Elizabeth.
Hand Mary over to the Scottish nobles.	Mary could be executed. She was a queen and cousin of the English queen. Elizabeth did not believe it was right to risk execution.
Meet Mary.	Mary had claimed the English throne when she became the Dauphiness. A meeting might be seen as supporting this claim.

DON'T FORGET

Mary's arrival in England was an unwelcome problem for Elizabeth. Mary was a threat. Catholics believed that she was the rightful queen of England. Elizabeth had a number of options for how to deal with her.

VIDEO LINK

Go to the Digital Zone to watch a clip and learn more about Mary in England: www.brightredbooks.net/N5History.

ELIZABETH'S RESPONSE

Elizabeth did nothing. Instead, Mary was kept confined in castles in the Midlands of England – far enough from London to ensure that there was little opportunity for a meeting of the two queens.

In 1568, Elizabeth eventually agreed to hold a conference to look at the accusations that the Scottish lords had levelled at Mary. The Earl of Moray brought a number of letters which he claimed had been found in the possession of one of Bothwell's servants at Carberry Hill. They were referred to as the **Casket Letters,** as they were found in a box or casket. It was claimed that the letters were written by Mary to Bothwell.

The casket that the letters were kept in

Source A shows extracts from one of the Casket Letters. Darnley was being treated for illness and was taking medicine and having regular baths as part of his treatment. Craigmillar was a castle near Edinburgh. It was where Darnley was originally going to stay on his return to the capital. These extracts may suggest that Mary and Bothwell are looking for a less obvious way of killing Darnley.

> *Cursed be this pocky fellow that troubles me thus much.*
>
> *Send me word what I shall do, and whatever happen to me, I will obey you. Think also if you will not find some invention more secret by physick (medicine), for he is to take physick at Craigmillar and the baths also, and shall not come forth of long time.*
>
> *Burn this letter, for it is too dangerous, neither is there anything well said in it, for I think upon nothing but upon grief if you be at Edinburgh.*
>
> *Love me always as I shall love you.*

Mary's defence was simple. The letters were forgeries. She also stated that some of her letters to Darnley had been altered to make it appear that they were written to Bothwell. The investigation dragged on for some time before it was ended. No decision could be reached. The original letters were returned to the Earl of Moray. They disappeared some years later, and only copies are left. Mary was to remain in prison for the next nineteen years.

DON'T FORGET

The Protestant lords would have benefited if Mary had been found to have been involved in the murder of Darnley. She may have been executed. This would have removed her as a threat to the Protestant lords.

MARY AND CATHOLIC PLOTS

By 1586, Mary was becoming desperate. She had been moved from one castle to another to prevent her involvement in plots. However, her presence in England continued to be a threat to Elizabeth. A number of events increased this threat:

1569 – The **Northern Rising**. A group of English nobles, led by the Catholic Duke of Northumberland, rebelled against Elizabeth. They believed that they were being persecuted due to their religion. Their solution was to free Mary and put her on the English throne. The uprising failed, and Northumberland was executed.

1570 – The pope issued a decree, **'Regnans in Excelsis'**, releasing Catholics from their allegiance to Elizabeth. English Catholics did not need to obey her.

1571 – The **Ridolfi Plot** was an attempt to assassinate Elizabeth and to put Mary on the throne. Ridolfi was a Catholic banker who had hoped to gain support from Spain for his plans. The Duke of Norfolk became involved. He would marry Mary and put her on the throne. The plot was discovered, and Norfolk was executed. Although there was evidence of Mary's involvement, Elizabeth refused to take action against her.

1572 – The **St Bartholomew's Day Massacre** of Huguenots (French Protestants) by French Catholics terrified many in England.

1584 – William the Silent was **murdered** by a Catholic assassin. He was the leader of the Dutch Protestants, who were rebelling against the Spanish.

1584 – The English Parliament introduced a **Bond of Association** which meant that any person who plotted against Elizabeth was to be executed.

1586 – James VI of Scotland signed the **Treaty of Berwick** with Elizabeth. This allowed for the two Protestant countries to cooperate against any threat from Catholic enemies. James also indicated that he would not accept his mother back as queen.

 **DON'T FORGET**

Some historians believe that James wanted to be recognised as the successor to Elizabeth. This was why he signed an agreement with the English queen.

 ONLINE

Go to the Digital Zone to read more about Elizabeth I of England: www.brightredbooks.net/N5History.

 THINGS TO DO AND THINK ABOUT

1. Why was Mary's arrival in England a problem for Elizabeth?

2. Evaluate the usefulness of Source A as evidence of Mary's involvement in the murder of her husband, Lord Darnley.
   (You may want to comment on who wrote it, when they wrote it, why they wrote it, what they say or what has been missed out.)

3. Explain why the Casket letters did not result in Mary being found guilty of having murdered Darnley.

4. Explain why Mary Queen of Scots was a threat to Elizabeth.

5. Why might the murder of William the Silent in 1584 have worried Elizabeth?

6. Explain why the Bond of Association and the Treaty of Berwick were serious blows to Mary's ambitions.

 ONLINE TEST

To take a test on this topic, go to the Digital Zone: www.brightredbooks.net/N5History.

MARY'S TRIAL AND EXECUTION

THE BABINGTON PLOT

In 1586, Mary became involved in another plot. A young nobleman, Sir Anthony Babington, planned to assassinate Elizabeth and to put Mary on the throne. He and Mary exchanged coded letters that were smuggled in barrels of beer into Chartley Manor, where Mary was being kept. What neither realised was that the letters were being carried by an English spy, who was handing them to Sir Francis Walsingham. He was one of Elizabeth's secretaries, and organised spies to protect her. He quickly found the evidence which showed Mary's involvement.

Source A is an extract from one of Mary's letters to Babington. When Walsingham read the letter, he drew a small gallows in the margin beside this quote.

> *The affairs being thus prepared and forces in readiness both without and within the realm, then shall it be time to set the six gentlemen to work taking order upon the accomplishment of their design, I may be suddenly transported out of this place, and that all your forces in the same time be on the field to meet me in waiting for the arrival of foreign aid.*

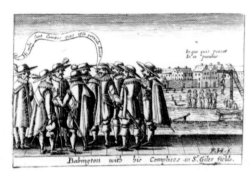

A contemporary drawing of the Babington plotters

Mary was put on trial in October 1586 at Fotheringhay Castle in Northamptonshire. She was not allowed a lawyer or to call witnesses. Nor did she know how much evidence had been gathered against her. She was unaware that Walsingham had deciphered her letters or that Babington had confessed under torture. Although she defended herself well, the verdict did not come as a surprise to the English nobles who were judging her. She was found guilty and sentenced to death.

a b c d e f g h i k l m n o p q r s t u x y z
o ‡ ⋏ ⧻ ᴑ ⊏ θ ∞ ɩ ᕒ ⋊ ∥ ⌀ ▽ ꙅ ꟽ ꜰ △ ℇ ꞓ 7 8 9

The code used by Mary and Babington

ELIZABETH SIGNS THE DEATH WARRANT

It took three months for Elizabeth to sign the order for Mary's execution. This was for several reasons:

- Mary was her cousin.

- Mary was a queen. Elizabeth was not keen to execute another queen in case it undermined the idea of royal authority. Others may have used it to justify their attacks on Elizabeth.

- Elizabeth was concerned about the reaction of other countries – Spain and France in particular.

- Elizabeth hoped that others would kill Mary without a death warrant. The Bond of Association allowed for this to happen.

Eventually, Elizabeth signed the death warrant. It was contained in a pile of other documents which needed to be signed. Afterwards, she blamed her secretary for allowing this to happen and had him thrown into prison for a time.

ONLINE

Go to the Digital Zone to learn more about the Babington Plot and the codes used by Mary: www.brightredbooks.net/N5History.

MARY'S EXECUTION

Mary was executed at Fotheringhay on 8 February 1587. She entered the great hall accompanied by a handful of servants who assisted her. Before being executed, she removed her black dress to reveal a red petticoat. Red was the symbol of martyrdom. She was indicating that she was dying for her religion.

Source B is an account of the execution, written by an eyewitness, Robert Wynkfielde.

> *Then lying upon the block most quietly, and stretching out her arms cried, 'In manus tuas, Domine', three or four times. One of the executioners holding her slightly with one of his hands. She endured two strokes of the other executioner with an axe, she making very small noise or none at all, and not stirring any part of her from the place where she lay. The executioner cut off her head, saving one little gristle, which being cut asunder, he lifted up her head to the view of all the assembly and bade 'God Save the Queen'. Then, her dress of lawn falling from off her head, it appeared as grey as one of threescore and ten years old, cut very short. Her lips stirred up and down a quarter of an hour after her head was cut off.*

This picture of Mary's execution was drawn at the time. It shows several stages of the execution. It shows Mary entering the great hall in the top left-hand corner. It also shows Mary having her black dress removed to reveal a red petticoat. Finally, the executioner can be seen in the top right-hand corner.

Mary was buried in Peterborough Abbey. Her son prevented Scottish nobles from attacking England. He spent a day in mourning. In 1603, Queen Elizabeth died. She was succeeded by Mary's son, James.

THINGS TO DO AND THINK ABOUT

1. Use Babington and Mary's code to encode Source A.

   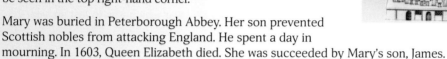

   a b c d e f g h i k l m n o p q r s t u x y z

2. Why do you think Walsingham drew a gallows sign in the margin when he read the quote shown in Source A?

3. Explain why Queen Elizabeth ordered the execution of Mary Queen of Scots in 1587.

4. Why did Elizabeth take several months to sign Mary's death warrant?

5. Describe the execution of Mary.

ONLINE

Learn more about the execution of Mary, Queen of Scots at the Digital Zone: www.brightredbooks.net/N5History.

DON'T FORGET

The source describes how Mary was executed. She was struck three times with the axe. When the head was picked up to display to the crowd, it was discovered she was wearing a wig. Her hair was short and grey.

DON'T FORGET

After 1603, James was known as James VI of Scotland and I of England. It can get confusing, as English historians often refer to him as James I.

ONLINE TEST

To take a test on this topic, go to the Digital Zone: www.brightredbooks.net/N5History.

REGENCIES AND CIVIL WAR

THE REGENCIES, 1567–1578

In 1567, Mary had surrendered to the Scottish nobles at Carberry Hill. She was forced to abdicate. She was replaced by her son, James. However, as he was too young to rule, a **regent** was appointed. A series of nobles filled this position over the next eleven years.

Noble	Tenure
James, Earl of Moray – Mary's half-brother. He was assassinated in Linlithgow by a member of the Hamilton family. They supported Mary.	August 1567 to January 1570
Matthew, 4th Earl of Lennox – Darnley's father. After the death of Moray, he was seen as the natural choice. However, he was unpopular. He was seen as being very closely involved with the English. He was also disliked as an individual.	January 1570 to September 1571
John, 6th Earl of Mar. He died of illness.	September 1571 to October 1572
James, 4th Earl of Morton.	November 1572 to March 1578

The Regents' biggest problem was the continuing support for Mary Queen of Scots. This led to two groups forming within Scotland and to a civil war which was to last six years.

The king's party

This was a group of nobles who wished to see James on the throne. They had the young king in their possession. However, when James was crowned at the Church of the Holy Rude in Stirling, many nobles failed to attend. The king's party claimed that they were fighting a war of religion.

The queen's party (or Marians)

There were a number of nobles who believed that Mary should not have been forced to abdicate. Some simply disliked Moray. Some families, such as the Hamiltons, saw James on the throne as evidence that their rivals, the Lennoxes, were increasing their influence. This group saw advantages in having Mary back. Many outside of Scotland saw this group as having 'just cause'.

CIVIL WAR

The fighting between the two groups continued for some time. The Marians held a number of castles around the country. These included both Dumbarton and Edinburgh. The king's party found it difficult to capture them without support from the English. However, Elizabeth of England was slow to give recognition to the Regents. She did not want to encourage the idea of rebellion among her own nobles.

Eventually, Dumbarton Castle fell to the king's party in April 1571. However, this setback only inspired the queen's party to make a daring raid on Stirling in September. If it had gone to plan, it could have ended the war. A group of around 400 soldiers were sent to Stirling to capture the leaders of the king's party, including the Regent, the Earl of Lennox. The plan was to take them prisoner and force them to agree to the demands of Mary's supporters.

DON'T FORGET

Politics at this time could get confusing. Some of the important individuals changed sides regularly. One example of this was Maitland of Lethington. He had been Mary's secretary. He had turned against her when she married Bothwell. However, he joined the Marians when the Casket Letters were taken south by Moray. He did not like the idea of a Scottish monarch being tried in an English court.

contd

In **Source A**, Sir James Melville describes the reasons for the failure of the raid in his *Memoirs*, published after his death.

> *The forces were at Stirling before four of the clock in the morning, and entered the town of Stirling at a little passage, led by a townsman called George Bell. They divided their men, and selected some to wait at every Lord's lodging, and a company with Captain Halkerston to wait at the market-cross, to keep good order, and to preserve the town-houses from being robbed.*
>
> *But because Captain Halkerston was not in time with his company to stand where he was appointed, a number of soldiers broke into merchants houses, and run here and there in disorder after the riches. Their masters were left all alone, after they had taken out all the lords from their lodgings. The masters were leading their captives down the steep causeway of Stirling on foot, intending to take their horses at the nether port, and ride to Edinburgh with their prisoners.*
>
> *But those within the castle being alarmed with the noise of the townsmen, crying out because of the riches taken from them, and seeing the disorder of their enemies, they came down upon them, and rescued all the prisoners save the Regent, who was shot in the back.*

In **Source B**, Melville describes the reaction of William Kirkcaldy of the Grange, who had planned the raid on Stirling.

> *'If he knew who had done that foul deed, his own hand should have revenged it.' For he knew the regent was inclined to peace, and was only driven on by the Earl of Morton.*

The death of Lennox was more of a blow to the queen's party than it was to the king's. It meant that the Marians' plans to force a settlement were in tatters. The new Regent, the Earl of Mar, died after a year. He was replaced by the Earl of Morton, who received assistance from England to bring the conflict to an end.

In February 1573, the English ambassador arranged a settlement known as the **Pacification of Perth**. Mary's supporters were allowed to keep their lands as long as they recognised Morton as Regent. They also had to end their attempts to restore the queen.

Around 1500 soldiers were sent north under Sir William Drury to capture Edinburgh Castle. They brought with them a large number of cannon and supplies of gunpowder.

The guns were used to destroy many of the castle's defences. By the end of May 1573, the 'Castilians' were forced to surrender. Although the ordinary soldiers were allowed to go free, their leaders were kept in prison or executed. Mary's old secretary, Maitland of Lethington, died in prison. William Kirkcaldy of the Grange was hanged at the Mercat Cross in Edinburgh. He had held Edinburgh Castle for Mary through the 'lang siege' of three years. His death marked the end of the civil war in Scotland.

 ONLINE TEST

To take a test on this topic, go to the Digital Zone: www.brightredbooks.net/N5History.

 THINGS TO DO AND THINK ABOUT

1. Explain why some Scottish Nobles were described as "Marians"

2. Which castles were held by the Marians?

3. Why was Queen Elizabeth reluctant to help the Kings party?

4. Explain why the Marians' raid on Stirling was a failure.

5. Describe the terms of the Pacification of Perth.

6. How important was English support in bringing about a victory for the king's party?

SCOTLAND BY 1587

JAMES VI

James was brought up under the control of the king's party. He was brought up as a Protestant and was influenced by his two tutors, Peter Young and George Buchanan. James received an education which included subjects such as Greek, French and arithmetic. He was also taught how to inform, persuade or motivate his subjects. James described his teachers' approach to education as:

'They made me speak Latin before I could speak Scots.'

James also learned a number of other lessons from his tutors.

James was encouraged to believe that his mother had murdered his father. Despite the education by Buchanan, James also believed that Mary's abdication was because she had allowed the nobles too much influence. He was determined to ensure the domination of the crown over all influences.

Until 1578, he was virtually ignored as king. It was the Regents who made the decisions affecting the country. The Earl of Morton took several measures to deal with the problems facing the country. He made several important decisions.

- Morton was a Protestant and would ensure that Scotland would be a Protestant country. His regency was the first stable government to pursue this. However, there would be growing tension between the Reformed Church and the state. This became more of a problem after the Regent appointed ministers to be archbishops of St Andrews and Glasgow in 1571. The new Reformed Church was not consulted.

- Scotland would continue to pursue friendly relations with England. Morton copied some of the Acts introduced in England.

Source B is an extract from the English version of the **Oath of Supremacy** of 1572. Any person who was appointed to Church or public office had to swear loyalty to the monarch. Failure to do was regarded as treason.

I ____ now elect bishop of ____ do utterly testify and declare in my conscience that the Queen's Highness is the only supreme governor of this realm.

Source C is an extract from the Scots version of the Oath of Supremacy of 1572.

I _____ now elected bishop of ____ utterly testify and declare in my conscience that your majesty is the only lawful and supreme government of this realm.

- The country experienced a shortage of money. To solve the problem, Morton reduced the amount of silver in coins. This was called **debasement**. Taxation was also raised to pay for government spending.

In 1578, Morton was forced to resign as Regent. He managed to retain some power. However, in 1581, Morton's enemies managed to have him arrested, tried and executed for his part in the Darnley murder. In his place, the young king turned to Esme Stuart, who was a cousin of Darnley. He became the king's favourite and was rewarded with the title of the Duke of Lennox and was showered with gifts. He became a member of the Privy Council. One of Esme Stuart's friends, James Stewart, was created the Earl of Arran. Together they effectively controlled Scotland.

THE RUTHVEN RAID

A number of Protestant lords were worried by the amount of influence that Lennox and Arran had over the young king. Some believed that they were trying to restore Catholicism within the country. They were also concerned by Lennox's spending. In 1582,

contd

ONLINE

Go to the Digital Zone to read more about James's relationship with his mother: www.brightredbooks.net/N5History.

George Buchanan wrote a book about Mary Queen of Scots which was titled *A detection of the actions of Mary Queen of Scots, concerning the murder of her husband, and her conspiracy, adultery, and pretended marriage with Earl Bothwell.* **Source A** is an extract from this book.

She a young Woman, suddenly advanced to the highest degree of authority, when she had never seen with her eyes, heard with her ears, nor considered in her heart the form of a Kingdom governed by Law, and thereto was given extreme advice by her Kinsmen, who themselves attempted to set up a tyrannical rule in France, endeavoured to draw right, equity, laws and customs of Ancestors to her only beck and pleasure!

VIDEO LINK

Go to the Digital Zone to watch a clip about the childhood of James VI: www.brightredbooks.net/N5History.

William Ruthven, the Earl of Gowrie, kidnapped James and demanded that changes be made. Ruthven forced Lennox to go into exile. For ten months, he controlled Scotland. Eventually, James escaped his control. Arran returned to power, which he held for three years. In 1585, James finally took direct control of his country.

ANDREW MELVILLE AND THE CHURCH

Andrew Melville was to play a key role in establishing the nature of the Church in Scotland. He was the son of an Angus laird and had graduated from St Andrews University in 1564. He had travelled abroad, where he had continued to study and teach. In 1574, he had returned to Scotland as the principal of Glasgow University. Six years later, he had moved to St Andrews University, where he set up St Mary's College. This was to produce the ministers who were desperately needed to carry out the work of the Reformed Church.

Melville believed strongly that there should be no bishops in the Reformed Church. These had existed after 1560 because many reformers, including Knox, thought that ministers needed to be supervised. However, Melville argued that this would set some ministers above other ministers and this would be wrong. Ministers in the Reformed Church were to be regarded as equal. In 1578, Melville was able to have his ideas approved by the General Assembly.

The new Church was experiencing problems after 1567. It lacked funds and ministers. Furthermore, not everyone attended the new Church. The new parishes could be large; and some of the ministers were former priests. They would often offer Catholic ceremonies when required.

The Church was to play a large role in shaping Scottish society. The Kirk Session was able to punish those in the local community who it felt had committed an offence.

1576   Every householder worth 300 marks annual rent, and every yeoman or burgess having stock valued at £500, was compelled to buy a Bible and a Psalm-book, under a penalty of £10 (Scots).

1577   Sunday markets were forbidden. The penalty was the seizure of goods.

1579   The Presbytery of St Andrews prevented ministers from marrying all persons who could not recite the Lord's Prayer and the Ten Commandments.

THE BLACK ACTS, 1584

These were introduced by the king because of the Kirk's support for the Ruthven raid. They stated:

- The king was the head of the Kirk
- No assembly could meet without his permission
- Bishops were to be appointed by the crown
- Ministers were not to preach politics.

PRESBYTERY –
This would supervise the work of Ministers.

KIRK SESSION – This would make decisions which affected the local community.

MINISTER – This would be chosen by the Congregation

ELDERS – These were elected by the Congregation to help run the Church

CONGREGATION – This was members of the Church or Kirk.

THINGS TO DO AND THINK ABOUT

1. Why was Andrew Melville against having bishops in the reformed Church?

2. What do the following words mean: (a) Congregation (b) Elders (c) Presbyteries?

3. What influence did the Kirk have over people's lives after 1567?

4. Explain why the king and the Church of Scotland were disagreeing by 1584.

DON'T FORGET

Melville was responsible for writing the *Second Book of Discipline* (1581). This outlined his views that the Kirk received its authority from God. This was seen as a higher authority than the state. It also outlined his opposition to bishops. This was to cause conflict with James.

ONLINE TEST

To take a test on this topic, go to the Digital Zone: www.brightredbooks.net/ N5History.

GLOSSARY

THE ERA OF THE GREAT WAR, 1910–1928

Artillery   Heavy guns

Assassination   A murder

Battalions   A unit of soldiers – often 800 to 1000 men

Censorship   A method of preventing harmful or useful information from becoming widespread.

Constitutional Monarch   A King or Queen who is head of state. However their powers are limited. Most decisions are taken by Parliament and the Prime Minster.

Franchise   The right to vote

Khaki   The colour of British army uniforms

Lyddite   An explosive

Munitionettes   Women who made shells and bullets

Observation   Watching the enemy to learn about their strengths.

Patriotism   An attachment or love for one's own country.

Propaganda   A method of influencing your opinion. This often involves posters and newspapers.

Rationing   Used when food is in short supply. It means that everyone gets a supply of food.

Reconnaissance   A method of gaining information on enemy forces.

Recruiting   Getting people to join the armed forces.

Revolution   This means a rapid change. Often connected with a change in Government.

Snipers   A highly trained marksmen

THE WARS OF INDEPENDENCE, 1286–1328

Barons   A title which indicates that the person is a wealthy and powerful landowner.

Chronicle   A written record of events.

Earls   An important member of the nobility.

Excommunicated   This means being thrown out of the Church. A person who is excommunicated cannot take communion and therefore cannot go to heaven if they die.

Guardians   A person who looks after a property or person for someone else.

Knight   Groups of wealthy landowners who will fight for the Monarch when required.

Lodgings   Temporary accommodation.

Nobles   A term used to describe Knights, Barons and Earls.

Palisade   A wooden fence

Realm   A country ruled by a King or Queen.

Siege   Surrounding a fort or castle and forcing its surrender or capture through starvation or attack.

Sovereign   The ruler of a country

Succession   This involves the replacement of a King or Queen by the next in line to the throne – often their eldest male child.

MARY QUEEN OF SCOTS, AND THE REFORMATION, 1542–1587

Begrimed   Dirty

Burgh Commissioners   Men who were elected or appointed to represent an area such as a town.

Dauphin   The heir to the French throne.

Forgeries   This is where a document such as a letter is produced with the hope it will deceive people.

Medieval   A time period in History. Also known as the middle ages. It lasted from around the5th to the 15th Century.

Oath   This means that the person will remain loyal to their country or monarch.

Privy Council   A small group of advisors to a King or Queen.

Regent   A person who rules a country because the King or Queen is too young or incapable of making decisions.

Renaissance   A period in history. It dates from the 14th to the 17th Century. It marked a rebirth in interest in learning and the arts.

MIGRATION AND EMPIRE, 1830–1939

Agricultural   Farming

Colony   An area or territory which is under the control of another country.

Crofters   Farmers who lived in the Highlands and owned a small amount of land and a few animals.

Famine   A shortage of food.

Fertilisers   Material which is added to the soil which improves the amount of crops grown.

Immigrants   People who settle in a new country.

Industry   Factories or other sectors of the economy which produce or make items.

Missionary   A person who goes to other areas to spread their religion as well as education. They also encourage improvements in health.

Navigators   A term used to describe the workers who built canals and railways. It was usually shortened to Navvies.

Pogrom   An organised massacre.

Presbyterian   A branch of the Protestant Church.

Propaganda   A method of influencing your opinion. This often involves posters and newspapers.

Tenement   A housing block which contains a number of flats.

ACKNOWLEDGEMENTS

Permission has been sought from all relevant copyright holders and Bright Red Publishing are grateful for the use of the following:

Contains Parliamentary information licensed under the Open Parliament Licence v1.0:

(http://www.parliament.uk/site-information/copyright/open-parliament-licence/):

Two extracts from Hansard: HC Deb 07 August 1913 vol 56 cc1744-5 (p 7) and HC Deb 02 December 1925 vol 188 cc2232-3 (p 37).

Contains public sector information licensed under the Open Government Licence v2.0 (http://www.nationalarchives.gov.uk/doc/open-government-licence/version/2/):

A table from 'History of the Great War Based on Official Documents' by Committee of Imperial Defence (p 22); An extract from 'History of the Ministry of Munitions: Man power and dilution' Volume 4, H.M. Stationery Office, 1922 (p 35); The Bryce Report: Report of the Committee on Alleged German Outrages, May 12, 1915 (p 36); An extract from a speech made to the General Assembly of the Church of Scotland in March 1938 © National Archives of Scotland (p 63); An extract from Poor Law Enquiry (Scotland), Appendix 11. Minutes of Evidence, Synod of Glenelg, Parish of Duirinish (Scottish Record Office 1843) (p 70); Two extracts from National Records of Scotland, Miscellaneous Gifts and Deposits: GD1/813/15 & GD1/620/66 (p 76); An extract written on 4 February 1836, by George Mackenzie, taken from National Records of Scotland (Seaforth Muniments: GD46/13/198) (p 78); A letter written by J. A. Dick, 8 April 1892, taken from National Records of Scotland (Murray Beith and Murray WS: GD374/18/5) (p 78); A letter written by D. S. Murray, 1839 taken from National Records of Scotland (Lintrose Writs: GD68/2/140/1) (p 79); Drawing of the scene of Kirk o'Field, 1567 Public Record Office London (p 126); Painting of Carberry Hill from the National Archives: Catalogue reference: MPF 1/366 (p 128).

Photographs © CSG Glasgow Museums and Libraries Collections (pp 35, 47, 52, 64, 66 & 84);

Extracts from the Glasgow Herald © Herald & Times Group (pp 9, 15, 26, 33, 37, 38, 40, 41, 47, 69 & 71);

Extracts from 'Forgotten Scottish Voices from the Great War' by Derek Young, published by Tempus 2005 (p 12, 13 & 19);

Extracts © Johnston Publishing Ltd: The Scotsman (p 15) and the Kirkintilloch Herald (pp 38, 39 & 45);

Extracts from 'War Diary of the Fifth Seaforth Highlanders, 51st Highland Division', by D Sutherland published by John Lane, London, 1920 (pp 16 & 25);

Images © Imperial War Museum 'The Kitchen is the Key to Victory' poster (PST 6541) (p 33); Defence of the Realm Act poster (PST 8363) (p 34) and the painting 'Shop for machining 15-inch Shells: Singer Manufacturing Company, Clydebank' by Anna Airy (ART 2271) (p 44);

Extracts from 'The Scottish Nation 1700–2000' by T.M. Devine (Allen Lane and the Penguin Press 1999, Penguin Books 2000). Copyright © T.M. Devine, 1999 (p 67, 72, 76, 84);

Extracts from 'The Scots Overseas' by Gordon Donaldson, published by Greenwood Press, 1976 (pp 74 & 77);

Extracts from 'The Scottish empire' by Michael Fry, published by Tuckwell, 2001 (pp 79 & 84);

Extracts from 'William Wallace' by Andrew Fisher, published by Birlinn, 1986 (pp 100 & 101);

An extract from 'The Scottish Suffragettes (Scots' Lives)' by Leah Leneman, NMSE - Publishing Ltd (11 Dec 2000) (p 10); An extract from 'Norman Collins, Last Man Standing:The Memoirs of a Seaforth Highlander During the Great War' edited by Richard Van Emden, Pen & Sword Books Ltd, 2002) (p 13); An extract from 'The First Hundred Thousand: Being the Unofficial Chronicle of a Unit of "K (1),"' by Ian Hay, published by Houghton Mifflin Company (1916) (p 17); An extract from the Wigtown Free Press of 6 July 1916 © Stranraer & Wigtownshire Free Press (p 17); An extract from 'Road to St. Julien: The Letters of a Stretcher-bearer of the Great War by William St Clair', published by Leo Cooper Ltd 2003 (p 20); The picture 'Hop-picking in Flanders', 1917-1918. World War I Sketchbook Collection, Volume 2, Page 19, Special Collections, University of Victoria Libraries (p 20); Photo courtesy East Dunbartonshire Information and Archives (p 21); An extract from 'Promise of Greatness – the 1914 – 18 War' edited by George A. Panichas, published by John Day Company, 1968 (p 22); An extract from 'The Seventeenth Highland Light Infantry (Glasgow Chamber of Commerce Battalion) During the First World War 1914-1918' by John W. Arthur and Ion S. Munro, published by D.J. Clark, Glasgow (p 23); An extract from 'Scotland's Forgotten Valour' by Graham Ross, published by MacLean Press 1995 (p 23); A photo from 'Covenants with Death' by T.A. Innes and Ivor Castle, Daily Express 1934 (p25); An extract from 'Band of Brigands: The First Men in Tanks' by Harper Perennial (September 1, 2008) (p 27); An extract from 'History of the 16th Battalion the Highland Light Infantry (City of Glasgow Regiment)' by Thomas Chalmers, published by Naval & Military Press 2003 (p 31); An extract from 'An English Wife in Berlin: a Private Memoir of Events, Politics, and Daily Life in Germany Throughout the War and the Social Revolution of 1918' by Evelyn Princess Blücher, published by Constable 1920 (p 31); Extracts from the Lennox Herald of 26 January 1918 & The Dumbarton Herald of 14 August 1915 © Trinity Mirror plc (p 33); An extract from 'Tommy's War: A First World War Diary 1913–1918' by Thomas Cairns Livingstone, published by HarperPress 2008. Reproduced with permission of Curtis Brown Group Ltd, London on behalf of Shaun Sewell. Copyright © Shaun Sewell 2008 (p 34); The cartoon "This is how I deal with small fry" by Louis Raemaekers, public domain (p 36); A poster courtesy National Library of Scotland (p 36); Photo reproduced with the permission of Leeds University Library (GB 0206 Liddle Collection CO 061) (p 39); Extracts from 'Voices from war and some labour struggles: personal recollections of war in our century by Scottish men and women' by Ian MacDougall, published by Mercat Press, 1995 (p 39); Advert for the Victoria Rubber Company, from www.aviationancestry.com (p 40); The painting 'Alexander Mackay from Dunbeath in Caithness' courtesy The Wick Society, Johnston Collection (p 41); The photo 'H.M.S. Hood 1924' by State Library of South Australia (CC BY 2.0)1 (p 42); The photo 'H.M.S. Argus' by the U.S. Navy, public domain (p 43); An advert taken from Grace's Guide (GFDL v1.2)2 http://www.gnu.org/licenses/fdl-1.2.html#SEC1 (p 43); Photo courtesy National Media Museum/Science & Society Picture

Library (p 46); An extract from 'The Cordite Makers' taken from 'The Young Rebecca: Writings of Rebecca West 1911-17' by Rebecca West © Viking Press (p 46); An extract from 'On the Health of Munition Workers in a Shell Filling Factory.' by Kennedy Dalziel. Glasgow Medical Journal 97, 1922 (p 47); An extract from 'A History of the Scottish Women's Hospitals' edited by Eva Shaw McLaren - London : Hodder and Stoughton, 1919 (p 48); An extract written by Winston Churchill, reproduced with permission of Curtis Brown, London on behalf of the Estate of Sir Winston Churchill. Copyright © Winston S. Churchill (p 48); An extract from War Memoirs of David Lloyd George: Volume 1 1918', published by Ivor Nicholson & Watson, 1933 (p 50); An extract from 'Modern Scotland 1914–2000' by Richard Finlay, published by Profile Books, 2005 (p 53); An extract from 'A Minstrel in France' by Sir Harry Lauder, published by Hearst's International Library Co, Inc 1918 (p 58); Photo © bpk, Berlin (p 62); An extract from 'Who belongs to Glasgow?' by Mary Edward, published by Luath Press Ltd, 1993 (p 65); An extract © Tony Jaconelli (p 65); Photo © U.S. Department of Agriculture (CC BY-ND 2.0)3 (p 66); An extract and image from the Illustrated London News, December 22, 1849 (public domain) (p 66);

An extract from 'The Irish in Scotland' by J. E. Handley, published by Cork University Press 1943 (p 68); A photo by Thomas Annan from 1868, public domain (p 68); A cartoon from Punch Magazine 1855, public domain (p 69); An extract from 'Scottish Voices, 1745-1960: An Anthology' by T. C. Smout and Sydney Wood, pushed by Harper Collins 1990 (p 70); An extract from Caledonia Australis: Scottish Highlanders on the Frontier of Australia', by Don Watson, published by Vintage Australia, The Random House Group (p 70); A poster © Canadian Pacific Archives (image no A.6199) (p 72); Photo by Francis M. Fritz 1907, public domain (p 75); Photo by Alexander Gardner, October 3 1862, public domain (p 75); Logo for Pinkerton Detective Agency, public domain (p 75); Photo by Canapress 1920, public domain (p 76); Photo by George Lancefield 1875, public domain (p 77); Photo by William James Topley 1908, public domain (p 77); Photo by John A. Cooper, 1901-2, public domain (p 77); Sketch by James & Edward Backhouse 1842, public domain (p 78); Poster from New Zealand Colony's Office, Glasgow, public domain (p 80); An advertisement: New Zealand. High Commission (Great Britain). New Zealand wants domestic servants; good homes, good wages. [ca 1912].. Information about New Zealand for domestic servants / issued by the High Commissioner for New Zealand...London, [ca 1912].. Ref: Eph-A-IMMIGRATION-1912-cover. Alexander Turnbull Library, Wellington, New Zealand. http://natlib.govt.nz/records/22908679 (p 80); An extract from the Otago News, December 1848, public domain (p 80); Logo © University of Otago (p 81); Photo by Grentidez, public domain (p 82); The logo of the British Indian Steam Navigation Company, public domain (p 83); Photo by Ghemachandar, public domain (p 83); Advertisement © Tony Hisgett (CC BY 2.0)1 (p 84); Photo © James Finlay Limited (p 85); Photo © The Black Watch Castle and Museum (p 86); Photo by Katie Chan (CC BY-SA 3.0)4 (p 86); Photo by Colin Smith (CC BY-SA 2.0)4 (p 90); A painting of William Wallace, taken from the collections of the Smith Art Gallery and Museum, Stirling (p 96); An extract from 'William Wallace: the true story of Braveheart' by Chris Brown, published by Tempus 2005 (p 101); An extract from 'Robert Bruce & The Community of the Realm of Scotland' by Geoffrey W. S. Barrow published by Edinburgh University Press (p 106); Painting of Cardinal David Beaton, courtesy Blairs Museum Trust (p 114); The drawing 'Burning of Patrick Hamilton at St. Andrews, 1528'. Illustration for The Scots Worthies (Blackie, 1879) © Look and Learn (p 115); The painting 'Henry VIII' by the artist Hans Holbein 1537. Courtesy National Museums Liverpool (Walker Art Gallery) (p 116); The Painting 'The Children of Henry VIII, c.1650-1680' © The Duke of Buccleuch, Boughton House/ PA photos (p 116); Photo © Peter Stubbs (www.edinphoto.org.uk) (p 116); Painting of Mary of Guise by Francois Clouet. Bequeathed by John Jones (public domain); digital image © Victoria and Albert Museum, London (p 118); An extract from 'Scotland before the Industrial Revolution: an economic and social history, c1050-c1750' by Ian Whyte, published by Longman 1995 (p 119); The painting 'Mary, Queen of Scots (1542-87) and John Knox (c.1512-72), Sidley, Samuel (1829-96)/© Towneley Hall Art Gallery and Museum, Burnley, Lancashire/The Bridgeman Art Library (p 121); The painting 'Henry Lord Darnley (1545-67) and Charles, Earl of Lennox (1555-76) after Hans Eworth (c.1525-c.1578)', Sullivan, Rhoda (fl.1905-10)/© Leeds Museums and Art Galleries (Temple Newsam House) UK/The Bridgeman Art Library (p 122); The painting 'The Murder of David Rizzio' by Sir William Allan/Scottish National Gallery – NG 1677 (p 124); The painting 'James Hepburn, 4th Earl of Bothwell, c 1535 - 1578. Third husband of Mary Queen of Scots'/Scottish National Portrait Gallery – PG 869 (p 128); The painting 'Queen Elizabeth I: The Darnley Portrait' © National Portrait Gallery, London (p 130); The drawing 'Babington with his Complices in St. Giles Fields', 1586 (engraving) (b/w photo), English School, (17th century) (after)/Private Collection/ The Bridgeman Art Library (p 132); Sketch from Robert Beale's 'The Order and Manner of the Execution of Mary Queen of Scots, Feb. 8, 1587 (p 133).

(CC BY 2.0)1 http://creativecommons.org/licenses/by/2.0/

(GFDL v1.2)2 http://www.gnu.org/licenses/fdl-1.2.html#SEC1

(CC BY-ND 2.0)3 http://creativecommons.org/licenses/by-nd/2.0/

(CC BY-SA 3.0)4 http://creativecommons.org/licenses/by-sa/3.0/

(CC BY-SA 2.0)5 http://creativecommons.org/licenses/by-sa/2.0/

Marie Theres Nölle

Formen der Darstellung in Hartmanns «Iwein»

Herbert Lang
Bern und Frankfurt/M.
1974

ISBN 3 261 01020 7

©

Herbert Lang & Cie AG, Bern (Schweiz)
Peter Lang GmbH, Frankfurt/M. (BRD)
1974. Alle Rechte vorbehalten.

THEMA

Mit unerklärlichem Reiz entzieht sich Hartmann von Aues "Iwein" jeder eindeutig fixierenden Interpretation. Das erste, womit man ihn einfangen zu können glaubt, ist: Märchenstimmung. Denn ähnlich wie das Märchen versetzt die Lektüre des "Iwein" den Leser in einen seltsamen Schwebezustand, schliesst ihn auf für Unwirkliches und Unvermitteltes. Aber das Märchen entspringt einem einhellig durchgehenden Formwillen; die Wirkung des "Iwein" hingegen geht von einem vielschichtig Zusammengefügten aus.

Wie in einem Kaleidoskopbild, in dem Glassteine von verschiedener Farbe und Schwere im richtigen Gleichgewicht erscheinen, sind hier objektiv gedachte Elemente, d.h. verfügbare Themen und Figuren, subjektiv gewählt und verdichtet. Der Eindruck unbeschreiblicher Anmut wird wiederholt durchsetzt von verfremdenden Effekten; die verschiedenartigsten Töne klingen zusammen, und weit entlegene Bereiche schieben sich ineinander.

Während das Märchen seine Welt fraglos, mit traumartiger Sicherheit entfaltet, schaltet sich im "Iwein" der Dichter immer wieder selbst zwischen das Geschehen, wundert sich, deutet es, relativiert es. Und obwohl der mittelhochdeutsche "Iwein" dem chrétienschen Text fast lückenlos folgt, gewinnt der Roman bei der Übernahme dennoch eine neue, wesentliche Dimension. Ohne den Stoff auffallend zu verändern, hat ihm Hartmann die eigene künstlerische Konzeption eingefärbt, welche die in seinen Legendendichtungen vertiefte Anschauung in subtiler Ausformung auch dem Artusroman unterlegt. In beiden Gattungsformen sind es Massstäbe von höchstem Rang und vollkommener Klarheit, die die Ausrichtung seiner Kunst bestimmen, Werte, welche in der Verlängerung auf absolute Kategorien zuzustreben scheinen: auf das Bonum, Verum und Pulchrum. Eindringlicher als Chrétien stellt Hartmann die Frage nach dem Guten und nach der verbindlichen Wirklichkeit seiner Erzählung und bringt, indem er sie solcherart erhellt und beschneidet, auch ihre Schönheit intensiver zum Leuchten.

Durch diese Zielsetzung, durch die Verbindungen über das Gesellschaftliche hinaus, erschöpft sich das Werk nicht in bestrickender und belehrender Unterhaltung, sondern ist gleichzeitig Öffnung auf das transzendente Sein, in dessen Bereich es teilhabend hineinragt und von da her, als schattenhafter Abglanz, seinen Wert gewinnt.

Auf die *Gutheit* ('güete') der Gegenstände und Motivationen, auf den exemplarischen Charakter der Figuren und Szenen, die 'moralitatis gratia', fällt in allen Werken Hartmanns besonders helles Licht[1]. Wo Hartmann einen Stoff übernimmt,

---

1 Dabei umfasst 'güete' wie alle zentralen höfischen Begriffe ein weites Bedeutungsspektrum, bezeichnet sowohl die Vortrefflichkeit weltlichen und ritterlichen Gutes als christliche Tugenden.
Schon im "Erec" ist Enites 'güete' stellvertretend der lichte Gegenpol zu Erecs schuldbefangenem Sein. Religiöse Vertiefung erfährt sie in den beiden ritterlichen Legenden: das präzisierende 'guot' im 'guoten sündaere' ("Greg." 176, 2552, 2606, 4001) meint seine Demut angesichts menschlicher Schuldhaftigkeit und ist Ansatz- und Kernpunkt der

verdeutlicht und idealisiert er. Er holt ihn aus der Unbefangenheit spontanen, spielerischen Erzählens hinein in seine eigene Schau und bezieht ihn auf eine im Sichtwinkel der Idealität erfasste Wirklichkeit. Stärker als bei Chrétien schimmert in Bild und Bewegung die Übereinstimmung mit christlich vorgezeichneten Grundfiguren durch.

Im Roman vom Löwenritter Iwein, der im Zauberbereich der Laudine durch das Quellenabenteuer Land und Herrin gewinnt, aus der unbekümmerten Sicherheit jählings ins Dunkle, in die Verbannung gerät und auf dem einsamen Weg der Demut und Hilfeleistung, vom Löwen begleitet, das Verlorene wiedererringt und dabei sich selbst in einer neuen Tiefe und Fülle des Wesens erfährt, taucht der zunächst noch unerschlossene Begriff der 'güete', gleich einem Siegel, schon in der über Chrétien hinausweisenden Eingangssentenz auf:

Iwein 1   Swer an rehte güete
           wendet sîn gemüete,
           dem volget saelde und êre[2].

Als durchgeistigendes Mass ist damit das Gute der Erzählung vorangestellt, und das Publikum, dem sich die Tragweite und Problematik dieser 'rehten güete' in den auslegenden Stationen von Iweins Weg, in Bild und Gegenbild enthüllen, tritt im Kunstwerk selbst in ihren Wirkkreis, wobei der Akzent in dieser Sentenz unüberhörbar auf der aktiven 'Wendung' liegt, die der Hörer vollziehen und mit der er dem Anruf der Dichtung antworten soll.

Die *Wahrheit*[3] dieses Werks: seine lebendige, geistige Kraft, wird vom Dichter nicht als persönliches, selbstverantwortetes Zeugnis konzipiert, sondern durch seine Inspiration in der Verborgenheit des vorhandenen Materials wahrgenommen und offenbar gemacht. Hartmann kommt dabei die Übersicht und Sammlung des Nacherzählers zu; klärend und erhellend durchdringt er den vorgeformten Stoff, markiert die Schwerpunkte und sucht den ihm angemessenen Ton. Indem er der Scheinwelt der Matière de Bretagne in umkreisenden Reflexionen auf den Leib

---

Interpretation; im "Armen Heinrich", bedeutet Heinrichs 'niuwe güete' (1254) Selbsterkenntnis und damit Selbstverzicht und kündigt seine entscheidende innere Umkehr an.
"Erec" hg. von Alb. Leitzmann, (3) Tübingen 1963 (ATB); "Gregorius" hg. von Herm. Paul, (10) Tübingen 1963 (ATB); "Der arme Heinrich" hg. von H. de Boor, Frankfurt 1963.
2 Wer seinen Sinn nach den "wahrhaften Gütern und Werten des Lebens" (Ruh) ausrichtet, dem wird [vor Gott und den Menschen] Heil und Ehre zuteil.
  Zitiert wird nach der Ausgabe von Hans Naumann und Hans Steiger, Leipzig 1933 (Deutsche Literatur in Entwicklungsreihen).
3 Der Begriff selbst tritt im höfischen Roman mit unterschiedlicher Bedeutungsintensität auf. Die Wahrheitsbeteuerung des Dichters ist rhetorischer Schmuck, die dem Erzählten Gewicht verleiht; als kontrastierendes Ornament, schillernd zwischen Ernst, nämlich wertmässiger Aufhöhung des Erzählten, und provozierender Ironie, ist sie beinahe mutwillig oft gerade dort eingesetzt, wo der Autor etwas Unglaubwürdiges oder Erfundenes vorträgt. Auf die Grundbedeutung: inneres Wesen (essentia) weist "Erec" 4837. Wolfgang Dittmann scheidet die 'wârheit' der Faktizität, an die der Dichter gebunden ist und die Dittmann als niedere, nichtssagende 'wârheit' bezeichnet, von der ranghöheren 'wârheit' der Deutung, die der Freiheit und Inspiration des einzelnen Dichters entstammt. " 'Dune hâst niht wâr, Hartman.' Zum Begriff der wârheit in Hartmanns Iwein", FG Ulrich Pretzel, Berlin 1963, 150–161.

rückt, sie beim Wort nimmt und mit der erfahrbaren Wirklichkeit in Beziehung bringt, schreitet er auf dem von Chrétien gewiesenen Weg voran, intensiviert er die Suche, so dass die Wahrheitsstruktur des 'maere' — und dazu gehört im christlichen Mittelalter auch seine Anwendbarkeit, sein Heilscharakter im Nachvollzug — in gesteigerter Helle entzifferbar wird. Das mit Bestimmtheit gesprochene 'ich weiz baz' (1875) zeugt von der Bewusstheit seines Gestaltens und ruft zu hellhörigem Wahrnehmen auf: Selbst geringfügige Abweichungen sind als geleistete Überformung zu werten und verändern die innern und äussern Proportionen des Werks.

Diese Proportionen aber sind es, in denen die *Schönheit* des mittelalterlichen Kunstwerks fassbar wird. Schön ist in der Anschauung dieser Zeit das Sichtbarwerden des Guten und Wahren[4].

In dichter, hellklingender Sprache, mit einem Höchstmass an claritas hat es Hartmann im "Iwein" erkennbar gemacht und nach einer eigenen, unvergleichbaren Gesetzlichkeit realisiert. Etwas von der poetischen Spontaneität, der französischen Lebhaftigkeit hat das Werk in der Umsetzung wohl eingebüsst; 'ebene unde sleht', in souveräner Einfachheit bietet es sich ruhiger delectatio dar, wobei der Kommentar des Dichters das bewegte Geschehen der Handlung immer wieder in den rechten Abstand besonnener Beschauung rückt. Dieser Wechsel zwischen vorgetragener Erzählung und fragender, deutender oder ironisierender Rede verleiht dem Werk einen neuen rhythmischen Reiz: Zur schimmernden Handlung gesellt sich die Reflexion. Der Roman hebt sich durch diese Stufung von der kontinuierlichen Erzählart Chrétiens ab, schafft Beziehungspunkte und Perspektiven und gewinnt so an geistiger Dynamik.

Denn für das mittelalterliche Publikum bedeutet die Begegnung mit Dichtung nicht blosses Registrieren, sondern aktives Weiterdenken, Umformen und Verbinden[5]. Jeder Text gibt Anstoss, über das Gegebene hinauszugehen, die Linien der Zeichen und Verkürzungen assoziierend weiterzuziehen, so dass ein immer weiteres geistiges Gelände aufgedeckt wird[6]. Der Versuch, solch schöpferischem 'erdenken'

---

4 Vgl. dazu Rosario Assunto, Die Theorie des Schönen im Mittelalter, Köln 1963. Die Einheit von Gut, Wahr und Schön, wie sie das Mittelalter begreift, kommt im "Iwein"-Prolog unmittelbar zum Ausdruck, wo die drei Eigenschaften, in enger Berührung, auf König Artus als Exempelfigur vereinigt werden.

5 Ein grundlegender Unterschied des modernen Kunstwerks zu dem früherer Zeiten liegt vor allem in seiner ästhetischen Ausrichtung. Valéry formuliert ihn im Hinblick auf die Malerei: "L'art moderne tend à exploiter presque exclusivement la sensibilité sensorielle, aux dépens de la sensibilité générale ou affective, et de nos facultés de construction, d'addition des durées et de transformation par l'esprit." Degas, Danse, Dessin. Paris (Gallimard) 1965, 179.

6 Klösterliche Schriftmeditation wirkt sich durch den Einfluss der Predigt und die Klerikerbildung der Dichter auch auf das Verständnis weltlicher Dichtung aus. In seinem "Didascalicon" gibt Hugo von Sankt Viktor Anleitungen zur rechten Art des Lesens: III, 9 (de studio legendi): "Modus legendi in dividendo constat. omnis divisio incipit a finitis, et ad infinita usque progreditur." (Lesen besteht im auseinanderhaltenden, vereinzelnden [Meditieren]. Dieses geht stets von den genannten, bestimmten Dingen aus und dringt zu den ungenannten, unbegrenzten vor.) Die kritische Ausgabe des Textes stammt von Charles Henry Buttimer: Hugonis de Sancto Victore Didascalicon. The Catholic University of America, Washington 1939 (Studies in Medieval and Renaissance Latin X).

("Parz." 1,17)[7] nachzuspüren, es einzuholen, wird dadurch, dass Orientierungspunkte meist fehlen, zu einem tastenden Vordringen ins Ungewisse, einem gebannten Eintreten ins Innere der Bilder und Formeln.

Der Kunstwerkcharakter des "Iwein" und die ihm zugrundeliegende Anschauungsweise sind Thema dieser Arbeit. Die Geschichte in ihrem Ablauf und mit ihrer Substanz ist Hartmann gegeben; die künstlerisch strukturierende Formung, mit der er den Stoff in jener einmalig unbeschwerten Durchlässigkeit für den inneren Sinn in Erscheinung bringt, ist deshalb von zentraler Bedeutung. Unter 'Strukturen' sind dabei nicht zahlenmässige, architektonische Gesetze verstanden, auch nicht jenes ideelle Grundschema, das Walter Ohly in seiner Dissertation für die Dichtungen Hartmanns herausgearbeitet hat[8], sondern wiederkehrende, verdichtende Muster der Darstellung, die zugleich Merkmale der Gestalt und der Sinnverdeutlichung sind und die ästhetische Wirkung auf den Hörer wesentlich bestimmen.

In der Gespanntheit der Problemstellung und der Ausgewogenheit des Enthüllens und Verbergens gilt der zwischen 1200–1205 entstandene "Iwein"[9] als das klassisch-repräsentative Beispiel des höfischen Artusromans. Die reiche handschriftliche Überlieferung[10] und auch das Hartmannlob des Dichterkollegen Gottfried ("Tristan" 4621–4637)[11], zeugen von seinem inspirierenden und massetzenden Rang. Als erster deutscher Dichter des Artusstoffes und der Romangattung hat Hartmann in vielfach noch experimentierender Pionierleistung die Modellform dieser Dichtung verwirklicht und der neuen literarischen Aussage und Technik damit entscheidende Akzente gesetzt. Seine Gestaltungsmittel, vor allem die souveräne Handhabung der 'colores rhetorici', werden von Wolfram und Gottfried in individualisierter und verfeinerter Artikulation weiterentwickelt, und seine moralisch-allegorische Sinngebung wird vertieft und überhöht[12]; die formale und thematische Antithetik des "Tristan" und Wolframs Humor im gesellschaftlichen Ton sind ansatzweise bereits bei Hartmann da.

Jene Formen der Darstellung, die ich im "Iwein" betrachte, weist z.T. auch schon die Vorlage auf, doch treten sie in der Fassung des deutschen Bearbeiters mit verstärkter Deutlichkeit hervor. Nicht im Einmaligen liegt für das Mittelalter die

---

7 hg. von Albert Leitzmann, Tübingen (7)1961 (ATB 12).
8 Walter Ohly, Die heilsgeschichtliche Struktur der Epen Hartmanns von Aue, Berlin 1958.
9 Der "Yvain" Chrétiens wird um 1170 datiert.
10 Der "Iwein" ist in 28 Hs. (10 davon fragmentarisch) aus dem 13.–16. Jh. überliefert. Auf die Heidelberger-Hs. A, aus der Mitte des 13. Jhs., stützt sich vor allem die Lachmannsche Ausgabe (7. Aufl., bearbeitet von Ludwig Wolff, Berlin 1968). Die älteste, B, ist zu Anfang des 13. Jhs., also noch zu Lebzeiten Hartmanns entstanden (Ausg. Emil Henrici, Halle 1891–93; Fotomechan. Nachdruck in Originalgrösse von Karl Bischoff, H. Matthias Heinrichs und Werner Schröder, Köln/Graz 1964). Nach Ansicht Hans Steingers liefern A und B in der Übereinstimmung den Urtext.
11 hg. von Friedrich Ranke, Berlin (7)1963.
12 Hermann Schneider erkennt im "Iwein" die unzweifelhafte Inspirationsquelle für Parzivals Läuterungsweg. Auch formal ist seine Gestaltung von Hartmann beeinflusst: von ihm hat Wolfram "die Technik der Symmetrie, des Parallelismus, des ruhenden Punktes der Erzählung erlernt". Parzival-Studien, München 1947 (Sitzungsberichte der Bayerischen Akademie der Wissenschaften, philos.-hist. Klasse) 40–45.

künstlerische Leistung, sondern in der inspirierten Darstellung, im bedeutungsreichen Einsetzen des verfügbaren sprachlichen und geistigen Materials. Schon
Chrétien, der grossartige Entwerfer, hat fremdes Erzählgut aufgegriffen[13] und,
verwurzelt in seiner Zeit und von ihr empfangend, seine Ausdrucksmöglichkeiten an
der Rhetorik geschult.

In einigen interessanten Arbeiten der letzten Jahre wurden neue Interpretations-
möglichkeiten und Fragestellungen zum "Iwein" gesucht[14]. Alle diese Studien, vor
allem aber die grundlegende, gültige Beschreibung und Deutung der Gattungsform
des mittelalterlichen Romans durch Max Wehrli[15] haben meine Arbeit richtungweisend und präzisierend bestimmt.

13 wahrscheinlich mündlich überlieferte keltische Geschichten, auf die er sich in V. 2687: 'ce
dit li contes' beruft.
Als Gegner der Keltisten vertritt Charles B. Lewis die Ansicht, dass die Artusdichtungen ihre
Motivik aus klassischer Mythologie und alten Religionspraktiken beziehen. Classical
Mythology and Arthurian Romance. A Study of the Sources of Chrestien de Troyes'
"Yvain" and other Arthurian Romances, Oxford 1932. – Der französische "Yvain" wird
nach der Ausgabe von Mario Roques, Paris 1965 (CFMA) zitiert. Diese Ausgabe richtet sich
nach der Abschrift des Schreibers Guiot, eines geübten Kopisten aus der ersten Hälfte des
13. Jhs., der dem Text jedoch häufig Modernisierungen nach eigenem Gutdünken
angedeihen lässt, während die ältere Edition von Wendelin Foerster, Halle 1888, die in
4. Aufl. auch der zweisprachigen Ausgabe in den Klass. Texten des Romanischen
Mittelalters, hg. von Hans Robert Jauss und Erich Köhler, München 1962, zugrundeliegt, das
gesamte Handschriftenmaterial einbezieht und nach einem auswählenden Verfahren die
Herstellung des Urtextes anstrebt.
14 Humphrey Milnes, The Play of Opposites in 'Iwein'. GLL 14 (1960/61) 241–256.
Hugh Sacker, An Interpretation of Hartmann's Iwein. GR 36 (1961) 5–26.
H. B. Willson, Love and Charity in Hartmann's Iwein. MLR 57 (1962) 216–227.
Wolfgang Dittmann, 'Dune hâst niht wâr, Hartman.' Zum Begriff der wârheit in Hartmanns
Iwein, in: FG Ulrich Pretzel, Berlin 1963, 150–161.
A. T. Hatto, 'Der aventiure meine' in Hartmann's Iwein, in: Mediaeval German Studies,
presented to Frederick Norman, London 1965, 94–104.
Kurt Ruh, Zur Interpretation von Hartmanns "Iwein", in: Philologia Deutsch. FS Walter
Henzen, Bern 1965, 39–51.
Thomas Cramer, Saelde und êre in Hartmanns 'Iwein'. Euph. 60 (1966) 30–47.
Rolf Endres, Der Prolog von Hartmanns "Iwein". DVjs 40 (1966) 509–537.
Johannes Erben, Zu Hartmanns 'Iwein'. ZfdPh 87 (1968) 344–359.
Xenia von Ertzdorff, Spiel der Interpretation. Der Erzähler in Hartmanns Iwein, in: FG
Friedrich Maurer, Düsseldorf 1968, 135–157.
Max Wehrli, Iweins Erwachen, in: Geschichte, Deutung, Kritik. FS Werner Kohlschmidt,
Bern 1969, 64–78.
Für die Bibliographie vgl. Peter Wapnewski, Hartmann von Aue, Stuttgart 1967 (Sammlung
Metzler).
15 Max Wehrli, Strukturprobleme des mittelalterlichen Romans, WW 10 (1960) 334–345.
Ders., Roman und Legende im deutschen Hochmittelalter, in: Worte und Werte. FS Bruno
Markwardt, Berlin 1961, 428–444.

I DURCHBROCHENE ERZÄHLOBERFLÄCHE

Eine Beobachtung

Als raffinierter Ausdruck höfischer Gesellschaftskultur, die im Erzählen leben-
stiftende Bedeutung wahrnimmt, entspringt im "Iwein" das 'maere' aus einem
'maere', wird das zentrale Geschehen durch den Bericht, durch das Erlebnis
Kalogreants ausgelöst, das als Unerfülltes Herausforderung ist und den Weg des
Helden präfiguriert.

Kalogreant betritt als erster jenen Ort der Quelle, der durch sein wiederholtes
Auftauchen im Roman dem magischen Bereich, den er vertritt, Bedeutung und
Präsenz verleiht[1]. Vom hässlichen Waldmann auf die Spur gebracht, hat er ihn am
Ende des aufsteigenden Pfades gefunden: einen seltsam entrückten Kreis, wo
wohltuender Zauber herrscht. Eine mächtige Linde überschattet das goldene
Becken auf dem leuchtenden Smaragdstein und spendet Kühle. Nie welkt ihr Laub;
doch vermöchte in diesem Augenblick keiner auch nur einen Fleck davon zu
erspähen: über und über ist der Baum mit Vögeln besät, und ihr Gezwitscher erfüllt
so vielfältig und betörend die Luft, dass eine Welle von Glücksgefühlen den
Lauschenden überflutet und sich selbst einem Verzweifelten der verdunkelte Sinn
wieder gelichtet hätte. Den Vögeln gelingt damit in vollkommener Weise, was
Hartmann selbst mit seinem Dichten anstrebt: durch eine wohlklingende Ordnung
der Lebenswirklichkeit etwas von ihrer Schwere zu nehmen[2].

---

1 Um die Bedeutung und Faszination einer 'âventiure' zu erhöhen, wird der gefährliche Raum
im höfischen Roman sehr oft als 'idealer Ort' ausgestattet. Der Topos des 'locus amoenus',
der in der antiken Literatur stets eine Stätte des Genusses evoziert, erhält dabei etwas
Schillerndes. Durchflochten mit märchenhaften Zügen und von Paradisesvorstellungen
beeinflusst, ist der Landschaftsausschnitt hier nicht Chiffre für eine seelische Gestimmtheit
wie im Minnesang, sondern ein Bezirk voll magischer Reize, aus dessen Hintergrund
unvermutet der Feind auftaucht. So scheint der Baumgarten von Brandigan ("Erec" 8698f.),
der durch märchenhafte Elemente als erhöhter Spielraum ausgezeichnet ist, gerade in seiner
freudenspendenden Gestalt zum erlösenden Sieg, zur Wiederherstellung der Identität von
Innen und Aussen aufzufordern.

2 Armer Heinrich 9   ob er iht des funde
                     dâ mite er swaere stunde
                     möhte senfter machen,
Der Topos 'Dichtung als Trost', eine Variation des horazischen 'delectare' (De arte poet.
333), fehlt sowohl in den antiken als mittellateinischen Rhetoriken, figuriert im 12. und
13. Jh. jedoch häufig in den expliziten Reflexionen der volkssprachlichen Dichter über ihre
Funktion. In dieser Zeit gesteigerter Wirklichkeitsnähe erschliesst sich eine neue, existen-
tielle Beziehung zur Kunst, die damit Funktionen übernimmt, die im frühen Mittelalter
einzig der Religion zukamen.
Gottfried, Tristan 73   daz si mit minem maere
                        ir nahe gende swaere
                        ze halber senfte bringe,
                        ir niht da mite geringe.
Ähnlich Wirnt von Gravenberc, Wigalois, der Ritter mit dem Rade, hg. von J. M. N. Kap-
teyn, Bonn 1926 (Rhein. Beiträge und Hülfsbücher 9) V. 126–128.
Marie de France, Prologue des Lais, hg. von Jean Rychner, Paris 1966 (CFMA) V. 23f.
Die nahe Verbindung zwischen Dichtung und Vogelsang ist durch die Minnesänger geläufig
geworden.

Die besondere Schönheit und die verwandelnde Kraft dieses Konzerts scheinen nun aber gerade darin zu liegen, dass jeder Vogel sich vom andern unterscheidet und eine eigene Weise intoniert:

Iwein 615   dern wâren niender zwêne glîch:
             ir sanc was sô mislîch,
             hôch unde nidere.

Nicht die als Einzellinie erkennbare Melodie, der einheitliche, reine Stil, sondern die Vielfalt, das Zusammenklingen verschiedenartiger Tonfolgen, Entsprechungen, ja vielleicht sogar Dissonanzen erscheint hier als Inbegriff des Schönen und Kunstvollen, als Prinzip einer anderen, höheren Harmonie.

Mit dieser winzigen, fast beiläufig schmückenden Schilderung Gedanken über mittelalterliche Ästhetik zu verknüpfen, scheint unproportioniert. Es kommt jedoch in diesem kleinsten Baustein eine grundsätzliche Eigenschaft mittelalterlicher Wahrnehmung zum Ausdruck, die die konkreten Beispiele aus der bildenden und der Wortkunst nur bestätigen: Gesetze der Perspektive, die unsern Blick geprägt haben, Schranken, die wir gewohnt sind, zwischen Bereichen, Gattungen zu ziehen, müssen wir wieder aufzuheben versuchen, um in grösserer Freiheit Zusammenhänge schöpferisch und damaligem Werkschaffen entsprechend aufzudecken.

Dies gilt als Voraussetzung auch für das Verständnis der Artusromane. In anderer Weise erscheinen auch sie vielschichtig und unerschöpflich an Ansätzen und Sinngebungen. Schon dadurch, dass ihr Stoff einer älteren Erzählschicht angehört, greifen Übernommenes und Selbsterdachtes ineinander, werden Bewegungen der Handlung und Deutung in verschiedener Richtung wirksam. So treten antikes Erbe, Märchenmotivik und die mythische Gesetzlichkeit des keltischen Stoffes im "Iwein" mit der höfischen Darstellung und dem christlichen Sinnhintergrund in ein spannungsvolles Kräftespiel[3].

In seinem Abbild der Welt, die das Mittelalter nicht einfühlend als organischen Zusammenhang, als gegenseitige Verflochtenheit der Dinge, sondern als bezugreiche geistige Ordnung begreift, strebt auch der Dichter nach einer Vielstimmigkeit, einer consonantia, die Entferntes, ja Widersprechendes teilhaben und mitklingen lässt.

Der kausale und psychologische Zusammenhalt ist dabei von minderer Wichtigkeit. Zwischenräume, die sich zwischen den prägnanten Situationen, zwischen Charakteren und Handlungsmomenten ergeben, bleiben unausgefüllt; es werden nicht Entwicklungen gezeigt, sondern Zeichen gesetzt. Immer wieder durchbricht der Dichter den Handlungsablauf, um sich einer Einzelheit zuzuwenden, sie zu bedenken und mit Eigenschaften auszustatten, wobei Christliches und Zauberei, Fabulierfreude und Wahrheitsbeteuerung nebeneinander bestehen, ohne sich gegenseitig zu schmälern.

---

3 "Es ist geradezu die Voraussetzung und die Chance des Romandichters, dass er bewusst mit mehreren Traditionen und Schichten arbeitet und versucht, Heterogenes einer neuen Einheit, einer neuen Totalität, dienstbar zu machen." Max Wehrli, Strukturprobleme des mittelalterlichen Romans. WW 10 (1960) 336.

Figur und Motiv erhalten so eine unerschöpfliche Vieldeutigkeit. Immer wieder fällt auf eine andere ihrer Bedeutungsflächen Licht; nie ergibt sich ein eindeutiges Profil, auf das man sich festlegen könnte. Auch der Dichter selbst, der zwischen Partien intensiver Sinndurchdringung immer wieder völlig zurücktritt, 'blinden' Quellenbericht übermittelt, ohne früher aufgedeckte Beziehungen aufzunehmen und weiterzuführen, wird nicht eigentlich greifbar.

Der mittelalterliche Roman bleibt seiner Form nach offen und bietet fortwährend Einfallswinkel zu denkerischer Bewegung und Erweiterung des Erzählten. In dieser Bewegung und in der verwandelnden Wirkkraft auf das 'gemüete', nicht in sich selbst, erreicht der Roman sein Wesen und seine Vollendung.

1. Präsenz der Erzählerfigur

Zunächst sind es vor allem die Sprünge aus der Handlungswirklichkeit in die unmittelbare Gegenwart, die dem Zusammenhang des Erzählten entgegenwirken. Immer wieder brechen Fragen, Zwischenbemerkungen, kommentierende und persönliche Zugaben des Dichters den Spannungsbogen, und der Bericht öffnet sich auf eine andersartige und anders verbindliche Wirklichkeit hin[4]. Der Erzählende tritt nicht hinter das Erzählte zurück, richtet vielmehr das Licht bald voll auf den evozierten Märchenraum, bald auf den Kreis der sie Betrachtenden und Bedenkenden, wobei sich die beiden Bereiche in wechselseitiger Spannung und Bezogenheit gegenüberstehen. Gottfried vollzieht diesen Perspektivenwechsel mit raffinierter Geschmeidigkeit; unauffällig gleitet der Gedanke zwischen dem Schauplatz und dem Publikum hin und her, während bei Hartmann das Überschwenken zuweilen noch etwas Abruptes hat; es erwirkt Zäsuren, die den inneren Rhythmus der Erzählung unterbrechen und stets neu bestimmen.

Dass ein Publikum angesprochen und einbezogen wird, entspringt der Vortragssituation selbst[5]. Auch im Heldenlied und in der sogenannten Spielmannsdichtung rücken affektive Einsprengsel, Apostrophen und Beteuerungen die Handlung

---

4 In einer interessanten Dissertation, "Zwischenrede, Erzählerfigur und Erzählhaltung in Hartmann von Aues 'Erec' (Studien über die Dichter-Publikums-Beziehung in der Epik)", München 1965, untersucht Günter Mecke Art und Funktion solcher Stellen im "Erec" und erschliesst damit einen neuen, fruchtbaren Betrachtungswinkel für den höfischen Roman. Seine Überlegungen gelten auch für den "Iwein", wo das Beziehungsspiel zwischen Erzähler und Publikum allerdings stark zurückgedämmt ist. – Vgl. auch Swantje Ehrentreich, Erzählhaltung und Erzählerrolle Hartmanns von Aue und Thomas Manns, dargestellt an ihren beiden Gregoriusdichtungen. Diss. Frankfurt 1964. – Klärenden Aufschluss über das grundsätzliche Verhältnis von dichterischer Fiktion und dem Anteil des Erzähler-Ich vermittelt das Kapitel "Die epische Fiktion" in Käte Hamburgers "Logik der Dichtung", Stuttgart 1957, 21–114.
5 Die höfischen Dichtungen setzen sowohl Hörer als Leser voraus (vgl. "Armer Heinrich" 22 'swer .. sî hoere sagen oder lese'). Die reich entfaltete Publikumsbeziehung im Roman lässt annehmen, dass dieser ursprünglich im Kreis der Gesellschaft vorgetragen wurde.

suggestiv näher und steigern ihre Dynamik[6]. Doch kommt diesen rhetorischen Einschüben dort weder formbestimmende Bedeutung, noch subjektive Aussagekraft zu. Auch in der vorhöfischen Epik gelangen die ans Publikum gerichteten Anreden und Fragen nicht übers Formelhafte hinaus, und vereinzelte spruchartige Erklärungen erweitern und verstärken das Erzählte, ohne jedoch Gegenspiel zu sein[7].

Die Romandichter der Blütezeit beleben all diese Spuren mit der Kraft eines neuen Beginns. Mit dem Aufbruch des individuellen Bewusstseins und unter Einfluss von Predigtstil und Rhetorik gewinnt das Subjektive in der Dichtung an Tragweite und Differenzierung. Der Weg wird frei zur Mitteilung von Persönlichem, und der Erzählton erreicht nüancierte Spontaneität. Lehrend und spielend mischt sich der Dichter in die Erzählung ein, intensiviert oder verfremdet sie und trägt dabei, der eigenen Art durchaus bewusst, sich selber, seine Einsicht, sein Persönliches, bei; die mit Kunstverstand gesetzten Einschaltungen werden zu einem inhaltlichen und künstlerischen Teil des Werks, einem Mittel der Profilierung und Modulation.

Auch im Erzähltext bleibt die Gegenwart dessen, der die Geschichte aus seiner Gesamtschau heraus wertet und deutet, spürbar; selten sprechen die Vorgänge selbst. Aus- und Zwischenrufe, wie auch das bekräftigende 'zwâre' oder das höfische 'waenlich', das einen Vorgang in behutsamer Schwebe hält, suggerieren persönliche Beteiligung. In ähnlicher Weise verfremdend wirken Metaphern und Hyperbeln.

An vielen Stellen wird die Handlung durch Einfügungen des Dichters jedoch merkbar unterbrochen — vielmehr: der Ablauf des mittelhochdeutschen Romans ist grundsätzlich gar nicht als zusammenhängende Linie konzipiert. Was Chrétien in natürlicher Folge als Ereignis beschreibt, wird bei Hartmann sehr oft mit Erklärungen, persönlichen Bemerkungen oder mutwilligen Digressionen durchsetzt, vor allem im "Erec", dem ersten deutschen Artusroman, wo Zugaben und Kommentare besonders zahlreich sind. Das hat zunächst einen praktischen Grund: Ein Werk, das im nordfranzösischen Kulturkreis und in einer konkreten Gesellschaft verankert, aus ihr entsprungen ist, bedarf vor dem deutschen Publikum einer Einführung. Die Matière de Bretagne war an den nordfranzösischen Höfen aus keltischen Sagen bereits bekannt; Hartmann aber hat den neuen Stoff und das höfische Programm dem deutschen Publikum erst vorzustellen[8]. Sein Dichten ist

---

6 "Graf Rudolf", hg. von Peter F. Ganz, Berlin 1964 (Philologische Studien und Quellen 19) B 18 'als ich han gehort sagen'; F 33 'nu nimet dirre rede goume'; Fb 51 'ir ne gesahet nie so vechte'. δ46—δb8: abschweifende Betrachtung über die eigene Zeit.
"Nibelungenlied", hg. von H. de Boor, Wiesbaden 1963, 183,1 'Ich sag' iu . .'; 1036,1 'Iu enkunde niemen daz wunder volsagen'. Der überblickende und arrangierende Dichter wird zudem in den zahlreichen zeitlichen Vor- und Rückblenden bewusst.
7 Dass sich erst in der höfischen Dichtung eine bewusst gestaltete Beziehung zum Publikum bildet, ist Teilergebnis der vergleichenden Untersuchung von A. van der Lee, der Stil von Hartmanns Erec verglichen mit dem der älteren Epik. Diss. Utrecht 1950, 115–143.
8 Kurt Ruh nimmt für Hartmanns Wirken den zähringischen Fürstenhof unter Berthold IV. (1152–86) und Berthold V. (1186–1218) an, dessen Machtbereich sich bis nach Frankreich (Burgund, Provence) erstreckt und Beziehungen zur französischen Kultur damit sichert. (Höfische Epik des deutschen Mittelalters, I Von den Anfängen bis zu Hartmann von Aue, Berlin 1967, 104–105.)

Initiation, und seine Rolle die des tonangebenden Lehrers, der seinen Hörerkreis nicht nur literarisch, sondern als höfische Gesellschaft heranbildet und formt.

Schon aus diesem Grunde ist es erforderlich, dass der Dichter seine Hörerschaft wahrnimmt und zu ihr in Beziehung tritt. Diese didaktische Zielsetzung lässt ihn in zahlreichen Zwischenbemerkungen alle Register des Humors und der Ironie, der eindringlichen Deutung und der persönlichen Einmischung ziehen. Stellen, an denen der deutsche Dichter ein Stück allgemeine Artuskunde einflicht, Tatsachen begründet oder mit einem Allgemeinen in Zusammenhang bringt, bleiben noch im Erzählstoff und im Tempus der Handlungswirklichkeit drin; häufig jedoch löst sich der Autor vom Geschehen, betrachtet es aus Distanz oder lässt durch die Fäden der Handlung hindurch sein Dichter-Ich in Erscheinung treten:

Iwein 3097   im wîssagete sîn muot,
als er mir selbem dicke tuot:
ich siufte, sô ich vrô bin,
mînen künftigen ungewin.
sus nâhte im sîn leit.

Solche bewussten Einschaltungen, die sich durch den Wechsel ins Präsens, die Aussage in Ich-Form oder die Anrede ans Publikum auch formal vom Erzähltext deutlich abheben, übernehmen neue Funktionen als Mittel der Publikumsverbindung und der Wahrheitssuche. Mit ihnen gewinnt das 'maere' eine neue Dimension: Ein Subjekt tritt erkennbar dem imaginären Geschehen gegenüber, durchdringt es und hebt es ins Aktuelle.

In erster Linie ist es in einem Werk der *Prolog,* der den Dichter ins Rampenlicht setzt und ihn im Rahmen der Werbung zur Formulierung seiner Absicht veranlasst. Die Prologe der höfischen Romane, in denen der Dichter über seine Aufgabe, sein Publikum und das Ziel des Kunstwerks reflektiert, zeigen gegenüber dem anonym wirkenden Heldenlied eindeutig einen geistigen Neueinsatz[9]. Der Rahmen des objektiv geschlossenen Erzählwerks ist gesprengt; seinen Hörern und dem Stoff steht der Dichter bewusst gegenüber und spielt diese Beziehung gedanklich und gesellschaftlich aus.

In Hartmanns "Iwein" ist der ganze Anfang umstrukturiert. Das Subjektive manifestiert sich hier nicht nur, wie in der Vorlage, stilimmanent; bewusst ist es vor und zwischen die Fabel gesetzt. Gegenüber Chrétien, der schon mit dem ersten Satz, in die Erzählung einmündend, das Pfingstfest am Artushof umreisst[10], setzt

---

9 Der Prolog ist jedoch nicht Gattungsmerkmal ausschliesslich des Romans; auch der Legendendichter äussert sich im Eingang über seine causa scribendi, doch kommt Bedeutsamkeit hier ausschliesslich dem Bericht, nicht der Person des Schreibers zu.
Umfassend orientiert Hennig Brinkmann über die theoretischen Richtlinien für die Prologtechnik nach der Gerichtspraxis und ihre Anwendung bei Chrétien, Wolfram, Gottfried und Rudolf von Ems: Der Prolog im Mittelalter als literarische Erscheinung. Bau und Aussage. WW 14 (1964) 1−21.

10 Vgl. die Quellenanalyse von Wolfgang Babilas, Chrétien de Troyes: 'Yvain', Verse 1−6, in: Arch. f. d. Stud. d. neuer. Spr. u. Lit. 196 (1960) 296−315, die den Traditionszusammenhang und die rhetorische Funktion dieser Verse aufweist.

sich im deutschen "Iwein" der Prolog vom Erzähltext deutlich ab. Das Artuslob, das Chrétien im 'ordo naturalis' mit dem Festbericht verflicht, ist bei Hartmann aus der Erzählung herausgelöst; wie ein erster Sinnkreis oder Vorspann, oder wie die 'propositio'[11], mit der der Gerichtsredner zu Beginn sein Beweisziel skizziert, markiert und beglaubigt es den Wertbereich des Höfischen, sammelt die Denkkraft darauf und gibt sie wieder frei[12].

Unvermittelt, ohne gedankliche Verbindung, tritt Hartmann darauf in eigener Sache vor. Er stellt sich seinem Publikum vor, baut selbstbewusst, mit ruhiger Sicherheit die eigene Person als Stütz- und Beziehungspunkt in die Erzählung ein und bekennt sich damit gleichzeitig, den Regeln der Gerichtsrhetorik gemäss, für die 'inventio' des 'maere', seine Verarbeitung und Glaubwürdigkeit verantwortlich[13]. Vornehmlich-vertraulich, von unübertroffener Einprägsamkeit ist die Intonation:

Iwein 21
    ein riter der gelêret was
    und ez an den buochen las,
    swenner sîne stunde
    niht baz bewenden kunde,
    daz er ouch tihtennes pflac
    (daz man gerne hoeren mac,
    dâ kêrt er sînen vlîz an:
    er was genant Hartman
    und was ein Ouwaere),
    der tihte diz maere.

Ohne mit Redegewandtheit zu prunken, mit souveräner Bescheidenheit, zeichnet Hartmann seinen Umriss[14]. Er nennt Bildung, Stand und Dienstzugehörigkeit[15], beleuchtet gezielt seine berufliche Kompetenz (Quellenstudium[16], Eifer und

---

11 Vgl. Heinrich Lausberg, Elemente der literarischen Rhetorik, München 1963, 27, § 43,2a.
12 Für diese Möglichkeit, die Dichtung mit einer Sentenz und der Veranschaulichung durch eine Exempelfigur einzuleiten, ist in der antiken Rhetorik kein Vorbild gegeben. Es handelt sich um eine typisch mittelalterliche Anfangsfigur, die sich wahrscheinlich unter Einfluss der Predigt herausgebildet hat. Vgl. dazu die beiden Hauptvertreter der literarischen Poetik des 13. Jhs.: Matthaeus von Vendôme, Ars versificatoria I,16 und Galfredus de Vinosalvo, Poetria nova 142 (s. Edmond Faral, Les arts poétiques du XIIe et du XIIIe siècle. Recherches et documents sur la technique littéraire du moyen âge. Paris (Champion) 1924, S. 113, 201–203).
13 Wie der Richter will auch der Dichter die Aufmerksamkeit und das Urteil der Hörer in eine bestimmte Richtung lenken. "Mit dem Blick auf die Gesprächssituation bei einer Gerichtsrede hat die Rhetorik ihre Anweisungen für die Gestaltungen des Prologs entwickelt." Brinkmann a.a.O. 4.
14 Schlichtheit (modestia) wird dem Redner von Quintilian empfohlen (Institutio oratoriae, hg. von Ludwig Radermacher, Leipzig 1959, 4,1,54–57); bei Hartmann ist sie über die Zweckbestimmung hinaus bewusstes ästhetisches Prinzip.
15 Die in der Gerichtstopik der Beglaubigung dienenden 'adiuncta personis' (Quintilian 4,1,30).
16 Der Plural 'buochen' weist auf allgemeine Belesenheit, hat aber auch wörtliche Geltung, da der eingeschobene Bericht vom Raub der Königin (4530–4726) im "Iwein" aus anderer Quelle stammt. Hartmann von Aue, Iwein, hg. von C. F. Benecke und K. Lachmann, Bd. 2 Handschriftenübersicht, Anmerkungen und Lesarten, S. 13.

Hingabe), um seine Materie und sich selbst dem Hörer nahezubringen, gleich wie der Gerichtsredner in seiner captatio benevolentiae verfährt. Mit einer kleinen Referenz (V. 26)[17] – oder ist es versteckte Provokation? – bezieht er das Publikum als sein geachtetes Gegenüber, als Aufforderung und Massstab in sein Werk und den Schaffensprozess mit ein und bekennt sich auch dort zum Hof und zum Ritterdienst, wo er die Kunst den müssigen Stunden zuweist: 'swenner sîne stunde / niht baz bewenden kunde' – doch färbt ein kaum an die Oberfläche dringendes Lächeln dabei seinen Ernst. Der Ton sagt bei Hartmann meist mehr aus als die Mitteilung, und gerade an ernsten Stellen klingt of eine unüberhörbare, in Balance versetzende ironische Heiterkeit mit, lässt das Einfache, 'cristallîne' seiner Sprache ein Wechselspiel verschiedener Sinnreflexe zu.

Dieses Spielerisch-Heitere bildet einen Grundzug der Hartmannschen Kunst, der nicht nur die Stimmlage der Erzählung bestimmt, sondern hier auch den persönlichen Aussagen etwas von ihrem Gewicht nimmt. Denn obwohl Hartmann bei all diesen Äusserungen vor seinem Publikum steht, spricht er von sich in der 3. Person und bannt sich, dem Romanpersonal gleich, in die Vergangenheit[18]. Das Imperfekt ist Tempus der Fiktion; indem es Hartmann für seine eigenen Mitteilungen in Anspruch nimmt, tritt er, wie ein Mitspieler, wenn auch auf höherem Podest, in den Raum der Erzählwelt ein. Seine Person vermischt sich mit der Rolle einer mobilen Dichterfigur, die, bald ins Vergangene, bald ins Gegenwärtige greifend, die Erzählung dem Publikum präsentiert[19].

Verglichen mit den Eingängen seiner Legendendichtungen, drückt der knapp formulierte, konzise Prolog des "Iwein" starke Zurückhaltung aus: im "Gregorius" sind es 176 Verse, in denen Hartmann das Thema ankündigt, es mit der eigenen Person, dem Sinn und Zweck seines Dichtens in Verbindung bringt und Hinweise gibt für die Interpretation. Auch der Prolog des "Armen Heinrich" (1–28), aus dem einige Gedanken im "Iwein" wieder aufgenommen sind, ist lockerer, weitatmiger als der des Spätwerks. Die Rückführung auf den knappen Ausdruck, auf die einfache, klar umrissene und konzentrierte Form ist das hervorragende Merkmal von Hartmanns geläutertem, nach innen vielfältig werdenden Stil in seinem letzten Werk[20].

17 Ästhetisches Kriterium der Kunst ist das Gefallen. "Pulchra sunt quae visa placent." Thomas von Aquin, ST I,5,4 ad 1.
18 Es sei denn, ein anderer als der Dichter selbst habe das Werk vorgetragen. Dagegen sprechen jedoch die vielen spontanen Ich-Einschaltungen im Roman, sowie die Stellen V 2974 und 7027, wo sich der Dichter von einem fiktiven Gegenüber mit 'Hartman' anreden lässt. Der Prolog des "Wigalois" mit seinen ausgedehnten Bescheidenheitsbeteuerungen ist im Präsens gehalten (141 'er heizet Wirnt von Grâvenberc').
19 Mecke interpretiert die Dichterfigur als Fiktion. "In den (fingierten, 'gespielten'!) Zwischenreden spricht also keine 'Dichterpersönlichkeit' . . ; sondern eine vom Gegenstand ausdrücklich und sehr oft ironisch distanzierte Erzählerfigur spielt mit einem fingierten Publikum Beziehungsspiele." a.a.O. 7.
20 Die These Werner Schröders, der sich auf die Studien Zwierzinas und Schirokauers stützt und die ersten 1000 Verse des "Iwein" früher, kurz nach dem "Erec" ansetzt (Zur Chronologie der drei grossen mhd. Erzähler, DVjs 31 [1957] 281), ist nicht gesichert. Eine vergleichende Untersuchung der Einschaltungen des Dichters, die im "Erec" noch durchwegs häufiger und ungezwungener sind, weist nicht in dieser Richtung. Vgl. dazu Wapnewski a.a.O. 16–19.

Der Prolog endet mit der Nennung von Namen und Stand; gleich einem Stichwort ruft 'diz maere' (30) der einsetzenden 'narratio'; die Geschichte hebt an. Mit der topischen Schilderung des Pfingstfestes am Artushof malt sie den Goldgrund für das erwartete Geschehen, weckt Hochstimmung und belebende Freude; doch bleibt der Blick nicht auf die eine Ebene gebannt; unmerklich wird der Bildausschnitt immer wieder geöffnet und ausgeweitet[21], und bereits in V. 48 stellt sich der Dichter mit einer ersten persönlichen Überlegung vor die heraufbeschworene Szene hin. Der Klage über die vergangenen arturischen Freuden antwortet er mit dem hoffnungsvollen *Bekenntnis zur eigenen Zeit:*

Iwein 48   mich jâmert waerlîchen,
                             und hulfez iht, ich woldez clagen,
                             daz nû bî unseren tagen
                             solch vreude niemer werden mac
                             der man ze den zîten pflac.
                             doch müezen wir ouch nû genesen.
                             ichn wolde dô niht sîn gewesen,
                             daz ich nû niht enwaere,
                             dâ uns noch mit ir maere
                             sô rehte wol wesen sol:
                             dâ tâten in diu werc vil wol.

Mit diesem Gedankengang tritt Hartmann, die Selbstverständlichkeit der Fiktion aufhebend, aus der Erzählung heraus und unterbricht sie. Was eben als entrückende Illusion zu wirken begann, wird als Vergangenes, als Gegenstand der Kunst in Distanz gerückt und der Gegenwart gegenübergestellt. Nicht nur in der Motivierung der einzelnen Handlungsteile, sondern als Rechtfertigung der Dichtung überhaupt, ist der realistische und moralische Nutzen, das Utile, von entscheidender Bedeutung für Hartmann. Von Anfang an hält er der Scheinwelt der Erzählung die geistige Wirklichkeit seiner eigenen Zeit als Gegenkraft hin und lässt es zu einem spannungsvollen Wechselspiel kommen zwischen 'nû' und 'dô', zwischen den vergangenen glanzvollen Taten und dem jetzigen Erkennen, zwischen vita activa und vita contemplativa, die er in leiser Andeutung typologisch, im Sinne einer Steigerung, verstanden wissen will: Was sich damals unmittelbar in Fest und Bewegung erschöpfte, wird jetzt, im Kunstwerk, ins Geistige emporgehoben und in der ihm eigentümlichen Schönheit, Bedeutsamkeit und Problematik erkannt[22]. Während sich Chrétien an dieser Stelle lediglich über den Verfall der Minne äussert

---

21 Iwein 38 *deiswâr* dâ was ein boeser man
                in vil swachem werde,
                wan sich gesament ûf der erde
                bî niemens zîten anderswâ
                sô manec guot riter alsô dâ.
22 "Typologie setzt in der Zeit Getrenntes in den Sinnbezug der Steigerung des Alten in das Neue. Das Neue hebt das Alte, das Alte lebt im Neuen. Das Alte wird erlöst ins Neue, das Neue baut sich auf dem Grund des Alten." Friedrich Ohly, Synagoge und Ecclesia, in: Miscellanea Medievalia 4, Berlin 1966, 357.

und in oberflächlich-illusionistischer Erzählhaltung verharrt[23], durchkreuzt Hartmann die 'laudatio temporis acti' mit einem Antitopos[24] und konfrontiert die Sage mit der Wirklichkeit. Wohl ist die Welt des Artus voll wundersamer und erstaunlicher Ereignisse und von der Vollendetheit der Ferne geprägt, doch: 'müezen wir ouch nû genesen.'

Es ist die neue Leistung dieses Dichters, dass er das Gegenwärtige, die zu bewältigende Realität und die anwesende Gesellschaft in seine Kunst hineinnimmt; seine Dichtung zielt damit über blosse Unterhaltung hinaus, wird zu einer Suche nach dem Realen und nach dem Heil. Die reflektorische Ausbuchtung an dieser Stelle steht richtungweisend für das ganze Werk. Sie fordert den Hörer auf, das Erzählte an der erfahrbaren Wirklichkeit zu verifizieren und seine Wahrheit umzurechnen in die eigene aufgegebene Zeit. Dynamisch reicht das Spannungsfeld dieser Dichtkunst damit ins Leben der Gesellschaft und des Einzelnen hinein: Als exemplarisch Gemeintes fordert sie auf das 'dô' ein 'nû', auf den geistigen Entwurf den existentiellen Vollzug.

Im Vergleich mit dem "Erec" sind die leutseligen und ablenkenden Zwischenreden im "Iwein" stark verringert. In intensiverer Geistigkeit und Ausgewogenheit wirkt er als Kunstwerk weit mehr aus sich selbst[25], während die Hauptabsicht Hartmanns im Erstlingsroman noch darauf gerichtet war, der neuen höfischen Literatur ein Publikum, einen heiter-animierten Raum zu schaffen. Noch immer aber bilden die Zwischenreden des Dichters, als deutliche Spur seines Mitdabeiseins, auch im "Iwein" ein unübersehbares formales Element. Wie feine Marken setzt Hartmann die Zeichen seiner persönlichen Beteiligung ein; es sind vorwiegend Figuren, die die Rhetorik zur Erregung des Mitgefühls und zur Verlebendigung der Rede empfiehlt[26]:

23 Yvain 29 Mes or parlons de cez qui furent,
    si leissons cez qui ancor durent,
24 Der Stolz, in der eigenen Zeit zu leben, erscheint als literarischer Topos bereits bei Ovid: Ars amatoria, hg. von E. J. Kenney, Oxford 1961:
    III,121 prisca iuuent alios, ego me nunc denique natum gratulor: haec aetas moribus apta meis
    127 quia cultus adest.
25 Gerade diese Läuterung und Verdichtung ist die Form von Hartmanns "Anteilnahme" am Werk, die Helmut de Boor (Geschichte der deutschen Literatur, II Die höfische Literatur, München 1953, 80) und Peter Wapnewski (a.a.O. 17) im "Iwein" vermissen.
26 Vgl. Leonid Arbusow, Colores Rhetorici, Göttingen 1948, 48–62.

Parteinahme	6660 daz ims doch got niht lône
	6675 deiswâr, dazn wirt mir niemer leit.
Zustimmung	2400 ich waene si rehte tâten,
	1585 doch enhât sî hie niht missetân,
	wir sulen sî genesen lân. (Minne)
das Publikum wird	7041 nû wil ich iu bescheiden daz,
ins Vertrauen gezogen	
fiktive Fragen	3309 waz welt ir daz der tôre tuo?
	3735 nû wer möhte diu sper
	elliu bereiten her
	diu mîn her Iwein dâ brach?
fiktiver Zweifel	6522 ich versihe mich wol zewâre,
Vorwegnahme eines	6574 swer daz nû vür ein wunder
Einwands (prolepsis)	im selbem saget
gespielte Ungeduld	6977 sît daz der kampf wesen sol,
	sô zimt in daz beiden wol
	daz sî enzît strîten.
	wes mugens iemer bîten?

Mit solchen Anreden aktualisiert der Dichter jedesmal in einer Gebärde zur Gesellschaft hin seine Verbundenheit mit ihr. Diese ständige Verbindung, das Einbezogen- und Angesprochensein des Publikums, kommt aber auch ohne direkte Apostrophe im Urteil des Dichters, in seinen Mutmassungen und Gedankengängen zum Ausdruck. So ist die wohlwollend idealisierende *Verteidigung der Frauen* (1869—1888), die sich Hartmann, in leicht ironischer Gegenposition zur Quelle, aufdrängt, kurz bevor sich Laudine so erstaunlich schnell trösten und überreden lässt, den Töter ihres Gatten zum Hüter der Quelle zu machen und ihm ihre Minne zu schenken, weniger ein Beitrag zum Romangeschehen als ein Kompliment an die Damen der versammelten Hofgesellschaft. Dem Urteil des Franzosen stellt sich Hartmann galant entgegen: Manch einer kreide den Frauen ihr vielgestaltiges Trachten, das stets dem Guten das Bessere vorzuziehen wisse, an, mache ihnen zum Vorwurf, dass sie ihre Versprechen brechen; wer solches aber Wankelmut, 'unstaetekeit' (1874) nenne (so Chrétien: Yvain 1439 'D'or en droit ai ge dit que sages, / que fame a plus de cent corages'), vergehe sich:

Iwein 1875	ich weiz baz wâ von ez geschiht
	daz man sî alsô dicke siht
	in wankelem gemüete:
	ez kumet von ir güete.

Ist das hier Ernst oder Scherz? Dass der im Eingang als zentral gesetzte Wert den Frauen ausgerechnet in Zusammenhang mit Laudine, der schnell getrösteten Witwe, zugesprochen wird, macht jedenfalls stutzig[27]; wir haben es auch hier mit einer Art

27 Allerdings ist gerade der Bedeutungsraum von 'güete' bei Hartmann reich gestuft. Das Hineinragen dieses Leitbegriffs in den religiösen Bereich hat vor allem der "Arme Heinrich"

Unterbrechung, einem gewichteverlagernden Umschlag zu tun. Gerade wo sich der Dichter selbst zu Wort meldet, ist immer auch die gesellschaftliche Situation im höfischen Kreis miteinzubeziehen, die den Dichter in spielerischer Kommunikation zu Seitensprüngen aus dem Ernst der Handlung heraus, zu heiteren "à parts" mit dem Publikum, verlockt. Die Interpreten, die Hartmann an dieser Stelle Unverständnis vorwerfen[28], haben sie vielleicht doch zu ausschliesslich als in die Erzählung verspannte Rechtfertigung Laudines gedeutet und den Teil an gesellschaftlichem Zugeständnis in der "gutgläubigen"[29] Beteuerung Hartmanns verkannt, der dieses Lob, seiner Hof- und Dienstpflicht eingedenk, mit verstohlenem Schalk geäussert haben mag. Mit einer herzgewinnenden Verneigung –

Iwein 1885   swer in danne unstaete giht,
                      des volgaere enbin ich niht.
                      ich wil in niuwan guotes jehen,
                      allez guot müez in geschehen. –

schliesst er die Klammer des kleinen Intermezzos, in dem, wie so oft im "Iwein", Ernst und versteckte Ironie ungreifbar ineinander verwoben sind[30], und nimmt die unterbrochene Unterredung zwischen Laudine und Lunete wieder auf.

Amusement und Publikumsverbindung sind jedoch nicht die einzigen Funktionen, die den Zwischenbemerkungen und Gedankeneinschlägen des Dichters, neben ihrer informativen Bedeutung, zukommen. Die fortwährenden Einschaltungen bestimmen grundsätzlich die Darstellungsart des Werks und damit auch die Haltung und die Art der Wahrnehmung, die ihm das Publikum entgegenbringt. Wo der Dichter, bald wortführerisch und verbindlich, das Steuer der Erzählung ergreift: 'ouch sag ich iu ein maere' (2565), 'und ich sage iu war an' (2716), – oder sich in scheinbarer Unbeteiligtheit hinter seine Quelle zurückzieht[31]: 'als ich vernomen habe' (1113), 'als diu âventiure giht' (3026), rufen solche Äusserungen immer wieder den Erzähl- und Vergangenheitscharakter der Handlung in Erinnerung. Der Hörer vermischt sich nicht mit dem Erzählten, sondern bleibt gegenüber. Wo Hartmann im Handlungsablauf einhält, um das Vorgefallene zu kommentieren, wo er die Aussage durch ein Zwiegespräch mit einem erfundenen Gegner belebt:

evident gemacht, doch schliesst er Tüchtigkeit im Kampf (afz. 'proesce', vgl. "Yvain" 2), aber auch Ausrichtung auf das Gute, also Klugheit, ebenso ein, wie Mitgefühl, Mitleid und die Wendung zu Gott, die Rolf Endres (Der Prolog in Hartmanns 'Iwein' a.a.O. 519) als Hauptgehalt herausarbeitet.

28 U.a. Kurt Ruh, Zur Interpretation von Hartmanns "Iwein", a.a.O. 47: "Hartmann aber verstösst gegen die Grundkonzeption der Dichtung, die er als Ganzes ja durchaus übernommen hat, wenn er Laudine zu rechtfertigen unternimmt;"

29 Endres a.a.O. 517.

30 W. Ohly erkennt in der Ironie dieser Einlage verhüllte Kritik an Laudine und der übereilt zustandegekommenen Minne. "Man geht am Wesentlichen vorbei, wenn man meint, dass Hartmann aus mangelnder Gestaltungskraft oder einem unglücklichen Schwanken zwischen Freiheit und sklavischer Ergebenheit gegenüber seiner Quelle die Entlastung nicht glaubhaft machen *könne; er will* es in Wirklichkeit gar nicht." a.a.O. 108.

31 Besonders auffällig an der zentralen Stelle, wo Iweins Schuld manifest wird und die in Abhängigkeit von 'man saget daz' (3052f.) berichtet wird.

23

Iwein 7027   'ich waene, vriunt Hartman,
dû missedenkest dar an . . .

oder dem Publikum ein Vorurteil unterschiebt:

Iwein 2581   und der herre Keiî
swie boese ir waenet daz er sî,

um mit einem Gegenbeweis zu triumphieren; wo er sich schliesslich offen von seiner Quelle distanziert:

Iwein 1548   ez ist der wunden alsô gewant,   (Topos der Minnewunde)
sî *wellent* daz sî langer swer
danne diu von swerte ode von sper,

oder sich mit Skepsis zu einem Sagenmotiv äussert:

Iwein 1355   nû ist uns ein dinc geseit
vil dicke vür die wârheit:
swer den andern habe erslagen,
und wurder zuo im getragen,
swie langer dâ vor waere wunt,
er begunde bluoten anderstunt.
nû sehet, alsô begunden
im bluoten sîne wunden,

verschafft er dem Hörer jedesmal, schon durch die Verlangsamung des Erzähltempos, Distanz und Freiheit zu eigener Anschauung und fordert ihn zu selbständigem Urteil auf. Denn diese Dichtung begreift sich nicht als Endgültiges, sondern sie ist dem Vollzug des Hörers anheimgestellt, ist Anlass und " 'figura' einer noch unerreichbaren Erfüllungswirklichkeit"[32].

Verfremdend wirken auch jene Äusserungen, mit denen der Dichter eine erwartete Darstellung verkürzt und dem Hörer dadurch die Dimension des künstlerischen Vorgehens, des so-oder-anders-Präsentierens, ins Bewusstsein rückt. Wenn Hartmann kurzerhand abbricht mit 'waz sol der rede mêre?' (2416) oder dem auf Kampfesschilderungen erpichten Publikum überlegen (da er Höheres zu bieten hat) ein Schnippchen schlägt:

Iwein 1029   ich machete des strîtes vil
mit worten, wan daz ich enwil,
als ich iu bescheide:

— weil nämlich keiner dabei gewesen sei, der den Hergang getreulich rapportieren könnte[33] — oder ähnlich

---

32 Erich Auerbach, Figura, in: Neue Dantestudien. Istanbuler Schriften 5 (1944) 57.
33 Humoristisch gefärbter Verkürzungstopos, wie ihn auch die mlat. Dichtung kennt; vgl. den Schluss des "Waltharius" (1451f.), den Ekkehard mit dem stumpfgewordenen Griffel begründet.

Iwein 6939   machet ich diz vehten
               von disen guoten knehten
               mit worten nû vil spaehe,
               waz töhte diu waehe?

so lösen solche launigen Schnörkel überraschte Heiterkeit, Enttäuschung oder aber kultiviert-eingeweihtes Augenzwinkern im Publikum aus, lassen den Bericht jedenfalls vielfältig, um Möglichkeiten bereichert, werden, denn nun stellt sich der Hörer den Kampf in Gedanken vor, vernimmt gleichzeitig jedoch den Gegenzug des Dichters, durch den, in unterschwelliger Wirkung, der gesamte Vordergrund der Geschichte ironisiert und das Schwergewicht dadurch auf eine andere Ebene verlagert wird. Indem solche Stellen der Erwartung eines einzigmöglichen, unverrückbaren Geschehens zuwiderlaufen, wirken sie relativierend auf die Märchenhaftigkeit der Erzählung ein.

Auffälliger noch als solche topischen Zwischenbemerkungen ist in dieser Beziehung der improvisierte *Disput des Dichters mit Frau Minne,* die unerwartet auftritt, als sich Iwein von Laudine trennt, um sein Rittertum erneut unter Beweis zu stellen[34]. In einem sich über 58 Verse erstreckenden Zwischenspiel zitiert sie den Dichter vor die Schranken, stellt ihn über sein Dichten zur Rede und erteilt ihm in eigener Person eine Lektion in Minnetheorie.

Iwein 2971   dô vrâgete mich vrou Minne
               des ich von mînem sinne
               niht geantwurten kan.
               sî sprach 'sage an, Hartman,
               gihestû daz der künec Artûs
               hern Iweinen vuorte ze hûs
               und liez sîn wîp wider varn? '
               done kund ich mich niht baz bewarn,
               wan ich saget irz vür die wârheit,
               wand ez was ouch mir vür wâr geseit.
               sî sprach, und sach mich twerhes an,
               dune hâst niht wâr, Hartman'[35].

Der zugrundeliegende Bescheidenheitstopos ist hier zu einer zweistimmigen demonstrativ-belehrenden Reflexion ausgebaut, die in lebhaftem Hin und Her mit These und Antithese operiert. Unterschlagung, Unverständnis wirft ihm Frau Minne vor; wohl hat er berichtet, wie die Liebenden unter Schmerz sich trennten, nicht

---

34 Das Streitgespäch (disputatio) ist als literarische Form und denkerische Methode zu dieser Zeit hoch im Kurs. Im höfischen Roman tritt es vereinzelt als dramatisch belebendes Schmuckstück oder als Mittel feinsinnig-theoretischer Erörterungen auf, vgl. das Gespräch zwischen Frau Aventiure und dem Dichter im "Parzival" 433,1–434,10. Dass dem in den Artes, und damit auch in Dialektik geschulten Hartmann diese Gattung entspricht, beweist seine "Klage", die als 'strît' zwischen Herz und Leib das Wesen der Minne zu ergründen sucht.
35 Vgl. dazu Dittmann a.a.O.

25

aber, der Quelle getreu, dass Iwein sein Herz bei Laudine zurückliess und das ihre mit sich führte. Offenbar übersteigt solche Metaphorik der Innerlichkeit Hartmanns Vorstellungskraft, denn — so wendet er naiv-listig ein: wie sollte sich Iwein mit einem zarten Frauenherz in der Brust auf dem Turnierplatz behaupten[36]?

Wer Hartmanns Stutzen an dieser Stelle jedoch für bare Münze nähme[37], für ein ernsthaftes Problem und überlegte Kritik an der Quelle, liesse sich narren. Der durch die Troubadours aufgekommene Herztausch-Topos ist in der Literatur des 12. und 13. Jhs. längst als rhetorische Figur geläufig, und Hartmann verwendet sie in seinen früheren Werken, ohne Anstoss zu nehmen[38]. Seine plötzliche Pedanterie im "Iwein", mit der er den kleingläubigen Rationalisten mimt, sein Wörtlichnehmen einer metaphorischen, 'uneigentlichen' Redeform, ist unterhaltsamer, auflockernder Überraschungseffekt, Didaktik im Gewande des Spiels.

Einen Heiterkeitsaufschwung erreicht dieses vor allem da, wo sich der Dichter dem schmähenden Tadel seiner Richterin aussetzt, wo er gezielt und mit einer Selbstironie, die ihm sein Wertbewusstsein erlaubt und welche wohl humoristisch ist, aber offenbar im Werk doch ihren Platz haben muss, sein Dichten selbst in Frage stellt.

Iwein 3011   dô zêch mich vrou Minne,
                ich waere kranker sinne.
                sî sprach 'tuo zuo dînen munt,
                dir ist diu beste vuore unkunt.

Wer mit so schwachem geistigem Vermögen ('vuore' = Weg, Art und Weise) nur die Oberfläche, den Literalsinn der Vorgänge fasst, verdient den Namen Dichter nicht. Wie aber soll Hartmann in Dingen der Minne bewandert sein? Hat sie ihn selbst doch nie so leidenschaftlich ergriffen, dass das Umstrittene ihm zur Erfahrung geworden wäre.

36 Anlass zu diesem rhetorischen Einfall ist Chrétien, der sich mit dem erwachenden psychologischen Interesse des 12. Jhs. über den metaphorischen Ausdruck beugt und den Umstand, dass Yvain sein Herz bei der Geliebten zurückliess, als 'mervoille' bezeichnet, als Wunder, das noch keiner sah (2650). Ähnlich reflektiert er im "Cligés" in einem fingierten Zwiegespräch über den Wirklichkeitsgehalt dieses Bildes (Ausg. Alexandre Micha, Paris 1967 (CFMA) V. 2779f.).
37 So Arthur Witte, Hartmann von Aue und Kristian von Troyes, I. Teil: Yvain und Iwein. Beitr. 53, Halle 1929, 155.
38 Erec 2364   der vil getriuwe man,
                ir herze vuorte er mit im dan,
                daz sîn beleip dem wîbe
                versigelt in ir lîbe.
   Greg. 651   ein getriuwiu wandelunge ergie,
                dô si sich muosen scheiden hie:
                sîn herze volgete ir von dan,
                daz ir bestuont bî dem man.
Ähnlich "Greg." 1966, "Le Chevalier de la Charrete", hg. von Mario Roques, Paris 1958 (CFMA) V. 4697f., "Lancelot und Ginevra", Nacherzählung von Ruth Schirmer, Zürich 1961, S. 166. Vgl. auch "Heloissae et Abaelardi Epistolae", I: "Non enim mecum animus meus sed tecum erat." (Dt. Übers. von Eberh. Brost, 3. Aufl., Heidelberg, S. 85).

26

Iwein 3015   dichn geruorte nie mîn meisterschaft:
              ich bin ez Minne und gibe die kraft
              daz ofte man unde wîp
              habent herzelôsen lîp
              und hânt ir kraft doch deste baz.'

Ein solches Bekenntnis vor versammeltem Publikum gleicht einer verschmitzten
Provokation, die auf ein Echo wartet[39]. Worauf zielt nun aber hinter dieser ganzen
Belustigung die beabsichtigte Wirkung? Denn auf der Ebene des Romanhaften
nimmt das Geschehen unbehelligt seinen Gang, lässt ihm Hartmann, kleinlaut
geworden, sein Recht widerfahren —

Iwein 3023   daz wunder das gesach ich nie,
              doch ergienc ez nâch ir rede hie. —

und wo die Quelle später an die vertauschten Herzen anknüpft, folgt Hartmann ihr,
ohne sich darüber aufzuhalten: 'daz in diu niht erkande / diu doch sîn herze bî ir
truoc, / daz was wunders genuoc.' (5456f.)
      Die Bedeutung liegt auch hier nicht so sehr in einer nach vorn weisenden
Erkenntnis, als in einem Näherführen zum Wahren: einer Bewusstseinsschärfung im
sprachlichen und sinnmässigen Erkennen des Werks. Sprachlich: denn hinter aller
Komik macht Hartmanns gemimte Begriffsstutzigkeit doch blitzartig etwas vom
Wesen der Sprache, von ihrer Leistung und Täuschung bewusst und von der Kluft,
die den Bereich der Wörter von dem der Lebenswirklichkeit trennt. Hinter der
Oberfläche weitet sich der sprachliche Ausdruck zur Vielfalt seines inneren Sinns.
So auch die Aussage der Geschichte selbst: Denn dass die Liebe zwischen Iwein und
Laudine dieses leicht spöttische In-Frage-Stellen des Dichters verträgt, heisst doch
wohl, dass sie nicht mehr, wie im "Erec", den endgültigen Mittelpunkt des Romans
darstellt, sondern dass der volle Ernst einer anderen Ordnung gilt. Die Minne, die
Laudine einflösst, und ihre unbedingte Forderung, die sie stellt, sind wohl reales
Geschehen, stehen aber auch zeichenhaft für jenen totalen Anspruch im Leben des
Ritters, der Anlass zu seinem Heilsweg wird. Eine andere, geistige Ordnung birgt
sich hinter dem wörtlichen Sinn, und die feinen ironischen Signale des Dichters
fordern den Hörer auf, zu dieser gewichtigeren Ordnung, zu diesem grösseren Mass
in eigener Suche durchzudringen und sie im Gewand des sinnlich Realen zu
erkennen.
      Eine unüberhörbare Zäsur markiert den Einsatz des Minnedisputs. Gegen Ende
des Romans, vor allem beim Zweikampf mit Gawan, wechselt Hartmann jedoch
häufig und unauffällig die Ebene des Spiels. Bericht und dichterisch-allegorische
Reflexion gehen fast gesprächsartig ineinander über, so als ob das Ende von Iweins
Läuterungsweg oder auch die komplizenhafte Verbundenheit, mit der hier Dichter
und Hörer hinter die geschlossenen Visiere der sich bekämpfenden Freunde sehen,
die gesprächige Geselligkeit des Dichters erhöhte. Fast löschen Sentenzen, Refle-

---

39 Ähnlich werben auch Wolfram und Gottfried um die Sympathie des Publikums: "Parz."
130,14f., 554,4f., 807,5f.; "Tristan" 12187f.

xionen und Gleichnisse die konkrete Szene auf dem Turnierplatz aus[40]; flüchtig nur sieht man Pferde laufen und Lanzen aufblitzen. Den Kampf selbst, dessen Bedeutung ja nicht im Ausgang liegt, sondern im Aufzeigen von Iweins ritterlichem Wert, in der Bestätigung seiner wiedererlangten 'êre' durch das Bestehen vor Artus' bewährtestem Held, ficht Hartmann bildlich, in gleitenden Übergängen zwischen realem und allegorischem Bereich, zwischen objektivem Bericht und belehrender oder humoristischer Abschweifung aus.

All diese kommentierenden und umspielenden Glossen, Ich-Äusserungen und Betrachtungen prägen die Gestalt von Hartmanns Roman. Bedingt z.T. durch die Nachdichtungssituation, die dem Übernommenen die eigene Anschauung und Absicht entgegenstellt, wird in ihnen die Eigenart und Ausrichtung des Dichters offenbar, der nicht Halt macht vor dem Bild und der Formel, sondern sie beharrlich nach ihrer Aussage und Vorbildlichkeit und nach dem Verbindenden zum eigenen Leben befragt. Diese besinnliche Haltung charakterisiert auch die Romanfiguren selbst, die nicht mehr wie die Recken des Heldenlieds in Entscheidung und Handlung aufgehen, sondern sich fragend über ihr Inneres beugen und den 'homo interior' monologisch ins Sichtbare heben.

Im Gegensatz zur Heldendichtung, wo der Sänger die Sage in völliger Eindeutigkeit ausbreitet, bildet sich im höfischen Roman ein eigentliches dichterisches Selbstbewusstsein aus, das sich in der bewusst geäusserten Überlegenheit und Distanz dem Stoff gegenüber und in der Suche nach seinem Sinn manifestiert[41]. Das Werk erscheint als das eines individuellen Dichters, der erweiternd und unterweisend in das Geschehen eingreift und das Publikum fortwährend in den Erzählvorgang integriert[42].

Bei Chrétien steht die szenische Darstellung, die Anschaulichkeit der Handlung und der Figuren im Vordergrund; in kunstvollem Aufbau folgen sich die bedeutungsreichen Bilder, wechselnd zwischen gleichmässiger Ruhe und spannender Turbulenz. Auch Chrétien setzt Werturteile und rhetorische Beteuerungen ein. Doch kommt es nicht wie bei Hartmann zu jener gemischten Erzählweise, in der, alternierend zur Handlung, immer wieder die Stimme des Dichters vernehmbar wird, die auf einen Vorgang seine Deutung oder eine Reflexion darüber folgen lässt[43].

40 'minne und haz' (7015f.), 'borgen und gelten' (7147f.). Hartmann vergleicht die Kämpfenden zwei geizenden Händlern: 7189 'sî wâren zwêne maere / karge wehselaere' und schiebt zwischen den Kampfbericht scheinbar allen Ernstes eine Reflexion über Freizügigkeit im Borgen ein; nur die spielerischen Wortwiederholungen an dieser Stelle decken seine wohlige Heiterkeit und sein verstecktes Lächeln über die eigene moralistische Neigung auf. Das geistreiche rhetorische Spiel an dieser Stelle fehlt bei Chrétien.
41 Vgl. dazu Erich Köhler, Zur Selbstauffassung des höfischen Dichters, in: Der Vergleich. FG Hellmuth Petriconi, Hamburg 1955, 65–79.
42 "So gehört zum Stil auch der ritterlichen Dichtung die dauernde Einbeziehung des geselligen Publikums, damit das erzählerische Tun seinen Sinn und seinen Ort immer wieder erhalte." Max Wehrli, Wolframs Humor, in: Überlieferung und Gestaltung. FG Theophil Spoerri, Zürich 1950, 20.
43 Auch die Antike kennt den epischen Bericht mit eingestreuter Rede, hauptsächlich in der Nachfolge Platos, der die mimische Dichtung als Täuschung und Lüge aus dem Staat verbannen will ("Staat" 393–396) und nur die berichtende Erzählung gelten lässt, in der die Präsenz des Dichters unverkennbar bleibt.

Indem Hartmann das Tun der Romanfiguren motiviert, beurteilt oder es zur eigenen Erfahrung in Beziehung setzt, verlängert er das Geschehen in die Reflexion hinein und hält die flüchtigen Bilder zurück. Die Wahrheit von Hartmanns Werk ist nicht eine andere als bei Chrétien, aber sie ist greifbarer und vermittelnd in die Nähe des Hörers gerückt. Immer wieder wird der Bogen zum Menschlich-Realen geschlagen. So fügt Hartmann mitten im fabulösen Kampf zwischen Löwe und Drache eine Überlegung, eine Art Spruchweisheit über die Unberechenbarkeit aller, auch menschlicher Dankbarkeit ein:

Iwein 3854   wan alsô ist ez gewant,
                als ez ouch under den liuten stât:
                so man aller beste gedienet hât
                dem ungewissen manne,
                sô hüeter sich danne
                daz ern iht beswîche.
                dem was diz wol gelîche.,

und auch aus dem Märchenmotiv von Iweins Rettung durch den unsichtbar machenden Ring zieht Hartmann, sinnend, es nicht dabei belassend, noch die Lehre, dass auch das wunderbare Geschenk immer nur dem Unerschrockenen zufällt:

Iwein 1298   bî sîner genist nim ich war,
                unz der man niht veige enist,
                sô nert in ein vil cleiner list.

Seine Betrachtungen über die Wirkung der Minne (1566f.), die Gastfreundschaft (2683f.) oder die Dankbarkeit (2731f.) runden die stilisiert gezeichneten Vorgänge ab, verleihen ihnen subjektive Färbung und Verbindlichkeit und holen sie in den Raum menschlicher Wirklichkeit hinein.

Die Geistigkeit, die das durchreflektierte Werk damit erreicht, überträgt sich unmittelbar auch auf die Haltung des Hörers. Schlussfolgerungen und Hinweise auf den Bedeutungskern eines Vorfalls sollen den Hörer immer wieder dazu anhalten, sich von den Vorgängen zu lösen und auf das Wesentliche: die spirituelle und moralische Realität des Geschehens, zu besinnen[44]. Zu Beginn der Erzählung Kalogreants, die miniaturartig die Situation des höfischen Dichters in seinem Kreis abzeichnet, fordert der Ritter von seinen Hörern die rechte Einstellung; der Bericht seines unrühmlichen Misserfolgs kann nur dann einen Sinn haben, wenn er weiterführt.

Iwein 245   'sô vernemt ez mit guotem site
                unde mietet mich dâ mite:
                ich sag iu deste gerner vil,

---

44 Arthur Witte, der in seiner vergleichenden Charakteristik einseitig dem Franzosen Beifall zollt, ohne die Blickeinstellung, die Hartmanns Werk in seiner künstlerischen Eigenart erfordert, zu suchen, verurteilt gerade diese deutende, der Unmittelbarkeit Chrétiens entgegengesetzte Darstellung, durch die Hartmann "ein kunstwerk zerstöre". (a.a.O. 191)

ob manz ze rehte merken wil.
man verliuset michel sagen,
man enwellez merken unde dagen.
maniger biutet diu ôren dar:
ern nemes ouch mit dem herzen war,
sone wirt im niht wan der dôz,
und ist der schade alze grôz,
wan si verliesent beide ir arbeit,
der dâ hoeret und der dâ seit.

Auch für den Hörer ist wahres Erkennen der Dichtung 'arbeit', die sich nicht in passivem Vernehmen, nicht in Hingerissenheit erschöpft, sondern die in innerem Bedenken und Anverwandeln schöpferisch wird. Zu solchem Weiterdenken vom Text aus ist die Inkohärenz der Erzählart, sind die fortwährenden Seitensprünge, Unterbrechungen und Gedankeneinschiebungen des Dichters Voraussetzung. Mit Hartmann ist die Richtung gegeben, in der Wolfram, freimütiger und weiter ausgreifend, mit dem ihm eigentümlichen Humor, seine Erzählung durchflechten wird.

2. Vielfalt der Perspektiven

Das fortwährende Absetzen und Neueinsetzen ist als Eigenart jedoch tiefer in der mittelalterlichen Denk- und Dichtform verwurzelt, als dass es sich einzig in den Einschaltungen aus höfischer Warte in die Stoffwelt ausprägte. Ein Weiteres wirkt am Eindruck des Unverbunden-Vielfältigen dieser Romane mit.

Es scheint, als schlage der Erzählgang darin innerlich, seiner dichterisch-gedanklichen Gesetzlichkeit nach, unerwartet immer wieder eine andere Richtung ein, stosse in Bereiche von veränderter Resonanz und neuer atmosphärischer Färbung vor und setzte unbehelligt die Schilderung oder Argumentation über mühelos vollzogene Sprünge und Wendungen hinaus fort. Bildschichten und Ausdrucksformen verschiedenen Ursprungs und von ungleichem Gewicht in ihrer Aussage erscheinen ineinandergefügt, und Bedeutungen in mehrfacher Richtung machen sich geltend, spannen ein verzweigtes Netz thematischer Ansätze, Verbindungslinien und Übereinstimmungen aus oder leuchten auch nur punktuell, an isolierter Stelle auf.

Im Gegensatz zu jeder "perspektivischen" Dichtung, in der der Autor einen festen Standort einnimmt, oder allenfalls den Wechsel mit Absicht zum Spiel erhebt, und von da aus, mit dem Blick aufs Ganze, die Erzählwelt als einheitliche entwickelt, fällt im höfischen Roman eine solcherart sich ergebende Durchschaubarkeit aus. In uneingeschränkter Wirkkraft besteht hier die Fabelwelt mit ihren Verkürzungen und Verdichtungen neben eindimensionalen Partien der Reflexion und der Nachbildung äusserer Wirklichkeit, besteht das Undurchsichtige, Rätselhafte zusammen mit dem grundlegenden Willen zu klärender, oft ins Spitzfindige geratender Analyse. "Stimmigkeit", sachliche und gedankliche Kohärenz, können in einer Dichtung, die gerade an zentralen Stellen das Wort und die Szene als Gleichnis setzt, deren letzte Gestalt also über das Beschriebene hinausdrängt, gar nicht angestrebt sein.

So wie die bildliche Darstellung dieser Epoche als Beziehungsfeld angeordneter Aussageexponenten, nicht als künstlich proportionierte, täuschende Raumordnung erscheint[45], sind es auch hier vielfältige Sichtwinkel, von denen aus der Stoff abgeschritten und nach seiner geistigen Wahrheit befragt wird. Unablässig sieht sich der Leser von einem Unerwarteten: einem Sprung im Handlungsablauf, einem Wandel des Schauplatzes oder einem neuen Aspekt in der Beurteilung überrascht und auf eine andere Ebene versetzt.

Im "Iwein" gehört dieser Perspektivenwechsel, dieses Spiel der fortwährenden Übergänge und Zusammenklänge, mit zum besonderen Reiz des Werks.

Zu Beginn haben sich vier Ritter, Standfiguren des Artuskreises, um Kalogreant, den Neffen Iweins, versammelt, um seine aussergewöhnliche 'âventiure' zu vernehmen; noch ein fünfter hört, wenn auch nur mit halbem Ohr, zu: Keii, der sich, schläfrig und unbekümmert um höfische Etikette, zur Wand gedreht hat. Die Feststunde ist fortgeschritten, über alles Zeremoniell hinaus; die einzelnen Gruppen haben sich, ihren Liebhabereien nachgehend, verzogen. In der königlichen Kemenate wacht die Königin von Kalogreants Stimme auf; da lässt ihr die Neugier keine Ruhe: 'sî lie ligen den künec ir man / unde stal sich von im dan' (99f.).

Allen andern zuvorkommend, eilt ihr Kalogreant mit galanter Verneigung entgegen. Diese Auszeichnung, dieser Beweis vollendeter, geistesgegenwärtiger 'hövescheit' genügt, um dem streitlustigen Keii, dem jedes andern 'êre' ein Stachel ist, allen Schlaf blitzartig zu vertreiben; gehässig und spöttisch sich spreizend, greift er Kalogreant an.

Iwein 108
      do erzeiget aber Keiî
      sîn alte gewonheit:
      im was des mannes êre leit,
      und beruoft in drumbe sêre
      und sprach im an sîn êre.

Zu allem Höfischen, Gemässigten und Kultivierten ist Keii immer wieder der polternde Gegenton, der Eckige innerhalb einer harmonisch geglätteten Sozietät; sein Name löst, wie der von Artus oder Gawan, eine ganz bestimmte Erwartung aus: Angriffig, draufgängerisch, überheblich − gefürchtet und verspottet zugleich, liefert er unermüdlich Schauspiele der Lächerlichkeit; seine hochtrabenden Reden und das darauf unweigerlich folgende Misslingen (vgl. 2454f.) geben jedesmal Anlass zu Witz und Gelächter, in dem sich die Spannung der hochgehaltenen höfischen Idealität, des reibungslos funktionierenden Zeremoniells entlädt. Hartmann knüpft hier an die literarische Kenntnis seines Publikums an; aus andern Artusromanen, aus dem "Erec" zumindest, ist ihm Keiis ruppig-dissonante Art, die Rolle des erfolglos um-sich-Schlagenden bekannt − sie ist 'gewonheit' (148, 204).

45 Vgl. dazu Wilhelm Messerer, Einige Darstellungsprinzipien der Kunst im Mittelalter. DVjs 36 (1962) 157−179.

Solche 'gewonheiten', d.h. zum vornherein festgelegte, gleichbleibend wirksame Einrichtungen, Figuren und Themen, bilden verfügbare Bausteine des Artusromans. Typische Szenen, die für menschliche Grundsituationen stehen: das Fest des Königs, die Herausforderung, der Kampf mit dem Verräter oder dem Monstrum, der Zwischenhalt auf der Burg und die Konfrontation mit dem nicht mehr erkannten Freund, aber auch undurchsichtige, in der Sage wurzelnde Motive, wie die Jagd auf den weissen Hirsch, die Überforderung der 'milte' des Königs oder der Automatismus der Zauberquelle im "Iwein", sind als Bildmuster und Ausdrucksmittel für eine innere Station immer wieder eingesetzt[46]. Wo dabei die märchenartige Gesetzlichkeit solcher Vorgänge mit dem aufbrechenden Willen des Dichters zu realistisch-psychologischer Erfassung zusammenstösst, entsteht etwas eigentümlich Gemischtes.

Als eine solche Figur, an der verschiedene Aspekte gleichzeitig zur Geltung kommen, erscheint der Ritter *Keii* in Hartmanns Darstellung. Chrétien zeichnet ihn als geschlossene, eindeutige Figur, als 'vilain' (90) am Hof: "unleidig, hinterlistig, scharfzüngig und giftig"[47] schilt er ihn, und der zu Tage tretende, stereotyp reagierende Charakter stimmt damit überein. Auch bei Hartmann bildet die 'gewonheit' den Grundton; noch bevor Keii in Aktion tritt, wird er, wie mit einer Kennmarke versehen, als 'zuhtlôs' (90) vorgeführt, und in all jenen Episoden, in denen er in den Mittelpunkt rückt, spielt er, wie es der Roman und der Fortgang der Handlung erfordern, seine Rolle als komisch-kontrastierende Gegenfigur[48]. Doch bleibt es nicht bei dieser Eindeutigkeit. Hartmann lässt ihn seine undankbare Rolle zwar spielen, verlängert aber den Blick und gibt den Hörern, aus dem deutlichen Bestreben heraus, möglichst viele Aspekte eines Phänomens mitzuberücksichtigen, die Kühnheit und den unberechnenden Einsatz, die Keiis Unternehmen immerhin auszeichnen, zu bedenken; so unmittelbar nach seiner schmählichen Niederlage an der Quelle:

Iwein 2565 ouch sag ich iu ein maere:
swie schalkhaft Keiî waere,
er was iedoch vil unervorht.
enhaet in sîn zunge niht verworht,
sone gewan der hof nie tiurren helt.

Aber auch schon in der Streitszene zu Beginn meldet sich Hartmann mit einem Gegenzug. Das eindeutige Schwarz-Weiss, wie es bei Chrétien erscheint, ist in einer komplexeren Darstellung ausgestaltet und aufgehoben, die Stilisierung durchbrochen. Hartmann geht auf die Figuren ein. Vor allem äussert sich eine

---

46 'Gewonheiten' ('coutumes') in der Bedeutung von Rechtsbräuchen stellt Erich Köhler unter soziologischem Deutungsaspekt zusammen in: Le rôle de la 'coutume' dans les romans de Chrétien de Troyes. Rom. 81 (1960) 386–397.
47 69 Et Kex, qui molt fu ranponeus,
fel et poignanz et venimeus . . .
48 H. B. Willson erblickt in Keii den gewohnheitsmässigen Sünder, die Verkörperung der superbia. (The Role of Keii in Hartmann's 'Iwein', Med. Aev. 30 (1961) 145–158).

Verschiebung in seiner Auffassung und Wertung Keiis. Der Spötter zeigt sich hier schuldbewusst und versöhnlich (160–184), und trotz der einmütigen Missbilligung, die die Gesellschaft ihm zollt, scheint es zuweilen fast, als liege der verbindliche, menschliche Akzent bei ihm:

Iwein 171
'ir strâfet mich als einen kneht:
gnâde ist bezzer danne reht
ichn hân iu solhes niht getân,
ir möhtet mich wol leben lân . . .

Den Bösewicht mit dem hölzernen Herzen versieht Hartmann mit einer inneren Dimension[49]. Einen Augenblick lang sind die Rollen beinahe vertauscht: der 'zuhtlôse' ist es hier selbst, der die Königin an Zucht und Milde gemahnt (167–170).

Stufenweise nimmt der Hörer das Vorgezeigte wahr: grundierend die Andeutung der 'gewonheit' und in den ausführenden Farben darüber gelagert den vermenschlichten Keii, der seine Eigenart gegenüber der Gesellschaft behauptet[50]. Die Änderung ist nicht allein mit Hartmanns 'mâze' zu erklären. Vielmehr deutet die leichte Akzentverschiebung, in der der Artushof mit seinen durchscheinend-zierlichen Figuren unmerklich aus dem Sattel der Unangefochtenheit gehoben ist, bereits hier auf den Stellenwert, den das Menschliche gegenüber dem rein formal-Höfischen einnimmt. Der Anspruch des Artushofes ist reduziert; seine Rolle ist nur noch eine poetische. Auf der Stufe der hellsichtiger und intensiver gewordenen Suche nach dem 'saelden wec', die der "Yvain" als Vorläufer des Gralsromans darstellt, ist das Artusreich als Wertzentrum schon nicht mehr völlig ernst genommen[51]; der blosse Massstab des Höfischen genügt nicht mehr, und deshalb erscheint auch der Aussenseiter Keii bei Hartmann in einem anderen Licht.

In einer Interpretation der Bluttropfenszene im "Perceval" verurteilt Reto R. Bezzola mit Blick auf Wolfram solche "Einmischungen der Denktätigkeit" des Erzählers[52]. Auch Hartmann hebt sich in ähnlicher Weise von Chrétien ab; in jedem der beiden Iwein-Romane drückt sich ein anderer Stilwille aus. Chrétiens Gestaltung

---

49 Auch im "Erec" ist Keii gegenüber der Vorlage gemildert. Die Erklärung für sein widersprüchliches Gebaren findet Hartmann in einer eigentümlichen Gespaltenheit seines Wesens: 'sîn herze was gevieret' (4636f.) — sowohl guter Wille ('groziu triuwe') als Boshaftigkeit und Falschheit, kühner Mut und Feigheit wohnten darin und gelangten an verschiedenen Tagen abwechselnd zur Wirkung.
In der Artusliteratur ist Keii, Artus' Ziehbruder, überhaupt eine zwiespältige Figur, schwankend zwischen der Wertschätzung des Königs, die schon seine Stellung als Seneschall bedingt, und seinen Charakterzügen, mit denen er seit Chrétien zum Antitypus des höfischen Helden gestempelt ist. Eigenmächtiger und eindeutiger als Hartmann ist Wolfram in seiner, wie oft, opponierenden Rechtfertigung ("Parz." 296,16f.); Keii erscheint hier als scharfsichtiger, von der Konvention unverbildeter und geachteter Kritiker.
50 Vgl. zu dieser Ambivalenz Humphrey Milnes, The Play of Opposites in "Iwein", a.a.O. 243f.
51 Vgl. Walter Ohly a.a.O. 99–104. "Nach der Entlarvung des brüchigen Untergrundes einer sich selbst autark setzenden Welt in den beiden Legenden kann die Welt des Artushofes nicht mehr den Rang einer in sich ruhenden innerweltlichen Heilssphäre haben." (104)
52 Liebe und Abenteuer im höfischen Roman, Hamburg 1961, 32–33.

ist reiner, von leuchtender Prägnanz und Symbolkraft. Die Stilbewegung, mit der Hartmann das umgrenzte Bild, die symbolische Formel aufbricht, ist ein Wegrücken vom "intuitiven Symbolismus" des Franzosen. Sie bedeutet aber gleichzeitig ein Weiterschreiten, ein Ausgreifen im literarischen Erfahren menschlicher Wirklichkeit. Gerade in der bei Hartmann angedeuteten Komplexität und Mischung, im Bereichern der Gesichtspunkte, von denen jeder einzelne seine Bedeutung ungemindert behält, im Ausweiten und Anfüllen der Bilder mit Gedankengängen ist seine dichterische Leistung zu fassen.

Mit der Beendigung des Streits ist der Kreis dieser Episode geschlossen; in den höfischen Rahmen schiebt sich mit Kalogreants Bericht ein magischer Raum von traumartiger Färbung. Von einem zeitlich und räumlich fixierten Punkt, dem Pfingstfest in Karidol (Wales), wo der Hof, wenn auch romanhaft-imaginär, angesiedelt ist, sind wir, über das trennende Meer hinweg, hineinversetzt in den Wald der Verheissung und der gefährlichen Abenteuer, der ungerufen auftauchenden Begegnungen und des Feenzaubers, wo die Schranken der Wirklichkeit, die Gesetze von Raum und Zeit nicht mehr gelten; der Name Breziljân (263) eröffnet das Märchen. Auf engem, beschwerlichem Steig reitet Kalogreant durch die Wildnis, fern von Menschen und menschlichem Bezirk, ohne bestimmtes Ziel, der Erprobung entgegen.

Die innere Unbegrenztheit des Waldes verengt sich wieder, als Kalogreant beim Hereinbrechen des Abends Rast hält auf einer Burg. Aus dem weiten Raum des unbegrenzt Möglichen wird der Blick zurückgeführt auf höfische Realität, auf Alltagssphäre, die den Hörern vertraut ist und die voll Interesse am Detail, an Kleidung, Brauch und Einrichtung beschrieben wird[53]. Die Gastfreundschaft ist mit höfischer Selbstverständlichkeit gewährt; hier befindet sich Kalogreant noch im Gewohnten. Eitel Wohlbefinden herrscht hier, unerwartetes, müheloses Glück fällt ihm zu. Doch ist dieser Aufenthalt nur reizvoll ausgestattetes Zwischenstück, und die wohltuende Begegnung mit der lieblichen Tochter gleicht im Geschehnisrhythmus einem hellen Vor- und Gegenton zur kommenden Bedrohnis. Voll Unruhe drängt Kalogreant weiter.

Die Schwelle des Realen ist hinter dieser Station überschritten; der Ritter dringt in die innersten, geheimnisbergenden Kreise vor. Auf einer Einöde, 'in dem walde verborgen' (400) sieht er sich plötzlich vor einem Unheimlichen: einem buckligen, finster aussehenden *Waldmann,* der, mit einer schweren Keule bewaffnet, stumm und unbeweglich zunächst, inmitten wild sich bekämpfender Tiere verharrt. Von furchterregender Grösse und Hässlichkeit, 'einem môre glîch' (427)[54], bannt die Erscheinung, die auf 43 Versen (425–468) beschrieben wird, den Blick.

---

53 Vgl. die meisterhafte Beschreibung dieser Übergänge bei Erich Auerbach: Mimesis, Bern (3)1964, VI. Kap. "Der Auszug des höfischen Ritters" (120–138).
54 Im kymrischen Mabinogion, d.h. in der von den in Wales lebenden Kelten im 14. Jh. aufgezeichneten Prosafassung "Owain und Lluned" ist laut Rud. Zenker (Forschungen zur Artusepik, I. Ivainstudien. ZfrPh 70 [1921] 324) nicht nur der Waldmann schwarz; auch der Quellenhüter erscheint in schwarzem Gewand, mit schwarzer Lanzenfahne, auf schwarzem Ross, und selbst der Löwe ist schwarz. Zenker nimmt dies als Indiz dafür, dass das Reich, in das der Held auf seiner Fahrt entrückt wird, in der irisch-keltischen Sage mit dem

Kein grösserer Kontrast als der zwischen der lichten Erscheinung des glanzvoll gerüsteten Ritters, der sich, noch angetan mit den Farben gesellschaftlicher 'vröide' und 'êre', aus dem Gesicherten gelöst hat und auf der Suche ist nach seiner Verwirklichung[55], – und diesem verwilderten, abstossenden Ungetüm, das, den unbändigen Tieren zugeordnet, an die verlassene Wildnis gebannt scheint, und das Kalogreant, der seinem Stand nach so ganz auf Schönheit und Harmonie Ausgerichtete mit sichtlicher Bekümmernis 'eine swaere ougenweide' (404) nennt. Sowohl die Sage, wie schon die antike Erzählung kennen den wilden Waldmenschen, den 'silvaticus', der die Ahnungslosen erschreckt. Typisch mittelalterlich ist hier jedoch, wie die Figur ausführlich und mit jener Faszination vor dem Absonderlichen und Grotesken, wie sie auch in der bildenden Kunst der Romanik oder in Fabelwesen der Buchmalerei zum Ausdruck kommt, geschildert wird. Der Kopf des Tierhüters, von dem das Haar verrusst und verfilzt zu Berge steht, ist grösser als der eines Auerochsen, das Kinn zur Brust herabgezogen und mit ihr verwachsen. Erleichternd und ergötzlich mischen sich humoristisch-burleske Farben ins Spiel: Wie Wannen sind die Ohren dieses Ungetüms, das Gesicht ist breit, 'mit grôzen runzen beleit' (438), und die Zähne sind die eines Ebers: 'ûzerhalp des mundes tür / rageten sî im her vür, / lanc, scharpf, grôz, breit.' (457f.).

Solch rätselhafte Sonderlinge, spannungssteigernde Ankündiger einer drohenden Gefahr oder eines Umschwungs, gehören als Repräsentanten eines bestimmten, vielseitig ausdeutbaren Bereichs zum Artusroman und wirken in ihrer dynamisch wirkenden Hässlichkeit mit an seiner Schönheit[56]. Es ist etwas in ihnen zusammengeballt, zu gesteigerter Ausdruckskraft verdichtet, mit der sie den Hörer in innere Bewegung versetzen und ästhetisch ein wirkungsvolles Gegengewicht zu allem Hellen und Geklärten bilden.

Gewohnt, mittelaltergemäss das Äussere als Zeichen eines Innern zu nehmen, erwarten wir Unheil, unentrinnbare Gefahr. Doch als dieser Ungeheure aufsteht und Iwein entgegentritt, bestürzt uns sein reiner Ton. Souverän ist seine beruhigende Geste: 'niene vürhte dir,' (516) zu dem verängstigten Ritter hin, und sein Hilfeangebot: 'ob du iht von mir geruochest, / daz ist allez getân.' (522f.) ist in vollkommen höfischem Ton gesprochen; auch hier hat Hartmann verändernd eingegriffen. Wohl sind dem Waldmann 'âventiure' und ritterliches Wesen fremd,

---

Totenreich gleichgesetzt war. Das Verhältnis zwischen dem Mabinogion und Chrétiens Roman und die Frage, ob beide evt. aus einer gemeinsamen Quelle schöpften, sind noch nicht geklärt.

55 Zur Gegenüberstellung des suchenden, strebenden Ritters mit dem Ungerührten, als Bild der Suche im religiösen und literarischen Schrifttum der gotischen Epoche vgl. Friedrich Ohly, Die Suche in Dichtungen des Mittelalters. ZfdA 94 (1965) 171–184.

56 Vgl. die Beschreibung Cundries ("Parz." 312,26f.), Malcreatiures ("Parz." 517,15f.), der hässlichen Ruel ("Wig." 6286f.).
Cramer (a.a.O. 35–36) erinnert an die Darstellung der Kainssöhne, z.B. in der Wiener Genesis (Ausg. Viktor Dollmayr 1932, V. 1292–1317), die im Mittelalter als Verführer zum Bösen galten und mit dem Waldungeheuer in einigen Zügen in Übereinstimmung stehen.
In den mittelalterlichen Poetiken figurieren neben den Richtlinien für die Idealisierung des Wohlgebildeten auch Modelle stilisierter Hässlichkeit. So Matthaeus von Vendôme, s. Faral a.a.O. 130–131.

den Weg, der zum Abenteuer führt, aber weiss nur er, und in geheimnisvoller, unaufgeklärter Weise ist dieser Wilde, dem die Tiere zitternd gehorchen, auch Eingeweihter: 'ich weiz wol' (562) und Mittler zum Laudinereich.

Eine symbolische Erklärung, die hier vom zurückstossenden Äussern bündig auf eine Verkörperung des Bösen und Unwahren schliesst, greift zu kurz. Reicher, komplexer sind die poetischen Gebilde der höfischen Kunst. Das 'uzen' und das 'innen' ("Tristan" 4623) einer Figur besteht offenbar nicht nur in symbolischer Übereinstimmung zwischen Zeichen und Inhalt, sondern kann eine Spannung in sich schliessen und ist vom mittelalterlichen Hörer gesondert, wie eine zwiegeteilte, zweistimmige Botschaft vernommen worden, in der den beiden Stimmen Eigenwert zukommt. Auch Cundrie ist schliesslich Abgesandte des Grals, und im "Gregorius" stimmen einige Züge des heiligmässigen Mannes, des Büssers auf dem Stein, fast wörtlich mit dem Waldmann im "Iwein" überein[57].

Ausdrücklicher als Chrétien hat Hartmann auch hier die hässliche Figur in den menschlichen Bereich, der nun allerdings die eng gezogenen Grenzen eines höfischen Zirkels sprengt, hereingenommen und integriert. Denn hier fällt dem 'walttôr' (440) nicht nur die Rolle des unheimlichen Wegweisers und des unterhaltsam-spannenden Widerparts zu; aus der Übersicht der Erzählung hat Hartmann noch eine andere Bedeutung in ihm erweckt: Bis in die lexikalische Bezeichnung hinein ist er in seiner Isoliertheit und seiner wüsten Gestalt Präfiguration des verstossenen Iwein, der in seinem Wahnsinn in die Tiefe des menschlichen Untergrundes hinabsinkt und als Genoss der Tiere, sinnentleert, nackt und schwarz, "in der Fremde des entstellten Ebenbildes"[58] durch die Wildnis irrt – Figur also jenes anderen, des 'edelen tôren' (3347). Wie der Waldmann wird auch Iwein 'griulîch' (3507), 'gebûre' (3557, 3573) und 'glîch einem môre' (3348) genannt. Hartmann hat damit dem 'ungehiuren' (526), der bei Chrétien noch mehr einem tierisch-dämonischen Zwischenreich angehört und dessen Bedeutung nach dieser Episode verstummt, seinen Platz angewiesen und mit unauffälligem Schöpfergeist eine neue Ordnung über die Materie erstellt.

Unablässig vollziehen sich Übergänge, nicht nur in den Erzählräumen, die der Dichter wechselnd durchschreitet, sondern auch in der Darstellung der Figuren, die sich immer wieder zu neuen Sinnhorizonten öffnen und deren Wahrheit stufenweise, Schritt um Schritt, sich zusammensetzt und offenbar wird. Denn gleichzeitig verkörpert der Waldmensch auf Iweins Weg der Selbstentwicklung eine wichtige und

57 "Gregorius"   "Iwein"
    3423 Der arme was zewâre
          erwhasen von dem hâre,
          verwalken zuo der swarte,   435 verwalken zuo der swarte
          an houbet und an barte:
          ê was ez ze rehte reit,
          nû ruozvar von der arbeit.   433 ein ragendes hâr ruozvar
    3439 diu ougen tief trüebe rôt,   451 diu ougen rôt, zornvar
    3441 mit brâwen behangen   445 granen unde brâ
          rûhen unde langen,   lanc, rûch unde grâ
58 "in regione dissimilitudinis", Augustinus, Confessiones VII,10,16 (lat.-dt. Ausg. von Joseph Bernhart, München (2)1960. Vgl. dazu "Iwein" 3358 'dem ist er nû vil ungelîch'.

36

unumgängliche Station: Er fordert vom Ritter die Auseinandersetzung mit den dunklen Mächten der Seele, die Konfrontation mit einer ursprünglichen inneren Formlosigkeit und Einsamkeit. Dadurch, dass Iwein diese hier herausgelöst dargestellte Seinsverfassung in seinem Waldleben an sich selbst erfährt, scheint erst der entscheidende Durchbruch in seiner Menschwerdung geleistet. Auch damit erweist sich der erzieherische Wert der höfischen Welt im Hinblick auf ein tiefer und ernster gefasstes Menschenbild psychologisch als ergänzungsbedürftig.

Auf dem Weg, den ihm der fremdartige Hüter weist, gerät Kalogreant nach drei Meilen zur verheissenen Quelle, deren Geheimnis ihm, im Gegensatz zum französischen Roman, noch verborgen ist; doch weiss er, dass dieses Abenteuer ein Wagnis ist auf Leben und Tod.

Sinnverwirrend und beglückend, hat der Ort zunächst die Wirkung eines Paradieses[59], in welchem er all das wiedererkennt, was ihm der Waldmann vorausgesagt hat: die Kapelle, die dichtbelaubte Linde und darunter, beschützt und ihr Geheimnis nicht preisgebend, die rätselhafte Quelle. Kalt, rein und völlig unberührt ist ihr Wasserspiegel — schimmernde Oberfläche, doch abgründig und voll unheimlicher Kräfte[60]. Auf den ausgehöhlten Smaragdstein daneben, der mit funkelnden Rubinen geschmückt ist[61] und auf vier marmorenen Tieren ruht, giesst Kalogreant nun, nach der Weisung des Waldmanns, Wasser aus dem goldenen Becken.

Hochempfindlich und unabsehbar — wie Laudine selbst! — reagiert ihr Reich, ihre Zauberquelle auf diesen Einbruch; ein gewitterartiger Aufruhr, eine wahre Entfesselung der Elemente ist die Antwort: schlagartig verfinstert die Sonne sich, der Wald bricht nieder, Donner und Blitz werfen den Herausforderer mit Gewalt zur Erde, und was vom Wild und den Vögeln sich nicht retten kann, ist verloren[62]. Als

59 Kalogreant nennt es in V. 687 'daz ander paradîse' (fehlt bei Chrétien). Die Vorstellung mehrerer Paradiese, meist einer Dreizahl: eines irdischen mit stets blühenden Bäumen, eines spirituellen, in das sich die kontemplative Seele gehoben fühlt, und des himmlischen, erscheint häufig bei den Viktorinern. Vgl. dazu auch Jean Daniélou, Terre et Paradis chez les Pères de l'Eglise, in: Eranos-Jb. 22 (1953) 433–472.
60 Phantastischer bei Chrétien: hier siedet die Quelle und ist doch kälter als Marmor (380f.). Im Märchen bedeutet die Quelle oder der Brunnen sehr oft den Durchgang in eine andere Welt. Vgl. Hedwig von Beit, Symbolik des Märchens, Bern 1952, I,36–38.
61 Edelsteine stehen in geheimer Verbindung zum Wasser; beiden kommen wunderbare, schützende oder zerstörende Kräfte zu. Häufig sind Brunnen mit Edelsteinen verziert, oder es finden sich heilkräftige Steine auf dem Grund von Quellen, vgl. Albrecht von Scharfenberg, Der jüngere Titurel, hg. von Werner Wolf, Bern 1952 (Altdeutsche Übungstexte 14) V. 6129–31.
Bei dem ähnlichen Abenteuer, das Simplicissimus am Mummelsee heraufbeschwört, indem er Steine in den See wirft (V, 12), wird ihm von den auftauchenden Wasserwesen ein durchsichtig grüner Stein überreicht, der ihn mit magischer Kraft hinab und auf seine wundersame Unterwasserfahrt zieht.
In den Lapidarien gilt der Smaragd u.a. als Bewahrer vor Ausschweifung und Sturm.
62 Die sturmauslösende Quelle ist ein verbreitetes Sagenmotiv, das auch in der Naturgeschichte, bei Konrad von Megenberg, in seinem "Buch der Natur" (1350) verzeichnet ist: 'Ez sint prunnen in dem grôzen land Britannia, wenn man der wazzer geuzt auf ainen stain nähen pei, so kümt regen und donr und ungewiter.' (Ausg. Franz Pfeiffer, Stuttgart 1861, S. 484). Ausformungen dieses Motivs in keltischen Sagen und in der mhd. Literatur stellt Nikolaus Patrzek in seiner Diss. "Das Brunnenmotiv in der deutschen Literatur des Mittelalters" (masch.), Würzburg 1956, zusammen.

der Hüter der Quelle darauf mit Getöse heranreitet und seine Zornesstimme grimmig, gleich einem Horn erschallt, erwarten wir ein Wesen aus einer anderen Welt. Doch mit dem ersten Vorwurf, den er Kalogreant entgegenschleudert, sind wir unversehens, in lautlosem Sprung, wieder auf höfische Ebene zurückversetzt: 'riter, ir sît *triuwelôs*' (712) hallt es ihm aus der Ferne entgegen. Obgleich die Quelle allen offensteht, ja geradezu zum Abenteuer verlockt und das Aufgiessen des Wassers als ihr 'reht' (556, 565; 'son droit' Y, 373), also als das, was ihr zukommt, bezeichnet wird, stösst der Zauber, die nach ungekannten Spielregeln vollzogene Geste, plötzlich zusammen mit höfisch-ritterlichem Wertmassstab, wird das Wagnis zu einem Vergehen wider ritterliches Recht.

In seiner hier aktualisierten Bedeutung meint das 'triuwelôs' zunächst eine fehderechtliche Verschuldung, ein Missachten der geltenden Regeln: Der Vorwurf des Wächters geht darauf, dass Kalogreant in sein Reich eingedrungen ist und ohne jede Herausforderung, aus dem Hinterhalt brechend, also unritterlich, seinen Wildpark und sein Land verwüstet hat. Hinter der vordergründigen Bedeutung aber öffnet sich der weite Bedeutungsraum dieses Worts. Die unerwartete Anschuldigung kündigt ein erstes Mal, wie ein Leitmotiv und in noch äusserlichem Sinn, die zentrale Thematik des "Iwein" an: 'triuwelôs' wird später Iwein nicht nur bei der Wiederholung des Abenteuers, sondern vor allem bei der ausbrechenden Krise von der beauftragten Botin in verdreifachtem Schlag gescholten (3174, 3183, 3186). Auch diese Stelle spielt zunächst auf ein formales Vergehen an, auf den gebrochenen Eid und die versäumte Frist. Das Wort meint aber noch mehr und weist über den konkreten Anlass hinaus, ist stellvertretend eingesetzt und vom Ganzen her auszulegen. Iwein vermag die 'triuwe' andern gegenüber nicht zu leisten, weil er sich selber noch nicht gefunden und begriffen hat, weil er noch unaufgeschlossen ist und in höfischer Konvention verharrt, mit deren Ungenügen er hier brutal konfrontiert wird und der er erst durch die Schuld hindurch und in der langen Gesellschaft mit dem Löwen, als Geheilter, ein Neues entgegensetzen wird[63].

Nicht nur die einzelne Szene, auch das einzelne Wort kann so, gleich einem eingesetzten Stein[64], aus dem Kontext herausgelöst, seinen objektiven Wert haben als Kennwort, von dem her der Sinn aufzubauen ist, das vorausweist und in dem sich das Ganze widerspiegelt. Solchen Beziehungsspielen, mit denen Hartmann die Erzählung ausschmückt, kommt der durchsichtige, zur Abstraktion hin tendierende

---

63 "Schliesslich gewinnt der Begriff der Treue, der Tugend, die Iwein offenbar vor allem zu lernen hat und deren eigentlicher Träger der Löwenritter ist, von hier aus eine neue Bedeutung: sie ist auch Treue und Huld zu sich selbst im Sinne der frommen, seelischen Erschlossenheit, wie sie vor allem die Aufgabe Parzivals wird." Max Wehrli, Iweins Erwachen a.a.O. 70.

64 Eingesetztem Schmuckwerk vergleicht Matthaeus von Vendôme gewisse Wortfiguren: "Siquidem, sicut in constitutione rei materialis ex appositione alicujus margaritae vel emblematis totum materiatum elegantius elucescit, similiter sunt quaedam dictiones, quae sunt quasi gemmarum vicariae, ex quarum artificiosa positione totum metrum videbit festivari." (So wie beim Herstellen eines materiellen Gegenstandes das Geschaffene durch Beifügen einer Perle oder Einsetzen von Intarsien verschönt zur Geltung kommt, so wird auch durch kunstvoll eingesetzte Formulierungen, wie mit Edelsteinen, der ganze Vers festlich belebt.) Ars Versificatoria, s. Faral, a.a.O. 154,11.

Charakter seiner Sprache weitgehend entgegen[65]. Dort wo sich Chrétiens Temperament in buntausgeschmückten, nüancierten Schilderungen äussert, wählt Hartmann vorwiegend den einfachen, allgemeinen Ausdruck, der damit auch weit genug ist, eine Vielfalt von Bedeutungen in sich aufzunehmen und zu verbinden.

Während Kalogreant, mit Schande beladen, an seinen Ausgangspunkt zurückkehrt, dringt Iwein durch und überschreitet die Grenze. Er bleibt Sieger im Zweikampf mit Ascalon und verfolgt den tödlich Getroffenen auf schmalem Weg bis hinein in seine Burg, wo er zwischen den Falltoren des Eingangs eingeschlossen bleibt[66]. 'Zwischen disen porten zwein' (1128), wie zwischen zwei Welten, ist er, ohne jede Möglichkeit, zu entrinnen, dem Abenteuer, mit dem er sich eingelassen hat, ausgeliefert[67]. Es ist zunächst kein Feenzauber, der ihn gefangenhält, sondern das sachlich beschriebene 'slegetor' (1080); Iwein befindet sich ganz offensichtlich in einer realen ritterlichen Burg. Aber dieser Palast, dieses ganze Reich ist so leicht zu handhaben, so schwerelos, dass sich ohne Mühe alles darin verschieben und verwandeln lässt. Das abgesperrte Ende des Burgwegs, in dem sich eben noch die beiden Pferde drängten, verwandelt sich plötzlich in einen prachtvollen, golden ausgemalten Saal, in dem sich auch, so wie man es benötigt, ein kostbares Bett befindet, 'daz nie künec bezzer gewan' (1215)[68], und, prompt wie im Märchen, zeigt sich unversehens in der Notlage auch schon die Rettung an: Durch eine kleine Tür schlüpft Lunete, die Zauberkundige, die ihn kennt und beim Namen nennt.

Märchenlogik und Realismus spielen schillernd ineinander. Denn Lunete besitzt zwar den Zauberring, ist daneben aber eine sehr realistische und feinsinnig abwägende Ratgeberin; sie ist blosse unscheinbare 'maget', die am Artushof keiner Beachtung würdig ist, und verkörpert doch die Macht, die Iweins Leben rettet und ihm schon zu Beginn und wieder am Schluss das verschlossene Tor aufbricht, durch das er auf das ihm zugedachte Geschick zutritt. Die Figuren in diesem Roman sind Anlass, um verschiedene Themen anklingen zu lassen. Sie sind nach anderen als organischen Gesetzen gestaltet, besitzen keinen einheitlichen Charakterkern und keine davon abgeleitete Folgerichtigkeit.

Mit allen ihm verfügbaren künstlerischen Ausdrucksformen und aus wandelbarer Perspektive tritt der Dichter an den Stoff heran. So ist z.B. mit der lyrisch-pathetischen *Totenklage* Laudines am Grab ihres Gatten ein völlig neuer Ton angeschla-

65 Vgl. dazu Hans J. Bayer, Untersuchungen zum Sprachstil weltlicher Epen des deutschen Früh- und Hochmittelalters, Berlin 1962, 20 (Philologische Studien und Quellen 10).
66 Dasselbe Motiv, verknüpft mit dem des Zauberrings, auch im "Chevalier de la Charrete" V 2320f.
67 'porte' kann ähnlich wie 'wec' symbolische Bedeutung annehmen, vgl. "Armer Heinrich" 406 'die saelden porte'. Im "Iwein" markieren die Tore deutlich eine Grenze zwischen dem wohlbekannten, durchschaubaren Reich des Artus und dem anderen, unergründlicheren der Laudine. Um dieses 'andere Reich', von dem das noch Ungekannte und Ersehnte, die stärkere Lebensäusserung erwartet wird, dessen Eintritt aber schwer zu erkämpfen ist, dreht sich auch im "Chevalier de la Charrete" das Sinnen des Dichters, vgl. V. 618.
68 Im Mabinogion (fz. Übers. von J. Loth, Les Mabinogion, tome II, Paris (2)1913; engl. Übers. von G. und T. Jones, The Mabinogion, London (2)1957) sind solche Sprünge ausgeglichen; der Gefangene wird von Lluned aus dem Torverliess befreit und in ein schönes Zimmer in einem dem Schloss gegenüberliegenden Gebäude geführt.

gen, der sich von der bisherigen Stillage und dem Sprechton der Figuren deutlich abhebt. Der Einsatz rhetorischer Stilmittel ist hier verstärkt: Apostrophe, Anapher und Ausruf verleihen ihr dramatische Ausdruckskraft und einheitliche Form, und zahlreiche Alliterationen und Hyperbeln schmücken sie aus[69].

Iwein 1454   sî sprach 'geselle, an dir ist tôt
der aller tiureste man,
der riters namen ie gewan
von manheit und von milte.
ezn gereit nie mit schilte
dehein riter alsô volkomen.

ouwê, wie bistû mir benomen,
ichn weiz war umbe ode wie?
der tôt möhte an mir wol hie
büezen swaz er ie getete,
und gewerte mich einer bete,
daz er mich lieze varn mit dir.

waz sol ich, swenne ich dîn enbir?
waz sol mir guot unde lîp?
waz sol ich unsaelec wîp?

ouwê daz ich ie wart geborn!
ouwê wie hân ich dich verlorn?
ouwê trûtgeselle!

got versperre dir die helle
und gebe dir durch sîne kraft
der engel genôzschaft,
wan dû waere ie der beste.'

Den kurzen Abschied bei Chrétien hat Hartmann in eine kunstvoll komponierte, formal geschlossene Klage ausgebaut, in der Laudine in expressiver Trauergebärde wie in ein Bild gebannt erscheint. Dieses rhetorische Meisterstück ist als kostbare Einlage in die Erzählung eingesetzt und entspricht in seiner formalen Vollendung dem hoheitsvoll entrückten Wesen, das in der Zeichnung Laudines als Hauptzug heraustreten soll. Mit der Anrede des Toten beginnend, steigert sie sich zu effektvollen, antwortlosen Exklamationen und gipfelt in dem rhythmisch verkürzten 'ouwê trûtgeselle'[70]. Das Abweichen vom unmittelbar-natürlichen Sprech-

---

69 Galfredus de Vinosalvo schreibt für affektische Reden, die Zorn, Empörung, Schmerz, Liebe, Hass oder Wahnsinn auszudrücken haben, die Wortfiguren der Anrede, der Wiederholung, der Doppelung des Ausdrucks, der Frage und des Ausrufs, sowie zur Steigerung und Heraushebung die asyndetische, d.h. unverbundene Reihung gleichgerichteter Glieder vor. Summa de Coloribus Rhetoricis, s. Faral a.a.O. 325.
70 Beschwerte Hebungen als Ausdrucksmittel sind bei Hartmann keine Seltenheit. Vgl. dazu Kurt Schacks, Beschwerte Hebungen bei Otfried und Hartmann, in: FG Ulrich Pretzel, Berlin 1963, 76–85. "Die logische und emphatische Augenblicksbetonung ... ist

ton bedeutet dabei keineswegs, dass ihre Trauer als unecht zu werten sei. Laudine hat hier in voller Vorbildlichkeit zu erscheinen, und gerade durch die formale Würde, die Hartmann ihrer Klage verleiht, ist diese Aussage gewährleistet.

Ein neues Element schiebt sich darauf mit den *Minnereflexionen* Iweins ein. Der Ritter, der eben noch mit traumwandlerischer Sicherheit die Situationen passierte, beginnt in seinem Gefängnis sich selber und das, was in ihm vorgeht, zu betrachten und in Frage zu stellen. Dass gerade dieser innerliche Vorgang rational aufzuschlüsseln versucht wird, dass der Dichter ihn mit den geläufigen Topoi der Minnegefangenschaft (1537f.) und der Minnewunde (1546f.) beschreibt und analysiert, dass die Minne personifizierte Macht ist, auf deren Gesetzlichkeit und Gunst sich Iwein verlassen kann und dass schliesslich Hartmann die Stellung dieser Minne in der eigenen Epoche und Gesellschaft diskutiert (1557f.), wobei das überwältigende Geschehen wieder etwas merkwürdig Distanziertes und Schematisches erhält, ist zeitcharakteristisches Gedankengut, moderne Minnetheorie, die für den Dichter die neugewonnene und geleistete Erfahrung darstellt und die er als höfische Schicht in den Sagenstoff einbaut.

Auf ähnlich gelagerter Ebene befinden wir uns bei den Verhandlungen zwischen Lunete und Laudine, in denen es der rhetorischen Begabung Lunetes, ihrem Geschick und ihrer Überredungskunst obliegt, die Trauernde zur neuen Heirat mit Iwein umzustimmen[71]. Der auf Sagenstufe selbstverständliche Übertritt der Quellenfee zu demjenigen Kämpfer, der im Initiationsabenteuer den Sieg davonträgt, war einem Publikum, dem die Minne mit ihren Rechten und Forderungen zentraler Wert, verbürgendes Elitezeichen war, nicht so ohne weiteres glaubwürdig zu machen, wenn auch für solchen Gefühlswandel im altfranzösischen Thebenroman (ca. 1150) ein Vorbild gegeben war[72]. Doch das war antiker Stoff, dem die höfische Gesellschaft eine bewusste Gesinnung und Innerlichkeit entgegensetzte. Mit allem Scharfsinn versucht deshalb Lunete, ihre Herrin auf Iwein hinzulenken, sie von dem Gewinn an 'êre', ja von der Notwendigkeit dieser neuen Verbindung zu

---

Hartmanns Kennmarke. Durch dieses Stilmittel erscheinen bei ihm häufig knappe Verse, die er bei Heinrich von Veldeke kennengelernt hat, und die ihn von Wolfram und Gottfried unterscheiden." (84)

71 Vgl. dazu Rainer Gruenter, Über den Einfluss des Genus iudicale auf den höfischen Redestil. DVjs 26 (1952) 49–57.

72 Auch dort heiratet Jocaste, um ihr Land nicht unbeschützt zu lassen, schon am nächsten Tag den Mörder ihres Gatten, der die Sphinx besiegt hat. Es finden sich beinahe wörtliche Übereinstimmungen zwischen den beiden Romanen: "Le Roman de Thèbes", hg. von Guy Raynaud de Lage, Paris 1966 (CFMA):

V. 485   Le duel du roi est oubliez
                 cil qui mort l'a est coronnez.
Yvain 2167   Et li morz est toz obliez
                 cil qui l'ocist est marïez;
Iwein 2435   des tôten ist vergezzen,
                 der lebende hât besezzen
                 beidiu sîn êre und sîn lant.
Zu der möglichen Beeinflussung des "Yvain" durch den Thebenroman vgl. F. Whitehead, Yvain's Wooing, in: Medieval Miscellany presented to Eugène Vinaver, Manchester University Press, New York 1965, 321–336.

überzeugen. Diese Partie der Argumentation, des gedanklichen Hin und Her, in der sich die Klagende in raschem Umschlag zur Überlegenden und Abwägenden wandelt, gilt nun aber wieder nur bedingt, nur auf die momentane Situation beschränkt, als notwendiges Umstimmungsmanöver und spannender, spitzfindiger Disput. Auch wenn zunächst durchaus nüchtern berechnende Überlegungen in den Mittelpunkt rücken, indem etwa Lunete den Sieger als den Überlegenen preist und zu bedenken gibt, dass Laudine und ihr Land ohne Beschützer völlig hilflos jedem Eingriff preisgegeben seien, so will Hartmann doch den Bund, der zwischen Iwein und Laudine geschlossen wird, am Schluss als vollkommene Minnegemeinschaft verstanden wissen (2341f.). Über verschiedene Stadien, ohne dass diese gegeneinander abgeklärt sind, in einem "Gegeneinander von matière und san, von rede und meine"[73] rückt der Roman vor, und der Hörer hat mit grosser Beweglichkeit und der richtigen Intuition vom rein Äusserlichen auf das wesentlich Intendierte überzuspringen.

Unter den schwungvollen Bogen, die die Reflexion schlägt, aber walten Märchengesetze. Verkürzungen, wie sie die schnelle Heirat und Iweins Aufbruch gleich nach dem Fest darstellen, gehören dazu. Auch die Bedingung, die Laudine stellt und die mit starrer Pünktlichkeit eingehalten werden muss, gemahnt ans Märchen, und märchenhafte Züge haften schliesslich dem unheilvoll-dramatischen Auftritt der Botin an, die ihren Fluch über Iwein ausspricht und wieder davonjagt[74]. Die Spannung zwischen dieser untergründigen Gesetzlichkeit und der Deutung des Dichters ist Grundzug des geistigen und literarischen Aufbruchs, den der höfische Roman darstellt. Der Dichter tritt hier einer Bildwelt gegenüber, die er nicht selber entworfen, bereinigt und abgestimmt hat, sondern die ihm als objektive Wahrheit vorgegeben und mit all ihren Befremdlichkeiten zur Deutung aufgetragen ist, die ihr Recht behauptet und mit der er "fertigzuwerden" hat, nicht anders, als wie er die Welt selbst, in die er sich hineingestellt sieht, in eigener Leistung und durch den Glauben gekräftigt, als sinnhafte Ordnung zu erkennen hat[75].

Auf die vereinfachten und gerafften Geschehnisse erfolgt nach Iweins Verfluchung nun aber plötzlich ein vertikaler Einbruch. Alle Schalen der Stilisierung brechen auf und fallen ab. Mit ganzer Teilnahme rückt Hartmann unmittelbar an menschliche Existenz heran; alles Märchenhafte hat sich verflüchtigt. *Iweins Not* füllt den ganzen Raum aus, verdrängt alle Kulissen. Mitten in sein Schweigen hinein, in seinen 'seneden gedanc' (3083), trifft ihn das Urteil Lunetes, die ihn des Verrats

---

73 Max Wehrli, Strukturprobleme des mittelalterlichen Romans a.a.O. 335.
74 Vgl. dazu Max Lüthi, Das europäische Volksmärchen. Form und Wesen, Bern (2)1960, S. 29: "Was in der Wirklichkeit ein nicht durchschaubares Ganzes bildet oder in langsamem, verborgenem Werden sich entfaltet, vollzieht sich im Märchen in scharf getrennten Stationen. . . . der Held verliert die Gattin wieder – aber nicht so, dass sie sich allmählich von ihm abwendet; sondern ein bestimmter Formfehler, meist das Übertreten eines Verbotes, bewirkt, dass sie ihm mit einem Schlag entrückt wird."
75 Seine dichterische Leistung begreift Hartmann grundsätzlich als auslegende, ins Licht rückende Deutung, vgl. "Armer Heinrich" 16:
    nu beginnet er iu diuten
    ein rede die er geschriben vant.

und der Treulosigkeit anklagt und ihm das Bild seiner selbst in so verschärften Strichen, unausweichlich und unwiderruflich hinhält, dass er erschüttert und fassungslos verstummt. Reue und Scham und die plötzlich zum zehrenden Schmerz gewordene Liebe packen ihn mit so eisernem Griff, dass nichts mehr laut wird: keine Widerrede, keine Frage oder Erklärung. Seine innere Unansehnlichkeit, die er plötzlich und unter Qual erkennt, treibt ihn fort von den Menschen, querfeldein, dem bergenden Walddunkel zu. Selbst die Kleider, diese letzten Zeichen seiner Gesellschaftszugehörigkeit und Ehre, erträgt er nicht mehr an seinem Leib; in blindwütigem Zorn reisst er sie von sich. Was der Aufstieg gewährte und einbrachte, ist alles in einem Augenblick und in stummer Ablösung wesenlos geworden.

Iwein 3231   dô wart sîn riuwe alsô grôz
                          daz im in daz hirne schôz
                          ein zorn und ein tobesuht.
                          er brach sîne site und sîne zuht
                          und zart abe sîn gewant,
                          daz er wart blôz sam ein hant.
                          sus lief er über gevilde
                          nacket nach der wilde.

In eindringlich knapper Zeichnung wird Iweins Waldleben geschildert, die Reduktion seines Lebens auf die paar wenigen Gebärden, mit denen er aus dem Eimer des Einsiedlers Wasser trinkt und sein Brot isst und das Wild erlegt, das ihm über den Weg läuft; für niemanden mehr ist er verfügbar, auf niemanden mehr achtet er, und sich selber versagt er alle Nachsicht und Huld. Gerade die Existenz des exemplarischen Menschen im Artusroman erscheint nicht etwa in primitiv-vereinfachender Einseitigkeit als ausschliesslich strahlende, glückhaft-geglückte. Die Verlorenheit, das Ausgeliefertsein des Helden an die dunklen Kräfte in ihm wird thematisch, und zwar nicht nur in pädagogischer Absicht als zu überwindende Seite, sondern als notwendiger, intensiver Gegenklang, als der für jede Begnadung vorausgesetzte menschliche Tiefenraum. Christliche Sicht aktualisiert sich hier am Märchenstoff, indem die Erkenntnis der eigenen Unzulänglichkeit und Erlösungsbedüftigkeit einen Schwerpunkt und im Dreischritt des Artusromans die notwendige Voraussetzung zur ganzheitlichen Verwirklichung des Helden darstellt.

Durch verschiedene geistige und bildliche Räume wird dieser so vom Dichter hindurchgeführt. Der Roman erscheint als Gefüge, in welchem Töne und Erzählkreise von verschiedener Farbintensität ineinandergefügt sind, wobei sich die einzelnen Stationen und Episoden in sich selber runden, stets wieder einen anderen Erfahrungs- und Empfindungssinn ansprechen und eine neue Denkrichtung fordern.

Auch bei der Interpretation der Figuren selbst stellt man fest, dass hier verschiedene Bedeutungsebenen übereinandergelagert sind, die abwechselnd zur Geltung kommen. Vor allem erscheint *Laudine* in immer wieder anderer Beleuchtung: als hohes Ideal einerseits, das Iweins Weg bestimmt und von dem Hartmann deshalb zu Beginn die höchsten Tugenden, 'güete' und 'triuwe' (1602, 1603), aussagt; als irdisches Geschöpf, erregbar, verletzlich und voller Widersprüche im

Gespräch mit Lunete, und als hohe Minneherrin, als Gebieterin mit dem unerbittlichen Anspruch, wie sie die provenzalische Minneauffassung will und anerkennt, als Iwein die Frist versäumt. Auf Einheitlichkeit ihres Charakters kommt es Hartmann gar nicht an. Wenn er deshalb Laudine gegenüber Chrétien idealisiert, das Komödienhafte an ihr in mehr Schlichtheit verwandelt und vor allem am Schluss ihre Unnahbarkeit mit plötzlicher Reue und Einsicht vertauscht, so mögen solche Wandlungen einem an Zusammenhang glaubenden und auf Übereinstimmung pochenden Empfinden zuwiderlaufen und als "unwahr" erscheinen[76]. Aber das mittelalterliche Publikum urteilte wahrscheinlich nicht so. Hartmann richtet seinen Blick nicht auf einen psychologischen und kausalen Zusammenhang, sondern auf die Aussage, die die jeweilige Station erfordert, und so ist auch Laudines Demut, ihre endliche Erlösung zur Hingabe, auf die der Dichter zum Schluss in eigenmächtiger Neuerung einen Durchblick schafft, sinngemäss, wie es der Ausklang der Geschichte nach seiner Auffassung verlangt.

Ähnliche Inkohärenz stellen wir an der Figur des Königs Artus[77], an Keii und schliesslich an *Gawan* fest, der je nach dem Licht, das er auf den Haupthelden zu werfen hat, einerseits als Inbegriff ritterlicher Tugend ('her Gâwein was der höveschste man / der riters namen ie gewan' 3037f.) gepriesen wird und der dennoch im entscheidenden Moment zur Seite rücken muss, um Iwein die Bahn zu überlassen, der unauffindbar bleibt, da man seiner bedarf und sich für die ungerechte Sache einsetzt, so dass Iwein an seiner Statt eintreten und das Abenteuer bestehen kann. Gawan hat damit in erster Linie die Funktion, Iweins Weg deutlicher herauszuheben; er zeichnet ihn mit seiner Freundschaft aus, hat aber gleichzeitig den ungenügenden Massstab und die eintönige Folie zu verkörpern, von der sich Iwein abhebt, die er durchbricht und mit einer lebendigeren Wahrheit überhöht. Der wohlgemeinte Rat des Musterritters reicht für Iwein nicht aus, ja er wird zum unmittelbaren Anlass seiner Krise und seines Sturzes ('her Gâwein sîn geselle / der wart sîn ungevelle.' 3029f.)

---

76 "unorganisch aufgepfropft und daher unwahr", Wapnewski a.a.O. 68. Laudines Niederknien bei der Rückkehr Iweins ist von den meisten Kritikern missbilligt worden. Vgl. Hendricus Sparnaay, Laudine bei Crestien und bei Hartmann. Neophil. 4 (1919) 318; einleuchtender ist die Kritik von Kurt Ruh, Zur Interpretation von Hartmanns "Iwein" a.a.O. 47. Auch hier gilt die Bemerkung des inspirierten Mittelalterforschers Alois Haas: "Die 'Entwicklung' ist mittelalterlich uninteressant, weil das Ziel, der Endpunkt interessanter ist als die Kausalität des Weges." Parzivals tumpheit bei Wolfram von Eschenbach, Berlin 1964, 323.

77 Auf die Diskrepanz zwischen dem Bild, das Hartmann im Prolog von König Artus entwirft, und der Haltung, die er ihn im Roman einnehmen lässt, hat Rolf Endres aufmerksam gemacht (Der Prolog von Hartmanns Iwein a.a.O. 530). Brinkmanns Untersuchungen über den Prolog (a.a.O.) haben jedoch gezeigt, dass der mittelalterliche Prolog nicht in direkter inhaltlicher Übereinstimmung steht mit dem Werk selbst, sondern eine Einheit für sich bildet, eine Vorstufe, die den Hörer einstimmen und gewinnen will, wozu die Berühmtheit des Königs von Britannien günstiger und wirkungsvoller Anlass ist. Der ernstzunehmende Akzent liegt auf dem Aufruf zur 'güete'; ihre Vertreter sind austauschbar.

Wapnewski spricht bei der Interpretation des "Iwein" von fehlender Integration, vom Aufeinanderprallen unvereinbarer Welten[78]. Das Sprunghafte in Hartmanns Darstellung, welches sich sowohl im kleinen wie im grossen manifestiert, scheint jedoch zur Struktur seiner Kunst zu gehören und fordert uns auf, andere als die gewohnten Wege zu seinem Werk zu suchen. Der höfische Dichter geht schwungvoller und unpedantischer mit seinem Stoff um. Ohne die Ränder aufeinander abzustimmen, fügt er Verschiedenartiges zusammen, lässt er Zwischenräume bestehen und überspringt sie. Nicht auf die genaue Begründung, auf eine nachrechenbare Folgerichtigkeit ist sein Sinn gerichtet, und dem Hörer ist es offenbar ein Selbstverständlich-Vertrautes, in jedem einzelnen Baustein, auch wo sein Spannungsverhältnis zum Ganzen nicht harmonisiert und eingeebnet ist, die bewegende Kraft der Schönheit und bruchstückhaft die Verkündigung des Sinnes zu erkennen[79].

78 "Zufolge solcher Überschneidungen der sich notwendig wandelnden Konzeptionen (Laudine als Sagenfee und als höfische Minnedame), die zu Kompromissen und poetischen Verzweiflungsaktionen führen, wie sie jeder inneren und äusseren Wahrhaftigkeit Hohn sprechen, entbehrt der "Iwein" in seiner höfischen Fassung eines organisch gestalteten, logisch durchgeführten, konsequent entwickelten Grundproblems." a.a.O. 69.

79 Die Konzentration auf das jeweilig Vorgezeigte, auf die einzeln heraustretende Bildgruppe, die sich der ungebunden assoziierenden Betrachtung öffnet, bestätigen auch jene Szenen, die, über das Mass ihrer Funktion hinaus, Raum gewinnen. Es sind vor allem zwei Episoden, die in dieser Hinsicht auffallen: das Bild des verkümmerten, kleinlich klagenden und freudlosen Landmanns, das Gawan mit Beredsamkeit und Humor zur Geltung bringt, um Iwein vor dem 'verligen' zu warnen (2807–2858), ein Meisterstück witziger descriptio, das mit seinen humoristischen Tönen auch der höfischen Mahnung etwas von ihrer Verbindlichkeit nimmt, – und daneben die Geschichte vom Raub der Königin Ginover aus dem Lancelot-Roman, die Chrétien nur zweimal kurz streift, um die Abwesenheit Gawans zu rechtfertigen, und die Hartmann auf 195 Verse erweitert (4530–4725), als 'vremdez maere' (4528) vorträgt. In keiner der beiden Episoden wird der innere Sinn des Romans verändert oder direkt mitbetroffen. Hartmann hat sie der Erzählung als in sich geschlossene Bilder, als belebende und unterhaltende Einlagen eingefügt.

II MERKMALE DER GESTALT

Dass der höfische Roman keine planlose Bilderfolge, keine willkürliche Reihung beliebter Motive darstellt, ist längst allgemein gewordene Erkenntnis. Auch wo wir sie nicht durchschauen, spüren wir im Auftauchen und Verstummen der Episoden Kunstgesetze am Werk. Doch handelt es sich dabei um andere Gesetze als die der Kontinuität, des lückenlosen Handlungsablaufes und der konsequenten Entwicklung der Figuren. Schon der kunstvolle Gesamtaufbau, die thematisch verankerte Zweiteilung und die Art, in der die Aventiuren ineinander verfugt sind, sich steigernd aufwärtsbewegen und Vorausgegangenes widerspiegeln, weisen auf das ausgeprägte Gestaltungsbewusstsein der höfischen Dichter. Gerade im Aufbau, im Gestalten nach Proportionen und nach einander entsprechenden Bildmustern, liegt die neue und eigene Leistung der höfischen Epoche. Denn Rhetorik und Poetik liefern lediglich Beispiele für den sprachlichen Schmuck und Richtlinien für die Gesprächsführung oder die Beschreibung, nicht aber für die Anordnung und Durchgestaltung der Szenen.

In vielen mittelalterlichen Dichtwerken lässt sich ein innerster Bauplan herausschälen, der ganz durch die Zahl bestimmt ist, d.h. dass die einzelnen Teile in der Zahl der Verse aufeinander abgestimmt sind oder dass die Proportionen dieser Teile zahlensymbolische Bedeutung haben. Auch wo sich diese objektive Zahlenstruktur dem Hörer nicht unmittelbar enthüllt, sondern erst vom Leser oder Forscher wahrgenommen wird, erhöht sie durch ihr blosses Vorhandensein nach dem damaligen Kunstverständnis den Wert und die heilsame Schönheitswirkung des Werks.

Einen solchen Grundriss nach proportional übereinstimmenden Erzähleinheiten, die sich spiegelbildlich um eine Symmetrieachse ordnen, haben Hans Eggers und Heinz Rupp im "Iwein" in unabhängigen Vorschlägen nachzuzeichnen versucht. Hans Eggers weist für den "Iwein" die Grundzahl 120 nach, auf der die Erzählabschnitte mit dazwischenliegenden zahlenmässig variablen 'Moventien' aufgebaut sind, wobei sich die Elemente im 2. Teil symmetrisch um die Mittelachse ordnen, die auf die Suche der jüngeren Tochter des Grafen vom Schwarzen Dorn fällt[1]. Nach dem Schema von Heinz Rupp ordnen sich Erzählabschnitte in proportionaler Übereinstimmung spiegelbildlich um einen Mittelteil, der die Heilung Iweins, das Löwenabenteuer und die Szene mit Lunete am Brunnen einschliesst[2]. Eine weitere Werkgliederung versucht Hansjürgen Linke, wobei er auf den in den Handschriften erkennbaren Erzählabschnitten aufbaut[3]. Untersuchungen der zah-

---

1 Hans Eggers, Symmetrie und Proportion epischen Erzählens. Studien zur Kunstform Hartmanns von Aue. Stuttgart 1956.
2 Heinz Rupp, Über den Bau epischer Dichtungen des Mittelalters, in: Die Wissenschaft von deutscher Sprache und Dichtung. Methoden, Probleme, Aufgaben. FS Friedrich Maurer, Stuttgart 1963, 366–382.
3 Hansjürgen Linke, Epische Strukturen in der Dichtung Hartmanns von Aue, München 1968. Günther Schweikle kritisiert in seinem Aufsatz "Zum 'Iwein' Hartmanns von Aue" grundsätzlich die Arbeit von Linke, und zwar sowohl die Fragwürdigkeit des Ansatzes wie

lenmässigen Struktur bleiben, wiewohl von aufschliessendem Wert, notwendig spekulativ. Die Gefahr des eigenmächtigen Kombinierens und Kalkulierens ist kaum zu umgehen, und das Ergebnis ist durch nichts kontrollierbar.

Nicht diese innere, zahlenmässige Harmonie soll uns hier beschäftigen, sondern die unmittelbar wirkende Gestalt des Romans selbst, deren besondere Merkmale sowohl Licht auf die Absicht, wie auch auf den ästhetischen Massstab des Dichters werfen und richtungweisend für das Verständnis sind. Zu den auffälligsten Gestaltungsmerkmalen im "Iwein" gehören die Wiederholung, der Kontrast und die Spiegelung. Dies sind Mittel, die auch in den anderen höfischen Romanen eingesetzt sind, doch lassen sie sich gerade an der durchsichtigen Komposition des "Iwein" besonders gut erkennen und untersuchen.

1. Wiederholung, Typologie

Der ritterlich-menschliche Weg, den Iwein durch die verschiedenen Lebenszonen hindurch abschreitet und der ihn, nach vollzogener Richtungsänderung, zu seiner Identität, zu dem ihm zubestimmten Löwen und schliesslich an sein Ziel führt, ist nicht ein Fortgang ins Unendliche zu je neuen, sinnverwirrenden Abenteuern und Begegnungen, sondern orientiert sich immer wieder an den gleichen Fixpunkten. Kalogreant, der als erster eine Spur durch Wald und Wildnis zieht bis hin zum Entscheidungspunkt, schreitet nach seinem Misslingen diesen Weg auch wieder zurück; er kehrt, nachdem er den Harnisch ebenso wie seine gespannte, hoffnungsvolle Erwartung von sich abgeschüttelt hat, wieder ein auf jener Burg, von der er des Morgens ausgezogen war und wo sich nun für das Burggesinde über das Bild des Vielversprechenden der Schatten seiner Begrenzung legt. So tauchen die Stationen des beschrittenen Weges rückläufig noch ein zweitesmal auf, nun ergänzt um die Seite der neuen Erfahrung.

Eine ähnliche Wiederholung, ein zweitmaliges Abschreiten von Wegstationen, liegt dort vor, wo die Tochter vom Schwarzen Dorn, auf den Spuren Iweins, nach einem Kämpfer für ihre Sache im Erbschaftsstreit sucht. Damit fällt ihr die Rolle zu, die vorausgegangenen 'âventiuren' Iweins, diese untrüglichen Zeichen seines ins Rechte geratenen Lebens noch einmal aufleuchten zu lassen, sie gleichsam zu unterstreichen. Von der Vorsehung gelenkt (5798), folgt das Mädchen ihm nach und passiert rekapitulierend all jene Stationen, die Zeugen seines Wirkens und seiner Mühsal waren: die Burg, auf der er den Riesen erschlug, die Quelle, an der er kämpfend für Lunete einstand, und sein mühsames, beharrliches Weiterziehen danach mit dem wunden Löwen bis zu jenem Schloss, wo ihnen heilende Pflege widerfuhr. Der Hörer erkennt Vertrautes wieder, sein Geist ruht darauf aus, und die

---

den vorgeschlagenen Plan. (In: Probleme des Erzählens in der Weltliteratur. FS Käte Hamburger, hsg. von Fritz Martini, Stuttgart 1971, 1–22). In seiner eigenen Analyse, die erst nach dem Abschluss meiner Arbeit herauskam, sucht Schweikle vom Inhalt her nach wahrnehmbaren und sinngebenden Ordnungsfaktoren im "Iwein", nach "strukturalen Korrespondenzen und Oppositionen, Motivresponsionen und Begriffsfiguren" (S. 5).

Freude, die sich dadurch mit hineinvermischt, erhöht den Glanz des Erzählten und sichert seine Einprägsamkeit.

Vor allem ist es nun aber der Weg zum 'brunnen' selbst, diese unruhige Suche nach der Lebensquelle, die im "Iwein" wiederholt ins Bild gebannt wird. Der weichenstellende Anfang, dieser mutige Aufbruch ins Unbekannte und die Konfrontation mit einer fremden, für Iweins Selbstverwirklichung so wesentlichen Macht, wird als Grundthema immer wieder angeschlagen. In einer ersten Figuration kündigt Kalogreant dieses Thema an; doch er stösst an seine eigene Grenze, kehrt ins Gleiche zurück und schafft damit die Erwartung für die Steigerung und Überhöhung durch Iwein. Beim Auszug Iweins zehn Jahre später, findet dieser unverändert alles wieder. Er dringt auf den gleichen, von Kalogreant geschlagenen Spuren vor, erfährt die beglückende Gesellligkeit auf der Burg und, kontrastierend dazu, den gespensterhaft-bedrohlichen Waldmann, wobei sein Weg auch in sich selbst noch einmal gedoppelt ist, als gedankliche Vorausnahme und wirklicher Vollzug.

Zur Wunderquelle zieht später König Artus selbst, hoch offiziell und mit versammelter 'massenîe', doch sieht auch er, vielmehr der stellvertretende Keii, sich einem Stärkeren gegenüber, und das Abenteuer, das für Iwein den Eingang zu einem neuen Lebensraum dargestellt hatte, offenbart nun bestätigend, dass dieser das Errungene auch vollkommen beherrscht. Immer wieder und in verschiedener Farbbrechung führt das Geschehen ins Quellenrevier zurück, das in spürbarer Spannung dem Artusreich entgegensteht. Eine geheime Sehnsucht nach diesem komplementär wirkenden Reich, eine Vorbestimmung dafür, scheint schon früh und noch unbewusst in Iwein eingesenkt zu sein: als einziger Ritter hat er sich am Hof der von Laudine abgesandten Botin zugewendet. Ihr Reich erweist sich als seine eigentliche Heimstatt, zu der er auch aus der Verbannung unwillentlich, ohne sie zu suchen (3923), wieder zurückgezogen wird. Aber inzwischen hat sich der Ort seines früheren Aufstiegs in eine Stätte des Leids und der Klage verwandelt. Als Ausgestossener und Entfremdeter steht Iwein vor der Quelle, und der bezaubernde Vogelsang erreicht ihn nicht mehr.

Erst am Schluss seines Leidensweges, nachdem sich die Erlösung an ihm selbst und durch ihn vollendet hat und ihm die innere Gewissheit wird, dass die Zeit dafür gekommen sei, richtet er seinen Weg wieder zu seinem Ausgangspunkt zurück; er entfesselt erneut das schlummernde Ungewitter, das sich ihm nun lichtet zum 'östertac' (8120)[4] seiner Freude und zum angedeuteten Märchenende: 'ez was guot leben waenlich hie, / ichn weiz aber waz ode wie / in sît geschaehe beiden.' (8159f.).

Durch solche Wiederholungen eines Typischen, einer Grundsituation unter stets verändertem Vorzeichen, ist jedesmal Rückblick geboten. Der Hörer erkennt deutlich Zusammenhänge, und es bildet sich ihm das wohltätige Gefühl, dass all dieses Erscheinende in einer sinnvollen Ordnung aufgehoben sei, dass hinter der

---

4 Vgl. dazu Werner Fechter, Ostern als Metapher in mhd. Dichtungen. Beitr. 85, Tübingen 1963, 289–296.

Vielfalt eine Einheit walte, eine vollkommen einfache Grundfigur, auf die sich alles zurückführen lasse. So wie der Reim dem Vers Halt, aber gleichzeitig beschwingte Leichtigkeit gibt, so verliert auch ein Motiv, wo es wiederholt wird oder wo ihm eine innere oder äussere Entsprechung antwortet, unwillkürlich etwas von seiner Wirklichkeitsschwere; es wird leicht und nähert sich dem verfügbaren Zeichen und Ornament.

Durch die Abwandlung, die eine Episode in der Wiederholung erfährt, durch Veränderung oder Umkehrung, durch das Zerlegen in mehrere ihrer Aspekte, erhellt und berichtigt sie sich selbst. Der Wert der Wiederholung liegt damit vor allem in einer Aktivierung der Imagination und Erinnerung des Hörers. Sie ist bequemes Mittel, innere Veränderung, Entwicklung aufzuzeigen und den Wert der sinntragenden Stationen zu verstärken. Die Absicht zur Verstärkung wird auch dort ausgezeichnet verwirklicht, wo ein Ereignis in die vorausnehmende Beschreibung und die darauf folgende Bestätigung auseinanderfällt, was dem Hörer nicht nur Stützpunkte für sein Verständnis liefert, sondern ihn auch entspannt und befreit und seine Aufmerksamkeit auf Einzelnes hinlenkt. So wird die Zauberquelle im "Iwein" schon im voraus, noch mitten in der ungastlichen Einöde vom Waldmann eingehend beschrieben, so dass Kalogreants Finden zu einem Wiedererkennen wird: 'ich vuor des endes unde vant / der rede eine wârheit' (600f.). Auch im kleinen wird dabei der Roman von einem unverkennbaren Streben nach Steigerung gelenkt; denn nun wird die Quelle mit den Augen eines Ritters gesehen, was gegenüber dem unwissenden Tierhüter notwendig höhere Einsicht bedeutet. Kalogreant erblickt nicht nur das Äussere, seinen Schein, sondern erkennt sein Wesen und weiss den 'harte zierlîchen stein' (582) zu benennen, dessen Heilkraft ihm, als dem ritterlich Eingeweihten, nicht verborgen sein kann: 'ein smareides was der stein. / ûz iegelîchem orte schein / ein alsô gelpfer rubîn' (623f.)[5]. – Ähnliches Wiedererkennen, Vorfinden eines Angekündigten, widerfährt dem gefangenen Iwein im Torhaus, wo die tüchtige Lunete alles vorausbedenkt, was sich demnächst um den Unsichtbaren abspielen wird: wie die Burgknechte verbissen und verzweifelt nach ihm suchen und wie sie mit den Schwertern in die Luft hauen werden, ohne ihn zu finden, so dass die Hörer zweimal in den Genuss dieser grotesk-dramatischen Szene gelangen: in der Schilderung Lunetes und später in Wirklichkeit selbst, denn 'nû widervuor im allez daz / daz im sîn vriunt diu guote maget / vordes hâte gesaget.' (1302f.)

Obwohl nun aber die Wiederholung als künstlerisches und erzähltechnisches Element eine so zentrale Rolle im "Iwein" spielt, würde sich das anspruchsvolle höfische Publikum die ausdrückliche Wiederholung eines Berichts gelangweilt verbieten. Der Dichter selbst kommt dieser Gefahr eines 'taedium' mit souveräner Geste zuvor. Als der arme Fischer im "Gregorius" den hergereisten Römern

---

5 Dieser erkenntnismässige Unterschied ist bei Chrétien noch verstärkt. Hier gesteht der 'vilains' offen von dem Stein: 'je ne te sai a dire quel, / que je n'en vi onques nul tel' (391f.); auch bezeichnet er das Becken über der Quelle als eisernes (386), während es Kalogreant als 'del plus fin or' (420) identifiziert.

Auskunft erteilen soll über den seit 17 Jahren auf dem Stein gefesselten Büsser, wehrt Hartmann kurz entschlossen ab:

Greg. 3321   ich waene ez unnütze waere,
      ob ich daz vorder maere
      iu nû aber anderstunt
      mit ganzen worten taete kunt:
      sô wurden einer rede zwô[6].

Wo deshalb der Dichter mit Doppelung arbeitet, wo er zwei Geschehen unter einem gleichen Zeichen zu einer Einheit verklammert, kommt seinem Vorgehen sinnerweiternde Bedeutung zu. Anders als im Märchen, wo Zauberformeln und Wünsche oft im Wortlaut wiederauftauchen und auch ganze Handlungsteile: die Ausreise von drei Brüdern oder ein Abenteuer, das stets die gleiche Belohnung oder Strafe einträgt, sich gleichförmig folgen[7], liegt der Reiz der Wiederholungen im höfischen Roman meist gerade in der Variation, in der Umkehrung oder Steigerung, die ein Motiv bei der Wiederaufnahme erfährt. In dieser Hinsicht ist die Wiederholung im "Iwein" auch bereits differenzierter gehandhabt als im "Erec", wo der Läuterungsweg des Ritters durch die sinnfällige Verdoppelung des Räuberabenteuers, der Erprobung Enites, des Zwergenkampfes und der Wundenheilung in einem eigentlichen "doppelten Kursus" (Hugo Kuhn) dem Endpunkt zustrebt.

Im "Iwein" sind solche Übereinstimmungen verhüllter; oft fordern nur flüchtige Referenzen den Hörer zu vergleichender Besinnung auf. Als reizvolle und wohlgezielte Entsprechung wirkt es, wenn Lunete, die einstige Retterin Iweins, nun ihrerseits gefangen und den Burgleuten preisgegeben, in der Kapelle liegt und der Gerettete in vertauschter Rolle zum dankbaren Befreier wird. Eine ähnlich polare Umkehrung erfährt das Grussmotiv. Als Lunete zum erstenmal, fremd und unerkannt, an den Artushof kommt, da ist Iwein der einzige, der ihr Gruss bietet, und diese bescheiden-höfische Ehrerweisung wird denn auch Anlass zu seiner Rettung. Gerade er aber ist der Begrüssung Lunetes unwürdig, als diese wieder, diesmal mit unheilvollem Auftrag, am Artushof erscheint, mitten in die versammelte Festrunde sprengt und Iwein verflucht. (3114f.)[8]

Als Bau- und Kunstprinzip spielt die Wiederholung in der gesamten mittelalterlichen Literatur eine wesentliche Rolle. In den Spielmannsepen werden blockartig Ausfahrt, Werbung und Kampf wiederholt und führen in wechselnder Konstellation

---

6 Ähnlich verschmäht es Gottfried, die Zerlegung des Hirsches durch Tristan vor dem König noch einmal zu wiederholen:
3466 nu waene ich wol und dunket mich,
    daz ez undurften waere,
    ob ich iu zwir ein maere
    nach ein ander vür leite.
7 Die starre Wiederholung gehört wesensmässig zum abstrakten Stil des Märchens. Vgl. dazu Max Lüthi, a.a.O. 45f.
8 Nur Hartmann lässt, vielleicht gerade dem Reiz dieser Motiventsprechung nachgebend, Lunete als verfluchende Botin auftreten. Bei Chrétien ist es eine weiter nicht näher bestimmte Rechtssprecherin (2707).

zu verschiedenen Zielen. Im höfischen Roman erfährt dieses Stilmittel nun aber von der *typologischen* Deutungsmethode her, in welcher der Hörer jener Epoche durch die Lesung und Auslegung der Bibel eingeübt war, einen neuen schöpferischen Impuls[9]. Diese Denkstruktur, die alles menschliche Geschehen als Vorentwurf und Erfüllung, als Hinführung und lebendige Wahrheit begreift und damit auch dem Unvollkommenen und noch Verkappten in einer Heilsordnung seinen Sinn zuerkennt, wirkt sich modellhaft auch auf die dichterische Nachbildung aus.

Eine Steigerung vom Niederen zum Höheren kann sich dabei im Roman zunächst in einem durchaus äusserlichen Sinn manifestieren[10], so etwa, wenn sich Iwein nach der Heilung zuerst einem einzigen, im Kampf mit Lunetes Verleumdern aber drei Gegnern gegenübersieht; wenn er auf der Burg von Gawans Schwager erst einen Riesen (Harpin) und bei der Befreiung der gefangenen Geiseln ('Pesme Aventure' Y.5103) gleich deren zwei erledigt; oder wenn der Löwe, der seinem Herrn in drei Abenteuern zur Seite steht, seinen Einsatz über wachsende Widerstände beweist.

Überhöhung in einem inneren Sinn drückt bereits das Ringmotiv aus. Dank dem unsichtbarmachenden Zauberring der Lunete rettet Iwein sein Leben (1202f.). Der Ring jedoch, den ihm später Laudine schenkt, ist nicht mehr Märchenring, obwohl auch er die Kraft hat, 'saelde' zu verleihen. Er ist 'geziuc' (2946), Zeichen und Unterpfand ihrer Liebe und wird ihm unweigerlich entzogen, als seine Treue in allzu grosser Selbstgewissheit gedankenlos wird. – In ähnlichem Sinn wird auch die Wunde, die Iwein dem fliehenden Ascalon schlägt, im Rückblick zu einem Vorzeichen. Denn Gefangener ist Iwein bald in doppeltem Sinn: er ist gefangen und gebunden von der Minne, ist selber 'tôtlîchen wunt' (1546), an einer Wunde leidend, die, wie die Minneerfahrenen wissen, kein Arzt zu heilen versteht. Durch die motivische Übereinstimmung wird dabei im Neuen stets die Erinnerung an das Vorausgegangene wach, dieses wird nun bereichert um seine Gegenseite und erhält in der Zusammenschau seinen Platz in einer neuen Wertordnung.

Als Präfigurationen im eigentlichen Sinn, als vorbereitende und hinweisende Figuren, wirken Kalogreant, dessen Ansatz Iwein zur Vollendung führen wird, und ebenso der dunkle Waldmann, an dem der Hochgemute zunächst eilig vorbeistrebt und den er später in eigener Begegnung in sich erfahren und integrieren muss.

Der wichtigste Sinnbezug spannt sich jedoch über Iweins Weg selbst, der nach dem Schema aller Artusromane zweigeteilt ist. In leichtem, kühnem Anstieg führt er zu Glück und Besitz. Doch wiewohl diesem sieghaften Abenteuer blendende Farben anhaften, erweist sich das Errungene als unbeständig, als Vorspiegelung und 'wân' (3540). Obwohl Iwein im Gegensatz zu Kalogreant weiss, dass das Abenteuer

---

9 Erich Auerbach, Typologische Motive in der mittelalterlichen Literatur, Krefeld 1953, 16–17: "Es ist meine Überzeugung, dass die typologische Exegese .... mit ihrer unendlichen Fülle von Kombinationen und Anspielungen, Motivkreuzungen und Metaphern, das eigentliche Lebenselement der christlich mittelalterlichen Dichtung bildet."
Ebenso Max Wehrli, Sacra Poesis, in: Die Wissenschaft von deutscher Sprache und Dichtung. Methoden, Probleme, Aufgaben. FS Friedrich Maurer, Stuttgart 1963, 27f.
10 Elise Richter weist auf den Stilzug des Parallelismus und der Steigerung auch bei Chrétien, gerät aber mit dem Materialnachweis oft ins Willkürliche. "Die künstlerische Stoffgestaltung in Chrestiens Ivain", ZfrPh 39 (1919) 385–397.

an der Quelle Einbruch und Landzerstörung bedeutet, begiesst er bedenkenlos den Stein und verfolgt den verwundeten Hüter, 'âne zuht' (1056). Hartmann hat gegenüber Chrétien diese Schuld noch verdeutlicht; nur bei ihm fügt Iwein dem Fliehenden vor dem Niederfallen des Schlagtors schonungslos die letzte tödliche Wunde bei[11]. Ohne der andern zu achten (vgl. 1440f.), steuert Iwein auf das Begehrte zu, jagt es wie eine Beute (3525). Widerrechtlich dringt er ins fremde Reich ein; unbarmherzig erschlägt er seinen Wächter, und die Frist, die ihm die unbeschützte Laudine stellt, überschreitet er. Zeichenhaft stehen diese Verfehlungen für seine Grundhaltung in diesem ersten Teil, für sein unerhelltes Befangensein in sich selbst.

Im Wald, nachdem ihn die Salbung heil und neu gemacht hat, erwacht Iwein aus der Dumpfheit zu einem Neubeginn. Alles Scheinhafte fällt von ihm ab. Dem alten Stand setzt Iwein nun ein neues Leben entgegen, den Weg des christlichen Ritters, als Kämpfer für das Recht, als Erbarmender und als Trost aller Wehrlosen und Unterdrückten. Durch zahlreiche Anklänge, thematische Kreuzungen und Rückverweise erscheinen die beiden Wege wie Positiv und Negativ, heben sich voneinander ab und bedingen sich doch gegenseitig. Der einstigen Selbstmächtigkeit antwortet nun vollkommene Demut. Iwein legt seinen Namen ab und überlässt sich dem Weg, der ihn führt:

Iwein 3825   unde suochte dâ zehant
                den naehsten wec den er vant,

Iwein 3923   dô truoc in diu geschiht
                (wande ern versach sichs niht)
                vil rehte an sîner vrouwen lant,

Iwein 4370   nû kam mîn her Iwein dar,
                als in der wec lêrte.

Iwein sucht die Abenteuer nicht; märchenhaft, doch auch als Ausdruck des Glaubens, dass sich das Heil dem Demütigen schenke, werden sie an ihn herangetragen. Allen, die vorübergehen, die ihn suchen und die seiner bedürfen, gewährt er Hilfe. Er nimmt ihre Sorgen wahr, achtet auf Verpflichtungen und Fristen, ganz von 'erbaermde' durchdrungen.

In tätiger Tugend, äusseres und inneres 'ungeverte' erduldend, schreitet Iwein den Weg der Erlösung ab. Zerstörung und verursachtes Leid waren an seinem Anfang gestanden; nun bringt er Trost und Heil, wendet Not und kehrt Trauer in Freude. Er besiegt den Angreifer der Frau von Narison, den er, wie damals Ascalon, auf schmalem Burgweg kurz vor dem Eingang einholt, doch diesmal in rechtmässiger Verteidigung und dankbarem Dienst am Nächsten. Er macht den jämmerlich klagenden Löwen aus der Umschlingung des Drachen frei und tritt vor Lunetes Verrätern und am Artushof als Kämpfer der Gerechtigkeit auf; Gott und

---

11 In diesem Totschlag, nicht in der Fristversäumnis, sieht Wapnewski etwas kurzsichtig Iweins Hauptschuld, a.a.O. 66–67.

das Recht (d.h. sowohl die Unschuld Lunetes als auch der Löwe[12]) sind auf seiner Seite (5169). Das schweigsame Reiten des 'Gesalbten' durch die Wildnis und die ruhige Beständigkeit seiner 'triuwe' zu seinem Gefährten, dem Löwen, und zu allen, denen Hilfe mangelt, haben ihm soviel unbesiegbare innere Kraft verliehen, dass die rohe und bedrohliche Übergewalt der Riesen vor ihm weichen muss und er den Bann über den gefangenen Weberinnen, in den sie durch die 'kintheit' ihres Herrn und seine leichtsinnige Suche nach 'âventiure' (6330) geraten waren, lösen kann[13].

In typologischer Entsprechung und Spannung stehen sich die beiden Teile von Iweins Weg gegenüber. Das Anfängliche, das gaukelnde Versprechen, wird bildhaft von der Wahrheit beantwortet und überformt. Iweins Sturz und seine Schuld erweisen sich damit als notwendig und heilsam; in seiner Erniedrigung zeichnet sich strahlend die Erhöhung ab[14].

2. Der Kontrast

In verschiedener Gestalt und Funktion wird der Kontrast, der in der Schöpfung selbst, in Farben und Formen, in der Äusserungsweise und im ständigen Wechsel allen Lebens vorgegeben ist[15], immer auch künstlerisches Element der Dichtung sein. Er ist ein Mittel intensiver, spannungsvoller Darstellung, das dynamisch auf den Erkenntnisvorgang wirkt. Im Kontrast rücken zwei entgegengesetzte Möglichkeiten, eine Teilwahrheit und ihr Gegenprinzip, gleichzeitig ins Blickfeld. Diese Gegenüberstellung hebt die Eigenart sowohl der einen wie der andern Seite stärker hervor; beide tragen zu ihrer wechselseitigen Abgrenzung und Erhellung bei und drängen gleichzeitig zu einer Auflösung der Spannung, einem Ausscheiden oder einer Synthese hin[16].

Es ist gerade in der durchsichtigen Komposition des "Iwein" nicht zu übersehen, dass Hartmann den Kontrast sehr bewusst als sinnverdichtendes und profilierendes Element einsetzt[17]. Er intensiviert sowohl die Bildkraft wie auch die Deutlichkeit

---

12 Vgl. dazu Friedrich Ohly, Vom geistigen Sinn des Wortes im Mittelalter, Darmstadt 1966, 19.

13 Dieser Weg der Demut und der Erlösertaten, bei denen Iwein durch die Hilfe des Löwen stets der Sieg zuteil wird, hat seine Parallele im asketischen und durch Wunder ausgezeichneten und bestätigten Leben des Heiligen in der Legende. Vgl. dazu Max Wehrli, Roman und Legende, a.a.O. 436.

14 "Descendite ut ascendatis", Aug. Conf. IV,12,19.

15 Vgl. Eccl. 33,15.

16 Aus seinem ganzheitlichen Denken heraus erkennt Augustin im Kontrast ein zentrales Schönheitsprinzip: "Ita quasi ex antithesis quodammodo, quod nobis etiam in oratione jucundum est, id est ex contrariis, omnium simul rerum pulchritudo figuratur." (De ord. I,7). "So entsteht geradezu aus den Antithesen, d.h. aus den Gegensätzen, die uns auch in der Prosa gefallen, zugleich auch die Schönheit aller Dinge." (Zitiert nach Rosario Assunto, Text-Dokumente a.a.O. S. 125.)

17 "Die Wirkung des Kontrastes ist in der deutschen Dichtung vor Hartmann nicht als charakteristisches Kompositionselement anzusprechen." Siegfried Grosse, Die Wirkung des Kontrastes in den Dichtungen Hartmanns von Aue. WW 15 (1965) 29–39 (31).
Zu den Gegensätzen im "Erec" vgl. Rolf Endres, Studien zum Stil von Hartmanns Erec. Diss. München 1961, 57–83.

der Aussage. Gerade in der Gegenüberstellung mit dem hässlichen Waldmann oder der kläglichen Gestalt des Krautjunkers 'mit strûbendem hâre, barschenkel unde barvuoz' (2820f.), die Gawan heraufbeschwört, gewinnt der Ritter mit seinem Auftrag seine volle Leuchtkraft. Erst Keii lässt höfische Gesittung sichtbare Kontur annehmen, und wo sich auf dem duftenden Rasen im Baumgarten (6522f.) der Sinn der beiden Alten nur um den nahenden Winter und um fuchspelzgefütterte Kappen dreht, erscheint die sommerliche Freude der Jungen in noch hellerem Licht.

Mehrmals treten Bild und Gegenbild in befremdlich abruptem Umschlag zusammen. Das tönende Paradies an der Quelle wandelt sich auf Iweins Herausforderung hin schlagartig in eine verfinsterte Stätte wild tobender Zerstörung. Angesichts dieses entwicklungslosen Umschlags stellt sich dem Hörer unwillkürlich die Frage nach dem Zusammenhang der beiden Erscheinungsweisen, nach der Bedingung ihrer Zusammengehörigkeit, und er beginnt, die Hintergründigkeit des anfänglichen 'locus amoenus', seine Vorläufigkeit und sein Gefälle zu einer integrierenden Veränderung hin zu ahnen.

Um einen ebenso verdichteten und unvermittelten Vorgang handelt es sich, als Iwein nach seiner Fristversäumnis aus der vom Lobpreis der Ritter umhüllten Versonnenheit jäh herausgerissen und in die Wüste verbannt wird und der Boden der vermeintlichen 'êre', des eingespielten Glücks immer mehr einsinkt. Indem sich die Wirklichkeit des Helden so plötzlich und widerstandslos in ihr Gegenteil verkehrt, tritt die Brüchigkeit der ahnungslos geglaubten Sicherheit — d.h. jeder Sicherheit, die sich nur auf das Selbst stützt — mit aller Deutlichkeit hervor. Dabei liegt für den Dichter der Sinn einzig im Wahr oder Falsch der Haltung, des Zustandes; das Phänomen der Entwicklung, des Prozesses interessiert ihn nicht. Dies gilt auch als Interpretationshinweis: Der Leser soll, vom Kontrast ausgehend, interpretieren, d.h. in der Tiefe jedes Bildes seinen geistigen Sinn suchen und nicht einer psychologischen Verkettung nachspüren, die zur Zeit Hartmanns nur sekundär und in geringem Masse relevant war.

Bei näherem Zusehen zeigt sich, dass der Weg, den Iwein von seiner Ausfahrt bis zum Wiederfinden Laudines zurücklegt, auch als Bilderfolge vom Kontrastprinzip her aufgebaut ist. Er erscheint als stetiger Wechsel zwischen der hell beleuchteten und belebten Szenerie des Hofes und dem unwegsamen Wald, zwischen Begegnung und Vereinzelung, zwischen dem 'wunschleben' (44), der Gesellschaft und dem 'ungeverte', das die in der Wildnis verbrachten Tage und Nächte bringen. Aus der glanzvollen Glätte des höfischen Rahmens entspringt Kalogreants Fahrt ins fremdartige Reich. Scharf hebt sich der Auserwählte von der übrigen Ritterschaft ab, die turnierend, musizierend und erzählend den Hintergrund ornamentiert; 'dô slâfennes zît wart' (383), denkt Kalogreant ans Weiterreiten und taucht aus der gastlichen Burg zurück in die dornenvolle Wildnis des Waldes.

Seine überzeugende Wirkkraft kommt dem Kontrast in diesem Roman zu, weil er nicht als blosser Schmuck aufgesetzt ist, sondern als Ausdruck einer geistigen Grunderfahrung den Sinn massgebend mitbestimmt. Das auffallend Neue dieser Romane ist es ja, dass hier der Held nicht wie derjenige des Heldenepos oder der antiken Dichtung in unbeirrtem und ununterbrochenem Voranschreiten auf einem

Weg, durch alle Wechselfälle des Lebens hindurch, an sein Ziel gelangt, sondern dass dieser Weg nach der christlichen Grunderfahrung von Tod und neuem Leben eine scharfe Zäsur erfährt. Zu Iweins erstem Aufstieg, aber auch zu seinem Heilsweg, zu all seinen bedrängenden und reizvollen Begegnungen und der abschliessenden Ehrenkrönung am Artushof, steht sein Waldleben in unauslöschlichem Kontrast; es bildet das dunkle, untergründige Fundament, aus dem erst die wahre Schönheit erwächst.

Durch die Auseinandersetzung mit Mächten, die Iwein noch fremd und dem Höfischen entgegengesetzt sind, die er nicht nur aussen, sondern in sich selbst wahrnehmen lernt, führt sein Weg, der in 'ungewizzenheit' (859) beginnt, schliesslich zu einer Ganzheit des Menschenbildes. Immer ist dabei das äussere Geschehen auch Zeichen einer inneren Station. Iwein begegnet sich selbst; er erlöst das Tier und macht es durch dieses fraglose Einstehen zahm und zutraulich; er sieht sich mit der ungebärdigen Rohheit von Riesen, mit Armut, Unterdrückung und Untröstlichkeit konfrontiert und muss auf all das kämpfend und entgegentretend antworten. Denn dieser Ritter, der 'nâch âventiure' auszog, muss den Menschen in sich, den Wissenden und Erkennenden, der die Not wie auch die Gnade kennt und beidem standhält, erst erfahren und erschaffen[18].

Die für Hartmann so zentrale Erfahrung von der Brüchigkeit des menschlichen Lebens und seiner Versprechungen – 'wir sind von broeden sachen'[19] – und von der Spannweite der Pole, zwischen denen es auseinanderklaffen kann, lässt ihn immer wieder, zu eindringlicher Vergegenwärtigung, die Gegensätze zeichenhaft zusammenrücken. Iweins Reaktion nach dem Urteil Lunetes ist kein langsames Absinken, kein fuchtelnder und protestierender Rückzug, sondern ein augenblicklicher Einsturz, eine plötzliche, vollkommene Umkehrung.

Iwein 3257   der ie ein rehter adamas
                 riterlîcher tugende was,
                 der lief nû harte balde
                 ein tôre in dem walde.

Wie Seite und Gegenseite einer einzigen, in dramatischer Spannung aufleuchtenden Schönheitsfigur sind Hell und Dunkel zueinanderhingeordnet. 'Heil und unheil' (3927) sind für Iwein aus dem Abenteuer an der Quelle entsprungen, und 'heil und unheil' hat auch die Salbung gebracht (3682). Dynamisch wirken die Gegensätze aufeinander zu. Gerade weil Iwein einst Glück und Freude besass, wird ihm der Verlust zum beunruhigenden Schmerz.

18 Als ein Streben nach Ganzheit der Menschennatur bezeichnet Hugo von Sankt-Viktor den menschlichen Bildungsweg: "Omnium autem humanarum actionum seu studiorum, quae sapientia moderatur, finis et intentio ad hoc spectare debet, ut vel naturae nostrae reparetur integritas vel defectuum, quibus praesens subiacet vita, temperetur necessitas." De studio legendi I,V,1. (Ziel und Zweck aller menschlichen Unternehmungen oder Studien, welche von weiser Erkenntnis gelenkt werden, sollen darauf gerichtet sein, die Ganzheit unserer Natur wiederherzustellen oder doch die zwingende Not der Schwächen, denen unser gegenwärtiges Leben unterliegt, zu mässigen.)
19 "Armer Heinrich" 105.

Iwein 3979   waere mir niht geschehen heil
                  und liebes ein vil michel teil,
                  sone west ich waz ez waere.
                  âne senede swaere
                  sô lebet ich vrîlîchen als ê,
                  nû tuot mir daz senen wê.

Diese Sehnsucht, dieser ständig verspürte Mangel, gibt ihn nicht mehr frei, bleibt ihm als fortwährende innere Last. Und doch ist gerade diese schmerzende Erinnerung Antrieb zur weiterstrebenden Suche. Denn anders als der Waldmann, empfindet Iwein, trotz seiner 'swarzen lîch' (3595) mit innerster Gewissheit: 'daz ich hie ungerne bin' (3633). Unvergänglich sind ihm die Spuren des einst besessenen Paradieses eingeprägt.

Als wichtiges Merkmal der Gestalt und ihrer Schönheit prägen sich die Konstrastbilder des "Iwein" dem Sinn unlöschbar ein und akzentuieren spannungsvoll das ästhetische Erlebnis. Ja vielleicht liegt das Geheimnis der unerklärlichen Bannkraft dieses Werks gerade darin, dass − in höchst hintergründigem Kontrast − die eindringlich gemeinte Aussage dem so leichten und unbeschwerten Ton und der durchfärbenden humoristischen Ironie anvertraut ist.

3. Spiegelungen

Die gestalt- und sinnmässige Ordnung seines Werks schafft Hartmann nicht neu und eigenmächtig, sondern in deutendem und verdeutlichendem Nachvollzug. Seine Leistung ist es, Sinnbezüge herauszuarbeiten, aufleuchten zu lassen. Die Vielfalt solcher "Spuren" im "Iwein", die den Deutungsfreudigen weiterlenken und durch die der Roman auf alle Seiten hin offen und teilhaftig wird, ist in der Tat unerschöpflich.

Szene und Wort öffnen sich dabei nicht nur in die Tiefe, auf eine moralische und allegorische Sinnschicht hin; an der Erzähloberfläche selbst entfaltet sich ein vielfältiges Spiel bildlich-motivischer Konkordanzen, und an einzelnen Stellen wirft diese Oberfläche spiegelnd Bildthemen zurück, in denen Gedankenkreise aus der Heilsgeschichte, aus antikem Erzählgut oder aus andern höfischen Werken auftauchen und die, bald stärker, bald schwächer durchschimmernd, mit der Episode auf gleicher Ebene ineinanderspielen. Gewohnt, die Wahrheit nicht anders als in Bruchstücken und wie "durch einen Spiegel" zu erkennen[20], wagt es der Dichter, von jeder Erscheinung aus eine Brücke zu einem Vorgeprägten zu schlagen und es seiner Deutung dienstbar zu machen.

Dass solche Spiegelungen, solch bildliches Ineinander im Dichtwerk jedoch möglich wird, fordert nun allerdings, dass dieses auch mit den Qualitäten eines Spiegels ausgestattet sei, also über die Eigenschaft verfüge, Bilder aufzufangen, ohne

20 1.Kor. 12,13.

sie zu fixieren. Dazu scheint gerade mit Hartmanns durchsichtiger, einfacher Darstellungsweise und mit seiner 'cristallînen' Sprache, die nicht durch farbige Oberfläche besticht, sondern vielfältigen Deutungsmöglichkeiten offen bleibt, ausgezeichnete Voraussetzung gegeben.

Dem Interpreten aber ergeht es vor diesem Phänomen wie vor dem fluktuierenden Wasserbild: greifen und festhalten lässt es sich nicht. Denn nirgends sind solche Spiegelungen konsequent durchgeführt oder auch nur eindeutig unterstrichen. Wo man deshalb umschreibend auf sie eingeht, treten die Konturen unwillkürlich stärker heraus als im Werk selbst.

So sind auch die zahlreichen Entsprechungen, mit denen der *"Erec"* schattenhaft noch einmal durch Hartmanns neuen Roman geistert, nicht so sehr als hinweisendes Paradigma für eine Deutung zu nehmen, sondern als liebenswürdiges, humorvollwitziges Echospiel. – Als das Fest, das bei der Einkehr des Königs Artus auf Laudines Schloss gefeiert wird, zu Ende geht, tritt Gawan auf den Haupthelden zu und zieht ihn beiseite, 'von den liuten sunder' (2769); die Absonderung der zwei ausgezeichneten Ritter kündigt Gewichtiges an, dem Hartmanns Aufmerksamkeit mehr gilt als dem nur kurz resümierten Festbetrieb. Mit der Mahnung Gawans zu unablässiger ritterlicher Übung, zu Turnier und 'âventiure', knüpft er an die bekannte Problematik des "Erec" an:

Iwein 2791
> 'kêrt ez niht allez an gemach,
> als dem hern Ereke geschach,
> der sich ouch alsô manigen tac
> durch vrouwen Enîten verlag.
> wan daz er sich erholte
> sît als ein riter solte
> sô waere vervarn sîn êre.
> der minnete ze sêre.'

Bei Chrétien fehlt dieser explizite Bezug. Hartmann jedoch signalisiert damit einen Drehpunkt, von dem aus die beiden Romane parallel und kontrapunktisch miteinander in Übereinstimmung zu bringen sind, wie Variationen eines selben Themas. Beide Helden gelangen in siegreichem Anlauf zu einem glückhaften, sie vor allen andern auszeichnenden Ziel. In leicht ironischem Kontrast treten dabei die scheue, arme und hingebungsvolle Enite und die mächtige, unduldsame Witwe auseinander. Ebenso klingt die an Erec geübte Kritik – 'der minnete ze sêre' (2798) – in ironischer Drehung als Vorwurf nach, als Iwein von den ritterlichen Anforderungen so ganz in Beschlag genommen wird, dass er Eid und Termin vergisst. Erec und Enite treten ihre Abenteuerfahrt gemeinsam an; Laudine aber tritt völlig zurück, wird unerreichbar, und der Löwe hat neben all seinen realen und symbolischen Funktionen sozusagen auch noch ihre Stellvertretung zu übernehmen. Erheitert stellt man allerhand Analogien zwischen ihm und der treuen Enite fest: beiden obliegt in der Nacht das Wächteramt; beide greifen eigenmächtig und ausschlaggebend ein, wo der Held in Gefahr gerät, und beide sind bedenkenlos und voreilig zum Selbstmord entschlossen, da sie den 'herren' tot wähnen, der in

Wirklichkeit in einer Ohnmacht liegt. Den zwei Räuberabenteuern im "Erec" entsprechen Iweins Kämpfe mit den Riesen, und die Treueprobe, die Enite vor Galoein und Oringles zu leisten hat, wird nun für Iwein aktuell: wo immer er kämpfend eintritt, schlägt er den 'lôn', Minne und Besitztum, aus, ja ist nicht einmal versucht, ihn anzunehmen, so fraglos ist ihm jetzt, da er zu sich selber gekommen ist, die Verknüpfung seines Wesens und Geschicks an Laudine geworden. Auch das grosse Erlösungsabenteuer am Schluss und der Kampf mit dem verkannten Freund haben ihr Pendant im "Iwein". Offenbar kannte Hartmann bei der Abfassung des "Erec" (ca. 1180) den "Iwein" bereits, denn das Abenteuer der 'hovesvröide' im "Erec" ist über Chrétien hinaus mit dem Motiv der gefangenen Witwen und ihrer Erlösung durch den Helden gekoppelt und mit der dadurch gewonnenen anagogischen Sinnstufe in seiner Schlusswirkung erhöht. Einen Widerschein des Zaubergartens mit seinem Hüter Mabonagrin, den noch keiner bestand, erkennt man schliesslich in Iweins Anfangsabenteuer.

Solche Übereinstimmungen können nun zufällig sein oder schon bei Chrétien mitgewirkt haben. Wesentlich ist einzig, dass auch sie als latenter, verborgener Reichtum den Roman zu einer unerschöflichen Quelle für die Phantasie und Kombinierlust der Hörer machen und ihn, bis ins Spielerische hinein, als Zeugnis einer allumfassenden Teilhabe erscheinen lassen.

Nach Spiegelungen biblisch-legendarischer Vorbilder im "Iwein" zu suchen, ist man bei dem Dichter des "Gregorius" und des "Armen Heinrich", trotz der Schwerelosigkeit und Diesseitigkeit seines letzten Artusromans, im geheimen immer wieder versucht. Es sind denn auch Anzeichen dafür da, dass Hartmann im Blick auf die Figur des *Adam* Inspiration schöpfte für die Gestaltung seines Romans und ihm damit eine allegorisch-anagogische Sinnspur einwirkte.

Der innere Weg des Helden, zu dem alle übrigen Figuren in funktionaler Abhängigkeit stehen, ist mittelaltergemäss nicht von individueller Auffassung her bestimmt, sondern auf das Typische, Vorbildhafte ausgerichtet und transparent auf den heilsgeschichtlichen Erlösungsweg der Menschheit. In letzter Rückführung ist dieser Weg exemplarisch und präfigurativ schon in Adam vorgezeichnet; denn der aus dem Paradies Vertriebene ist auch gleichzeitig Bedingung und Ankündigung des Kommenden, des zweiten Adam, der ihn erfüllt und erlöst[21]. Ausblick auf diesen Ersten und diesen Letzten, auf den Menschen und seinen Erlöser, der wiederum Menschensohn ist, und die Hartmann beide eng zusammenrückt, ja in ein und derselben Figur vereinigt, gewährt die zentrale Stelle von Iweins Heilung.

Da Iwein verstört, wild und ohne Erinnerung im Wald lebt und auf niemanden mehr achtet, finden ihn eines Tages drei ritterliche Frauen nahe bei der Landstrasse, in tiefen Schlaf versenkt.

21 1.Kor. 15,22.

Iwein 3359 er lief nû nacket beider
der sinne und der cleider,
unz daz in zeinen stunden
slâfende vunden
drî vrouwen dâ er lac,
wol umb einen mitten tac,

Der Schlaf ist hart, denn weder das Pferdegetrappel noch das Gespräch der Frauen vermögen ihn zu wecken, und als eine der Frauen später wiederkehrt, findet sie ihn 'dannoch slâfende' (3459). Lähmende Schwere, die zu keinem Ziel mehr einen Ausblick lässt, hält ihn gefangen – verstärktes und gleichzeitig letztes Zeichen von Iweins Beladenheit und Entfremdung. Aber es ist Mitte des Tages, Zeichen zur Umkehr[22].

Aufmerksam beugt sich eine der Frauen über den Schlafenden. Da ist er so missgestaltet, so unkenntlich und armselig geworden, dass sie über ihn weint (3387f.). Nackt ist Iwein[23], wie Adam, und schwarz am ganzen Leib – auch das vielleicht ein Zug, der auf den aus Erde Gestalteten deutet, den sich das Frühchristentum schwarz vorstellte[24]. Vor allem aber ist auch Iweins Schlaf selbst, dieser Schlaf, der den alten Menschen vom neuen scheidet und im Erwachen zu neuer, erleuchteter Erkenntnis führt[25], ein Zeichen, das dem Mittelalter als Hinweis auf Adam noch vertrauter war als uns. Als Gott aus der Rippe des Adam den zweiten Menschen schuf, liess er einen Tiefschlaf über ihn fallen (Gen. 2,21); dieser Schlaf des Adam erscheint in der Exegese der Väter als Figur des Todesschlafs Christi. Augustinus, Bernhard und später Dante legen ihn als Schlaf der Kontemplation aus, denn "wenn Adam erwacht, beginnt er zu prophezeien." (Gen.

22 Mittag als Metapher für geistige Erleuchtung: 'sicut meridies' Aug. Conf. X, 5,7, nach Is. 58,10. Auch Enite konfrontiert Erec 'umbe einen mitten tac' (3014), da die Sonne durch das Fenster der Kemenate ihren Dienst wohl versieht, mit der Wahrheit über ihn selbst. Im "Armen Heinrich" steht 'mitten tac' für Heinrichs Hochgefühl (154); oft dient der Ausdruck aber auch blosser formelhafter Zeitbestimmung, so "Iwein" 3284.
23 Iweins Nacktheit ist Signum seiner Entpersönlichung, aber auch Möglichkeit eines Anfangs. – Das Kleid hat in der mittelalterlichen Dichtung hohen symbolischen Wert. Die Torenkleider Parzivals, seine rote Ritterrüstung und später sein Büssergewand markieren äusserlich die Stufen seines inneren Weges. Repräsentativen Charakter gewinnt das Kleid der Enite am Artushof (1530f.) und auf ihrer Aventiurenfahrt (3054f.); ebenso für das Bauernmädchen auf der Reise nach Salerno ("Armer Heinrich" 1034f.). – Die Entwicklung zur Allegorie, schon in der Bibelsprache vorgeprägt, so: Hiob 29,14 "Ich kleidete mich in Gerechtigkeit, sie ward mein Kleid, in das Recht, wie in Mantel und Turban.", liegt nahe; vgl. "Greg." 103f., "Tristan" 4563f., 4991f. – Im "Wigalois", wo unter der faszinieren farbigen Oberfläche kaum mehr ein 'innen' ausgeformt ist, hat das Modische bereits einen gewissen Selbstzweck.
24 Vgl. Hugo Rahner, Griechische Mythen in christlicher Deutung, Darmstadt 1966, 216: "Noch auf den Mosaiken der Vorhalle von San Marco in Venedig kommt diese durchaus antike Denkweise zu bildlicher Gestalt. Da wird Adam von Gott gebildet als vollkommen schwarze Gestalt. Und erst von dem Augenblick an, wo dem schwarzen Adam der Geist Gottes eingehaucht wird, die Seele, wird Adam weiss und schön."
25 "Ich war eine Weile weg von mir und Schlummer legte sich auf meinen Wahn (insania). Und dann erwachte ich in Dir und sah Dich als den anderswie Unendlichen, und dies war nun ein Sehen, das nicht aus dem Fleische kam." Aug. Conf. VII,14,20.

2,23–24)[26]. Nun ist auch Iweins Schlaf durchaus nicht ein Heilschlaf, der Vergessen bringt, im Gegenteil: Bei seinem Erwachen ist Iwein wissend geworden. Zum erstenmal seit seinem sehnenden Verdenken am Artushof und der Verfluchung Lunetes durchbricht er seine Stummheit; Erinnerung ist ihm zurückgegeben; er erkennt sich selber und das Vergangene in neuer Bewusstheit[27]. Das herrliche Selbstgespräch Iweins, das Hartmann dem Erwachen folgen lässt, das plötzliche Auftauchen aus 'wân' und Traum zur Wahrheit (3509–3583)[28], das bei Chrétien völlig fehlt, ist in seinem kontemplativen Charakter vielleicht mit inspiriert vom Wissen um die Bedeutung jenes zeichenhaften Schlafes, in dem Adam der Wahrheit näherkommt.

Wohl ist es vordergründig die Zaubersalbe der Feimurgan[29], die Iwein verwandelt hat, doch sein neu erschlossenes Wertbewusstsein wurzelt im Traum: 'mich hât gelêret mîn troum' (3569). Er hat ihm sein 'rîchez leben' (3514) als trügerische Wahrheit ('dazn ist allez niht wâr' 3536), als 'wân' (3540)[30] enthüllt. Die Einsicht in sich selbst, die Iwein durch diesen Traum zuteil wird, steht als erfahrene Begnadung, als mitvollzogene Heilung komplementär und überformend zur automatischen Märchenwirkung. Der Traum hat ihm sein 'altez reht benomen' (3572); nicht länger verweilt Iwein in Wildnis und Verlorenheit. Über den alten Menschen, über den schwarzen Leib, zieht er die bereitliegenden scharlachroten Kleider an (3453)[31]. Das Märchenmotiv der Salbung wird dabei durchsichtig auf einen vielfältigen geistigen Sinn[32]. Sie bedeutet, wie die Salbung der Taufe, Wiedergeburt; sie ist Anfangszeichen und Ostererfahrung[33].

26 Auf das Motiv des Adamsschlafes in der Bibelauslegung und in der mittelalterlichen Literatur macht Erich Auerbach aufmerksam. "Typologische Motive in der mittelalterlichen Literatur", a.a.O. 19–29 (20).
27 Max Wehrli macht anhand dieser zentralen Stelle den "Weg zum Selbst" als Grundthema in Hartmanns Werken und als die faszinierende und grundlegende Erfahrung dieser Zeit offenbar. "Iweins Erwachen", a.a.O.
28 Vgl. die analoge Stelle im "Wigalois", V. 5800f., wohl vom "Iwein" inspiriert.
29 Die Fee Morgane, Schülerin des Zauberers Merlin, ist in der Heil- und Zauberkunst bewandert. Bei Hartmann hat sie sogar Macht über Teufel ("Erec" 5194f.). Ihr Pflaster heilt die Wunde Erecs (7225f., 5243f.), und im Lancelot-Roman heilt sie den Helden eigenhändig von seiner Krankheit ("Lancelot und Ginevra" a.a.O. S. 227).
30 Vgl. "Armer Heinrich" 400 'sus trouc ouch mich mîn tumber wân'. Heinrich meint damit seinen 'hôchmuot' (404), die fehlende demütige Ausrichtung auf Gott, die in unausgesprochener moralischer Sinnschicht auch im "Iwein" nachklingt.
31 Rot gilt in der bildlichen Darstellung oft als göttliche Farbe. So erscheint Christus meist in rotem Gewand, während Maria über dem roten Kleid den blauen Mantel der Menschlichkeit trägt. Im Ritterroman ist das scharlachfarbene Gewand jedoch auch einfach Zeichen der Erhöhung oder Initiation, die einem Ritter widerfährt.
32 Aus Predigt und Bibelkommentar hat die Salbe (< salve) häufig allegorische Bedeutung. Bernhard spricht von der bitteren Salbe der 'contritio', von der heilsamen Salbe der 'devotio', mit der der Bekehrte die erfahrene Gnadenwirkung allen Bedürftigen mitteilt, und bezeichnet Gott selbst als den 'veritatis doctor', der mit seiner Salbung Erleuchtung schenkt und die Nebelschatten der ignorantia zerstreut. (Sancti Bernardi Opera I, Rom 1957, sermo 10: III,4; IV,5; sermo 12: VII, 10) Bei Origenes wird Christus 'Narde' genannt, mit der die durch Gnade Angerührten zu Christen gesalbt werden. (Geist und Feuer. Ein Aufbau aus seinen Schriften von Hans Urs von Balthasar, Salzburg [2] 1938, 310).
33 Auf die Anklänge an die Osterszene mit den drei Marien und an die Salbung Magdalenas haben A. T. Hatto, 'Der aventiure meine' in Hartmann's Iwein a.a.O. 94f., und H. B. Willson, Love and Charity in Hartmann's Iwein a.a.O. 216f. aufmerksam gemacht.

Ein Widerschein dieser Adam–Christus–Verbindung spiegelt sich bei Hartmann noch einmal im Löwenabenteuer ab, das als wahrhafte Epiphanie die Verwandlung Iweins bestätigt. Es ist gleichzeitig das Abenteuer, das sich von den übrigen ritterlichen Kämpfen vollkommen abhebt, das speziell Iwein zukommt und in ähnlichem Sinn Kennzeichen seiner Erlösergestalt ist, wie der Gral für Parzival[34].

In seiner neuen Verfügbarkeit lässt sich Iwein nach dem Aufenthalt auf der Burg der Frau von Narison von einer rauh klagenden Stimme zu einem Kampfplatz leiten, wo ein Löwe sich verzweifelt aus der Umschlingung eines Drachen zu befreien sucht. Iwein stellt sich dem Kampf. Nach der frei geschenkten Wandlung durch die Zaubersalbe beweist er nun aus eigener Haltung und mit neugewonnener Kraft, dass er sich für das Gute und das Gerechte entscheidet:

Iwein 3846 hern Iwein tete der zwîvel wê
       wederm er helfen solde,
       und bedâhte sich daz er wolde
       helfen dem edeln tiere.

Zum erstenmal ganz auf sich selber gestellt, löst Iwein in diesem Abenteuer mit neuer Bewusstheit und Einsicht den Löwen aus den Fängen des Drachen, löst das Gerechte aus der Umschlingung und Vermischung mit dem Bösen[35], und legt damit gleichzeitig seine eigenen guten Kräfte frei, befreit sie aus einer möglichen Umklammerung durch die bittere Verstocktheit des Zurückgestossenen und Gedemütigten. Wie das Gelingen all seiner Kämpfe ist der Sieg über den Drachen dabei Bestätigung der 'saelde', die ihn aufs neue, noch verhüllten Antlitzes leitet, ja sie gewährt ihm hier den vollen Beweis seines richtig gewählten Weges: denn der befreite Löwe, der König unter den Tieren, legt seine Wildheit vor Iwein ab und unterwirft sich dem Königlich-Gesalbten in friedlicher Dankbarkeit[36].

Bei Chrétien, der die ganze 'mervoile' (3349) malerischer und weitläufiger beschreibt, stellt sich der Löwe dabei auf die Hinterbeine, legt die Tatzen aufeinander, beugt das von Tränen überströmte Gesicht demütig zur Erde und kniet schliesslich sogar nieder, um Yvain so seine Ergebenheit zu bezeugen (3388f.)[37].

34 In der "Queste del Saint Graal", einem stark religiös-moralistisch ausgerichteten Prosaroman des 13. Jhs., ist das Löwenabenteuer auch Perceval gewährt. (Ausg. Albert Pauphilet, Paris 1923 [CFMA] S. 95)

35 Bei Chrétien tritt die symbolische Bedeutung noch deutlicher hervor: 3355 'et li serpanz est venimeus, / si li saut par la boche feus, / tant est de felenie plains.' (Und der Drache ist giftig; Feuer fährt aus seinem Rachen, so sehr ist er mit Bosheit angefüllt.)

36 Die Erzählung vom dankbaren Löwen taucht zum erstenmal auf in der antiken Sage vom Löwen des Androcles (2. Jh.n.C.), der ihn von einem Dorn befreit, später bei Hieronymus, wo der Löwe als zahmes Haustier im Kloster bleibt. Im Mittelalter, wo der Ritter als Helfer auftritt, tritt der Drachenkampf an die Stelle der Verletzung. – In leicht variierter Version flicht Petrus Damianus (11. Jh.) die Geschichte in einer Epistel ein als Exempel des 'ordo caritatis' und der getreuen Unterwerfung unter Gottes Gesetze (Liber VII, Ep. V; Paris 1610, S. 472–473).

37 Löwen mit menschlichem Antlitz, meist in Gesellschaft von Einsiedlern, finden sich häufig in der byzantinischen Malerei. Vgl. Lacarrière, Les hommes ivres de Dieu, Paris (Arthaud) 1954, 258.

Hartmann lässt all diese verspielten Details weg; sein Löwe ist keine Märchenfigur, keine Karikatur; er behält die Ausdrucksformen des Tier'sinns'.

Iwein 3869

> sich bôt der lewe an sînen vuoz
> und zeiget im unsprechende gruoz
> mit gebaerde und mit stimme.
> hie liez er sîne grimme
> und erzeiget im sîne minne
> als er von sînem sinne
> aller beste mohte
> und eime tiere tohte.

Hier mutet das Bild viel eher wie eine Erinnerung ans Paradies an, da Adam noch in friedlicher Gemeinschaft mit den Tieren lebte und sie ihm untertan waren. Und so wie Adam im Stand der Unschuld über sie herrschte (Gen. 1,26; Ps. 8,7–9) und ihnen Namen gab (Gen. 2,19–20), so werden die wilden Tiere auch dem, der die verlorene Gottebenbildlichkeit zurückgewinnt, wieder gehorsam sein – so sagen es die Propheten von den messianischen Zeiten voraus[38]; in den apokryphen Evangelien gebietet auch Jesus häufig über wilde Tiere[39].

Iwein steht als zweiter Adam damit in einer Reihe mit all jenen Gestalten in Legenden, Mönchsviten und Vätergeschichten, denen ein anhängliches Tier als Trost in die Einsamkeit und als Zeugnis ihrer Begnadung zugesandt ist und deren vertrauter Umgang mit der erlösten Tiernatur nicht nur die Erinnerung an die einst besessene wahre Natur bekräftigt, sondern auch einen lichten Vorausblick auf die einst vollendete Erlösung gewährt[40]. Dass die ritterliche Welt diese Auszeichnung an dem fremden, namenlosen Ritter wahrnimmt, fügt Hartmann, wenn auch in durchaus höfischer Sprache, eigens hinzu:

Iwein 4811

> sî prîsten sêre sînen muot.
> er dûhte si biderbe unde guot,
> in allen wîs ein hövesch man.
> daz kurn sî dar an
> daz der lewe bî im lac
> und anders sites niene pflac
> niuwan als ein ander schâf.

---

38 Is. 11,6–9 "Beim Lamm wird Gast sein der Wolf", ff. Ebenso Is. 65, 25.
39 Vgl. August Nitschke, Tiere und Heilige, in: Dauer und Wandel der Geschichte. FG Kurt von Raumer, Münster 1966, 71.
40 Jean Daniélou, Sacramentum futuri, Paris 1950 (Études de Théologie Historique) 9: "La domination sur les animaux restera dans la littérature des Pères du désert, l'un des traits marquant la restauration de l'état paradisiaque chez ceux qui sont transformés par l'Esprit-Saint."
Vgl. zu diesem Thema auch Hugo Rahner, a.a.O. 187; Wilhelm August Schulze, Der Heilige und die wilden Tiere. Zeitschrift für neutestamentliche Wissenschaft 47 (1955) 280–283; Joseph Bernhart, Heilige und Tiere, München 1937, 24; Ludwig Bieler, Das Bild des "göttlichen Menschen" in Spätantike und Frühchristentum, Wien 1935, 109f.

Iweins Weg erstreckt sich in der Zeit als ein mühseliger Weg der reparatio, sowohl an ihm selbst wie an der bedrohten und bedürftigen höfischen Welt. In seiner Gemeinschaft mit dem Löwen aber ist stetig, als Zeichen und als Versprechen, das Ende dieses Weges, die vollzogene Erlösung und die wiederhergestellte Ordnung und Harmonie schon angekündigt und gegeben.

Mit der Wachsamkeit des Löwen —

Iwein 3911   her Iwein leite sich und slief,
                    der lewe wachet unde lief
                    umbe sîn ros und umb in. —

ist jedoch gleichzeitig ein neuer Hinweis gegeben, wonach der Löwe, in Übereinstimmung mit der allegorischen Deutung des "Physiologus", selber Symbol Christi ist. Denn seiner Natur nach schläft der Löwe mit offenen Augen, so wie Christus durch seinen Todesschlaf hindurch wach zur Auferstehung blieb[41]. Als nächster und einziger 'geselle' auf seinem Weg, ist der Löwe gleichzeitig auch Vorbild und die eigentliche Macht, mit der Iwein sieghaft wird; denn keines seiner Abenteuer besteht er aus eigener Kraft; immer wieder ist er auf die Hilfe seines Gefährten, auf dessen Unbesiegbarkeit und unverbrüchliche Treue angewiesen; der Löwe entscheidet Iweins Sache. Iwein legt seinen eigenen Namen ab und beruft sich auf den Stärkeren.

Iwein 5496   er sprach 'ich wil sin erkant
                    bi mînem leun der mit mir vert.'

Das Auffällige an der Sinnerweckung in mittelalterlichen Texten ist, wie hier frei und ungehindert scheinbar Getrenntes nahe zueinandergebracht werden und sich verbinden kann: der Ostermorgen und Magdalenas liebende Salbung in der Heilungsszene; der erwachend erkennende Adam und der Auferstandene; die unterworfene Tiernatur und Christus selbst. Alle Schranken einer eingerichteten Ordnung fallen vor solchem freudigen Erschauen und Erkennen dahin.

An seinem Löwen lernt und übt Iwein Treue, Zuwendung und Hingabe, denn der Löwe lebt sie ihm vor.

---

41 "So der Lewe slaeffet, siniu ougen er haltit offen. daz sculen wir suochen gescriben an den buochen: 'ich slief genote, min herze wachote.' (HL 5,2) von diu bezeichent er den heiligen Christ, got her. wand er in dem vleische entslief, diu gotheit in anrief. do erwachot er aber ze der zeswe sines vader, also gescriben ist: 'stande uf, min ere du bist. got den entslafot niht, wande er Israhel behuotet unde siht." Der altdeutsche Physiologus, Millstätter Reimfassung, hg. von Friedrich Maurer, Tübingen 1967, (ATB 67), S. 5.
Zum Löwen als Christussymbol vgl. Julian Harris, The role of the lion in Chrétien de Troyes Yvain. PMLA 64 (1949) 1143–1163. – Der Aufsatz von Giuseppe Sansone, Il sodalizio d'armi del leone e di Ivano, in: Studi in onore di Italo Siciliano, Firenze 1966, 1053–1061, trägt nichts weiter dazu bei.

Iwein 3877   er antwurte sich in sîne pflege,
             alser in sît alle wege
             mit sînem dienest êrte
             und volget im swar er kêrte
             und gestuont im zaller sîner nôt,
             unz sî beide schiet der tôt.

Dabei leistet der Löwe nicht nur Beistand, sondern fordert selbst auch den Schutz und die Teilnahme Iweins. Ein inniges Verhältnis bildet sich zwischen den beiden heraus, eine vollkommene, liebevolle Solidarität. Gerade in jener Zeit, da Iwein niedergeschlagen, mit verhängtem Visier von Laudine wegreitet, die ihn nicht erkannt hat, bedarf der im Kampf mit dem Truchsess verwundete Löwe seiner besonderen Pflege. Hinkend und wund – der Löwe am Leib und Iwein im Herzen – schleppen sich die beiden durch die Wälder, und da der Löwe nicht mehr weiterkann, bereitet ihm Iwein eigenhändig in seinem Schild ein weiches Lager aus allerhand Moos und weichem Laub und hebt ihn zu sich aufs Pferd!

Iwein 5564   nû was der leu sô starke wunt
             daz er michel arbeit
             ûf dem wege mit im leit.
             dô er niht mêre mohte gân,
             dô muoser von dem rosse stân,
             und las zesamene mit der hant
             mies und swaz er lindes vant.
             daz leit er allez under in
             in sînen schilt und huop in hin
             ûf daz ros vür sich.
             daz leben was gnuoc kumberlich.

Alle Tugenden, die für Iwein wesentlich werden: Treue, Mitleid und Gerechtigkeit, sind vorbildhaft im Löwen verkörpert. Und doch ist anderseits diese symbolische Fracht, die ihm aufgebürdet ist, wieder so leicht und beweglich, dass er in der Episode am 'brunnen' unversehens auch wieder in ein neues Spiel treten kann. Dorthin sieht sich der Löwenritter als erstes und ohne es zu wollen hingelenkt, und im Angesicht des verlorenen Paradieses und seiner eigenen Schuldhaftigkeit erfasst ihn eine solche Bitternis am ganzen Leib, dass ihm noch einmal Kraft und Bewusstsein schwinden. Doch sieht der vom Gram Bezwungene sich bald und zu seiner eigenen Aufrichtung einem noch grösseren Leid gegenüber: In der Kapelle liegt Lunete, gefangen und von den gedemütigten und erbosten Untertanen Laudines zum Tode verurteilt. Noch unerkannt zunächst, treten der Verfluchte und seine Richterin, beide in klagender Not zueinander. Durch einen Riss in der Kapellentür ruft Lunete den verzweifelten Ritter an:

Iwein 4018   und dô er dirre clage pflac,
             dô sach sî hin vür
             durch eine schrunden an der tür.
             sî sprach 'wer claget dâ, wer? '

Unwillkürlich weckt die Spalte[42], durch die die Unterhaltung stattfindet, die Erinnerung an *Pyramus und Thisbe*. Mitten in der Erzählung von Iwein taucht damit plötzlich die Episode aus Ovids "Metamorphosen" auf[43]. Da ist an Stelle des Maulbeerbaumes, unter dem die Liebenden sich das Stelldichein geben, die dichtbelaubte Linde, da ist die kühle Quelle, und da ist auch der Löwe, doch nicht blutrünstig und wild, "von frischem Blute geschlagener Rinder das schäumende Maul noch besudelt,"[44] wie das antike Raubtier, sondern als Gegenbild dazu die Verkörperung sanfter Anhänglichkeit; ja seine Treue reicht geradezu an die Pyramus', des vorbildlichen Liebenden heran, denn wie dieser wäre auch der Löwe bereit gewesen, Iwein in den Tod zu folgen: 'er rihte daz swert an einen strûch / unde wolde sich stechen durch den bûch,' (3953–54)[45].

Durch die Ritze an der Tür werden hier nun allerdings nicht Liebesgeständnisse gelispelt, sondern Iwein vernimmt erneut von der ahnungslosen Lunete sein eigenes Urteil und erkennt erst jetzt das Ausmass an Leid, das sein Versagen nicht nur über ihn selbst, sondern über Laudine und auch über diese schuldlose Magd, die ihm einst das Leben rettete, gebracht hat. Wie Pyramus, hat auch Iwein Grund, sich anzuklagen und sein eigenes Leben zu verfluchen[46]:

Iwein 3995   'mîn lîp waere des wol wert
daz mich mîn selbes swert
zehant hie an im raeche
und ez durch in staeche,'

Iwein 4223   'jane müet mich niht wan daz ich lebe,
ouch sol ich schiere tôt geligen.'

42 Das Motiv der Spalte, durch welche eine wichtige Botschaft vernommen wird oder sich ein überwältigender Anblick bietet, besitzt in der mittelalterlichen Dichtung hohen Reiz. Durch einen Zwischenraum der Wand verfolgt der gefangene Löwe Iweins Kampf mit den Riesen (6715f.), und 'durch die schrunden' erblickt Heinrich das nackte opferbereite Mädchen (1245). Vgl. auch die Unterhaltung 'par mi une creveüre de la tor' in "Aucassin et Nicolette" XII, 35, kritischer Text von Hermann Suchier, Paderborn 1932, und das Gespräch durch das schmale Burgfenster zwischen Lancelot und seiner Befreierin: "Le Chevalier de la Charrete" 6447f.
H. B. Willson (Love and Charity in Hartmann's Iwein a.a.O. 220) vermutet als Inspirationsquelle solcher Stellen Hoheslied 2,14 "Meine Taube in felsigen Klüften, im Verstecke der Steilwand! Lass deinen Anblick mich schauen, deine Stimme mich hören! "
43 Vgl. "Erec" 7709–7713; "Tristan" 3615–3617; "Le Chevalier de la Charrete" 3820–3821. Zur afz. Umdichtung "Piramus et Tisbé" et quelques romans français du XIIe siècle, in: Recherches sur les sources latines des contes et romans courtois du moyen âge, Paris (Champion) 1913, S. 5–33. Chrétien war Ovid aus eigener Übersetzerarbeit vertraut, vgl. "Cligés" 1 'Cil qui fist d'Erec et Enide / Et les Comandemanz Ovide / Et l'Art d'Amors en romanz mist . . .'
44 Ovid, "Metamorphosen", lat.-dt. Ausg. von Erich Rösch, München 1964, IV, 96–97.
45 Treue über den Tod hinaus bekundet auch der Löwe des Einsiedlerabtes Gerasimus (5. Jh.); er stirbt am Grab des toten Freundes. Joseph Bernhart a.a.O. 58.
46 Ovid a.a.O. IV, 109–110: "doch meine Seele ist schuldig; denn *ich* hab, du Arme, zugrund dich gerichtet."

Doch steht dem tragischen Ende der antiken Geschichte ein hoffnungsreicher Ausblick gegenüber. Iwein entreisst sich der Besinnungslosigkeit, und auch der Löwe wird gerettet: Iwein 'rihte sich ûf unde saz / und erwante dem lewen daz / daz er sich niht ze tôde stach'. (3957–3959). Durch die 'schrunde' aber vernimmt Iwein eine Botschaft, die ihm Auftrag ist und die seinem Leben, das eben noch sehnsuchtsvoll in die Vergangenheit versenkt war, eine neue Richtung gibt und ihm im Abzahlen seiner Schuld, im demütigen und rückhaltlosen Einsatz für den Nächsten einen Sinn offenbart.

Nur flüchtig schimmert die Erinnerung an Ovid in der Erzählung auf, ohne dass der Dichter eigens darauf hinweist und auswertend darauf beharrt. Solcher Hinweise bedurfte das zeitgenössische Publikum offenbar auch nicht. Das blitzschnelle Deuten und Kombinieren, das kontemplative, eindringende Erkennen war ihm selbstverständlicher Kunstvollzug.

SCHLUSSBEMERKUNGEN

Hartmann hat sich sehr spärlich über seine Kunstauffassung geäussert. Ohne theoretischen Rückhalt, wie ihn etwa Gotfried in seiner Literaturschau geliefert hat, müssen wir den Aussagewillen des Dichters, auch als Stilwillen verstanden, aus seinem Werk selbst herauslesen. Bei einem nochmaligen Überblick über Hartmanns Iwein-Roman zeigt sich der Weg des Helden deutlich als ein nach Stufen klar gezeichneter Entwicklungsweg, der nicht individuell, sondern exemplarisch für den Menschen allgemein zu verstehen ist.

Die erste Stufe, die Iwein zu bewältigen hat, ist die Emanzipation von den Massstäben, die ihm der Artushof gesetzt hat. Gerade die Werte, die er sich am Hof angeeignet hat, darunter vor allem die durch Tüchtigkeit im Kampf erworbene 'êre' und das elitäre Selbstbewusstsein der auf sich selbst konzentrierten und geschlossenen Hofgesellschaft, lassen ihn scheitern. Für Iweins Menschwerdung weiss der Hof weder Rat noch Hilfe. Iwein muss zunächst auf sich selbst zurückfallen und Menschlichkeit in sich selbst entdecken. Erst nachdem alle äusserlich einordnenden und abschirmenden Insignien von ihm abgefallen sind und er die 'persona' des Artusritters von sich abgestreift hat, ist die Voraussetzung gegeben, dass er hinter diesen verstellenden Standeszeichen sich selbst wahrnimmt.

Der neue Weg beginnt mit dem Zweifel an der eigenen Identität und der Echtheit der bisherigen Wirklichkeitserfahrung. Gemessen an der jetzt erfahrenen Existenz, erweist sich der Artushof als Scheinwelt. Iweins Waldleben, das der Artusgesellschaft als peinlicher und peinvoller Zwischenfall erscheinen muss, ist für Iwein notwendiger krisenhafter Durchgang und schliesslich Neugeburt, und der Löwe, den er kurz nach seinem Erwachen rettet und der sein Begleiter wird, ist die sichtbar gewordene Gnade, die er in sich selbst gerettet hat. In Demut, Treue und bedingungsloser Hilfsbereitschaft aller Kreatur gegenüber ist er auf den Weg jener 'rehten güete' geraten, die Hartmann im Prolog von einer nur scheinbaren absetzt, mag diese sich auch auf imponierende und verlockende Weise äussern und von der Gesellschaft anerkannt sein.

Das Erkennen neuer Massstäbe setzt das Durchschauen der alten voraus. Hartmann reflektiert den Begriff der 'güete', der durch die Ausbreitung der höfischen Kultur eine so verflachende und grenzenverwischende Ausweitung erfahren hat, und versucht, ihn neu zu fassen. Seine Auffassung ist seit den Legendendichtungen nicht mehr ausschliesslich an einer höfisch-weltlichen Werteskala orientiert, sondern an einem Menschenbild im Horizont christlichen Geistes. Das Gegebene, nämlich von der Hofgesellschaft Vorgelebte erweist sich als Engpass, keiner Vertiefung fähig; es muss grundsätzlich durchbrochen werden. In einer fundamentalen Besinnung, zu der eigentlich nur eine vorausgegangene Krise führen kann, muss der Held zu einer tieferen Quelle durchdringen, aus der heraus sich ganz andere Möglichkeiten des Mensch- und Personseins erschliessen. Als neuer Adam, erlöst und erlösend, gelangt Iwein auf den Weg, der am Schluss zu Laudine zurückführt.

Die Figur Laudines ist nicht eindeutig, wohl aber die Rolle, die sie in bezug auf Iweins Entwicklung spielt. Sie wirkt als Herausforderung und Antrieb zu seiner Selbstfindung, und wenn sich Iwein beim Eindringen in ihren Bereich mit einer völlig fremden, rätselhaften Macht einzulassen glaubt, so wird er durch diese Begegnung imgrunde nur mit sich selber konfrontiert. Die etwas nachlässige Behandlung, die Laudine als Figur in der Zeichnung ihres Charakters und den Motivationen ihres Verhaltens widerfährt, lässt den Schluss zu, dass ihre Bedeutung nicht so sehr in ihr selbst als in ihrer Funktion liege. Sie könnte als eine Art Anima Iweins aufgefasst werden, die seinen Reifungsprozess veranlasst und bestimmt und die er früh erahnt (Begrüssung Lunetes), von der er gewaltsam Besitz zu ergreifen sucht, um sich plötzlich ihren Forderungen gegenübergestellt zu sehen. Nachdem er sich selbst gefunden hat, und das heisst im Horizont mittelalterlichen Denkens, nachdem er die ursprüngliche Selbst-sicherheit aufgegeben und die christliche Umkehr vollzogen hat, kommt Iwein zu Laudine zurück. Der Brunnen in ihrem Herrschaftsbereich, der dem Artushof deutlich entgegengestellt ist, erweist sich somit als wirkliche Lebensquelle, auch im christlichen Sinn. Dass auf dem Weg zu Laudine der 'ungehiure' steht und die Richtung weist, unterstreicht, dass in der gesuchten Lebensordnung die bisherigen Werte der Standeszugehörigkeit, der höfischen Erziehung und Kultiviertheit, innerhalb welcher es hauptsächlich auf die Bewährung in Turnier und 'aventiure' ankommt, durch andere ersetzt werden müssen. Der ungestalte Teil muss der Gestalt integriert werden, weil er, als Quelle der Erkenntnis erst den Umschlag von Erlösungsbedürftigkeit zu Erlöstheit ermöglicht.

Hartmann hat versucht, seine Sicht und Einsicht im märchenhaften Stoff von Chrétiens Roman fruchtbar zu machen und sie dem höfischen Publikum zu vermitteln, wobei der weltliche Stoff einer Bestätigung christlichen Glaubensgutes dient. Die bewusst angestrebte Vermittlung prägt den stilistischen Charakter des "Iwein" sehr stark, verleiht ihm eine dynamische Grundstruktur. Ausdruck davon sind die explizit publikumsbezogenen Stellen, in denen der Dichter das Werk oder sich selber relativiert und den Hörer immer wieder aus der Fiktion reisst und auf die Wirklichkeit verweist. Der Hörerschaft geht damit einerseits das Bewusstsein der Fiktionalität nicht verloren; sie bleibt in heilsamer Freiheit dem Stoff gegenüber. Andererseits werden auch ihre eigenen schöpferischen Kräfte dadurch unterstützt. Auf Schritt und Tritt ist der Hörer am Werk geistig mitbeteiligt, indem der Dichter Aussagen nur andeutet, die in der Rezeption ergänzt und vollendet werden sollen. Das Werk begreift sich so selbst als eine Art "Präfiguration". Die Symbolkraft des Quellenmotivs z.B. wird nicht erklärt; durch sein wiederholtes Auftreten als Bewährungsprobe kann sein tieferer Sinn erschlossen werden. Die Wiederholung oder die Variation eines Motivs tragen somit zur Sinnerhellung bei. Ebenso dienen Kontrastbildungen der Verdeutlichung.

Ein weiteres Merkmal der Darstellungsart ist der ornamentale Charakter vieler Erzählmotive. Sie wirken so, weil sie oft unkommentiert und unverknüpft mit der Handlung, scheinbar im Dekorativen, Unterhaltsamen bleiben und doch Schlüssel-wert besitzen (z.B. der 'ungehiure'). Sie treten wie Signale auf, ohne mit dem vordergründigen Zusammenhang genügend vermittelt zu sein. Bei eingehender Betrachtung zeigt sich, dass diese Motive jedoch selten so einschichtig sind, wie sie auf den ersten Blick erscheinen. Parallelen zu Bibelstellen, vom Inhalt oder vom Bild her, deuten sich an (Iwein—Adam), Anklänge an antikes Erzählgut oder an Erzählabschnitte aus früheren Dichtungen lassen uns ahnen, wie der mittelalterliche Hörer mit seinem uns nur teilweise bekannten Repertoire den Text assoziativ aufgenommen und verarbeitet haben mag. Immer wieder drängt sich Deutung vom einzelnen her auf, umso mehr, als die Handlung nicht organisch entwickelt wird. Das Werk wirkt vielmehr wie eine Komposition, in der Figuren und Motive als Muster eingesetzt sind, die variiert oder verdichtet werden. (Ähnlichkeit mit bildlichen Darstellungen: Buchillustrationen, Bildteppichen, Malereien, Reliefs.) Die geradezu abstrakte, unverbundene Handhabung von Figuren und Motiven bedingt auch, dass die Figur keinerlei persönliche Autonomie beansprucht; die Einheit der Figuren ist nicht angestrebt. Diese werden vielmehr von der Aussage beherrscht. Frühere Interpreten von Hartmanns Werken haben zwischen dem märchenhaft leichten Schlusswerk und den Legendendichtungen, in denen sie einen Gesinnungswechsel wahrnahmen, einen Widerspruch gesehen und sich dabei so beholfen, dass sie den "Iwein" als "blossen Zeitvertreib"[1] in dem der 'eigentliche' Hartmann nicht mehr zum Ausdruck gelange, abtaten.

Die schwerelose Sprache und der gattungsbedingte Schluss können jedoch nicht darüber hinwegtäuschen, dass die Stufen von Iweins Weg grundsätzlich völlig parallel zu denjenigen im "Gregorius" und im "Armen Heinrich" gesetzt sind: Anfängliches Gelingen im konventionellen Erfahrungshorizont, Schuld, Krise und schliesslich gnadenhafter Durchbruch zu einer neuen Lebenshaltung, bei der vor allem die christlichen Tugenden der Liebe und der Demut, als Leid- und Selbstbejahung verstanden, massgebend werden.

Zudem ist, gerade im Hinblick auf den gesteigerten Kunstcharakter des "Iwein", nicht zu übersehen, welche wesentliche Rolle das Schöne für Hartmann spielt und wie sehr dieses im Ethischen verwurzelt ist. So wird z.B. die Wandlung des armen Heinrich weder durch Gebet noch fromme Belehrung herbeigeführt, sondern im Betroffensein Heinrichs vor der Schönheit des sich opfernden Mädchens (1247f.). Ganz ähnlich wird Iwein während der Beerdigung Ascalons vom Anblick Laudines so berührt (1331f.), dass der eben noch Unbedenkliche, der in einziger Sorge um seine 'êre' ins Schloss eingedrungen war und den weder der Erschlagene noch das verzweifelt klagende Burggesinde zu rühren vermocht hatten, nun plötzlich Reue über sein Tun empfindet und, wie aus sich selbst herausgehoben, von einer neuen Lebensordnung, der Liebe, ergriffen wird (1338—54)[2]. Diese Verwandlung fehlt bei

---

1 So Helmut de Boor, Literaturgeschichte a.a.O. 83. Allerdings längst überholt durch Hugo Kuhn (in: Annalen der deutschen Literatur, hg. von Heinz Otto Burger, Stuttgart 1952, 133–135), Hugh Sacker, H. B. Willson, Wolfgang Dittmann, Max Wehrli.

2 In der Diss. von T. C. van Stockum, "Hartmann von Ouwes 'Iwein'. Sein Problem und seine Probleme", Mededelingen der Koninklijke Nederlandse Akademie van Wetenschappen, AFD Leterkunde N.R. 26/3, Amsterdam 1963, ist Iweins Erschauern vor der schönen Trauernden als negativ zu wertende Sinnlichkeit verbucht (16). Die Wandlung, die der Anblick in Iwein bewirkt, schliesst aber eine solche Beurteilung aus. Das stellenweise Sichtbarwerden des Körpers durch das Kleid ist Schönheitstopos (vgl. "Erec" 323f.).

Chrétien, ist Hartmanns idealisierende und bedeutungsvolle Zutat. Das Erschaute ist von solcher Macht, dass Iwein nicht länger auf sich selber besteht; sein Herz öffnet sich, wird lebendig und empfänglich, lässt den Schmerz der Trauernden zu seinem eigenen werden. Auf die kokett herausfordernde Frage der über die neue Wirklichkeit staunenden Laudine: "ouwî, mîn her Iwein, / wer hât under uns zwein / gevüeget dise minne? " (2341) antwortet Iwein selbst: "iuwer schoene und anders niht." (2355). Das Gewahrwerden der Schönheit, die als Abglanz und Botschaft einer vollkommenen Ordnung erscheint, in der alles Gabe ist, öffnet den verschlossenen Sinn, löst alle Versteifung auf, vermittelt neue Erkenntnis. Die Schönheit ist hier eine Erscheinungsform der Gnade. Sie bewegt den Menschen, überwältigt ihn, schliesst ihn auf für das grössere Mass, das durch sie offenbar wird. Sie drängt den Menschen hin zur 'güete', zu dem, was der Schöpfungsordnung gemäss ist, ja, sie ist dieses Gute selbst, dem man nicht anders als zustimmend begegnen kann. Wie für Heinrich ist auch für Iwein das Schöne entscheidende Begegnung auf dem Weg zu sich selbst und zu Gott.

Von diesem Standort und Einblick in Hartmanns Wertdenken aus spannt sich eine verlässliche Brücke über die Kluft, die seine geistliche Legende scheinbar vom abschliessenden Märchenroman trennt. Wenn dem Schönen so grosse Wirkkraft innewohnt, wenn es Mittel und Weg ist zur tieferen Einsicht und mehr als alles andere den Menschen zu verwandeln vermag, so wird auch der Dichter, dessen Wille zu verändernder, zum Guten hinlenkender Wirkung in all seinen Werken unverkennbar ist, versucht haben, diese Schönheit in der Kunst selber immer mehr zu verwirklichen und mitzuteilen.

Die kunstvolle Gestalt des Werks selbst wird damit Aussage, indem ihre helle Klarheit, die Lebendigkeit und Kraft ihrer Schönheit in den Betrachter eingehen und sich auf ihn übertragen. "Bonitas igitur bonificat, album albificat. Et ita de omnibus." (Nicolai de Cusa, De venatione sapientiae XIV, 41.)

BIBLIOGRAPHIE

1. Texte

Hartmann von Aue:
- "Die Klage", hg. von Herda Zutt, Berlin 1968.
- "Erec", hg. von Albert Leitzmann, (3) Tübingen 1963 (ATB 39).
- "Gregorius", hg. von Hermann Paul, (10) Tübingen 1963 (ATB 2).
- "Der arme Heinrich", hg. von Helmut de Boor, Frankfurt 1963.
- "Iwein", hg. von Hans Naumann und Hans Steinger, Leipzig 1933 (Deutsche Literatur in Entwicklungsreihen).
- "Iwein", hg. von G. F. Benecke und K. Lachmann, neu bearbeitet von Ludwig Wolff, (7) Berlin 1968, Band 1: Text, Band 2: Handschriftenübersicht, Anmerkungen und Lesarten.

Chrétien de Troyes:
- "Erec et Enide", hg. von Mario Roques, Paris 1955 (CFMA).
- "Erec et Enide", moderne Prosaversion von André Mary, Paris (Gallimard) 1944.
- "Cligés", hg. von Alexandre Micha, Paris 1967 (CFMA).
- "Le Chevalier de la Charrete", hg. von Mario Roques, Paris 1958 (CFMA).
- "Le Chevalier de la Charrette", französische Übersetzung von Jean Frappier, Paris (Champion) 1967.
- "Le Chevalier au Lion" (Yvain), hg. von Mario Roques, Paris 1965 (CFMA).
- "Yvain", altfranzösisch-deutsche Ausgabe nach dem Text von Wendelin Foerster; Übersetzung von Ilse Nolting-Hauff, München 1962 (Klassische Texte des romanischen Mittelalters).

2. Sekundärliteratur

(Dieses Verzeichnis umfasst all jene Studien, die mein Verständnis des "Iwein" allgemein, in ästhetischer Hinsicht oder in Einzelfragen förderten.)

Arbusow Leonid, Colores Rhetorici, Göttingen 1948.

Assunto Rosario, Die Theorie des Schönen im Mittelalter, Köln 1963.

Auerbach Erich, Mimesis, (3) Bern 1964, VI. Kap.: Der Auszug des höfischen Ritters, 120–138.
- Figura, in: Neue Dantestudien. Istanbuler Schriften 5 (1944) 11–71.
- Typologische Motive in der mittelalterlichen Literatur, Krefeld 1953.

Babilas Wolfgang, Chrétien de Troyes: 'Yvain', Verse 1–6. Arch. f. d. Stud. d. neuer. Spr. 196 (1960) 296–315.

Bayer Hans Jürgen, Untersuchungen zum Sprachstil weltlicher Epen des deutschen Früh- und Hochmittelalters, Berlin 1962 (Philologische Studien und Quellen 10).

Bayer Raymond, Von der Methode der Ästhetik, Darmstadt 1960.

von Beit Hedwig, Symbolik des Märchens, Bern 1952.

Bernhard Erwin, Abstractions médiévales ou critique abstraite? in: Studi Mediolatini e Volgari IX, Bologna 1961, 19–70.

Bernhart Joseph, Heilige und Tiere. Texte, München 1937.

Bezzola Reto R., Les origines et la formation de la littérature courtoise en occident (500–1200), Paris (Champion) 1958.
- Liebe und Abenteuer im höfischen Roman, Hamburg 1961.

Böckmann Paul, Formgeschichte der deutschen Dichtung I, (2) Hamburg 1965, Einleitung: Möglichkeiten und Aufgaben der Formgeschichte, 7–69; 1. Kap.: Das sinnbildende Sprechen in der höfischen Epik des Mittelalters, 71–166.

de Boor Helmut u. Newald Richard, Geschichte der deutschen Literatur, 2. Band: Die höfische Literatur, (6) München 1964, 63–90.

de Bruyne Edgar, Etudes d'esthétique médiévale, 3 Bände, Brugge 1946.

Cormeau Christoph, Hartmanns Armer Heinrich und Gregorius, München 1966 (Münchener Texte und Untersuchungen zur deutschen Literatur des Mittelalters 15).

Cramer Thomas, Saelde und êre in Hartmanns Iwein, Euph. 60 (1966) 30–47.

Curtius Ernst Robert, Europäische Literatur und lateinisches Mittelalter, (4) Bern 1963.
– Dichtung und Rhetorik im Mittelalter, DVjs 16 (1938) 435–476.
Daniélou Jean, Sacramentum futuri, Paris 1950 (Etudes de Théologie Historique).
Dittmann Wolfgang, 'Dune hâst niht wâr, Hartman'. Zum Begriff der wârheit in Hartmanns Iwein. FG Ulrich Pretzel, Berlin 1963, 150–161.
Drube Herbert, Hartmann und Chrétien, Münster 1931.
Eggers Hans, Symmetrie und Proportion epischen Erzählens. Studien zur Kunstform Hartmanns von Aue, Stuttgart 1956.
Ehrentreich Swantje, Erzählhaltung und Erzählerrolle Hartmanns von Aue und Thomas Manns, dargestellt an ihren beiden Gregoriusdichtungen. Diss. Frankfurt 1963.
Endres Rolf, Studien zum Stil von Hartmanns Erec. Diss. München 1961.
– Der Prolog von Hartmanns "Iwein", DVjs 40 (1966) 509–538.
Erben Johannes, Zu Hartmanns 'Iwein', ZfdPh 87 (1968) 344–359.
von Ertzdorff Xenia, Spiel der Interpretation. Der Erzähler in Hartmanns Iwein. FG Friedrich Maurer, Düsseldorf 1968, 135–157.
Faral Edmond, Recherches sur les sources latines des contes et romans courtois du moyen âge, Paris (Champion) 1913.
– Les Arts Poétiques du XIIe et du XIIIe siècle. Recherches et documents sur la technique littéraire du moyen âge, Paris (Champion) 1924.
Fechter Werner, Ostern als Metapher in mhd. Dichtungen, Beitr. Tübingen 85 (1963) 289–296.
Fourquet Jean, Le rapport entre l'oeuvre et la source chez Chrétien de Troyes et le problème des sources bretonnes, RPh 9 (1956) 218–312.
Frappier Jean, Chrétien. L'homme et l'oeuvre, Paris 1957.
– Le Roman Breton. Yvain ou le Chevalier au Lion. Centre de Documentation Universitaire, Paris 1952.
Friedman Lionel J., Occulta Cordis, RPh 11 (1957–58) 103–119.
Grosse Siegfried, Beginn und Ende der erzählenden Dichtungen Hartmanns von Aue, Beitr. Tübingen 83 (1961) 137–156.
– Die Wirkung des Kontrastes in den Dichtungen Hartmanns von Aue, WW 15 (1965) 29–39.
Gruenter Rainer, Über den Einfluss des Genus iudicale auf den höfischen Redestil, DVjs 26 (1952) 49–57.
Gsteiger Manfred, Note sur les préambules des chansons de geste, CCM 2 (1959) 213–220.
Hamburger Käte, Die Logik der Dichtung, Stuttgart 1957.
Harms Wolfgang, Der Kampf mit dem Freund oder Verwandten in der deutschen Literatur bis um 1300, München 1963.
Harris Julian, The role of the lion in Chrétien de Troyes' Yvain, PMLA 64 (1949) 1143–1163.
Hatto A. T., 'Der aventiure meine' in Hartmann's Iwein, in: Medieval German Studies presented to Frederick Norman, London 1965, 94–104.
Heselhaus C., Auslegung und Erkenntnis. Zur Methode der Strukturanalyse, in: Gestaltungsprobleme der Dichtung, FS G. Müller, Bonn 1957, 259–283.
Jolles André, Einfache Formen, (2) Halle 1956.
Kobel Erwin, Untersuchungen zum gelebten Raum in der mhd. Dichtung, Zürcher Beiträge zur deutschen Sprach- und Stilgeschichte 4 (1953).
Köhler Erich, Scholastische Ästhetik und höfische Dichtung, Neophil. 37 (1953) 202–207.
– Ideal und Wirklichkeit in der höfischen Epik. Studien zur Form der frühen Artus- und Graldichtung, ZfrPh Beih. 97 (1956).
– Zur Selbstauffassung des höfischen Dichters, in: Trobadorlyrik und höfischer Roman, Berlin 1962, 9–21.
– Le rôle de la 'coutume' dans les romans de Chrétien de Troyes, Rom. 81 (1960) 386–397.
Kölbing Eugen, Christian von Troyes' Yvain und die Brandanuslegende, Zfvgl. Litteraturgeschichte N.F.11 (1897) 442–448.
Kuhn Hugo, über Hartmanns "Iwein", in: Annalen der deutschen Literatur, hg. von Heinz Otto Burger, Stuttgart (2) 1952, 133–135.
– Hartmann von Aue als Dichter, DU 1953/H.2, 11–27.
– Stil als Epochen-, Gattungs- und Wertproblem in der deutschen Literatur des Mittelalters. 7. Kongress der Internationalen Vereinigung für moderne Sprachen und Literaturen, Heidelberg 1959.
Lausberg Heinrich, Elemente der literarischen Rhetorik, (2) München 1963.
Leclercq Jean, Aspects littéraires de l'oeuvre de st. Bernard, CCM 1 (1958) 425–451.

74

van der Lee Anthony, Der Stil von Hartmanns Erec verglichen mit dem der älteren Epik, Diss. Utrecht 1959.

Lewis Charles Betram, Classical mythology and Arthurian Romance. A Study of the Sources of Chrestien de Troyes' "Yvain" and other Arthurian Romances, Oxford 1932.

Linke Hansjürgen, Epische Strukturen in der Dichtung Hartmanns von Aue, München 1968.

Lüthi Max, Das europäische Volksmärchen. Form und Wesen, (2) Bern 1960.

– Es war einmal . . . Vom Wesen des Volksmärchens, (2) Göttingen 1964.

Meng Armin, Vom Sinn des ritterlichen Abenteuers bei Hartmann von Aue, Diss. Zürich 1967.

Mecke Günter, Zwischenrede, Erzählfigur und Erzählhaltung in Hartmanns Erec, Diss. München 1965.

Messerer Wilhelm, Einige Darstellungsprinzipien der Kunst im Mittelalter, DVjs 36 (1962) 157–179.

Milnes Humphrey, The Play of Opposites in 'Iwein', GLL 14 (1960/61) 241–256.

Nitschke August, Tiere und Heilige, in: Dauer und Wandel der Geschichte, FG Kurt von Raumer, Münster 1966, 62–101.

Ohly Friedrich, Vom geistigen Sinn des Wortes im Mittelalter, Darmstadt 1966.

– Die Suche in Dichtungen des Mittelalters, ZfdA 94 (1965) 171–184.

Ohly Walter, Die heilsgeschichtliche Struktur der Epen Hartmanns von Aue, Diss. Berlin 1958.

Piquet F., Etude sur Hartmann d'Aue, thèse pour le doctorat Paris 1898.

Quintilianus M. Fabius, Institutionis oratoriae libri XII, hg. von Ludwig Radermacher, Leipzig 1959.

Richter Elise, Die künstlerische Stoffgestaltung in Chrestiens Ivain, ZfrPh 39 (1919) 385–397.

Rigolot François, Valeur figurative du vêtement dans le Tristan de Béroul, CCM 10 (1967) 447–453.

Ruh Kurt, Zur Interpretation von Hartmanns "Iwein", in: Philologia Deutsch, FS Walter Henzen, Berlin 1965, 39–51.

– Höfische Epik des Mittelalters, I. Von den Anfängen bis zu Hartmann von Aue, Berlin 1967.

Rupp Heinz, Über den Bau epischer Dichtungen des Mittelalters, in: Die Wissenschaft von deutscher Sprache und Dichtung. Methoden, Probleme, Aufgaben. FS Friedrich Maurer, Stuttgart 1963, 366–382.

Sacker Hugh, Interpretation of Hartmann's Iwein, GR 36 (1961) 5–26.

Schacks Kurt, Beschwerte Hebungen bei Otfried und Hartmann, FG Ulrich Pretzel, Berlin 1963, 76–85.

Schneider Hermann, Parzival-Studien, Sitzungsberichte der Bayer. Akademie der Wissenschaften, philos.-hist. Klasse, München 1947.

Schröder Werner, Zur Chronologie der drei grossen mhd. Erzähler, DVjs 31 (1957) 264–303.

Schulze Wilhelm August, Der Heilige und die wilden Tiere, Zfdie neutestamentliche Wissenschaft 47 (1955) 280–283.

Schweikle Günther, Zum "Iwein" Hartmanns von Aue, in: Probleme des Erzählens in der Weltliteratur. FS Käte Hamburger, hg. von Fritz Martini, Stuttgart 1971, 1–22.

Schweitzer Bernhard, Vom Sinn der Perspektive, Tübingen 1953.

Sparnaay Hendricus, Hartmanns Iwein, in: Zur Sprache und Literatur des Mittelalters, Groningen 1961, 216–230.

Spitzer Leo, Le Lion arbitre moral de l'homme, Rom. 64 (1938) 525–530.

van Stockum Th. C., Hartman von Ouwes "Iwein". Sein Problem und seine Probleme. Mededelingen der Koninklijke Nederlandse Akademie van Wetenschappen, AFD Letterkunde N.R. 26/3, Amsterdam 1963.

Tschirch Fritz, Spiegelungen. Untersuchungen vom Grenzrain zwischen Germanistik und Theologie, Berlin 1966.

Wapnewski Peter, Hartmann von Aue, Stuttgart 1962 (Sammlung Metzler).

Wehrli Max, Strukturprobleme des mittelalterlichen Romans, WW 10 (1960) 334–345.

– Roman und Legende im deutschen Hochmittelalter, in: Worte und Werte, FS Bruno Markwardt, Berlin 1961, 428–443.

– Sacra Poesis, in: Die Wissenschaft von deutscher Sprache und Dichtung, FS Friedrich Maurer, Stuttgart 1963, 22–41.

– Iweins Erwachen, in: Geschichte, Deutung, Kritik. FS Werner Kohlschmidt, Bern 1969, 64–78.

Whitehead F., Yvain's Wooing, in: Medieval Miscellany presented to Eugène Vinaver, Manchester University Press, New York 1965, 321–336.

Willson H. B., The Role of Keii in Hartmann's 'Iwein', Med. Aev. 30 (1961) 145–158.
– Love and Charity in Hartmann's 'Iwein', MLR 57 (1962) 216–227.
Witte Arthur, Ywein und Iwein. Vergleich des Aufbaus und der Gestalten, Beitr. Halle 53 (1929) 65–192.
Zenker Rudolf, Forschungen zur Artusepik, 1. Ivainstudien, ZfrPh Beih. 70 (1921).
Zumthor Paul, Langue et techniques poétiques à l'époque romane (XIe-XIIIe siècles), Paris (Klincksieck) 1963.

EUROPÄISCHE HOCHSCHULSCHRIFTEN

Reihe I Deutsche Literatur und Germanistik